George Moore and the Autogenous Self

Richard Fallis, *Series Editor*

A sketch of George Moore by Sir William Orpen.
Courtesy of Mark Samuels Lasner.

George Moore and the Autogenous Self

The Autobiography and Fiction

Elizabeth Grubgeld

SYRACUSE UNIVERSITY PRESS

Copyright © 1994 by Syracuse University Press
Syracuse, New York 13244-5160

First Edition 1994

94 95 96 97 98 99   6 5 4 3 2 1

Portions of chapter 1 have appeared in *Biography* (14:4) Fall, 1991. © Copyright 1991 by the Biographical Research Center.

Portions of chapter 7 were first published by Swets & Zeitlinger in *English Studies* (67:4) 1986.

Quotations from the unpublished letters of George Moore. Copyright © 1994 by the estate of John Christopher Medley, by permission of Colin Smythe Ltd.

The paper used in this publication meets the minimum requirements of American National Standard for Information Sciences—Permanence of Paper for Printed Library Materials, ANSI Z39.48-1984. ∞™

Library of Congress Cataloging-in-Publication Data
Grubgeld, Elizabeth.
    George Moore and the autogenous self : the autobiography and
fiction / Elizabeth Grubgeld.
        p.   cm. — (Irish studies)
    Includes bibliographical references (p.   ) and index.
    ISBN 0-8156-2615-0
    1. Moore, George, 1852–1933—Criticism and interpretation.
2. Authors, Irish—Biography—History and criticism.   3. Ireland in
literature.   4. Self in literature.   5. Autobiography.   I. Title.
II. Series: Irish studies (Syracuse, N.Y.)
PR5044.G78   1994
823'.8—dc20   93-26584

Manufactured in the United States of America

THE ONLY ONE WHO KNEW ME in the days of the Cremorne and Argyle Rooms is dear Edward, and it always interests me to hear him say that I began myself out of nothing, developing from the mere sponge to the vertebrate and upward. I should have liked another simile, for Nature has never interested me as much as Art, perhaps I should never have paid any attention to Nature if it hadn't been for Art. I would have preferred Edward to have said that I was at once the sculptor and the block of marble of my own destiny, and that every failure to win a mistress in the Cremorne Gardens was a chipping away of the vague material that concealed the statue. But the simile would perhaps not have been so correct, for to say that a man is at once the sculptor and the block of marble means that he is a conscious artist, and I was not that in those days; I worked unconsciously.

—George Moore, *Hail and Farewell*

E LIZABETH GRUBGELD WAS EDUCATED at Lewis and Clark College and The University of Iowa. She is Associate Professor of Modern British and Irish Literature at Oklahoma State University.

Contents

Preface

> George Moore is ill from a nightmare in which he
> thought the Germans had invaded England and
> were storming his bedroom—he jumped out of bed
> with the intention of resisting to the last, and slipped
> right along the floor to the other end of the room,
> cutting himself all to bits. He wants Maud to get him
> the V.C. on the grounds that anybody can be brave
> when they're awake, but to be brave in one's sleep is
> the *real thing*.
>
> —Edward Marsh, Summer, 1916

I N *The Great War and Modern Memory*, Paul Fussell defines the modern perspective on war as that of grim irony. Although, as given in Edward Marsh's anecdote, George Moore's response to war is more playful than grim, he vividly enacts his view not only of war but of his own life as an ironic action of a specifically parodic nature.[1] Within the story, Moore appears as a paradigm of his autobiographical persona: the wise fool, driven for a time by the same kinds of starry ideals that inspire the other buffoons around him. However, what he elsewhere calls his "instinct" leads him eventually to recognize the delusive nature of dreams, and that self-consciousness sets him above his fellows: "To be ridiculous has always been *ma petite luxe*," Moore writes in *Hail and Farewell*, "but can anyone be said to be ridiculous if he knows that he is ridiculous? Not very well." The ridiculous man in Marsh's anecdote figures not merely as a partici-

pant in the story but—as one who shares a name with its author—
the creator of the dream in which he finds himself an actor. How
much more important, Moore asserts, to be brave in the dreams of
one's own creation than in the world of others' illusions! To claim
such an imperative is to make a proclamation of being which, like
the parody it is, dominates by means of its wit and for the brief
moment of its utterance, the very world beyond itself which it simultaneously acknowledges.

The paradoxical interdependence of the parodic figure and the
world that it parodies is central to Moore's conception of the self.
In the face of an Irish heritage he sought throughout his career to
repudiate, he maintains a principle of autogenous creation. In *Confessions of a Young Man* he begins the story of his life with the declaration that he had come into the world "with a nature like a smooth
sheet of wax, bearing no impress." Denying the claims of mother-
land or the inheritance of his father's role as a man of action, he
would deliver himself as if by miraculous birth. He professes the
capacity to reengender himself "in the womb of a new nationality,"
to become not the Catholic landlord from Mayo but a Frenchman,
an Englishman, or even a reincarnation of some anonymous writer
who lived in Greece two thousand years ago. Yet at the same time,
through the very vehemence of his denial of his own history and
heredity, Moore indicates how fully he is compelled by deterministic
theories of human behavior. His autobiographies and fiction frequently trace the powerful influences of heredity, class, culture, and
language upon the would-be autogenous character. In this sense, his
work incorporates within itself both a profound recognition of the
historical world and a declaration of his own self-determination.[2]

To accommodate this fundamental opposition between what his
experience has shown him and the autogenous life to which he aspires, Moore developed a self-reflexive mode of narrative, one that
typically queries its own explanations, thereby giving voice to both
perspectives and settling upon neither. His work also depends upon
such metaphorical explanations as his idiosyncratic concept of "instinct," a conceit that conflates various figures of determined and
self-creative being. His interest in physiognomy also reveals this per-
vading contradiction as he fixates upon the body as a source of character and a key to its interpretation, even as, by highlighting the role
of the interpreter, he suggests that real power lies in the act of interpretation, not in the body itself. His preoccupation with sexual identity, the question of nationality, and the function of the authorial

name also result in metaphoric figures that combine elements of these antithetical modes of explaining the origins of the self.

Throughout this study I have analyzed the ways in which formal literary structure carries the weight of his ambivalence. In Moore's early fiction, there is a notable disharmony between his postulation of the pure, instinctive individual and the formal mode of social realism with its emphasis on the ultimate power of economic relations. His attention to both psychological realism and linguistic indeterminacy in his *Celibate Lives* series guides his inquiry into the means by which sexuality is determined by physiology, language, and economic relations. Moore's theory of self-genesis is extended to a treatment of his ongoing concern with birthing—as biological process and as literary metaphor—and his concurrent preoccupation with the ambiguities of human sexuality. In his later fiction, he moves to an entirely different narrative structure, one that subverts the language of public, historical discourse by assimilating it to a vitalistic code of personal memory. In their dependence upon a sophisticated form of indirect discourse, the late novels place at their center the subjective consciousness of their protagonists who, through the act of remembering, come to a reconciliation with the world beyond the self.

In discussing Moore's autobiographies, I examine the multifarious substructures within each text and their relation to his construction of the autobiographical speaker. *Parnell and His Island,* which I take as his initial effort toward autobiographical inquiry, adopts an anonymous narrator and the method of episodic description typical of the genre of the travel memoir. This form permits Moore to indulge the necessary fiction of stepping outside of his homeland in order to disavow all that is depicted, including an alienated reflection of a cast-off younger self, the character "Landlord M——." I discuss *Confessions of a Young Man* as a parody of the conventions of Victorian autobiography, particularly in regard to biblical models of narrative and questions of heredity and nationality. In addition, through its intratextual self-reflexivity, *Confessions* anticipates the instability of the narrative perspective and the authorial signature which we find articulated in more recent autobiographical writing. Given its technical complexity and thematic richness, I devote two chapters to *Hail and Farewell* as an autobiographical comedy. In conceiving the autobiographical persona as a satiric one, Moore effects an unusual relation among author, narrating persona, and the past self. This relation is even further complicated as he suggests the parodic dimension of the autobiographical persona's voice. His explorations of these and many other questions produce a subtle meditation on the nature of the self and its relations with the surrounding world. In looking at Moore's essay-dialogues and his voluminous correspondence, I address the use of dialogue as a mode of self-creation and propose a number of different perspectives from which his correspondences might be considered acts of epistolary autobiography. I conclude with a discussion of his theories of memory and autobiographical process in the later novels and in *Memoirs of My Dead Life*.

In the midst of an explosion of interest in the field of autobiography, there have developed critical languages and approaches that allow us to read Moore's fiction and his fictive autobiographies with new insight. Putting aside previous preoccupations with sincerity and integration, readers can look afresh at the experimentations of his fiction and the duplicitous, highly ironic, and multigeneric performances Moore put forth as his life story. The writings of George Moore, like his life, abound in antithetical ideas, and accordingly this study abounds in the qualifying and contrasting phrase. During the late 1890s, Moore's ambivalences occasionally resulted in a morass of incoherence from which he feared he might never escape, but for the majority of his career his deeply ironic outlook enabled him to see the internal inconsistencies of the premises by which our lives are lived and explained. It is exciting to write about George Moore in the 1990s with such a multitude of critical tools at one's disposal: new questions, problems, and methodologies with which to approach Moore's long and varied career.

If at times this work seems to be written with a missionary zeal, I must confess to a hope that it will bring the achievements of George Moore to a broader readership. His writings are of value not only to readers of Irish literature and history but to all interested in autobiographical writing and late Victorian and early twentieth-century literature. Moore has been for much too long the focus of a small group of devotees while relegated by others to a variety of pedagogic categories as a doctrinaire naturalist, a Paterian stylist, or an unreliable opportunist who for a brief time exploited the ideas of Yeats and his circle. None of these reductive assessments accounts for the diversity and the complexity of his lifework. In 1891 Moore wrote to his friend Clara Lanza that "I am what I am; I don't know what that is and I am sure the reviewers know still less," and while I have suggested briefly what Moore is not, the explanation of what he is presents greater difficulties.[3] Is he a modernist steeped in Romanticism who asserts the autonomy of the privileged artist and his effete book? Or an early incarnation of the postmodern dismantler of narrative authority whose self-reflexive ironies emanate from an unstable text? Or a social realist who foregrounds the contextuality of language and the body through his dedication to an aesthetic of exteriority? He is all of these and much more, and therein lies the pleasure and the challenge that awaits the reader of George Moore's lifelong investigation into the construction of the self.

Elizabeth Grubgeld

Stillwater, Oklahoma
May 1993

Acknowledgments

P ORTIONS OF THIS BOOK were completed with the assistance of The National Endowment for the Humanities; The Oklahoma Foundation for the Humanities; The College of Arts and Sciences, Oklahoma State University; and the Department of English, Oklahoma State University.

Over the last decades, scholars of George Moore have produced many fine works of an editorial and interpretive nature, and like them, I have depended upon the groundbreaking labors of Edwin Gilcher and the late Helmut E. Gerber. Without their achievements in bibliography, editing, and criticism, my task would have been much more difficult, if not impossible. Like so many others who read and study autobiography, I am profoundly indebted to James Olney, who, perhaps more than anyone else, changed how we think about autobiography and opened the way to a whole new field of inquiry. I am grateful for his insights as a critic, an NEH Summer Seminar leader, and a reader of the present study.

Many friends and colleagues contributed their expertise to this book, and for their encouragement and a variety of assistance along the way, I must extend my warm thanks to Florence Saunders Boos, Frederick P. W. McDowell, Donald Jordan, Geoffery Pill, Mark Samuels Lasner, Adrian Frazier and Robert Stephen Becker. Seonae Ha-Birdsong proved an invaluable research assistant, while Shirley Bechtel provided secretarial help with unfailing efficiency. The staff of Syracuse University Press has been a pleasure to work with, and their helpfulness and professionalism have aided me throughout the process of publication. On numerous occasions, my colleagues in the American Conference for Irish Studies provided a forum for this study as a book-in-progress; their enthusiasm and interest have meant a great deal.

My parents, L. E. and Jane S. Grubgeld, have supported this effort in every imaginable way, and my children, Edward and Robert, have contributed their good cheer. From the beginning of it all, William Merrill Decker has served as editor, interlocutor, and the best of helpmates. Much of whatever is good about this work developed from our almost daily conversations about it. For all this and so much more, I offer my deepest appreciation.

A Note on Transcriptions, Translations, and Texts

T RANSCRIPTIONS OF MOORE'S LETTERS appear as given in the books, articles, and dissertations that reproduce them. Some editors correct Moore's erratic spelling and punctuation; others do not. Moore did not generally date his letters, and the dates given are frequently approximate dates established by the editors of his letters. I have followed Joseph Hone in referring to Moore's friends by their pseudonyms; George Russell and W. K. Magee thus appear throughout as AE and John Eglinton.

Any works that Moore would have read in French are cited in French. For the convenience of the reader, long quotations are followed by a translation. Quotations from French writers who postdate Moore are given in English. As Moore did not know German, quotations from German writers are given in the translation most likely to have been familiar to him.

Moore's many revisions of his books necessitate careful and informed textual choices on the part of the critic. An invaluable guide is Edwin Gilcher's *A Bibliography of George Moore* (DeKalb, 1970) and the 1988 *Supplement* (Westport, Conn.). No definitive edition of Moore's work exists, but when appropriate, references are to the Ebury (or Second Uniform) Edition published by William Heinemann. Selections of other editions have been made according to critical context and, in a few cases, general availability. References to less frequently cited works or other versions of the following texts are given in the notes to each chapter.

BK   Charles Burkhart, "The Letters of George Moore to Edmund Gosse, W. B. Yeats, R. I. Best, Miss Nancy Cunard, and Mrs. Mary Hutchinson," Ph.D. diss. Univ. of Maryland, 1959.

C   *Celibates.* London: Walter Scott, 1895.

CES   *Conversations in Ebury Street.* London: Heinemann, 1936.

CL   *Celibate Lives.* London: Heinemann, 1938.

CYM   *Confessions of a Young Man,* ed. Susan Dick. Montreal: McGill-Queens Univ. Press, 1972.

DM   *A Drama in Muslin.* Gerrards Cross: Colin Smythe, 1981.

EG   *Letters of George Moore,* ed. John Eglinton [W. K. Magee]. Bournemouth: Sydenham, 1942.

EW   *Esther Waters.* London: Heinemann, 1938.

GMP   *George Moore on Parnassus,* ed. Helmut E. Gerber. Newark: Univ. of Delaware Press, 1988.

GMT   *George Moore in Transition: Letters to T. Fisher Unwin and Lena Milman, 1894–1910,* ed. Helmut E. Gerber. Detroit: Wayne State Univ. Press, 1968.

HF   *Hail and Farewell,* ed. Richard Cave. Gerrards Cross: Colin Smythe, 1976.

L   *The Lake.* Gerrards Cross: Colin Smythe, 1980.

LGM   Joseph Hone, *The Life of George Moore.* New York: Macmillan, 1936.

LLC   *Letters to Lady Cunard 1895–1933,* ed. Rupert Hart-Davis. London: Rupert Hart-Davis, 1957.

MMDL   *Memoirs of My Dead Life.* London: Heinemann, 1936.

PI   *Parnell and His Island.* London: Sonnenschein, Lowrey, 1887.

STH   *A Story-Teller's Holiday.* London: Heinemann, 1937.

George Moore and the Autogenous Self

1

The Discourse of Repudiation
A Drama in Muslin
and Parnell and His Island

> For my part, I was by no means ill-pleased to
> alter, in these pages, both my name and my back-
> ground. By doing so, I acquired a much wider freedom
> to talk about myself, to indulge in self-accusation,
> self-praise, self-pity, self-complacency, and self-cast-
> igation at leisure. . . . This fictitious name did not
> disguise me; but it did signal my intention not to ap-
> pear. . . .
> I have been able to invent concatenations of cir-
> cumstance to supply the place of those which eluded
> me . . . but I am persuaded that no man ever told
> lies with a deeper concern for the truth.
> —Anatole France, *La Vie en Fleur*
> (as translated by Richard Coe)

U NLIKE ANATOLE FRANCE, George Moore could rarely resist
the temptation to appear. Even before publication of the first
English edition of *Confessions of a Young Man* (1888), he sought to
alter the name of his narrator from Edwin Dayne to George Moore.
However, in *Parnell and His Island* (1887), published in its final version only a year before, he chose to maintain the narrator's anonymity. Most important, he forcefully distanced himself from the world

1

depicted therein by presenting an alienated reflection of a cast-off younger self, the character "Landlord M——." *A Drama in Muslin,* the novel composed immediately before *Parnell,* reveals a similar disquietude as to the author's relation to the text. In these early works, Moore begins his lifelong autobiographical activity by demonstrating what he would not be; by his very unreadiness to appear, he defines himself in contrast to that which he depicts. While not until *Confessions of a Young Man* would Moore postulate a distinct autobiographical persona, his early works initiate the venture by clearing his path, portraying and subjecting to ironic scrutiny the lives he might have lived as an Irishman. He recognized early in his career a need to disclaim his Irish heritage (and the very principle of heredity) in order to affirm later that he was truly a man who "made himself because he imagined himself."[1] Before laying claim in *Confessions* to a miraculous autogenic appearance in the world of letters and cosmopolitan society, he establishes in his initial writings an active repudiation of the inherited historical world and those parts of himself that were susceptible to entrapment by that world.

Throughout his career Moore was to testify to the independence of the imagination so engaged in the activity of self-creation. Nonetheless, his wish to fully author himself is offset by a profound historical consciousness that cannot ignore the nagging probability of determinant forces outside the self. For the bearer of such a consciousness, any initial formulation of the self must continually measure its relation to its origins, even if the probable rejection of those origins is kept always in view. It is thus that Moore in his early works struggles with matters that turn on the question of his citizenship. By 1887 a self-proclaimed Irishman-turned-Frenchman-turned-Englishman, Moore wrote in an advertisement for *A Drama in Muslin* that the novel offered "a picture of Ireland all complete . . . and *painted by an Irishman*" (*LGM* 117). While the world of his birth is depicted with loathing in *A Drama in Muslin* and *Parnell and His Island,* he cannot disregard the question of genesis. His very schizophrenia of citizenship indicates his compulsion to assert identity in terms of nationality, even if by so doing he also asserts his privilege to discover the proper country of origin. The process of discovery is initiated through his narrator's dismissal of everything he sees in Ireland, as potential identities—lives that might have been the author's—are called up one after another to face the acid judgments of the narrative voice.

The narrative voice in the one book resembles that of the other,

but the precise forms of narration differ. *Parnell*'s narrator is unnamed, although identified as an Irishman now living outside the
country. The story includes vignettes whose intimate details could
not have been known by the speaker, but even when the narrative
slips into an omniscient perspective, the narrator's impassioned
judgment remains intensely felt. *A Drama in Muslin* is told through
third-person omniscience, although Moore occasionally lapses into
the first person.[2] As dissimilar as they are, both texts share a common rhetorical strategy: a repudiative discourse, initiated by a narrative voice that addresses the reader, comments upon, condemns—
and, on rare occasions, praises—what it displays. The formulation of
the narrative voice is not always consistent or controlled, but it represents a fundamental stage in the development of the autobiographical persona so masterfully culminated in *Hail and Farewell*
(1911–14). Although the voice acknowledges an intimacy with things
Irish, as in *Hail and Farewell*, the very intimacy is set up as a self-
evident rationale for the repudiation of those things that others,
Moore implicitly claims, are too blind to reject.

   Moore's discourse of repudiation proceeds with considerable vehemence. Yet in spite of its vehemence, it admits an undeniable ambivalence. At the heart of this ambivalence is Moore's recognition
that the oppositional life of the artist maintains links to, and may
even require the preservation of, that which it would replace. Ireland, repellent in almost every way, is constructed in Moore's text by
means of conceptual categories that are duplicated in the altogether
attractive world of art. In the imagistic language that *Parnell* and *A
Drama in Muslin* share, Ireland reeks of its own degeneration, with
food that is too coarse or too luscious, sexual relations that are too
brutal or too voluptuous, and money that bears the material traces
of its origins in peasant misery. Yet both books imply, as *Confessions*
makes explicit, that art too is to be imagined through metaphors of
decadence, food, sexual reproduction, and money. The correspondences between the rejected national life and the adopted life of the
artist reappear despite Moore's belief that art and Ireland can hardly
occupy the same thought. He cannot reject the possibility that art
may be unable to effect the desired deliverance from a failed national life. Again, the overt argumentation in his novels and autobiographies pleads for the autonomy of the life of the artist; yet seen
in juxtaposition, his works reveal a repeated questioning of the very
propositions they purport to evince.

   In *A Drama in Muslin* and *Parnell and His Island*, Moore acknowledges his contradiction at some level: of the four fictional characters who write, none is occupationally immunized from participation in the exploitative relationships that, to Moore, epitomize the nature of all relations—economic, sexual, and literary—within the Ireland of his memory. Neither Alice Barton nor John Harding of *Drama*, neither the Irish poet "Landlord M——" nor the anonymous narrator of *Parnell* escapes the reductive irony that encloses the text. If art opens the door to escape from Ireland, the road is very, very narrow. Before *Confessions of a Young Man*, Moore does not project a genuine artist with any ties, even repudiated ones, to Ireland. In *Confessions* and the works that follow it, only a few succeed in following the treacherous road of art: almost all are French painters, and none, save himself, are Irish writers. The failures of others actually enhance the ahistorical miracle of his own success. As will be seen in the discussion of *Hail and Farewell*, Moore refuses to grant even to his characters that right he reserves to himself: to be the only one who may use literary language properly, the only one with a right to linguistic capital.

Before examining the figures who repudiate Ireland, it is necessary to chart just what is being repudiated and why. In both *A Drama in Muslin* and *Parnell and His Island*, Ireland is no place for life because it is no place for art; art has no chance in Ireland because, in the Arnoldian terms Moore simultaneously borrows and mocks, no cultural occasion exists to encourage and support it. As the Land League rushes to a tumultuous future and the landlords cling to an ossified form of past life, no orderly progress is possible, and, without a future, no fecundity in art or cultural life can exist.[3] According to Moore, Ireland affords no opportunities for generative work of any kind. Potential forms of nurture or creative activity—food, sex, reproduction, art, or money—are distorted beyond redemption by the nation's inability to assert its will behind a cause of integrity, whether it take the form of the equitable distribution of land or a marriage of mutual affection and respect. In his first novel, *A Modern Lover* (1883), Moore traced creative failing to personal weakness, but *A Drama in Muslin*, like *Parnell*, traces creative failing to the collapse of national life. In the later two books creativity is measured not only by artistic productivity, as in *A Modern Lover*, but by the ability to manage one's lands and by the essential reproductive act of childbearing. The latter two options from this triad of productive possibilities were rejected by Moore, as well as by the young aesthete "Landlord M——" of *Parnell and His Island* (who is equally incapable of artistic achievement). We must again read Moore's emphasis upon social involvement and his interest in parenting as aspects of his autobiographical act as it is configured in 1886: a projection of paths not followed, in these instances, paths of deliverance that demanded entirely too close a relation with the historical world upon whose rejection the life of art appeared to depend for its fulfillment.

Sex and Starvation

In Moore's Ireland, the possibility of such fulfillment is restricted by convention and the conditions created by convention. Taking as his subject the horrors of the marriage market, Moore sees the stultification of a people's ethical and aesthetic capacity evident most vividly in the repression of young women. As was not uncommon for writers of the period, Moore compares the restriction of the upper-class female to the economic and cultural deprivation of the Irish poor and so effects the indictment of the landlord class for failures in nearly every area of life. In his essay on the novel, Paul Sporn notes that in *A Drama in Muslin* Moore exposes "the inherent irrationality and the violence of an exploitive society and its corrosive effect on women, ironically through marriage, which is the unit cell of its existence."[1] Only the novel's heroine is capable of sensing that the mores of the landed class restrict both women and peasants, although unlike her author she can never say this in so many words. Most of the girls subscribe to the very standards that repress them and view the rebellious tenants as sinister and alien. As Moore explains in a letter to the Dutch naturalist Frans Netscher, "The scene is laid in Ireland during the land agitation: while the girls are crying for white dresses, the peasants are crying for the soil."[5] The world of landlord society "in its last decadence" is held responsible for both the misery the girls endure and that of the exploited poor, although the correlation between their cries is directly articulated only by the narrator.

The peasants are never described in individual detail, but his "girl book," as Moore called it, depicts various psychological types among the debutantes: scheming, frivolous, sensuous, man-hating and, finally, the plain, pragmatic woman of integrity who is the central character. Repelled by the marriage chase and inspired by her encounter with the cynical English novelist John Harding, Alice Barton begins to write. Her pieces are conventional and marketable, and through her power to earn income she gains sufficient strength of will to resist her family and marry an earnest, peasant-born doctor with whom she escapes to the placidity of a London suburb, leaving the calamitous Ireland behind her.

"What could they do with their empty brains? What could they do with their feeble hands?" These questions, which *Drama*'s narrator poses to a landlord class terrified at the prospect of its own demise, address Moore's concern with the necessity of finding a productive vocation. When beginning *A Drama in Muslin*, Moore seems to have been interested not exclusively in Irish society, but in a more general question of the repression of the individual and the consequent incapacity to engage in worthwhile work. Long before he thought to set the book in Ireland, he conceived the novel as a comparison between the restrictive upbringing of English girls and the more useful and interesting lives of their French counterparts.[6] While the precise details of the Irish debutante's life and the tumultuous undercurrent of the land agitation give the novel its dramatic power and sociological richness, underscoring as they do the themes of exploitation and restriction, evidence suggests that the Irish materials did not dominate Moore's original conception of the novel as the story of a struggle of personal consciousness against the molding forces of historical life. In the midst of composition, Moore could write to Netscher a letter that practically ignores the political setting of his novel: "My new book deals with the question whether English girls (of whom there is now a surplus population of more than two millions) will take professions or continue to consider marriage as the only profession open to them. . . . The principal character is an atheist who is likewise a virtuous woman."[7] His girls, actually Irish, are concerned only with whether they will be able to root out enough tolerable beaux to keep the profession of marriage open to them. Alice stands unique in her questioning as to whether a woman may not have an occupation within marriage, or, barring that, some useful independent existence.

The description of Alice as a virtuous atheist, like the later characterization of her as "a puritan . . . but not a sexless puritan,"[8] indicates several other concerns that, while tangentially related to the political background, demonstrate Moore's preoccupation with characters, autobiographical and otherwise, who find themselves unable to accept given forms of life. In Alice can be seen Moore's emergent interest in the conflicting yet often inextricable powers of intellectual, religious, and sexual impulses, and his view of freethinking as a form of repudiation, ironically more morally justifiable—and therefore "virtuous"—than group standards of morality.

Alice's capacity for freethinking establishes her as one with some potential to escape the mindless conformity of her peers; through her ability to embrace ideas other than those she has been taught, she discovers "the divine power to create, and to live an interior life" (*DM* 102). Alice's one fault, according to the narrator, is a lack of sufficient selfishness. From an unwarranted loyalty to her family and an intrinsic inability to offend others, she retains a dutiful, if skeptical, allegiance to that which her intellect prompts her to reject. Alice defends her need to search out a balance among the life she leads, the ideas she holds, and the instincts she feels by explaining that her life's goal is "making the ends of nature the ends also of what we call our conscience" (*DM* 228). In her sentence, Moore has slightly altered an otherwise direct—although unacknowledged—quotation from Eduard von Hartmann's *Philosophy of the Unconscious*: "the principle of practical philosophy consists in this, TO MAKE THE ENDS OF THE UNCONSCIOUS ENDS OF OUR OWN CONSCIOUSNESS."[9] Moore has substituted the term, "nature," for what von Hartmann called "the unconscious." For almost any other writer "nature" would designate an inherited set of traits, but in Moore's usage—as will be discussed in the next chapters—"nature" is exclusive to the individual and bears no relation to the inherited world; as a transcendental category it justifies those actions that defy social mores and even social responsibilities. Here "nature" is set in contrast to "conscience," which Moore has substituted for von Hartmann's "consciousness"—a significant change in that "conscience" implies social duty and a complicity with learned morality. In *Hail and Farewell*, the narrator muses that "Alice Barton in *Muslin* is a preparatory study, a prevision of *Esther Waters;* both represent the personal conscience striving against the communal" (*HF* 275), yet his original phrasing in the novel suggests that Alice's own conscience is itself too communally determined. "Conscience," after all, is the despised and feared interlocutor of *Confessions of a Young Man*'s independent young protagonist. Alice has insufficient will or, to use a term that will also be more fully defined in the following chapters, insufficient "instinct" to ensure that conscience not override nature.

To be passionate and a freethinker, Moore suggests, is to have powers of both body and mind, but without some selfishness their victory is compromised. Consequently, Alice's final escape is qualified by Moore's ironic description of it: a conventional life of middlebrow literary societies, a well-kept home without pictures, and a kind, dependable, but unattractive husband. To be an authentic individual seems to require full repudiation of loyalties to any force outside of one's own "instinct." The necessity of selfishness is a principal theme of Moore's autobiographies, and it is revealing that the years in which Alice discovers her identity precisely correspond to those of Moore's own emergence as novelist: a role he considered to be both socially productive and necessarily selfish.[10] In *Parnell* as well as in *A Drama in Muslin*, the historical world operates as the foil against which individuality is defined, and against which the nonconformist must assert selfish will in order to achieve work of significance.

Moore thus struggles with the question of responsibility to others, even if—as in the case of the reluctant landlord of Moore Hall—that responsibility appears to contradict one's selfish interests. In *A Drama in Muslin*, the question manifests itself in Moore's preoccupation with the failure of sexual and parental relations (as well as the inadequacy of other forms of physical nourishment). Through the ironic method of implied contrast to what is actually depicted, Moore invokes paradigms of social responsibility in sexual behavior that is immune from financial motive or indiscriminant intemperance, and parenting that engages careful nurture. Each also involves devotion to something worthwhile and thus the espousal of a genuine vocation. Particularly in Moore's later work, female sexuality and effective mothering appear as forms of creative labor and, consequently, self-creation; as he would remark in *Hail and Farewell*, his icon of maternity, Esther Waters, finds her life's work in defying the accidents of chance and the fixed expectations of social determinism. In contrast, he relates twisted and inadequate sexual relations and parenting to insufficient will and intelligence. In motherhood, Moore identifies work that, at best, conjoins self-expression with ties to others outside the self; as will be later discussed, he finds it difficult to imagine similar models among males, although the issue of communal concerns remained for him irrepressible.

In the Ireland of *A Drama in Muslin*, marriage and motherhood do not function in any creative way; both relations stultify the individuals involved and prohibit autonomous identity, while at the same time promoting a narcissistic self-absorption much different from the necessary selfishness whose absence the narrator bemoans in Alice Barton. Moore's analysis of sexual and maternal roles echoes then current debate over the relationship between maternity and feminism. This debate is clearly articulated in Olive Schreiner's feminist novel *The Story of an African Farm* (1883), a book Moore was reading with apparent attention while composing *Drama*. Although the unreliable Frank Harris writes that Moore thought the book a "poor one," Moore's letters to Netscher indicate that he was deeply impressed by the novel. He was also in social contact with Schreiner and had ample opportunity to discuss her ideas.[11] In her novel, Schreiner sets forth, as Moore does throughout much of his career, Schopenhauer's belief that while all labor is ultimately fruitless and we are duped by our own will to live, nevertheless, it is labor that gives us whatever meaning we do have. According to Schreiner, to be married and the mother of children is a form of labor, one without which a woman must exist "without honour, without the reward of useful labour, without love."[12] In Alice Barton's mind, the unmarried state presents its most horrible aspect as "an aimless life of idleness" in which she "would have to live without any aim or object in life," "unillumined by lamp of delight or star of duty." While Alice is haunted by the probability that she will never experience sexual relations, she is even more distressed by the possibility that her desire to work will be unfulfilled. Despairingly, she cries out, "Give me a duty, give me a mission to perform, and I will live! . . . but, oh! save me from this grey dream of idleness!" (*DM* 91, 97, 98).

Those who are to do the work of mothers and wives need other traits, according to Schreiner, than an enfeebled intellect and runaway sensuality—the characteristics of the women who populate Alice Barton's world. In *The Story of an African Farm,* she writes that a woman requires "a many-sided, multiform culture; the heights and depths of human life must not be beyond the reach of her vision; she must have knowledge of men and things in many states, a wide catholicity of sympathy, the strength that springs from knowledge, and the magnanimity which springs from strength."[13] In this passage, the language of Matthew Arnold informs Schreiner's argument, echoed by Moore, as to the cultural life needed to render mothering a true act of creation and, by extension, of self-creation. Such terms resemble those Moore invokes when he argues for the cultural "moment" required by an artist. Of the women in *A Drama in Muslin,* only Alice has achieved some semblance of education and force of will, although both are developed in defiance of her culture and her potential remains not fully realized. But by eventually marrying she is seen to be "taking her part in the world's work" (*DM* 315). As Alice attempts to explain to her mother, only this partnership in labor is genuine marriage. The desire for it dominates even the erotic consciousness John Harding awakened in her. Although Dr. Reed does not physically attract her, she accepts him as a diligent, good man who offers her the opportunity to continue her writing and take up the fundamental work of motherhood.

Olive Schreiner suggests that true partnership is incompatible with the financial transactions by which marriage is most commonly constituted. In Moore's novel, men and women are bought and sold in open discussions of dowries and mortgages. Alice Barton refuses to chase after men for their money or title as most of her contemporaries do, yet she does find at least a close approximation of her proper mate. Her relationship with Edward Reed emerges slowly from friendship and mutual respect, and the recognition that they wish to marry comes upon them by surprise. Similarly, Schreiner writes, "when love is no more bought or sold, when it is not a means of making bread, when each woman's life is filled with earnest, independent labour, then love will come to her, a strange sudden sweetness breaking in upon her earnest work; not sought for, but found."[11] Again, all satisfaction proceeds from the initial discovery of one's vocation.

Proper work, including proper mothering, is hard found in Ireland. Parenting, nourishment, and sexuality are—except in Alice's case—all linked to no other purpose than the acquisition of money or title. Like Moore's other realistic fiction, *A Drama in Muslin* abounds in neglectful parents, both male and female. Children are inadequately nurtured in both country and city. Mrs. Gould wastes her time in gossip and ignores her daughter's dangerous flirtations. May Gould, the girl whose blooming sensuality is reined in by no moral conviction, thoughtlessly becomes pregnant and bears an infant who soon dies and for whom she has no feeling and does not mourn. The artistic dilettante, Mr. Barton, abdicates his paternal authority for fear of losing the allowance for brushes and paints dispensed by his domineering wife. Mrs. Scully finds her daughter a marquis, but it is a dubious marriage based on the lust for social position. Elderly Sir Charles has a "little dirty crowd of illegitimate children running about the stableyard." Among the Dublin slum-dwellers who come out to haunt the debutantes on the night of the Vice-Regal Drawing Room are "poor little things in battered bonnets and draggled skirts, who would dream upon ten shillings a week; a drunken mother striving to hush a child that dies beneath a dripping shawl." Mrs. Barton calls them "a lot of hungry children looking into a sweetmeat shop" but coming to the limit of her maternal sympathy, declares, "the police ought really to prevent it" (*DM* 171). While Mrs. Barton loves her own daughters in her constrained way, she teaches them nothing of ethical, intellectual, or artistic value.

Those hungry children looking into the sweetmeat shop would find nothing to sustain them in Dublin, for only the bone-thin Alice is capable of providing sustenance to anyone. When May hides in a Dublin boarding house during her pregnancy, it is Alice, with a hopeful sense of having some purpose at last, who works to feed her; and it is Alice who feeds her sick sister while gaining the love of Dr. Reed. In Moore's more overt use of food as metaphor of sex and the financial transactions that surround it, Alice, the giver of food, finds food repellent: her "sense of the moral degradation, to which she had been so cruelly subjected, came upon her like the foul odours of a dirty kitchen issuing through a grating" (*DM* 143). However, unlike Lady Cecilia whose hysterical antipathy to food symptomizes her equally hysterical antipathy to men, Alice exercises intelligent discrimination, as in one telling scene she rejects the strawberry ice Harding hands her without having first asked her preference.[15]

While in *Confessions of a Young Man* the consumption and excretion of food are metaphorically compared to the artistic process, in *A Drama in Muslin* the exercise of mechanical appetite speaks to the absence of art or anything else worth having. The narrator recoils at the watery potatoes of the poor or the "sloppy tea" poured out at the Calico Ball, an occasion whose real counterpart Moore described to his mother as "so low, so vile, so dirty" (*LGM* 102). No better are "the few dried oranges and tough grapes" that pass for dessert at the pretentious Shelbourne Hotel, where the aging girls around the table have seen so many years of disappointment on the marriage market. The lavish food served at Lord Dungory's or the Bartons' is fragrant, delicate, and exotic, but can hardly be enjoyed when discussion centers on the projected demise of the landed classes. As the narrator says of a dinner-party conversation dampened by discussion of the Land League, "their vision of poverty had become so intolerably distinct that they saw not the name of the entree on the menu, and the côtelettes à la réforme were turned to porridge in their mouths" (*DM* 44). As even further evidence of its metaphoric relation to corruption, such food is used as procurement, a vulgar enticement to be added to Olive's bosom and her reputed £20,000 dowry as a means of selling to the highest bidder.

One would expect to find a portrait of Ireland as a pinched, starved place, but instead Moore has depicted a land where appetites run out of control. Clothing which, like eating, is borrowed from Carlyle as a playful metaphor for art in *Confessions* (and is first so used in the 1886 preface to *Terre d'Irlande*) here points instead to a raw grasping at sex and money. The luxurious, seductive dresses of an Olive Barton appear grotesque when contrasted to the wet rags of the peasant and the cheap finery of the working class. Clothing exposes an excess of flesh, and flesh and sweat fill the novel's pages. Instead of a gracious scene at the long-awaited presentation night, the narrator relates that "in this beautiful drawing-room . . . the air grew hotter and more silicious." A muddle of perfumes and the "garlicky" smell of a fat chaperon's arms mix with "voluptuous shoulders," "dainty little shoulders," "chlorotic shoulders," and the "florid faces of the men" (*DM* 172–74). The predominance of the body in the novel underscores Moore's interest in physiognomy, a trend in fictional technique he learned well from the French natural-ists and one that is often used in *Drama*. Like his physiognomist de-scription, his emphasis on food and flesh dramatizes that which throughout Moore's work is at odds with the autogenous self: the determinist force of physical life, whether that amounts to being forced to live with others in a shared space, or forced to inhabit an inescapable body. Moore's belief in the power of personality strug-gles with his conviction that individuals are entrapped by their circumstances of birth, including the body in which they find them-selves. The best response to the body's appetites, he would discover in *Confessions of a Young Man,* is to become an epicurean, to discrimi-nate in food as well as sex, or, as he portrays in his relationship with "Stella" in *Hail and Farewell,* to be so driven by the vocation of the intellect as to subordinate the body's desires.

A similar argument would underlie his 1914 tale, "Euphorion in Texas," in which a beautiful young American, desiring to bring art to the new world, seeks Moore as a father for her child. His affair with the woman derives from his decision to act as the progenitor of American art, and he relinquishes any further attachment to her or the child they conceive. The story's absurd, comic plot takes Moore as close as he will ever come to imagining a male who combines the personal creativity and social engagement of maternity. Unlike his archetypal mother, Esther Waters, the narrator of "Euphorion in Texas" turns away from the physiological—or even psychological—grounding of sexuality. Sexuality has been completely subsumed by art; no longer a male propelled by inherited physiological desire, Moore acts only as the medium of literature. The appetite for food can also undergo a similar transformation. Oliver St John Gogarty, among others, thought Moore's obsession with the quality of his own food to be pure affectation; if so, the use of food as metaphor in his texts is all the more fascinating, for affectation is a deliberate form of self-construction. To be a connoisseur, but not a glutton, stands as another means to repudiation of the inherited world. Among Moore's most memorable characters are the fat and the promiscuous, while the autobiographical persona remains primarily a watcher of others' appetites.[16]

In the pages of *A Drama in Muslin*, however, flesh is plumped and reddened and set on display in the crowded ballrooms of Dublin, where breasts and ankles squeeze out of strategically tight dresses; in the scene of a tenant eviction, the rags a peasant man wears reveal his damp, hairy chest, while his wife's wet, torn skirt exposes her bare red legs. Toward both situations, the narrator registers as much disgust as Lemuel Gulliver toward the Brobdingnagians. An examination of the revisions made between *Drama*'s first appearance in *Court and Society Review* and its subsequent book publication demonstrates that Moore quite consciously emphasized this nauseating excess of flesh. Many of the revisions involve the addition of a more feverish sexual undertone, more explicit erotic remarks, and many more incidences of bare skin, if only the sight of Mrs. Gould's "fat thick legs" roasting by the fire while "there being no man present, she undid a button or two of her dress."[17]

Only thin, angular Alice is not sweaty nor damp nor overexposed. Yet she is observant enough to know that others are. Mrs. Barton's maneuvers are registered through Alice's increasing awareness of just what her mother's relations with Lord Dungory amount to. Even at the beginning of the book, as a naïve and hopeful Alice returns home from her convent education, she intuits that her family's fortunes are linked to her mother's flattery of the old lord. Alice finds that in her wakeful mind, "the figure of Lord Dungory again loomed in sight. Suspicion, dark, formless, and fragmentary, forced sleep from Alice's eyes" (*DM* 31). As in the short story "Agnes Lahens" (1895), Moore communicates through the daughter's innocent eyes a view of the inadequate mother who allows her gnawing need for money and admiration to make her just such an "elegant harlot." In both stories, French is used as a secret sexual code. The inexperienced Agnes, recalling her early meetings with the man who—unknown to her—has been her mother's lover, remarks to him, "very often you used to speak French to mother. I never could understand why—I used to think and think" (*C* 479). Although she has learned French from the convent nuns, she still fails to understand its employment in her own household. Unlike the timid Agnes—

who retreats from the aberrations of life to a convent—Alice knows enough about the language of art and life to know that in her household it is undergoing a great misuse; and it is Alice who grows to have sufficient control over literary English to effect her escape from that household. As in *Confessions of a Young Man*, language acquired in adulthood can become the means to remake one's nationality in a new and, Moore would have it, better place.

If Ireland's children are stunted, both rich and poor, whatever future can be hoped for them lies, at least in the first part of *Drama*, with the land movement. With breadth of vision surprising in a man who, because of the land revolution, made almost no money from his property for several years, Moore depicts the idealism of its early stages. For the most part true to his facts, Moore depicts the degeneration of the League into what Charles Stewart Parnell called in the fall of 1881, "mongrel revolutionary associations."[18] With some fairness, he traces its collapse to the imprisonment of the leadership and the mass evictions and arrests through the spring and summer of that year and the next, as well as to self-serving attitudes among both leadership and tenantry. Yet with the apocalyptic outlook typical of his attitude toward Irish affairs, he fails to mention that another reason for the League's demise was that its more moderate aspirations had been accommodated by the 1881 Land Act. Nor does he acknowledge that the League did not disappear, although its name and ideology underwent pragmatic changes.[19] As in *Parnell and His Island*, Moore eradicates the possibility of any successful change in the communal life. With leadership suspect and self-interest paramount, the brightest cause disintegrates. While the foolish Mr. Adair bores the debutantes with his plans for the amelioration of Ireland's woes, for the person of real ethical intelligence no reformist work is possible.

Moore punctuates with irony the scene in which Alice and her new husband, on their way to England, make the philanthropic gesture of paying an evicted family's rent. Other tenants crowd around them, offering to buy them a pint in a nearby tavern, hoping apparently to win such charity for themselves; the agents laughingly dismiss Dr. Reed by "coarsely" observing that "there are plinty more of them over the hill on whom he can exorcoise his charity if he should feel so disposed!" (*DM* 323). The couple's action, however, salves their consciences and makes them feel sufficiently intimate for the awkward Edward Reed to draw his arm around his bride. While opposed to the powers that be in Ireland, both default on any attempts at social responsibility beyond their isolated act of charity, believing, in Dr. Reed's words, "the fatality of all human effort." As Alice says to her husband, "of humanity we must not think too much; for the present we can best serve it by learning to love each other" (*DM* 324). In such a conclusion, Moore repudiates a common pattern of the Victorian social novel. Not only is Edward Reed no gentleman, but his altruism is essentially pointless, except to enhance his and Alice's sense of unity as fellow exiles. While no better alternative is presented, neither *A Drama in Muslin* nor *Parnell and His Island* is altogether confident about the integrity of the exile, particularly when the exile escapes by means of his or her chosen identity as a writer.

As lack of selfishness confines Alice to a complacent life in an aesthetically bland if pleasant suburb, so also is the literary work she does constricted by her lack of substantial imagination. This ending is hardly the triumph some commentators have found it to be. Even as a compromise, the remoteness of her situation from any wider historical life—as Paul Sporn suggests—diminishes the sense of historical change upon which the novel is structured.[20] Moore alludes to a "great tide of revolution that is now gathering strength far away, deep down and out of sight in the heart of the nation," which will sweep away the "dull well-to-do-ness" of Alice's new life, but the observation is a brief aside in a more convincing portrait of complete tranquillity. Alice's retreat seems to exist outside of time—time whose force has been so eloquently chronicled throughout the novel. Alice's escape, as Sporn argues, is "pragmatic and private, not dialectical where synthesis is always radical transformation."[21] Perhaps Moore's portrait of historical force in Ireland has been so convincing that such a private escape seems incongruous with the impact of the more dominant elements within the novel. In later works, Moore does project France and, to a lesser degree, England as nations offering release from the force of historical dialectic. But in *A Drama in Muslin*, Moore cannot wholeheartedly put forward any faith in such places. The sardonic undercutting of the Reeds' life in suburban London evinces Moore's deep ambivalence toward the possibility of Alice's liberation, much more so than in the depictions of his own escape given in his autobiographies. Moore portrays the flight from historical life most convincingly either as a form of neurosis (in, for example, his various versions of *Celibates*), or as part of the mock-heroic *Künstlerroman* of his autobiographies. Alice's escape is simply not the effective rebirth that *Confessions*'s protagonist undergoes, although even in his autobiographies Moore does not fully subscribe to the absolute power of the exile's life of art to exempt him from determining forces.

The Artist in the Mirror

In *A Drama in Muslin,* the focus of Moore's ambivalence may lie in the kind of art Alice produces, that is, in the nature and result of her labor. Unlike her author, who agonized over his prose and his inability to write quickly, Alice writes rapidly; her plain style and simple ideas bring her a good income and a ready audience. Unlike Moore's autobiographical persona, Alice is not sufficiently committed or talented to completely remake her world in her own self-made image; she so remains complacently (if comfortably) determined.

Similar limitations are ascribed to Alice's novelist friend, John Harding. It has been widely accepted that Harding is a self-representation of Moore, and I would agree insofar that he is an early manifestation of Moore's desire to create a figure whom readers would associate with the "George Moore" who already existed as an author before the reading public. Unlike many writers, Moore displayed a self formulated for public consumption, to be understood and "read" just as one would read his written word. He sought to connect his extratextual performances to his in-text appearances not only through autobiography but in countless self-referential letters to newspapers and, in later life, books like *Avowals* or *Conversations in Ebury Street:* modeled after Landor's *Imaginary Conversations* but featuring Moore himself and set in the present moment of their writing, as if transcribed by dictation. Very clearly, Moore was much enamored with the role of celebrity author. If the author's name, or "signature," is understood to designate a set of utterances rather than a private person, then Harding may be read as part of a rhetoric in which Moore conjoins a textual creation with his cultivated notoriety as a public figure to further develop the voice of "George Moore," the author.[22] From his letters both prior to and immediately following the novel's serial publication, it is evident that he had a strong sense of an immediate audience who would seize upon the work and react to it by seeing themselves and him reflected in it.[23] These readers would know enough about the author's public appearance to connect Harding with Moore as an extratextual referent.

Moore teases the reader with similarities between his own appearance and that of the fictional Harding, particularly in the feature that would most commonly signify personality: the hard, penetrating blue eyes. Many of Moore's acquaintances testify to the unsettling obduracy of his clear eyes, which Oliver St John Gogarty described as capable of examining one with "parrot scrutiny."[21] Harding has "cold merciless eyes—eyes that were like the palest blue porcelain." Alice observes "the sharp clean-cut nose, the pointed chin, the long wavy brown hair, and the cold, close-set, keen-sighted, passionless blue eyes." Moore decidedly wants the reader to associate himself with his character. But why? Harding is not a simple figure of wish-fulfillment or self-justification; rather, he is held up to prosecution and judgment. Moore's first novel, A Modern Lover, casts the moral and aesthetic trial of the artist in black-and-white terms: one becomes either an exploitative artist who uses women and his talent for financial and social gain or an artist whose first allegiance is to aesthetic principles. But Harding fits uneasily into either category. Harding is much less than the great writer Alice imagines him to be; during one evening with her, we are told, he has "over the intellectual counter . . . flaunted samples of everything he had in stock; and the girl saw God in the literary shopboy" (DM 154). In a later scene, a voice—it is unclear whether it is Alice's or the narrator's—comments that "he paraded his ideas and his sneers as the lay figures did the mail armour on the castle stairway" (DM 188). Like other Moorian self-representations, he is attractive to women while not conventionally handsome, susceptible to artistic wrong-turns, and capable of looking on life with little involvement, sometimes at the cost of others' pain. But while Hail and Farewell may toy with the tormenting notion that all such cruelty may be for no end at all, still, once its narrator is no longer lost on the wrong artistic road, the book justifies itself by its own material presence as the defining text of the nation it repudiates—or so Moore presents the case. In A Drama in Muslin, no such confidence can emerge given the novel's intrinsic doubts about art itself.

As has already been discussed, Moore indirectly and probably unknowingly undercuts his own doctrine of the autonomy and the redemptive role of art by describing the world it repudiates in the same language that he is, a year later, to use in defining the artistic process itself. But beyond even such already severe qualifications, art is also suspect as a form of voyeurism. As has also been argued earlier, Moore likens aesthetic production to sexuality and reproduction, and all three aspects of life are interfused, like every other form of life in Ireland, with exploitative practice. To seek one's pleasure from observation and "objectivity" (the naturalist keyword) becomes, in terms of *A Drama in Muslin,* a voyeuristic act that, like experiential voyeurism, isolates the watcher from active involvement in the lives of other human beings, and which, as an act in isolation, can never bring about generation. The capacity to watch, Moore links to the incapacity to parent. In contrast to Alice's earnings, which support the life of May Gould's illegitimate child (who, however, is soon to become another dead Irish infant), Harding's income goes to support no offspring at all. He is unlikely to marry and Alice correctly realizes that "honest or dishonest . . . he could love no one" (*DM* 188). Harding's tantalizing figure torments Alice because he—unlike her husband—affects her erotically, and she winces at her mother's query as to whether her feelings for Dr. Reed resemble those she possesses for Mr. Harding. As a novelist, Harding relies upon his skill at dispassionate observation, but once he enters into social intercourse with the girls he came to observe, this same talent leads to the severe compromise of Alice's passionate nature.

Through the motif of the mirror, Moore develops the idea of art as exploitative voyeurism. As it appears in Moore's work, the mirror suggests both the narcissism and the cruel impartiality of art. Among the women, the mirror is ever-present; most of the girls (and particularly Olive) spend a great deal of their time looking at themselves, and wall-mirrors decorate the rooms in which they search for husbands. The beautiful Olive Barton's self-cultivation is so narcissistic as to be oblivious to any perspective beyond her own; as a result, it fails to bring her what she wants. Once the "belle of the season," Olive languishes at the end of the novel as potential spinster seeking refuge from her mother's machinations in Alice's London home. Olive incorrectly regards the mirror as impartial; in terror that Violet Scully might steal from her the Marquis of Kilcarney, she jealously gloats that Violet once blanched at the sight of her emaciated ankles in the mirror. However, that same Marquis dreams adoringly of Violet's very thinness. There is no such thing as an objective mirror; a perceiver always looks into it and sees what he or she wishes to see. But the ostensibly controlling artist who "watches the watcher," as Moore describes himself in *Hail and Farewell,* looks with an intrinsically mocking eye at the passions of others caught in the act of self-reflection.

Yet even the mocking glance of the writer is itself perceived in mirrors by other eyes. When Alice initially sees the man who will introduce her to the world of literature, she glances away into the fire and imagines "as in a mirror" the features of his face. Like Olive's view of Violet Scully's ankles reflected in a glass, Alice's re-imagining of Harding's face distances her from the frightening physical presence of the real man and allows her to literally "make" a reflection of him, one she later realizes was composed by her own desires. In Moore's 1915 preface to his considerably altered novel, now retitled *Muslin*, he imagines his youthful self as seen, now by his elder self, in a mirror:

> And my thoughts . . . began to take pleasure in the ridiculous appearance that the author of *A Drama in Muslin* presented in the mirrors of Dublin Castle as he tripped down the staircases in early morning . . . his lank yellow hair (often standing on end), his sloping shoulders and his female hands—a strange appearance which a certain vivacity of mind sometimes rendered engaging.[25]

The young novelist so constructed appears in a mirror as if he had no independent existence or corporal being except as a perception. He is an image that lives in the eye of the seer alone, as the projection of his author's youth. But despite a consistency of name between viewer and image, the viewer's eye is much different from the youthful eye that would look on its own reflection. Subject not to an exalted self-image but to the harsh outside eye of the mature, repudiating self, the mirror of narcissism is superseded by the mirror of the realist. Both are turned against the vain young man who thought he was something because that was what he wanted to be—against the man who is now observed with the same "parrot-like scrutiny" with which he observed others.

Through this complicated image, Moore subjugates the aesthetic of solipsistic narcissism to the realist's perspective. In a well-known passage from *Studies in the History of the Renaissance*, a book to which Moore paid lifelong homage, Walter Pater suggests that all observation and expression is essentially solipsistic:

> Experience, already reduced to a group of impressions, is tinged round for each one of us by that thick wall of personality through which no real voice has ever pierced on its way to us, or from us to that which we can only conjecture to be without. Every one of those

impressions is the impression of the individual in his isolation, each
mind keeping as a solitary prisoner its own dream of a world.[26]

In the preface to *Muslin*, Moore adopts the rhetoric of empiricism to
observe a young man lost in his own dream of the world. That the
figure is observed as a reflection in a mirror confirms the figure's
primary existence as an image. No longer has the elderly author the
ability to create that young man; his identity is so fixed by his early
writings that the elderly man can only stand apart from him with
disdainful, if affectionate, repudiation.

While in the act of voyeurism the observer remains by necessity
unseen and protected by his anonymity, in Moore's work the observer is bound to become, in the next autobiographical representation, exposed to view. If the author of the 1915 *Muslin* observes the
yellow-haired youth, and the yellow-haired youth observes Harding,
then it is not surprising that the narrator of *Parnell and His Island*, an
unnamed variation on "Harding," observes a certain young Irish
poet identified only as "Landlord M——." In these early works, the
process of self-observation (and self-revision) is thus spread out between editions or, as in *Drama* and *Parnell*, between two different
texts. In later writings, the process is completed within one version
of the text. For example, in *Confessions of a Young Man*, the narrator
evolves from a frivolous youth to a serious writer and, in the book's
last sentences, sits at a table about to embark on the novels that will
culminate in *Confessions* itself. Similarly, by the conclusion of *Hail and
Farewell*, the narrator has repudiated his earlier follies and leaves
Ireland the emergent author of the text we just finished reading.
Whether from book to book, from revision to revision, or from one
section of a work to another, each later manifestation of the self
subsumes an earlier self inscribed in a now-supplanted text. Each
speaker moves from watcher to icon, from subject to object.

Were Alice a self-representation, she would very likely be last
seen writing the novel we have just finished, but Moore has not set
her up in this way. John Harding, on the other hand, leaves Ireland
about to begin a series of Irish sketches much like what Moore produced in *Parnell and His Island*. Harding, however, is not identified
as the narrator of *Parnell*. That he is not testifies to the embryonic
state of Moore's practice of self-representation in the early 1880s. It
is as unsettled as his choice of names for the narrator of *Confessions*.
Whether to be Edward, Edwin, or Eduard Dayne, or to be George
Moore? His final decision to use the latter name marks a leap in his

development as an autobiographer, but in *Parnell and His Island,* he calls himself nothing at all.

Dispossession and Degeneration

In later works, Moore fictionalizes his experiences as much as in *Parnell,* but attaches his own name to his narrators, as well as ruthlessly utilizing the names of actual persons whose conversations and actions are, for the most part, invented by him. In *Parnell*'s bitter recantation of Irish identity, the narrator is nameless, and the historical persons described therein are generally disguised by false names or blended into composite figures. However, *Parnell* reads most significantly as Moore's first autobiography, obligated by the nature of its method to discourage the identification of author with narrator: an autobiography that, by distortion, caricature, and rejection of all it depicts, defines its author by delineating that which he is not, particularly that manifestation of an earlier self, the Irish poet "Landlord M——." If there is any consistency in this collection of violent contradictions, slurs, ad hominem attacks, and alarmist scenarios, it resides in the implicit conviction that its author shall have no part of the world portrayed within it. Yet, as in *A Drama in Muslin,* its author finds himself uncomfortably associated with that which he leaves behind. To judge Ireland with the anger of *Parnell* is to reveal one's continuing relation to it, especially when the judgments are colored by a sense of culpability.

Moore's conflicting responses to the world depicted in *Parnell*— disgust, pity, despair, and guilt at the inaction despair legitimizes— lead to a portrait fraught with ambivalence. Moore himself hated the book and in *Hail and Farewell* disdains it as "mere gabble." In the 1921 preface to *The Lake,* he assigns its authorship to his rapscallion "disciple," Amico Moorini. Most readers have confirmed his own abjuration of the work. The astute commentaries of Malcolm Brown in *George Moore: A Reconsideration* (1955) and of Wayne Hall in *Shadowy Heroes* (1980) remain the only serious discussions of the text. It is easy to see why the book has been so generally disregarded. Critics of Moore have had to be his defenders, arguing for his secure place in literary history; for most, *Parnell* is an embarrassment—an often brutal diatribe against all things Irish, particularly offensive in its dependence upon bestial metaphor. But what goes unrecognized is that *Parnell* is also Moore's first act of autobiography (however disguised as satiric pamphleteering); it endures as a vivid, passionate analysis of the state of the Irish landholding classes and their tenantry; it commends itself as a study of the relationship between individual and community life and, by extension, of the relationship between its author and the region of his childhood.

Parnell and His Island first appeared during the summer of 1886 as "Lettres sur l'Irlande," a series of articles in *Le Figaro* translated by Felix Rabbe. With some additions and revisions, they were published in France as *Terre d'Irelande* in March 1887. Three months later, an expurgated English version appeared, and Moore never attempted further revisions. The essays are undeniably written in haste, but the unresolved contradictions are more than the result of careless writing. In truth, they appear as an uncontrolled proliferation of what Malcolm Brown identifies as the key component of Moore's writing and conversation: the "Moorism." In Brown's analysis, the "Moorism" is a statement that simultaneously and self-consciously denies its own proposition, and, in so doing, simultaneously condemns and justifies the speaker.[27] If the narrator despises the poor, he is also sympathetic to their condition; if he scoffs at a typical landlord's son who wastes his inheritance on fast living in London, "Landlord M——," who exits to Paris in search of art, is deemed nearly as profligate; if he renders all reformers as either opportunists or hopeless idealists, he cannot suppress his admiration of Lord Ardilaun's attempts to beautify Dublin and improve his own estate (as by the absence of criticism, he conveys his admiration of Michael Davitt's struggle for agrarian socialism). If Moore distances himself as a purely objective artist, he abounds in moral discriminations. And as he discerns with mordant irony in the portrait of the "Irish Poet," it will be difficult for any, including the landlord's artistically minded son, to elude the power of cultural and biological heredity or, still more tenacious and pernicious, the temptation of the money that waits to be extracted from Ireland—by the landlord, and by the artist.

As the vehicle of a repudiative discourse, the narrator stands outside the world he depicts. Using the techniques of travel literature, Moore sketches common Irish scenes for the reader, who is identified as French in the first versions and as English in the last. A collection of vignettes and commentaries, *Parnell* makes use of fictional situations and technique while purporting veracity as a guidebook to Irish life during the Land War. It attempts to critique almost every facet of Irish rural society in the 1880s by creating a grotesque representative who is then subjected to caustic lampoon. The chapters appear as a series of portraits: "The Landlord," "The Priest," "The Patriot." Interspersed are scenes of Mayo life: "An Irish Country House," "A Hunting Breakfast," "An Eviction." Despite his assurances to his mother that he had done no such thing, Moore depicts in explicit and damning detail the demesne of Moore Hall and the surrounding estates, as well as his relatives and acquaintances (*LGM* 127).

By retaining some actual names, Moore gives as history that which is largely a fictionalization; his distortions and inventions have sufficient factuality to blur the distinction between the invented and the recollected.[28] Yet readers of fiction and readers of history come to a text with different expectations: Francis Hart suggested in an early "anatomy" of autobiography that readers may accept fiction as communicative of "meaning" while assuming that history and autobiography communicate "historic identity." In other words, fiction allows for personal interpretive truth; history and autobiography necessitate a shared experiential truth.[29] Contemporary readers are more likely to place autobiography between fiction and history— closer to the former than the latter—and in doing so to allow for a kind of interpretive truth nearly parallel to that allowable in fiction. Moore himself makes quite clear in his statements about autobiography that he expects his own contemporaries to accept his lifewritings as fictions. In a letter of 1923, for instance, he perhaps most succinctly articulates the procedure he had been following as early as the 1880s. Chastising the author of an article about him for an overdependence on fact, Moore admonishes him to invent. Memory, he says, "plays us false"; the creative faculty, he implies, is less likely to do so, a well-wrought fiction being more true than a mere inadequate memory (*GMP* 645).

Moore's overtly autobiographical writings celebrate the subjectivity of the self and openly exploit an unreliable, ironic narrator. But his refusal to name a narrator or engage in overtly ironic narration encourages the reader's assumption of *Parnell and His Island* as history. Even the narrator's justification of his failure to synthesize erratic impressions takes as its defense the argument that he has thus duplicated the erratic state of "nature herself." In the conclusion to *Parnell*, the narrator remarks that he has

> sought the picturesque independent of landlords and Land Leaguers; whether one picture is cognate in political feeling with the one that preceded I care not a jot; indeed I would wish each to

be evocative of dissimilar impressions, and the whole to produce
the blurred and uncertain effect of nature herself. Where the facts
seemed to contradict, I let them contradict. (*PI* 234–35)

In spite of its pretext to history, however, the truths of the book are
internal and imaginative. As autobiography, *Parnell*'s inconsistencies
and deviations from fact reveal the consistencies of an inner life. It is
Moore's autobiographical activity, which proceeds, as he says of his
purported historical activity, through ambivalence and contradiction.

The ambivalences and contradictions in his portrait of Ireland
become immediately evident within the opening description of Dalkey Bay. Like the seascapes of Italy and France, the bay is voluptuous, amorous, and the surrounding mountains are "standing out
brutally in the strength of the sun, are as the mailed arms of a
knight leaning to a floating siren whose flight he would detain and
of whom he asks still an hour of love" (*PI* 2). But as the narrator
directs our eyes to a seated figure on a terrace, we are introduced to
a down-at-the-heels landlord from the West, who must deny his
pretty daughter the clothes and dowry that would bring her a husband. The abuses of landlordism negate the chance that this shore-
line might ever be like France or that the horizons might ever bring
real "knights and sirens" together. As a repository of human misery
for generations, the land offers no sentimental promise of rebirth.
The many scenes of rural poverty in *Parnell* are vivid and devastating, and the now decrepit eighteenth-century houses and gardens
offer no respite. Even when in good repair, the narrator argues,
their foundation is the crumbling hovel: "every glass of champagne
drunk, every silk dress trailed in the street, every rose worn at a ball,
comes straight out of the peasant's cabin"—and, he reminds us, they
always did (*PI* 8).

The landlord's exploitation of the tenants and the fields they
work stains the money that comes into his possession, and for
Moore, the much-handled bill appears as the primary symbol of the
land system. With keen concentration, he describes his landlord at
Dalkey pulling

> from his pocket a roll of bank-notes black and greasy, notes with
> worn-out edges, notes cut in two and stuck together, notes which
> smell of the smoke of the cabin, notes that are rancid of the sweat
> of the fields, notes which have been spat upon at fairs for good
> luck, notes which are an epitome of the sufferings of the peasant of
> the west of Ireland. (*PI* 9–10)

When Moore came to write of himself as landlord in other auto-biographies, some of these images would recur to indict his complicity in the system. In *Hail and Farewell*, he evokes the wonderment of his childhood, the sight of peasants coming to pay the rent, muttering in Irish, their "tall hats filled with dirty bank-notes which they used to give my father." In *A Story-Teller's Holiday* he reflects that the rents from peasant cabins allowed him to escape to Paris and begin his career. A famous passage of *Confessions of a Young Man* satirically expresses his outrage upon being called back to Ireland during rent strikes: "That some wretched farmers and miners should refuse to starve, that I may not be deprived of my demitasse at Tortoni's; that I may not be forced to leave this beautiful retreat, my cat and my python—monstrous" (*CYM* 123). In these passages from later auto-biographies, he discovers himself—as callow youth and elderly man—linked to the landlord class as one for whom those greasy bills, while not precious in themselves as they are for the peasant, are indeed precious for how far they can remove him from contact with their origin.

The landlord at Dalkey is one of many antithetical selves in *Parnell:* incarnations of men Moore might have become had he not fled Ireland, and therefore men against whom he defines himself. In spite of Moore's determination to distance himself from such Irishmen, his narrator identifies himself as "a landlord today"; his distinction, the book seems determined to prove, is that he recognizes and repudiates the use to which other landlords put their money, even if he does little about the conditions that produce that money. As in *A Drama in Muslin*, the dirty money of Ireland stands behind every other abuse, and Moore's angry satire targets the denigration of sexuality and the reproductive function, the appetite for food, and the clothing that displays either the most degrading poverty or the raw attempt to attract the opposite sex by overt display. By establishing his ethical and aesthetic superiority, Moore distinguishes himself from the forms of life in Ireland: social reformer, landlord, tenant, or perhaps worst of all, failed artist.

Through the invocation of the relentless determinist rhetoric, Moore denies the possibility of reform in Ireland.[30] As in *A Drama in Muslin*, the nation of *Parnell* has fallen into a state of irredeemable degeneration, and the scenes of his book are presented collectively as "an epitaph upon a tomb, the history of a vanished civilization" (*PI* 10–11). In Felix Rabbe's translation, a small difference in phrasing posits a civilization that is not "vanished" but "nearly vanishing" ("une civilisation près de s'évanouir").[31] Perhaps Rabbe merely took liberty with Moore's manuscript, but it may also be that Moore later altered the phrasing to suggest an even more adamant denial that any civilization has existed in Ireland within living memory, and a determination to reject any possibility of its being brought back from the edge of extinction.

Moore's postulation of Ireland's extinction parallels the extinction of the familial line of his Irish poet, "Landlord M——." Although *Parnell and His Island* makes no direct reference to George Henry Moore, its author's negation of reformist possibilities entails a rejection of heredity and the establishment instead of a self shaped—as in a distorted mirror—by repudiation of his activist father. Moore's father spent much of his energy fighting colonialism, religious discrimination, and—strangely, for a man of his wealth and position—landlordism. G. H. Moore died suddenly during a rent strike in 1870, and at his funeral "representatives of the gentry," remarks Joseph Hone, "were conspicuously absent."[32] The insult culminated the deterioration of a relationship that had been unraveling for more than twenty years due both to the nature of the elder Moore's opinions and to his caustic manner of asserting them. Historians of the period agree, as David Thornley states, that G. H. Moore's "ungovernable temper" and "incautiously stinging tongue" did as much to separate him from his neighbors as did his politics.[33] Although beginning his career in 1846 as the candidate of his predominantly Protestant and conservative landholding associates, G. H. Moore quickly began to attach his name to such causes as the campaign against Russell's "Anti-Popery" Bill of 1851, the Tenant Right Movement, Repeal and, it was rumored, Fenianism: causes disconcerting to the landlords who had first elected him and forced their tenants to vote accordingly. In a rejection of landlord power unprecedented in Mayo, he won the 1852 election as the candidate supported by the priests in opposition to a candidate chosen by the landlords. Five years later as an instrument in a power struggle between two archbishops, he aligned lower-class Catholics against upper-class Catholics. Despite the isolation it brought him, he asserted an identity vehemently Catholic and radical.[34] His opinions alienated the conservatives, and his opinionated aggressiveness alienated his fellow reformers. His eldest son, who was passing through adolescence during this period, was unsurprisingly repelled by the tumult of Irish politics.

Moore's rejection of the man-of-action role may also be traced to his sense of the uselessness of landlord participation in Irish national life. Although G. H. Moore asserted his love for his lands and a paternal sense of responsibility toward his tenants, he could never acknowledge the obsolescence of his position as a hereditary landlord. As Joseph Hone suggests, much of his declamation against the descendants of English Protestants as enslavers of the poor worked to sidestep objections to his own privileged position in Mayo. Lord Sligo, his cousin and onetime close friend, protested that the elder Moore had tried, impossibly, to be both radical and landlord when in a letter of 1852 he remarks that Moore actually hurt his tenants by refusing to evict the poorer ones.[35] G. H. Moore, Sligo suggests, attempted to play too many contradictory roles.

George Moore had no reason to attempt such a reconciliation of roles, since he strongly doubted any future for the old gentry and exhibited little desire to live in Mayo. His father's efforts thus appear to him wasted and pathetic. In *Hail and Farewell* and his preface to his brother's biography of their father, Moore expresses admiration for his originality, imagination, and adventurousness, but the admiration is often qualified by the expressed belief that his father was unappreciated and suffered the inevitable fate of idealists.[36] His admiration exists in tension with his pity, and his ambivalence characterizes his assessments of all reformist possibilities.

Throughout *Parnell and His Island*, Moore disputes the pragmatic effectiveness of the gentleman reformers as he questions the ethical validity of those reformers who emerged from the middle class of graziers and more prosperous farmers. In the description of a residence that, although unnamed, corresponds to Moore Hall, he finds grounds for his dismissal of the first group, of whom his own family were prominent members. Commenting on the house of young "M——" (revealed to be the landlord in spite of himself), the narrator observes:

Here we find traces of the riches of other generations—traces that in themselves are characteristic of Ireland. The original design as it shows through the wreck and ruin seems to indicate that from the first all had been undertaken on a scale a little above the fortune of the owner; and this in Ireland! The western Celt is a creature quick to dream, and powerless to execute; in external aspects and in moral history the same tale is told—great things attempted, nothing done; and the physiology and psychology of his country is read in the unfinished pile. (*PI* 55)

In this passage, Moore awkwardly applies the clichés of nineteenth-century racial theory to men who were by no means Celts. And while his grandfather might well be seen through a veil of pathos (his life-work, a history of the French Revolution, was never published), his father was hardly a pathetic figure, but instead a man of genuine consequence. Toward the end of *Parnell* the narrator identifies the father of Landlord M—— as one who had "wasted" the family fortune "in race-horses." With a liberty granted by his anonymity, the narrator belittles a man who is of no relation to him, but merely the father of his acquaintance, the "Irish poet." Thus alluded to, G. H. Moore becomes a figure of ironic reduction, one whose ambitions are inevitably negated by the determining factor of his genetic inheritance. Although Moore's sense of his father alters in later recollections, the final verdict is similar to this early representation. Moore's remarks in *Hail and Farewell* and his preface to his brother's biography cast his father as a figure of tragic irony. He laments that G. H. Moore "wasted himself in the desert of national politics" and that his personality was much greater than his nation could encompass. According to the maxim of Matthew Arnold which appears frequently in *Hail and Farewell*, G. H. Moore was an exceptional man who lived in an inferior "moment." His individual powers to create were thwarted by the shaping power of this "moment." In this context, the reformer is equally limited, if not by genetic inheritance, then by the larger history in which he finds himself.

Although he is twice alluded to, George Henry Moore is never mentioned by name in *Parnell*. But his presence is felt in the narrator's underlying theme of historical inevitability and in the consequent perception of all reformers as foolish idealists or wily opportunists. The only well-known figure who escapes condemnation is the peasant-born land reformer, Michael Davitt, who organized the Land League in Mayo. Never a politician, Davitt remained a utopian idealist until his death. Contrasted in *Hail and Farewell* with reformers like Gill and Plunkett (acerbically dismissed by the author as men without convictions), Davitt repeatedly appears as one with "a great nature" who is "immune from the temptations of compromise, whose ideas and whose actions are identical" (*HF* 305, 308). Such phrasing also constitutes Moore's explanation of himself, although he ascribes his own absence of subterfuge to an utter lack of abstract ideals. In *Parnell*, Moore's silence on the subject of Davitt, if construed as a form of approval, suggests his early reverence for the purely idealistic and his disdain for those he deemed hypocritical.

The narrator's assertions of his own amorality and indifference may then be identified as an incipient form of self-justification. As Moore would develop the analogue in *Hail and Farewell*, the guise of the man of utter frankness effectively associates with the autobiographical persona the integrity of the admirable idealist, although without the latter's susceptibility to misleading idealisms.

For those he judged hypocritical opportunists, Moore reserves his most vehement attacks; the most vicious caricatures in *Parnell and His Island* are of those who, historically, had the most to gain from the Land League's activities: the graziers and strong farmers who made up its leadership. He creates as their representative a composite figure bearing the name of one whom a historian of the era has called "the most influential man in Mayo by the late 1870s."[37] James Daly, the "patriot," is a "half-animal" who ascends from a peasant background to the writing of incendiary articles for the *Clare Telegraph*, and thence to a life as an Irish M.P. in London, embarrassing Parnell by his unpolished English and "thick, greasy brogue." Like the landlords of *A Drama in Muslin*, his lack of aesthetic discernment and moral sense is reflected in his appetites for food and sex. Recoiling from the sophistications of the city "like a dog from a vanille [*sic*] ice," he salivates over coarse food in a cheap eating-house: "his nostrils . . . filled with the rank smells of the dung-heap, the pig, the damp cabin, the dirty paraffin-oil odour of the West" (*PI* 143). In portions of the text expurgated from the English, this "Irlandais primitif" learns to find delight in the clean body of the common London prostitute since previously "ses amours s'étaient consommées dans un champ fangeux au milieu des bouses de vache, derrière les remparts de la ville du comté avec des mendiantes et des vagabondes qu'on ne saurait nommer ni concevoir."[38] A political flunky, he spends the remainder of his days between feeble imitations of English manners and fervent proclamations of his love for Ireland.

To understand the nature of Moore's repudiation of his homeland, it is necessary to establish the differences between what *Parnell* represents as the Ireland of the early 1880s and what may be ascertained from historians of the period. In drawing the portrait of "the patriot," Moore makes libelous use of the name of James Daly, editor of the *Connaught Telegraph*, as he incorporates into what is actually a composite figure the career of John O'Connor Power, a peasant M.P. from Mayo who was aligned with Daly. The historical Daly, like his fictional counterpart, had garnered some wealth through grazing, and was typical of the class who actually gained most from the efforts of the Land League. Daly's attacks upon Davitt, whom he felt to be an impractical militant, and his active participation in anti-landlord agitation would have provoked Moore's ire. But judging from the emphasis placed on what the fictional Daly stood to gain financially from following Parnell, Moore appears to be denigrating a class type more than simply an individual. Although he asserts in an 1885 letter to the *Court and Society Review* that "there are no middle classes in Ireland," his portrait of Daly betrays his knowledge that class structure in the West was much more complicated than the simple bifurcation between dissipated landlords and starveling tenantry that he elsewhere projects.[39] His precise antipathy to Daly—and to all those in Ireland whom, in contrast to Davitt and his father, he deemed opportunistic—is brought out in the narrator's insinuation that the Daly family has everything to gain from a transfer of lands: a transfer, that is, from the landlord to the new class of graziers and moderately prosperous farmers, not to the destitute tenants toward whom the narrator feels intense sympathy as well as disgust.

A similar motive may affect that part of his model derived from O'Connor Power. A contemporary described this man as "reeking of the common clay" and added that "Parnell's aristocratic sensitiveness recoiled" in his presence.[40] But he was a powerful personality and an excellent orator: by no means the buffoon portrayed in *Parnell*. Moore may have resisted him as unrefined, as he resisted Daly, but may also have accepted Michael Davitt's condemnation of Power as politically double-dealing and self-serving. By mid-1880 O'Connor Power had turned against Davitt, who found him "egotistical" and "miserably selfish."[41] The breach between Davitt and O'Connor Power immediately preceded Moore's own return to Mayo; in such a small community it seems likely that Moore would have been aware of such a well-publicized schism. Suspicious always of reformers, Moore again may be pitting idealist against opportunist. Through his oblique censure of those he deemed opportunistic, he once more seeks to establish his distance from the greasy bill and the exploitation that, in his estimation, accompanies any efforts made in Ireland.

We can, of course, only surmise Moore's true reasons for the excesses of "The Patriot." Yet his use of James Daly's name invites, if not provokes, comparison with the factual record. Such comparison is useful in that it exhumes from the crudity of *Parnell and His Island* what would become Moore's preoccupation with the relations of poor and rich, idealist and opportunist. We recover thereby an early manifestation of a lifelong ambivalence between, on the one hand, an urgent belief in the human capacity to make oneself and one's history anew, and, on the other, a doctrine of historical and personal determinism (with the consequent impossibility of valuable reforms).

While the narrator of *Confessions of a Young Man* enacts Moore's belief in the fluidity of the self, the anonymous narrator of *Parnell* expresses a conviction of historical inevitability. As in his comments on the genealogy of the "Irish poet," the narrator offers a pseudo-evolutionist explanation for Irish history in the crude notions of racial historiography that he voices in asides and in the bestial metaphors that darken his text with the troubled atmosphere of racialist harangue. Only the "Irish poet" escapes the bestial metaphor, and he is poisoned with other darts. The tenantry are "rats," "apes," and "newts"; the landlords "larvae," "oysters," and "flies." All are characterized by their foul eating habits and—particularly in the French edition—sexual intemperance with overt and grotesque animal associations.[12] Speaking of Dublin society and its response to the Land League, the narrator makes the following observation:

> Today it trembles with sullen fear, and listens to the savage howling of the pack in kennels set in a circle about the Castle, the Hotel, the Club, and the Shop; and as Gladstone advances, the barking springs to meet him; the fierce teeth are heard upon the woodwork. Will he lift the latch and let the hounds rush in on the obscene animal? (*PI* 34)

As purposeful rhetoric, Moore's analogy is a failure. In a book that openly criticizes Gladstone's reforms, the allusion to the group that opposed them as an "obscene animal" makes little sense. The idea that Gladstone holds the power to restrain the "hounds" of the Land League is inconsistent with Moore's deterministic thesis. The passage is clearly out of control; his rejection of constitutional reformers locks with his fear of secret organizations, and both collide with a bitter disdain of landlord society and a strident refusal to admit the tenantry as a desirable element. The only solution is a nonsolution: to let these assorted animals follow their inevitable degenerative evolution, and to remove himself from the historical time in which they are bound.

To do so, Moore turns to work. If the work is good, then one's depatriation is confirmed; if not, the writer is condemned to being

just what Moore portrays in *Parnell:* an "Irish poet." In discussing
Moore's views of Ireland, his valuation of art, and his own dread of
artistic failure, Wayne Hall offers the following hypothesis:

> Anxiety and guilt about his status as a landlord . . . com-
> pounded doubts about his talent as an artist. . . . If he would not
> rightfully earn . . . privileges by staying in Ireland to manage the
> family estate, then the burden fell on him of creating great art, of
> contributing to the spiritual worth of society as the tenant contrib-
> uted to the material. His recognitions of the injustices in the whole
> landlord-tenant system, like his fears of personal poverty, only
> added to anxieties about artistic failure.[13]

Hall is clearly correct in so characterizing the despair and guilt of
one who finds scenes of poverty "burnt for ever in my memory" and
who identifies as tenants of "Landlord M——," the inhabitants of "a
dwelling-place that strikes me as being the farthest possible limit to
which human degradation may be extended" (*PI* 74, 72). Art may
well be seen as an attempt at compensation, but only if successful.
The apparent futility of reformers like his father conjoins with
Moore's one great terror: that of producing nothing, of being finally
judged a dilettante, and, as such, an irredeemable Irishman.

His caustic portrait of himself as he was in the early 1880s delineates a silly little man who is, after all, only a type. Of "Landlord
M——" the narrator remarks:

> on the refusal of his agent to supply him with any more money he
> had come over from Paris with a few pounds, and a volume of
> Baudelaire and Verlaine in his pocket. Of all the latest tricks that
> had been played with French verse he was thoroughly master; of
> the size, situation, and condition of his property he knew no more
> than I did. . . . This type of man is not unfrequent in Ireland. (*PI*
> 53–54)

Moore reduces his artistic powers to familiarity with "the latest
tricks," and he diminishes to a stock type the man who wrote his
mother in 1883 that "I was born, I live, I shall die a peculiar man. I
could not be commonplace were I to try" (*LGM* 150). If, as has often
been suggested, the act of autobiography depends upon a sense of
oneself as completely unique, then Moore's presentation of the repudiated self as a mere type functions within his anti-autobiography,
or autobiography-of-what-he-is-not.[14] The manifestation of this

younger self as a character completely distinct from the narrator
serves to alienate this most dangerous of potential selves, the failed
artist. Similarly, the explicit designation of "Landlord M——" as a
poet identifies him with the author of *Flowers of Passion* (1878) and
Pagan Poems (1881), while distinguishing him from the author who,
by 1887, was known almost exclusively as a novelist.

It is crucial that Moore draw absolute barriers between himself
and one who would come of age in such an atmosphere, where "to
be considered a man of the world, it is only necessary to have seen
one or two plays in London before they are six months old, and to
curse the Land League" (*PI* 18). If George Henry Moore was, according to his eldest son, either a degenerative product or a good
man with the misfortune of living in the wrong moment, then like
him, the Irish poet's failures might also be blamed on heredity or on
his own "moment." Through the autogenic thesis, Moore would attempt in his very next book, *Confessions of a Young Man*, to step out
of his line of ancestry and out of his time. For the young "Landlord
M——," however, the confines of type—with all of the biological
inferences of such a term—prohibit such self-creation.

Moore defines himself against the reformer, the landlord, and
the Irish artist, and so too does his repudiative process renounce the
tenantry. The terms are similar to those in which the landlord class
is itself accused: unrefined and irresponsible sexuality, bad food, the
maltreatment of children. In peasant life, he saw only deprivation
and, when the financial status of the tenants rose, "dreadful hats and
shapeless mantles." As Matthew Arnold's famous vignette on the disastrous life of a workhouse inmate, "Wragg," expresses an outrage
at her poverty equaled only by his outrage at the woman's hideous
name, so Moore's analysis of the oppression of the poor is mingled
with his revulsion at the aesthetic poverty he finds among them.

But unlike the peasant, unlike the landlord who thinks Wagner
and Beethoven are livestock breeders, and unlike the pretentious
would-be artist, Moore in the guise of narrator gains power as the
storyteller of the tragic. As omniscient storyteller, he seals the separation between his adult being and his upbringing in County Mayo.
Instead of embodying potential and promise, the world of youth acts
as an emblem of sterility. The pathos of youth articulates the cruel-
ties of Ireland: Dublin is like a city constructed with blocks by a tired
child; St. Stephen's Green is a school-treat for charity children; the
moral distortions of poverty leave a young girl and her illegitimate
baby abandoned in a mud cavern. In a particularly telling scene, the

narrator wanders in back of the Irish poet's decaying mansion and encounters a "sun-dial that the sun has not seen these many years." Brushing away the overgrowth, he feels as if he were deciphering "an inscription upon a lost and forgotten Brahmin tomb." The scene may have been suggested by *David Copperfield,* where in book 1, chapter 2, the narrator recollects a sundial from the world of his childhood. Dickens (whose works, as he writes in *Confessions,* Moore "knew . . . by heart") remarks that the sundial allowed the young David to overcome his fear of the shapeless night (and, by implication, his fear of death). In *Parnell,* the narrator's discovery of the sundial suggests instead the closure of time upon the moribund world of childhood. Alice Barton makes a similar discovery after returning home when, in the midst of a reverie over "the dead life of childhood," she spots the "old-fashioned time-piece" that once called her to lessons: "Alice felt as if she had been apprised of the loss of a tried friend when one of the servants told them the clock had been broken some years ago" (*DM* 34–35). In a clock that has ceased to function, Moore creates in both texts the symbol of a lost childhood. Unlike Alice, the narrator of *Parnell* bears no intimate relation with the timepiece; the words written upon it are to him as the alien signs of a "forgotten Brahmin tomb." At the end of his own line and for all generative purposes, "a celibate life," Moore understands the sundial and the clock to mark the burial place of a dead life.

With terrible self-mockery, Moore describes his lost lineage when the Irish poet discovers that his ancestor's grave in northern Mayo has been pillaged for the lead coffin (a source for bullets). His companion, the narrator, muses:

> the bones of him who created all that has been wasted—by one generation in terraces, by another in racehorses, and by another in dissipation in Paris, lie scattered about the ground trodden by chance of the passing feet of the peasant.
>
> Notwithstanding his cynicism my friend was touched to the heart. Three days afterwards he began a poem on the subject, the chief merit of which lay in the ingenuity of rhyming Lilith with lit. (*PI* 76)

With such bitter images of sterility, Moore has silently returned to his opening scene at Dalkey Bay and the young woman who must live husbandless and childless. Without artistic achievement, Moore's fate will repeat hers.

Alice Barton left the west of Ireland in 1883; in the same year nearly eight thousand people emigrated from County Mayo alone. Moore was not singular in viewing departure as the one deliverance from the ravages of the Irish landlord's world. *A Drama in Muslin* and *Parnell and His Island* announce the imperative for the move, and in *Confessions of a Young Man,* Moore discovers his means.

2

The Autobiographical Pyramid
Confessions of a Young Man

At Moore's everyone becomes inspired to talk without any affectation. Moore is the most sincerely affected man I know. His mannerisms have become
real.
— Oliver St John Gogarty to G. K. Bell, 1904

T HE PROCESS OF REPUDIATION enacted in *Parnell and His
Island* culminates in the burial of childhood and the disap-
pearance of a lineage. *Confessions of a Young Man* both begins and
ends with the entombment of youth—regretted, cherished, but most
of all lost to the world of ongoing experience. Like the narrator of
Parnell, the young man of *Confessions* rejects most received forms of
belief and behavior. In the earlier text, those received forms are pe-
culiarly Irish and belong to a specifically familial, regional, and religious heritage. The pointed assaults of *Confessions* are aimed at the
morals and aesthetics of middle-class propriety in general, be it of
the British, European, or American variety. If the range of Moore's
scrutiny has broadened, the process of repudiation leads also to a
more ambitious end than the purgation of unacceptable alternative
identities evident in *Parnell* and *A Drama in Muslin*. The text recovers
a process of espousal as well as rejection. In the midst of its narrator's ostentatious iconoclasm stands a clearly defined autobiographical persona who may smash but who also spares and selects as his

emerging sense of literary vocation directs him. The young man may resemble "Landlord M——," but unlike the latter, he is no longer set apart from his narrator as a distinct being. The narrator here speaks as the older version of the young man, and he looks upon his youthful incarnation with indulgent affection. After 1889, the protagonist's name was changed from "Edwin Dayne" to that of his author, in accordance with what Moore says was his original intention to identify himself with his character.[1] Not only did Moore establish a resilient central character to undergo the process of disavowal and avowal, but he offered this character as the representation of himself.

The autobiographical status Moore overtly conferred upon his text remained for him one of its crucial elements, and he claimed its energetic call to life as the chronicle of his own discovery of vocation. Unlike *Parnell and His Island*, *Confessions of a Young Man* is a book of life, a joyous enactment of the very autogenesis it proclaims. Its vivacity may be checked by an intimation of final futility, but its fundamental narrative became for its author and his readership a central myth of recreation, its story retold in so many subsequent editions and repeated in so many other works as to become a ritual telling. Given the salvationist terms Moore himself adopts, his story's factual basis provides the substantive miracle to this myth of self-birth, proclaiming its author's faith in the self-generative capacity.

In its doctrine of the created self, *Confessions* resembles other fin de siècle texts, most notably the writings of Oscar Wilde. Yet its divergence from the common theme is considerable, for reasons that become clear if Moore and Wilde are compared. Two men who knew Moore well, Max Beerbohm and AE (George Russell) examine his resemblance to Wilde and return the similar verdict that while Moore was extraordinarily self-conscious and affected, "his mannerisms," as Gogarty affirms, "have become real." In Beerbohm's words, he presented "in the midst of an artificial civilisation the spectacle of one absolutely natural man." The personality of Wilde, in contrast, Beerbohm describes as "a conscious and elaborate piece of work."[2] In a letter to Moore, AE perceptively remarks that Yeats, like Wilde, wanted to create a mask that "would harmonise with the literary style." Yeats, writes AE, "said it was merely living artistically, and it was the duty of everybody to have a conception of themselves, and he intended to conceive of himself. . . . The error in his psychology is, that life creates the form, but he seems to think that the form creates life."[3] Moore, like AE, recognized the determining aspect of historical life in the form both his personality and his work would take.

As an Irishman, Moore belonged to what was popularly considered a distinct "race"; he was acutely aware of the force of historical condition, particularly that of economics. Wilde was also an Irishman and, as the social criticism within his comedies reveals, he too understood the formative role of money and class. Unlike Wilde, however, Moore was a novelist whose strength derived from his immersion in the naturalist tradition. Not surprisingly, then, the self-creative process celebrated in *Confessions* is counterweighted by an implacable determinism; each proclamation of freedom stands in tension with its denial. Taken as a totality, however, *Confessions* less demonstrates its author's vacillation between two theories of origin and development than it testifies to his startling power of assimilation. Through his always elastic and self-serving notion of "instinct," Moore appropriates the very language of heredity to his theory of autogenesis. As he twists the essential determinist principle to his own purposes, its entrapments—for the highly skilled few like himself—become, like Houdini's ropes, the very means of escape.

This story of development—of selections, rejections, liberations, and captivities—is presented through a minimal chronological overlay: childhood in Ireland, escape to Paris where Moore attempted painting, early efforts at literature, his financial crisis and subsequent move to London to become a journalist, and, finally, as youth is relinquished, the serious pursuit of a novelist's career. Selected from Moore's life are those details that most directly affect his development as a writer. Only those affiliations that have bearing on his emerging aesthetics warrant description, and rather than scenes from family life Moore depicts the café society of the artists he admired and emulated, men like Degas, Manet, and Villiers de l'Isle-Adam. In addition to the memorable conversation of the latter, Moore records the accents of landladies, aspiring actresses, hacks and third-rate publishers—uncouth but delightfully novel and intriguing to the narrator's receptive ear. Many extreme assertions about politics, the family, women, and religion are registered in the pages of *Confessions,* although only in conjunction with equally extreme assertions about aesthetics. All such vociferations are offered unconditionally, even aggressively, as if designed to shock the reader; many are contradicted elsewhere in the text in ways that allow us to measure the young man's development. As part of his attack upon conventional morality, the narrator flaunts his apparent heartlessness in addresses to the "hypocritical reader" as well as the comic dialogue with "Conscience" (added in 1889). With apparent relish, Moore adopts the guise of the cruelly yet naively self-preoccupied artist, a role he continued to exploit in later autobiographies.

Despite his assertion in the 1904 preface that "no one may re-write his confessions," Moore rewrote the text repeatedly. Ultimately, it would appear in seven distinct versions, and while the 1918 version had been thought to be the last, recent bibliographical discoveries suggest that he was again revising the text sometime after 1926.[4] In general, the revisions reflect his increasing stylistic skills and the prose style he developed about the turn of the century, which he came to call the "melodic line." His alterations in diction produced a less abrasive tone, perhaps to accord with his increasing affection for the narrator and a wish to render him more acceptable to the reader. In each revision he persistently interjected a sense of the present tense by adding new prefaces that comment upon the text and upon previous prefaces, thereby challenging the past into which the autobiographical act casts the writing "I." Within the prefaces and the story itself, he continued to incorporate new opinions about art while retaining the old ones; but true to the nature of his story, he made no attempt to reconcile these divergent ideas or to correct facts, translations, or citations.[5]

As a composite of multiple genres, tenses, topics, and rhetorical positions, *Confessions* flouts expectations of a self-integrated text. Yet underlying its surface diversity are two major organizational features: the narrative structure of the Exodus and a series of recurring metaphors about the construction of the self and the process of life-writing. Both are critical to *Confessions'* argument as to the nature of the self and the role that writing takes in its realization. The first of these features has often been defined as the dominant mode of British autobiography: the story of conversion, or exodus from the land of Egypt into the Promised Land.[6] Building upon the literal and symbolic motif of geographical movement, Moore's exodus not only follows the allegorical path from darkness to enlightenment, but delivers its protagonist from the Egypt of Ireland to the genuine "homeland" of France and, later, London. Ireland, Moore said, was merely an accident of birthplace; as he wrote to John Eglinton and to Ernest Boyd, Paris was his true "cradle," the "nest" of his life (*EG* 63; *GMP* 330). According to Moore's ideas of instinct, the move to the promised land is, as in the biblical story, less a discovery of that land than a recovery of one's birthright. Adapting the sacred paradigm to his secular narrative, Moore openly exploits the terms of conversion—spiritual death, rebirth, and baptism—in what he calls a parody of the *Confessions* of St. Augustine, a story not of "a God-tortured" but of "an art-tortured, soul."

Appropriate to a story in which the protagonist's rebirth is set in the Paris of the late 1870s, Moore superimposes upon the British pattern of bondage and deliverance a highly diversified, even fragmented, surface narrative that he identifies as French in origin. In so doing, he successfully disrupts reader expectations—producing the desired effect of shock and surprise—while he imitates the mixed genre and the digressive, episodic narrative structure of French essay-novels like J.-K. Huysmans's *A Rebours*. Through direct reference to *A Rebours* and other texts, Moore attempts to set his own book's avowal of artifice and individualism within a French, rather than English, tradition. His perversely proud recital of his selfishness seems to follow that of Jean-Jacques Rousseau's *Confessions*, although in the 1917 preface Moore denies any previous knowledge of Rousseau. Still, the tradition of Rousseau and the influence of avant-garde Parisian aesthetics should not obscure the fact that Moore's *Confessions* echoes the model of the Exodus. Through the religious connotations thus invoked, Moore prepares his reader to interpret his story as a parable of aesthetic dogma while underscoring how absolutely critical to personal and vocational salvation was the discovery and emerging mastery of his art.

Like *A Rebours*, *Confessions* posits "life" and "art" as oppositional categories and then proceeds to interfuse the two terms. The narrator probes into his character's "soul" in the act of discussing art and, conversely, verifies his aesthetics through discussion of his experience. As much a commentary on autobiography as the embodiment of one, *Confessions* advances Moore's ideas poetically with (as he wrote to his brother) an "irony and subtelty [*sic*] of expression" that he feared would not be understood.[7] Replacing systematic argumentation, a series of key metaphors about art as self-construction constitutes a second major organizational feature. These metaphors are then developed by the accumulation of corresponding images, anecdotes, and expository passages.

The Man of Instinct

The initial formulation of the persona whom Moore will henceforth put forward as the image of himself emerges from one such representation. It is the book's most striking metaphor, the one upon which all commentators have at some time remarked: that of the man of wax who wanders within the labyrinth of his own desires. Coming in *Confessions'* first sentences, the passage serves as the reader's entrance into what Moore would call the "instinctual" self.

> I came into the world apparently with a nature like a smooth sheet of wax, bearing no impress, but capable of receiving any; of being moulded into all shapes. . . . I have felt the goad of many impulses, I have hunted many a trail; when one scent failed another was taken up, and pursued with the pertinacity of an instinct, rather than the fervour of a reasoned conviction. . . . Intricate indeed was the labyrinth of my desires; all lights were followed with the same ardour, all cries were eagerly responded to. . . . But one cry was more persistent, and as the years passed I learned to follow it with increasing vigour, and my strayings grew fewer and the way wider. (*CYM* 49)

Moore freely borrows his image from Schopenhauer's "On Thinking for Oneself." In that essay, the philosopher postulates that the inferior intellect accepts thoughts as foreign to it "as is the seal to the wax whereon it impresses its stamp." In contrast, Schopenhauer contends, the original genius follows the impulses of his own mind. The only environmental factors that shape those impulses are those by which the mind, operating with the wisdom of "instinct," chooses to be affected.[8] Moore alters Schopenhauer's metaphor in several characteristic ways. First, as one warmly attached to his young man, Moore refuses to equate the man of wax with an inferior mind. Instead, he identifies such plasticity as a progressive stage for the original genius who learns through experience and instinct what impresses he should allow. Second, he broadens the metaphor's application. While Schopenhauer designates the intellect as waxen, Moore extends the referent to include his whole "nature" and, in doing so, admits the senses and emotions as receptive elements. Third, he renders the concept paradoxical by making his man of wax both passive ("I have felt the goad of many impulses") and active ("I have hunted many a trail").

While Moore neglects to state directly that he took on each impress with a fervor that more than warped the mold with the heat of the wax, his entire paragraph synthesizes figures of passive receptivity and active acquisition and in doing so suggests the nature of the instinctual self. He argues that "what I have . . . chance bestowed, and still bestows, upon me," but merges passive with active metaphors in arguing that his "soul" has "taken colour and form from the many various modes of life that self-will and an impetuous temperament have forced me to indulge in." In such phrases, Moore is using the deterministic language of novelists like Samuel Butler, Thomas Hardy, or George Gissing, but to unusual ends. By "chance," Moore means nothing uncustomary; it simply signifies unforeseen events, particularly those that influence financial circumstances. "Temperament," however, takes on new meanings. In the minds of many other late Victorians, "temperament" is associated with heredity's irreducible force: Hardy's Tess is perhaps the best-known embodiment of the idea. But to Moore, one's temperament, particularly if impetuous, finds release and expression only when hereditary forces are contained. In *Confessions,* temperament is decidedly aligned with the concept of idiosyncratic choice. The narrator remarks that chance sent no person into his life who did not contribute something to it, and in response to an imagined disputation of the idea, the narrator affirms that "chance, or the conditions of life under which we live, sent, of course thousands of creatures across my way who were powerless to benefit me; but then an instinct of which I knew nothing, of which I was not even conscious, withdrew me from them, and I was attracted to others" (*CYM* 62).

The process is not a matter of deliberate selection; in fact, Moore goes on to describe its workings through metaphors of digestion and elsewhere imagines the resultant art as "divine excrement." Like many of his contemporaries, he rejects the concept of individual moral choice central to the ethics (and aesthetics) of Evangelical Protestantism. But he uses deterministic language in a way that supports the primacy of individual will; while temperament—or instinct—leads the speaker without his knowledge, according to Moore it never leads him wrong; nor is it in any sense inherited.

As to the origin of this instinctual "temperament," Moore, never a systematic philosopher (in truth, a parodist of such thinkers), begs the question. In an 1889 insertion, he is as specific, if indeed inconclusive, as he will ever be about the issue: the narrator tells his "Conscience" that he has "drawn the intense ego out of the clouds of semi-consciousness, and realized it" (*CYM* 219). The question as to the origin of this semiconscious presence is never raised. Although like his Romantic predecessors, Moore depicts the self as transcendental, he refuses to assign it a transcendental origin. Wherever it comes from, he maintains, it does not derive from family or nationality. Family and nationality are, in fact, the most fearsome impediments to its development. In a countermove, Moore establishes himself as the father of his own country. In *Hail and Farewell,* for example, he recalls his horror at his father's plan to make of him a military man whose "lot might be to die in defence of his country, or be wounded in her defence, which was worse still." He goes on to comment, "It seemed to me that myself was my country" (*HF* 476). The life-affirming country of "I" here stands in diametric opposition to the call to death from father and nation. Citizenship in the country of "I" demands the denial of other sources of origin.

Besides being autogenic, the instinctive self is, according to Moore, essential and unchanging.[9] At the beginning of chapter 12, the narrator of *Confessions* scoffs at the assumption that character is developmental. Parodying lines from Tennyson's "In Memoriam," he mockingly associates the idea of moral development with outmoded notions of progressive evolution. Despite those variations in his opinions, which the text abundantly demonstrates, Moore insists in the 1904 preface that "no one has changed less than I." As an elderly man remembering his years in France, he reflected to a friend that "I already thought I knew a good deal: I was ignorant, of course, but I was already George Moore with something to say for myself though I did not know how to say it" (*LGM* 66). This egotistical entity called "George Moore," who existed even before his emergence as a Frenchman, is represented as immutable. Yet as a man of wax, this autobiographical protagonist absorbs a multitude of influences and chance events toward which he is drawn by his own static nature. As he concedes his involvement in historical life, he simultaneously defies its transformative power.

The metaphorical underpinning of *Confessions* directs attention to the process by which the young man sheds the conventions and avoids the obstacles that restrict the movement of this essential self. Again, Moore intertwines metaphors of passivity and activity. The young man is to plunge into life as if into water and to be carried like a boat through experience. The profligate Marshall, a talented but undisciplined painter and a parasitic companion, threatens to become "a shipwrecking reef." Aestheticism, naturalism, and symbolism are "shoaling waters," mud, and surf; the modern world is "putrefying mud." While the boat is a passive image of the self, getting into the boat to set off across the water is its own radical activity for a youth raised in an obscure corner of an obscure island. Such assertiveness is implied in a supplemental metaphor by which the narrator describes himself searching after literature "like a pike after minnows." The image depicts a being compelled to move through waters stronger than itself at the urging of its own self-interested, voracious appetite. In yet another metaphor, Moore describes his youth as running "into manhood, finding its way from rock to rock like a rivulet, gathering strength at each leap." While constrained by the rocks that chance places in his path, his youth finds its way with an abounding energy from an unidentified source.

To some degree, to be subject to one's own instinct is to be a victim of what Schopenhauer calls the great joke of the will to live: an impetus toward self-realization that leads inevitably to futility and despair. While not entirely dismissing this outlook, Moore alters such severe pessimism and places it in service of his autobiographical rhetoric. As has been shown, the notion of instinct serves a particular purpose in his theory of self-creation and in his politics of self-justification. Like the heroine of *Esther Waters*, Moore's autobiographical persona takes great satisfaction in the acts of discovery and creation, regardless of their hope for lasting significance; and if the autogenic man has been the victim of a joke, at least that joke has been partly of his own making and on something of his own terms. In addition, a belief in the dominance of instinct serves the apologetic aspect of Moore's autobiography: that is, the autobiography's function as a defense of actions. If the instinct, or will, is distinct from the ego and something to which the ego is subject, then in Moore's schema the ego is absolved of culpability for its actions. "Couldn't, with wouldn't," says the narrator of *Confessions*, "was in my case curiously involved; nor have I . . . ever been able to correct my natural temperament. I have always remained powerless to do anything unless moved by a powerful desire" (*CYM* 51). The man of wax may receive impressions, but only at the bidding of his unchanging understructure, the rigidity of which seems to surprise even him.

Moore presents as his autobiographical persona a naïve, even childish, figure caught in the passion of his notions, and innocently torturing those who stand in his way: a figure, in Joseph Hone's words, "of paradoxical simplicity." Often Moore's rhetoric is sufficiently persuasive and his tone so intimate as to prompt a thoughtful consideration of the notion in question. For instance, *Confessions'* attacks upon philanthropic reform and its advocacy of hedonism function in a fairly simple way to justify the narrator's ideas and character by attributing his apparent selfishness to a form of compassion more sophisticated than the philanthropist's. His resistance to increasing the salary of the abused servant, "Awful Emma," indicates, if anything, an awareness of how fully imprisoned within class structure she is: an imprisonment a small increase in money or a few holidays does nothing to eradicate, although such may salve the conscience of the self-proclaimed reformer.[10] Similarly, his affirmation to the "hypocritical reader" that a wicked life is a courageous and interesting one has a rhetorically persuasive appeal coming as it does at the end of a story brimming with lively bohemian adventures set in contrast to conventional society's preoccupation with money and appearances.

In such passages, Moore plays the relatively uncomplicated role of the amoral freethinker who proves to be more genuinely moral than proper society—all, ironically, within the confines of a morality dictated by bourgeois ideology. But much more frequently, Moore portrays himself as so fully at the mercy of his instinct that he acts in ways that are simply cruel. He exploits for the purposes of self-defense Schopenhauer's adage that the individual is ruled by his instinctual will and that "he must carry out the very character which he himself condemns."[11] The self-centered artist, in such terms, cannot help but place his will-to-be ahead of another's feelings or ahead even of his own attachments to others. Moore's autobiographies, for instance, exhibit a disregard for family that simultaneously taxes and engages the reader's sympathy with the protagonist. In a passage added to *Confessions* in 1889, the narrator confesses at length his true reaction to his father's death. He feels, he admits, an exultant sense of liberty since, freed from patriarchal constraints, financial and otherwise, he may now devote his time to art. Years later in *Memoirs of My Dead Life*, Moore acknowledges his squeamish disinclination to visit his dying mother in Mayo, and in *Hail and Farewell*, the narrator pitilessly and irrevocably estranges his brother Maurice ostensibly over nothing more important than the evaluation of Cardinal Newman's prose style.[12] Moore's letters to his brother during the period indicate that he in no way exaggerated his behavior when recreating it in *Hail and Farewell*. The letters depict the apparently senseless demise of a close brotherly affection through Moore's incessant, insulting obsession with the imagined offenses of his brother's religion.[13]

Because Moore's autobiographies generally do not demonstrate concern with fidelity to fact, the question arises as to why he would depict himself in such an unflattering way, particularly as the very depiction suggests that he realized the harshness of his past actions. The motive, perhaps, lies in his sense of the grim urgency of his self-identification as an artist, who, as demonstrated in *Parnell* and *A Drama in Muslin*, lives necessarily estranged from all calls of duty to nation or home. Such calls, for the artist, are as suspect as the self-seeking gabble of priests and politicians. Moore thus highlights his disregard for the feelings of others, particularly those of his family. But as he does so he also depicts his family members—and others—as impediments in his road to self-discovery and the disciplined self-creation that shall follow. Because the simultaneous enactment and documentation of that self-creation rest in the reader's hand, Moore is prepared to argue that father and brother must have been in the wrong and that his "instinct" must have been correct in overriding the claims of family. Moore appears to be arguing that even when instinct takes the form of folly or cruelty, it leads to an end that justifies its means precisely because its struggle has been successful. If the story of his emergent career as a writer is at the same time the story of the origin of the book we read, the book then acts as a testament of victory.

Life and Lifewriting: The Autobiographical Pyramid and the Portrait of the Artist

The unchanging, instinctual self is therefore contingent upon the activity of autobiography for its existence. As the following series of metaphors from *Confessions* implies, life and lifewriting exist interdependently. Metaphors first applied to youth are later extended to prose style. For example, a passage in the first edition describes the narrator's youth as "finding its way from rock to rock like a rivulet"; in the 1889 preface Moore observes that the early stages of his narrative "leaped like a rivulet from rock to rock, so narrow was the channel" and never, despite the author's efforts, "flow[ed] like a stream, lingering now and then, a quiet pool, beneath pleasant boughs" (*CYM* 35–36). Like so many others, the metaphors of rivulet and stream project as interchangeable referents the process of living and the process of writing. In his influential essay, "Autobiography as De-facement," Paul de Man asks whether "the autobiographical project may itself produce and determine the life"—if "the referent determine the figure, or is it the other way round"? Might the life be "no longer clearly and simply a referent at all but something more akin to a fiction which then, however, in its own turn, acquires a degree of referential productivity?"[11] As the man in the tow of his infallible instinct, Moore has formulated a description of himself that shapes future self-representations. If letters and the recollections of others can be admitted as evidence, Moore also exploited the description to justify almost any act of social behavior in his extraliterary life. The autobiographical persona seems to be directing all shows—within the text, in future texts, and in the lived life.

At his most radical point of aestheticism, Moore postulates a self that comes into being only with the acquisition of literary language and in the process of describing itself. His text seems to be an early intimation of de Man's idea that no autobiographical referent exists beyond the text itself. Yet I maintain that Moore's sense of history and audience is far too deeply ingrained to allow him to reside indefinitely within such purely self-referential boundaries. Just as he adapts the language of biological determinism to his own autogenic argument, so he modifies to fit his historical consciousness the language of literary self-murder and subsequent self-creation.

As it affects his ideas of the relation between the autobiographer and his subject, this process of modification appears most vividly in his metaphor of the pyramid and in his comments on textual and photographic portraits of the writer. Moore begins *Confessions* with a dedication to Jacques-Emile Blanche that takes the form of an extended metaphor that he calls in the 1904 preface "an epitaph upon myself."[15] It reads, in part:

> L'âme de l'ancien Egypien s'éveillait en moi quand mourut ma jeunesse, et j'ai eu l'idée de conserver mon passé, son esprit et sa forme, dans l'art.
>
> Alors trempant le pinceau dans ma mémoire, j'ai peint ses joues pour qu'elles prissent l'exacte ressemblance de la vie, et j'ai enveloppé le mort dans les plus fins linceuls. Rhamesès le second n'a pas reçu des soins plus pieux! Que ce livre soit aussi durable que sa pyramide! (*CYM* 33)

> [The soul of an ancient Egyptian was reborn in me when my youth died, and I developed the idea of conserving the spirit and form of my past in art.
>
> So, dipping my brush in my memory, I painted its cheeks so that they would capture the exact resemblance to life, and I enveloped my dead self in the finest shrouds. Rhamses II never had treatment so pious! Oh that my book would be as durable as his pyramid!]

Looking back on his text in the preface of 1904, the narrator concludes that "this epitaph dedication . . . informs me that I have embalmed my past" (*CYM* 37). As the embalmer, the writer has made of his younger self a kind of literary mummy that resides in the textual pyramid excavated by the revising author. This extended metaphor is, as Moore notes in the 1904 preface, "astonishing." As we shall see, it points to the inseparability of experienced life and the recollective process, particularly when recollection takes the form of autobiographical art.

Before returning to the metaphor of the subject self as a literary mummy, I must examine its house—the textual pyramid—because the metaphor of book as edifice also reveals the ambivalence in his judgment about whether art follows life or life follows art. As an architectural structure, the pyramid is particularly suited to its function in Moore's text. An alien form imposed upon an inhospitable landscape, the pyramid has not arisen naturally from its environment. It is gorgeous, overpowering, artificial, and has no function but to affirm the majesty of the pharaoh who lies within. As a literary structure its beauty, variety, and otiosity stand in contrast to the faltering moralistic efforts of such "houses" as Mrs. Humphry Ward's *Robert Elsmere,* a building made of "plaster of Paris" dismissed in *Confessions* as the by-product of a culture childishly obsessed with its conscience. The metaphor of book as an edifice further recalls Moore's preoccupation with place—either localities like Mayo or Paris, or constructed buildings like Moore Hall or his house on Ebury Street. In books, letters, and conversation, his self-portraiture dwells upon the necessity of replacing improper dwellings—like the archaic Moore Hall or the mud cabins of *Parnell* or *A Drama in Muslin*—with the right kind of house, decorated with impressionist paintings, beautiful furniture, and an Aubusson carpet. Like the pyramid in the desert of English letters, the chosen place functions as a fortress against the repudiated localities of historical necessity, which in *Confessions* are Ireland or the bourgeois "villa," and in later life becomes nearly all modern settlement outside the homes of a few friends.

Yet as W. B. Yeats knew about his own fortress against modernity, Thoor Ballylee, any structure—even a fortress—is founded in a cultural landscape. Moore himself became convinced of this when he failed to establish Upper Ely Place against the conservatism of Dublin. The bohemian apartment that *Confessions* places on Rue de la Tour des Dames or the house on Ebury Street can serve their function only in a Paris or London, cities that allow the kind of life Moore finds acceptable. In the first case, although Moore himself never actually lived on Rue de la Tour des Dames, he probably names the street for the same reasons he gives in *Memoirs of My Dead Life:* "because the name is an evocation. Those who like Paris like to hear the names of the streets" (*MMDL* 19). The fact that such a name could exist in Paris (as it certainly could not in Dublin or even in London) confirms his sense of the historical groundings of imaginative language. The landscape from which the literary pyramid rises cannot be then entirely inhospitable. In this sense, Moore's metaphor of literary buildings tempers the artifice of his aestheticism by linking language to the historical world from which it emerges.

Other aspects of the metaphor similarly point to Moore's ambivalence as to whether autobiographical art is objective and representational or, on the other hand, a primarily fictive mode. Echoing the naturalist credo that art is the precise observation of experience, the narrator of *Confessions* declares that he has constructed the textual pyramid as "l'exacte ressemblance de la vie." In a letter to Emile Zola he invoked the same explanation while trying to soothe Zola's indignation at having been mocked in certain sections of the book (*CYM* 242). That mockery, Moore pointed out, was balanced by praise in other sections and all such variations were included only to delineate accurately the variety of opinion expressed in the café milieu. Similarly, the narrator of *Parnell and His Island* advances his aesthetic of discontinuity on the grounds that an erratic book accurately mirrors an erratic national life. In all three contexts, Moore falls back on the rhetoric of realism to defend stylistic and ideologic variety, and it would seem that he is emphatically locating the power of controlling design outside his text. On the other hand, as Louis Renza suggests of Rousseau's similar claims, Moore may be attesting not so much to his fidelity to nature as his right to imagine himself without reference to any other models besides the one that comes into being with his own text.[16] In terms of his metaphor, the sheets that enwrap the corpse may be subject to its general dimensions for their own shape, but when the embalmer is through, the two become indistinguishable. Moore not only admits to but relishes the inaccessibility of the "corpse" in any form other than that of the mummy: a transformed, made object. The mummy functions as a representation, or sign, of the once-animated form; but it can never be a reproduction in the naturalist sense of being a copy or direct placement of experience into literature.

The dedication that begins *Confessions* makes clear that Moore disbelieves in the accessibility, not to mention the reproducibility, of any common truth about the self that has not been drastically altered by self-reflection. Readers of autobiography have become increasingly aligned with Moore's prescient view. Roland Barthes warned in 1966 that "the one *who speaks* (in the narrative) is not the one *who writes* (in real life) and the one *who writes* is not the one *who is*."[17] *Confessions* makes yet a further demarcation between the one who speaks and the one whose actions are remembered and related by the narrator. Moreover, because of Moore's many revisions and multiple prefaces, any reader who has familiarity with at least some of the various editions is faced with splitting each one of Barthes's designations into several more subentities. The precise relationship among these various images of the self has constituted a matter of major debate in autobiographical theory since the late 1960s.[18] On one extreme lies the classical notion of a historical self that is recalled and reproduced in the text, with primary valuation upon sincerity— or, at least, the attempt at such. At the other extreme, the Tel Quel theorists postulate the complete displacement of the author and life by the text.

To a point, Moore's position on the irreproducibility of the referent anticipates de Man's idea of the autobiographical activity as a kind of self-murder in which the language, becoming itself the referent, deprives the writer of his voice or the expression of his historical existence.[19] Looking again at the metaphor of the autobiography as a pyramid, the narrator of the 1904 preface informs us "that part of me was dead even when I wrote . . . that I have embalmed my past, that I have wrapped the dead in the finest winding-sheet" (*CYM* 37). Like Huysmans's des Esseintes who "s'abandonnait, regardant, plein de dégoûts et d'alarmes, défiler les années de sa vie défunte,"[20] Moore hints that the process of recollection and its reciprocal action, the re-creative process of writing, put to death the author-as-man. Yet, again, while he comes close to such a position, Moore pulls back from its full embrace, as is particularly evident when we compare his ideas about authorial portraits and the use of the author's proper name.

The first of these references to portraits of the artist is given in the preface of 1904 and seems to reinforce the idea that self-portraiture admits no referent beyond itself. Considering his pyramid, the writer of 1904 admits that he finds a few loose threads and coarse tissues in the young man's "winding-sheet" and acknowledges his "loving regard of the middle-aged man for the young man's coat (I will not say winding-sheet, that is a morbidity from which the middle-aged shrink)." In this attitude, he compares himself to an old prostitute who "sits by the fire in the dusk, a miniature of her past self in her hand" (*CYM* 37). This comparison draws together a number of Moore's ideas about the autobiographical activity. The "light-o'-love," a euphemism Moore prefers in order to render the prostitute's appeal less physical than aesthetic and nostalgic, existed even in her youth as a creature of artifice, an image made deliberately for consumption, to tantalize the customer as a surrogate for some other woman, real or ideal. She, failing in her powers as a created object (or representation), looks back on a representation of her self as a more successful representation. Like the "light-o'-love" when she "wears a wig and reddens her cheeks," the aging author invites ridicule if he imitates the language of his younger self; yet by analogy that language is deemed to have been studied artifice even at the time of inscription. Also by analogy, the language of that artifice reflects commercial needs and is rhetorical in origin rather than romantically self-expressive. At no point in the text's history is a sincere authorial voice accessible; with each revision, the narrator speaking and young man spoken about recede further into multiple self-reflecting representations.

In this analogy, as by the succession of prefaces Moore appends to his text, one soon-to-be dead life encloses the former life, which has already died. The past is recoverable only when part of a present self, who—with the exception of the static "instinct" that guides it—is always in flux. As the narrator explains of his former enthusiasms, for example, "my old rapture and my youth's delight I can regain only when I think of that part of Gautier which is now incarnate in me" (*CYM* 63). Moore frequently attempts to create the effect of a voice speaking to the reader in the present through sudden shifts into present tense, as in the sections of literary criticism, in "miniatures" like the evocation of "the woman of thirty," in the fragments from "Thoughts in a Strand Lodging," or in his addresses to the reader. These shifts in tense impose a present that encapsulates the past; that present then becomes the new past in the devouring mouth of a new present. The mummified young man as well as his aging recollector, the narrator, become in all their various manifestations the potential subjects of further revision. What, then, becomes of the author and the historical life to which Moore linked his narrator when he gave him his own name?

To the facts of that historical life Moore makes no vow of fidelity other than the dubious defense of realism with which he justified his criticisms of living persons like Emile Zola. He was just as capable of invoking an entirely different aesthetic as his defense in other situations. To Moore's acknowledgment of the autobiographer's limited capability ever to recover the face in the portrait—or even to do anything more than "impersonate" the revising author who looks at the portrait—must be added his essential disregard for any attempt to make that portrait a precise imitation of the lost face. Since the painted face and the observer are both beyond recovery, concern for verisimilitude is irrelevant to his purposes. Repeatedly, Moore expressed surprise when his contemporaries took offense at the dialogue and actions ascribed to them, and he protested that all concerned should have understood that his anecdotes and information were exaggerated and sometimes invented for dramatic effect. Such practice is in keeping with that of other memoirists of the same era. In the collection of pieces now called the *Autobiography*, W. B. Yeats likewise relates stories of admittedly dubious truth while only hinting at their uncertain origin; Oliver St John Gogarty, Max Beerbohm, and Edmund Gosse all openly acknowledge that their memoirs involve considerable fictionalization.[21] But again, why then write autobiography, even if openly "fictive"? Why ascribe to a character one's own proper name?

It is perhaps in this matter of the proper name that the answer lies, as it illuminates Moore's counteraction to that notion of autobiographical self-murder that he has come very close to fully espousing. The past life, which he has pronounced dead, is the property of a narrative voice that is also characterized as having belonged to a different time and hence no longer a living voice. By use of his proper name, Moore declares that this voice is intimately connected to the excavator of the pyramid, the author who presents himself to his reading public in the ever-emergent present. This self-presenting author requires that the reader acknowledge his designation of the narrative voice as his own younger self, a designation to be distinguished from calling one's narrator "Edwin." While in calling Edwin Dayne "George Moore" his author may tell the reader no more truth about his younger days than he had previously, Moore does make a statement about who he is at the time of composition (and revision) by declaring that he seeks to be identified with this character. To call *Confessions* its author's story is to agree that while the pharaoh's corpse will turn to dust outside of its pyramid, the architect /

excavator stands regenerate: at least as he stood in his last revision. This last qualification distinguishes Moore's use of the proper name from that which Philippe Lejeune employs in "The Autobiographical Pact." In arguing that the proper name is "the deep center" of autobiography, Lejeune identifies the name as a representation of its author, an assertion of a more solid identity than that of the first-person pronoun.[22] For Moore, however, the centrality of the proper name lies in its power as a rhetorical gesture. His textual pyramid offers itself as the expression—although by no means a sincere expression—of the public figure of "George Moore," still "alive" at the time of completion.

Completion of *Confessions,* as has been indicated, is a matter that seems never to come to a close. While the continual introduction of new prefaces results in their supersedure by yet newer ones, thus rendering their author yet another "dead life," nevertheless, the activity of preface-making can also be interpreted as a way of fighting against the tendency of autobiography to render subject into object or the speaker into the spoken-about. Louis Renza discusses the tension between "himself as he writes and the discursive 'I' passing seriatim through any sustained piece of writing," and argues that "the autobiographer must come to terms with a unique pronominal crux: how can he keep using the first-person pronoun, his sense of self-reference, without its becoming in the course of writing something other than strictly his own self-referential sign—a de facto third-person pronoun?"[23] That self-referential sign then becomes an icon that is lost in the past, itself observed and recollected. While Moore's work openly acknowledges this dilemma, his repeated attempt to interject by means of the fresh preface the present subject self into the lost past world of the object self speaks again to his reluctance to abandon a world of reference outside the text.

The assumption of continuity among the public figure of the author, the narrator, and the remembered self underlies Moore's remarks about two other authorial portraits. His comments appear in letters, some twenty-five years apart. Both concern photographs under consideration as frontispieces, one for the first and second English editions of *Confessions* and the other for his brother's biography of their father, *An Irish Gentleman.* Moore writes to Swan Sonnenschein, Lowrey, "I think it would be well to print my portrait in the confessions. It would attract attention for I have a photograph that is very like the author of the confessions."[24] His letter at once affirms and denies the existence of a referent outside the text. The photograph that will be attached to the book is his own—in fact, he would later suppress it because of its unflattering likeness. Yet he calls it a portrait not of "myself as a young man" but of "the author of the confessions."

A similar contradiction is evident in his condemnation of his brother's choice of a youthful photograph of himself to accompany his own book. Having examined the illustrations that were to accompany the biography, Moore writes to his brother Maurice, "I found a terrifying portrait of you—you, in all your youth and beauty, the darling of the garrison hacks. So now we know the light in which you wish people to see you! Lord have Mercy upon us sinners! It will make you and the book rather silly. Why did you not get Walter Osborne's portrait photographed? . . . If your's [sic] must go in I will propose to Werner Laurie to print opposite to it one of Max Beerbohm's caricatures of me as a sort of make-weight" (GMP 263). Some degree of malicious sibling rivalry is probably operative in Moore's exultant exposure of his handsome brother's vanity. However, he disavows any malevolence in a letter written two days later, remarking that "you gave me tit for tat this morning, and the tit was out of proportion to the tat for my letter was written to amuse" (GMP 264). A week later Moore protests again that Maurice has overreacted to a trivial matter, although he cannot resist suggesting that his brother's photograph has been touched up by the addition of "some curls" (GMP 267). While Moore's remarks were certainly written to amuse or to provoke, taken with his earlier ideas as to the frontispiece of Confessions and his mock-suggestion that he might be represented by a Beerbohm caricature, his comments further reveal his working theory of the relation between author and text.

The photograph chosen by Maurice Moore is simply an inappropriate illustration of the voice that speaks there; it will make a solemn, commemorative text look "silly," just as a Beerbohm caricature renders Moore a figure of ridicule. Had the colonel written a racy romance of garrison life, Moore might have found his brother's choice of self-presentation entirely appropriate; it was with this sense of the need to match photographic image with text that he suggested a picture of a younger self to illustrate Confessions. As he reminds Maurice in an unrelated quarrel a year previous, his concern for the overall effect of his study of the impressionists, Modern Painting, led him to include a portrait of himself by Manet that "in the opinion of many people made me look like a figure of fun" (GMP 248). The public's sense of a work's "author" must match the textual narrative voice and in that sense be a product of the narrative; one's vanity should be sacrificed to the integrity of the text. Moore satirically underscores this conviction in the "Prelude" added to the 1921 edition of *Memoirs of My Dead Life*. Ostensibly explaining to his publishers the advantages of a childhood photograph as frontispiece to the book, he writes that "it will persuade the prudes into reading the book in the hope of discovering in the stories traces of the dear little boy in the frontispiece . . . for on turning the pages to escape from some jarring incident or apophthegm, the prudes will come upon the portrait again, and of a certainty the winning features will bring belief that the little boy must have fallen into evil company or been neglected in his youth, for if he had been brought up properly he would be quite different from his book—no, not his book, his ascendant's book" (*MMDL* xiii). Here, Moore misleadingly suggests that the portrait's function is to encourage the interpretation of a sexually provocative text as an innocent one, while in actuality his remarks call attention to the sexual overtones of his stories. Still, the portrait is imagined as an extension of the text.

In Moore's view, the authorial portrait must, however, have some relation to the historical, publishing author: Moore never suggests using a photograph of someone else as an acceptable substitute for his own. His sense of the double nature of the authorial portrait—as the representation of the textual voice and, at the same time, a sign of an extratextual referent behind the authorial signature—complements the metaphor of the pyramid. The architect of the pyramid may find his past life a corpse and his autobiographical persona a mummy, but as excavator he insists upon remaining alive through the series of prefaces that allow him to bring all into a simultaneous present over which he reigns. In this process, we see his essential myth of self-creation and regeneration. If his myth has become its own referent, it is an engendering one that makes possible the production of other texts—those successes realized after its first edition and those promised in the future beyond the last preface.

Using the proper name as text, sign, and signature amounts—in Yeatsian terms—to choosing one's mask; this choice could be productive or it could be lethal. A pseudonym, too, functions as the sign of a calculated authorial portrait or logo of authorial presence, and in *Conversations in Ebury Street*, Moore reflects only half-facetiously on what he diagnoses as the disastrous effect of Mary Ann Evans's choice of one. Offering the "fantastic theory that the name we bring into the world or that we assume is accountable for all our acts and thoughts," he asks his interlocutor, "Do you think my writings would have been the same if I had adopted *Annie Grey* as my pseudonym?" (*CEB* 71, 70). Moore rarely published under a false name, and even *Confessions,* initially given as the story of "Edwin Dayne," bore his own name as the author of the tale. The first edition exhibits some befuddlement over the name of the narrator, which appears variously as Edwin, Edward, or Eduard. This confusion Susan Dick attributes in part to Moore's "lack of conviction in the use of a pseudonym in the first place" (*CYM* 2). Yet the notion of a pseudonym can extend much further than the signature on the title page. After having been granted the name of his author, the young man who narrates acts as a pseudonymic personality created to display George Moore to the reading public. When Moore bestowed his own name upon his character, he was also bestowing upon himself the character of the narrator. This process is perhaps not so different from Mary Ann Evans's choice of a decoy, or literary identity, in the name George Eliot. For Moore, however, it became crucial, for reasons just discussed, to affix his own name to this representation. Moore's identification with his narrator may account for the sense of accomplishment—even happiness—that exudes from the story despite its pessimist utterances and the morbidity of such images as corpses and mummies. By declaring a referent outside the text, the use of Moore's own name confirms both the story and the production of *Confessions* as the recovery of the promised land.

The Birthwaters of a New Nationality

In *Confessions of a Young Man,* the narrator's awkward grasp of French serves as his passport out of Irish culture. Dependent upon tenant rents, the young landlord's chances for permanent removal are as fragile as his hold upon the language. Yet by the end of the book, his command of a freshly acquired literary English has given him sufficient income to establish himself in London. And because the publication of *Confessions* followed *A Modern Lover,* Moore's first novel, even initial readers knew the eventual success of the fledgling writer who in *Confessions'* last lines surrenders his youth and sits in the icy morning "haggard and overworn" to work on his novel. Given the historical frame that autobiographical status confers upon the text, later readers of *Confessions of a Young Man* also know that the quest for language has resulted not only in the elegant book we hold in our hands but in the growing achievement of the author who presents himself in the prefaces.

The means to these transformations has been the acquisition of language. It is Moore's view of the cultural origins of language that acts as one of the most forceful counterweights to the admittedly more dominant theory of textual autogenesis—although, as we have seen, this theory too is fraught with contradiction and expressed through metaphors of both freedom and determination. To use the metaphor that Moore employs in the introduction to *Hail and Farewell*, he acts as his own midwife, delivering his books—and himself in the process—in the birthwaters of French, then English: languages to be acquired only in certain districts of Paris and London—and never in Ireland. Given opportunity, the essential nature Moore postulates will choose the right language instinctively: a process that, as has been described, is itself a curious amalgam of the free and determinative modes. Rooted in culture and nationality, the language has itself a determined aspect, although its sensuous character and its pliability render it an instrument to be shaped by authorial choice.

The instinct that leads finally to the recovery of "the intense ego out of the clouds of semi-consciousness" (*CYM* 219) first manifests itself when the child, George, experiences his initial moment of linguistic self-consciousness. In the Irish childhood this moment is divorced from the surrounding world of the "terrible brogue," local gossip, and mutterings over politics. Consider the scene in which the narrator records his discovery of literary language:

> A great family coach, drawn by two powerful country horses, lumbers along a narrow Irish road. The ever recurrent signs—long ranges of blue mountains, the streak of bog, the rotting cabin, the flock of plover rising from the desolate water. Inside the coach there are two children. . . . Opposite the children are their parents, and they are talking of a novel the world is reading. Did Lady Audley murder her husband? Lady Audley! What a beautiful name; and she, who is a slender, pale, fairy-like woman, killed her husband. Such thoughts flash through the boy's mind; his imagination is stirred and quickened. . . . The coach lumbers along, it arrives at its destination, and Lady Audley is forgotten in the delight of tearing down fruit trees and killing a cat. (*CYM* 49–50)

The road takes the center of this picture, and on it the coach—the only sign of life or motion in the silent morning and all the more precious for its singularity—enclosing young George who finds budding within himself the incipient fascination with the sensuous qualities of form. His artistic genesis comes only inside a closed coach, distinct from road and bog. Once returned to the rough life of Moore Hall, the aesthetic awakening is followed by a fury of destruction. Having been entranced by the story of a woman's murder of her husband, the child mutilates the fruit-bearing trees of his father, a gesture that must be seen in relation to Moore's guilty suspicion that his rebirth as an artist depended upon his father's death.

Moore's statement as to the genesis of his artistic identity is, again, tremendously ambivalent. Following the pattern of repudiation initiated in *A Drama in Muslin* and *Parnell and His Island,* the language of self-realization exists in an antithetical relationship to the language of County Mayo; because it is defined as being not-of-Mayo, it maintains dependency upon Mayo as its imaginative nemesis. On the other hand, Moore attributes his aesthetic birth to forces he specifically locates outside of any historical or familial influence. First, his theory of instinct plays a role in the acquisition of literary language: there sit two boys in the coach, both born of the same parents, but only one has ears to hear. Second, the child, George, is predominantly attracted to the formal properties of language, which Moore pointedly isolates from their context. The name "Audley" carries its own music; elsewhere in *Confessions* Moore describes the appeal of the "crystal name" of "Shelley." In his final recollection of youth, *A Communication to My Friends,* he recalls the marvelous "mysterious power" of sheer sound in the name "Tinsley," *Lady Audley's* publisher. The acquisition of literary language becomes, in this sense, an awakening from meaning into the more immediately persuasive world of sensuous experience. As originally recognized by the child in the coach, sound and form offer escape from historical contextuality. This aesthetic transcendence of history is in accordance with the more radical doctrines of French symbolism, and Moore has cast the story of his awakening to literature in the very terms designated by the symbolist art with which his narrator—at least temporarily—was enamored. The narrator would have us believe that history—at least Moore's own—is thus directed by literature.

As *Confessions* goes on, evidence mounts toward the independence of literary language, despite simultaneous expressions of its origins in historical life. Style, for example, is a kind of clothing, and fashions are easily interchanged. When the narrator leaves Paris to begin a writer's career in London, he describes himself as having been "as covered with 'fads' as a distinguished foreigner with stars.

Naturalism I wore round my neck, Romanticism was pinned over the heart, Symbolism I carried like a toy revolver in my waistcoat pocket, to be used on an emergency" (*CYM* 149). The young man admits to flashing at the London publishing world whatever seemed most suited to advance his fame. Moore puts to use a versatile wardrobe of styles in depicting the young man who deliberately imitates, adopts the dress of his new compatriots, decorates his apartments after bohemian fashions, and apes the ideas and behaviors of his multiple "maîtres."

As if to emphasize the indeterminacy of literary language, Moore inserts within the revisions of *Confessions* direct repudiations of passages found in other parts of the book, while retaining those passages in their original state. In an added chapter near the book's end, for example, the narrator engages in a dialogue with "Conscience" who taunts him by misquoting lines from earlier sections. Phraseology like "the perfumed darkness of the chamber" is repeated with some disdain by this voice of middle-class respectability, but its disdain does not even begin to equal that of the revising author who utilizes this dialogue to assert his superiority over his earlier authorship. And further twists develop. "Conscience" also openly attacks the affectations of the author figure with whom he is in dialogue. The aging author is absurdly made-up when he dabbles in his lost youth, but no more made-up and absurd than the younger man who rewrote, the even younger man who wrote initially, and that raw young fellow who is their subject. The opportunity for comedy here is never ceasing, begetting itself perennially in the infinitude of potential identities growing out of the repudiation of former identities. The ever-evolving discrepancies between that which was said and all that could be said equate revision with the essential freedom to self-create.

Writing (as rewriting) seems as malleable and full of possibilities as the identity it encloses; yet if language is also "cookery" and Moore with "one hand in every literary pie-dish" produces, as art, "divine excrement," these metaphors borrowed from Carlyle temper Moore's figures of linguistic indeterminacy with ones grounded in mechanistic functions such as digestion.[25] Similarly, his emphasis on French and English as formal structures of grammar and vocabulary highlights at once their free and prescriptive aspects. While they can be acquired systems of great malleability like the literary "fads" with which the young man decorated himself, languages also are rooted in specific places and point the way not only to new techniques but to "new nationalities." His years in France, the narrator writes, were spent, not as an "indifferent spectator, but an enthusiast, striving heart and soul to identify himself with his environment, to shake himself free from race and language and to recreate himself as it were in the womb of a new nationality, assuming its ideals, its morals, and its modes of thought" (*CYM* 129). At the chance mention of the single word, "France," the narrator recalls, he became suddenly aware that "I should, that I must, go to France, that I would live there, that I would become as a Frenchman" (*CYM* 53). The phrase offers a syntactical parody of Christ's admonition that those who follow him must become as little children. It draws attention to the underlying metaphor of being born again, the quasi-religious nature of the calling, and the ludicrous, childlike naïveté of a young man unable to learn French grammar ahead of time, so great was his impatience to tumble directly into French life. French nationality (and, by implication, the art resultant from such "repatriation") in his case results from immersion in the cultural life in which the language takes shape.

Near the book's end, the young man relates that having narrowly escaped the fate of becoming French and irretrievably alienated from the English language, he feverishly "washed myself clean" of French, relearned English style and rebirthed himself as an Englishman.[26] The act of choosing a "language" other than "the awful brogue" provides an entryway to a new place—ideally the promised land. Residency in the place of choice, however, is necessary to acquire and master the language itself: a crucial sign of repatriation and reconception.

To Moore's mind, self-genesis necessarily implies the repudiation and free espousal of any national origin, as the location of "instinct" within "the haze of semi-consciousness" implies the denial of any immediate hereditary source. National origin appears more susceptible to redefinition than does familial background. Redefining nationality involves, first of all, a conception of oneself with no birthplace at all, as a man "dipped in Lethe" to whom "the world always seems . . . more new, more wonderful than it did to anyone he ever met on his faring" while "himself seemed to himself to be the only young thing in the world" (*CYM* 37). The world seems new only to him who comes to it anew. Rescued from doddering irrelevancy, the world is then reconceived according to his own perception, as he discovers it and makes it fresh. Any nation, then, can be potentially the country of "I." For just this reason the title of the French edition, *Les Confessions d'un Jeune Anglais*, was singularly inappropriate, although Moore appears to have been enthusiastic about his transla-tor's choice.[27] The narrator's final identity as an Englishman is as provisional as his earlier insistence upon antenatal French citizen-ship or his claims to represent in A Drama in Muslin a true picture of Ireland "painted by an Irishman."

While self-birth also implies the elimination of any familial ante-cedents, Moore reveals just how inextricably he is tied to the genetic metaphor when the young man attributes his restlessness in Ireland to "antenatal" sympathy with the English or "atavistic" leanings to-ward France. Parentage proves to be an even more complicated problem than nationality. Alternately venerated and castigated throughout his autobiographical writing, his family—and, in partic-ular, his father—is not so easily dismissed. In the middle of Confes-sions, Moore grants considerable space to a tale of familial genocide adapted from Balzac's "El Verdugo"; his so doing attests to his un-easiness in regard to becoming one's own father. The story is pre-ceded by the narrator's ecstatic recollection of the Nouvelle Athenes —his university, he says—and it is followed by a debate between Manet and Degas as to whether art is natural or synthetic. A group of hushed café-goers listen while Villiers de l'Isle-Adam relates what is certainly a key "lesson" in the young man's education. It concerns the son of an old Spanish family that has been condemned by the occupying French army. At the father's pleading, this son is spared to carry on the family name, but for this immunity he must fulfill one condition: he must act as his family's executioner. The boy is appalled, but his family begs him to comply. He does so, but spends the rest of his life in complete seclusion without wife or heir (CYM 102–4). This version differs from the original in two significant ways. Although there is no evidence as to whether Moore simply repeated the details as given by Villiers de l'Isle-Adam, misremem-bered them himself, or intentionally altered them, in any case he did not choose to correct them in subsequent revisions and, perhaps most tellingly, he repeated the same variants when reciting the tale to Alec Trusselby in A Story-Teller's Holiday (1918). The son in Moore's version executes all his family. In Balzac's, he cannot bring himself to kill his mother whose role as his progenitor is emphasized by the otherwise silent boy's despairing protest that she had nursed him from her breast. In Balzac's story, the young man also eventu-ally marries and fathers at least one child. The tale ends as he wea-rily awaits the birth of his second son, a birth that will complete his duty to his family name and allow him to join the dead upon whom all his thoughts rest.

Not only does Moore erase the character's agonizing loyalty to his mother, but he releases the son from his duty to the family name. Although the son must bear the guilty knowledge of the murders he has committed, he refuses to redeem himself according to the pattern established by those who were responsible for his burden in the first place. The story, as Moore gives it, balances the patricide with childlessness: biological descent is aborted. The censure of human reproduction forms a recurrent motif in *Confessions,* and the narrator alternates between rantings against children in general and expressions of sympathy for unwanted children (Moore even wrote to the publisher W. T. Stead that the "dominant idea" of his book was "the population question").[28] Some of his phrasings are borrowed from Schopenhauer and some from Huysmans, but all call to mind Moore's early conviction that he would not himself produce an heir to Moore Hall. Taken in conjunction with Moore's adaptation of "El Verdugo," the cumulative effect seems to lead to des Esseintes's view that, as for nature itself, "tout n'est que syphilis."[29]

From the deliberate halt of historical life Moore turns his attention to art, which engenders an alternate life. In the café debate that follows Villiers de l'Isle-Adam's story, art is said to take on the reproductive function of nature. The same Schopenhauerian language that Moore applies with despair to the sexual drive and the urge to procreate, he uses during the café discussion to metaphorically describe Manet's method—except that for the great artist, the drive to produce results in triumph and power. Manet, he says, paints unconsciously, instinctively, "not by inclination, but by force." Driven by an aesthetic version of the "will to live," the artist has only to fear the death of his work: "Que ce livre soit aussi durable que sa pyramide!" As the author becomes his own parent, so the book, according to Moore, acts as the source of future representations.

The idea of the book as one's father and child is closely related to Moore's observations on the relationship between his father's death and his emergence as a writer. Mentioned in the 1888 edition of *Confessions,* the effect of G. H. Moore's death receives more extended treatment in the 1889 revision: "His death," admits the narrator, "gave me power to create myself . . . to create a complete and absolute self out of the partial self which was all that the restraint of home had permitted; this future self, this ideal George Moore, beckoned me. . . . Would I sacrifice this ghostly self, if by so doing I should bring my father back? . . . I shrank horrified at the answer" (*CYM* 196). This confession bears striking similarity to other autobiographical treatments of the death of the father. In his study of autobiographies of childhood, Richard Coe argues that many male autobiographers strive to demolish paternal power by the act of writing. While the son speaks, the father remains silenced; he lives on only because the son has engendered him through portraiture.[30] Patricide seems particularly prevalent in those autobiographies that struggle toward a proclamation of the self's complete independence from the historical world. In Jean-Paul Sartre's autobiography, *Les Mots* (The words), the narrator confesses his belief that the early death of his father "was the big event of my life: it . . . gave me freedom. There is no good father, that's the rule. . . . Had my father lived, he would have lain on me at full length and would have crushed me. . . . I left behind me a young man who did not have time to be my father and who could now be my son."[31] Not surprisingly, Sartre's autobiography presents a man who desires to "derive only from myself" and who finds his self-genesis in language (although by the end of the book he has disavowed the idea as a bourgeois illusion). If Moore's primary crime is the desire to murder his past, perhaps he offers the book as recompense.

However, another sign of Moore's own dissatisfaction with the totalizing theory of linguistic self-creation may be the central importance of sexuality and birth in the fiction written during the years leading up to and following *Confessions of a Young Man*. Paralleling this preoccupation, the most persistent theme in Moore's novels and short stories of the period involves, as has been frequently noted, the problem of creation, of the need to produce some work of value. From the iconographic mother of *Esther Waters* to the inadequate parents, celibates, and promiscuous characters who populate his short stories and other novels, birth of some kind is desperately sought: a birth that is understood to also precipitate the re-creation of the self, just as the birth of *Confessions* signals the regeneration of its author. Although it has been argued that Moore created "his autobiographical self on the grave of his mother [Ireland]" while seeking to "repeat and supersede the art of his fathers,"[32] in the light of his whole career, it is perhaps more accurate to assert that Moore seeks to supplant the functions of both the writing father and the parturient mother. Despite the potency he would attribute to the written word, the emphasis on sexual reproduction in his fiction testifies to Moore's enduring sense of the forces that drive us: sexual, psychological, but most emphatically, economic. The fiction of the period sets the self-creative man (or more frequently, woman) to a severe test, with varying verdicts as to the power of (re)generation.

3

Moore's Own Everlasting Yea

Sexuality and Production in the Fiction of the Middle Period

> Boccaccio's Calandrino was the first and last man
> who felt himself with child. Fatherhood, in the sense
> of conscious begetting, is unknown to man. It is a
> mystical estate, an apostolic succession, from only be-
> getter to only begotten. On that mystery . . . the
> church is founded and founded irremovably because
> founded, like the world, macro- and micro cosm,
> upon the void. Upon incertitude, upon unlikelihood.
> *Amor matris*, subjective and objective genitive, may be
> the only true thing in life. Paternity may be a legal
> fiction. Who is the father of any son that any son
> should love him or he any son?
> —James Joyce, *Ulysses*

I N HIS EARLY WORKS, Moore had traced the way constrictions of poverty and the obligations of family, church, and nation distort both sexual expression and the ability to work toward some constructive end. In opposition to these models of productive incapacity, *Confessions of a Young Man* offered the young protagonist who retains minimal ties to the world of social organization and biological reproduction. As Moore would have it, the young man observes the world beyond him and "transposes" it into literature. Without gesta-

64

tion in the flesh, an offspring is produced that bears minimal relations to culture and heredity. Being necessarily born in language, it originates in culture. Yet as was seen in the discussion of *Confessions,* Moore defines language as both a product of a particular culture and, at the same time, a matter of selection by the writer who may "recreate himself as it were in the womb of a new nationality." Nature generates the offspring only in that literature is a matter of "instinct" with all the peculiar ramifications of Moore's own autogenous sense of the word.

As was evident in the character of John Harding, this essentially autoerotic activity and its self-reflexive offspring leave the writer with a certain measure of anxiety and guilt. Increasingly in Moore's autobiographical writing, the writer becomes blatantly voyeuristic, while in his fiction Moore repeatedly returns to the relationship between sexuality and productivity. Between 1885 and 1927 he presented at least ten major characters, as well as numerous minor characters, who are celibates, homosexuals, or persons engaged in promiscuous heterosexuality. Through these portrayals, Moore inquires into the origin of sexual identity and its formative effect upon the personality. Mixing congenital, behavioral, environmental, and economic explanations as if to mock the possibility of definitive explanations for the origins of sexuality, Moore's final judgment on most forms of desire turns upon their relationship to the production of meaningful work and the achievement of the autogenous self.

Production and reproduction are central to Moore's most appreciated work, the novel he once imagined entitling *Mother and Child.* The unwed mother who is its heroine, Esther Waters, stands alone among his repertoire of fictional characters as a mediator between nature and self-creation. In this sense, she resembles the autobiographical persona, the humble "secretary" of Nature as he calls himself in *Hail and Farewell,* a man whose bodily form determines the comedy he is compelled to write. Moore allows Esther, as an inarticulate and illiterate woman, to exist in a less ironic relationship with a world her author defines as "natural." Yet while Moore would have her function as an icon of nature, he also projects his own idiosyncratic characterization of nature in tandem with his equally idiosyncratic definition of instinct. In Esther's practical intelligence, her passion, and her spiritual life, Moore creates a figure who abrogates exclusive categories of mind, body, and spirit, and who does so consistently in opposition to claims of church, family, and all communal life that would restrict her productive capacity.

To "Do the Duty which lies nearest thee":
Esther Waters and the Doctrine of Labor

From *Parnell and His Island* emerged a method of describing the self through the repudiation of potential identities, achieved in part by the dispersal of those potential identities into separate fictionalized figures who function in balance with one another. In *Esther Waters*, this mode of inquiry matures, revealing multiple sides of the protagonist by pairing Esther with analogous and antithetical doubles. The same framework that structures the autobiographies, beginning with *Parnell*, enriches the narrative of *Esther Waters* and marks it as another stage in Moore's continuing exploration of autobiographical questions. On the surface, there would appear to be few similarities between the distinctively Irish *Parnell* and a novel that Moore called "as characteristically English as *Don Quixote* is Spanish" (*EW* v). Yet *Parnell and His Island* exhibits in bold relief many of the issues that underlie Moore's fiction prior to 1901: the conflict between doctrines of social and biological determinism and an equally powerful belief in the capacity for self-creation, a fear of inheriting what he believed to be an Irish legacy of inefficacy and idleness, the denial of home in order to locate posterity elsewhere, and a troubled and complex reaction to the social dynamics of money and class. In *Shadowy Heroes: Irish Literature of the 1890s*, Wayne Hall offers the only previous analysis of the close relationship between the little-read *Parnell* and Moore's best-known work, *Esther Waters*. Because of the singularity and ambition of his attempt, Hall's essay deserves scrutiny. The parallels he draws between the two texts demonstrate the possibilities if also the pitfalls of using *Parnell* as an index to Moore's fiction.

Hall combines evidence from *Parnell* with biographical data to draw a picture of Moore as landlord. On the basis of this assemblage he interprets *Esther*, and, parenthetically, *A Drama in Muslin*. Much as Moore does, he depicts the landowning classes as alienated from their country, fearful of uncontrollable, random turns of fortune, and retreating from all decisive action. Hall then proceeds to find these characteristics in Moore and in Esther herself. The novel reads as a study in failure, the story of a woman whose actions are futile and who finally withdraws from the world in which her efforts are unrewarded. Esther's dependence upon twists of fate is likened to the landlord's dependence upon the relentless, unpredictable course of the land reform movement and the author's dependence upon the uncertain whims of the reading public. Her return to the ruined estate at Woodview is interpreted as the homecoming of the "dutiful child" Moore could never be at Moore Hall, and thus as an apology for the author's "errant nature." Her illiteracy, according to Hall, amounts to the wish-fulfilling fantasy of the literate, ironic author unable to find his own serenity. Esther's "retreat into peace, silence, and simplicity" is seen as the logical conclusion to a book about "exhaustion." Finally, Hall draws a parallel between her return to Woodview and Moore's immersion in folktales, myths, and romance during the last years of his career, a move castigated as escape into "the artificial monastery of his work."[1]

Hall has read *Parnell* with insight, for as Moore expressed so vehemently there, he found the "Irish Poet" irrelevant in his own country, and no more efficacious model of action appeared as an alternative to that irrelevancy. In *Hail and Farewell*, published some twenty-five years later, Moore repeats this theme, telling his brother Maurice that all efforts toward the restoration of Moore Hall are pointless, that "the landlords have had their day. We are a disappearing class. . . . Moore Hall is out of date, and it astonishes me that you don't feel it" (*HF* 634). From one perspective, Moore's removal to Paris and London conforms to the conventional perception of Irish landlords, and Moore himself provided variations on the type in "Landlord M——" and Tom Blake of *Parnell*, or Fred Scully of *A Drama in Muslin*. The model of the frivolous absentee appeared in fiction at least as early as Maria Edgeworth's *Castle Rackrent* (1800), and Michael Davitt's dramatic characterization of this figure in an 1879 speech confirms that it remained a popular conception: "The farmers must work from morn till eve to support themselves and their children, when in steps Mr Lazy Unproductive Landlord and demands almost half of the money so earned, to sustain himself in the licentious and voluptuous life he very often leads, not in Ireland but away in London, Paris, and elsewhere."[2] Moore may have enjoyed having others believe he lived a licentious and voluptuous life, but his routines were actually disciplined and austere. His choice to live a productive life admittedly made very little difference to his tenants; his ability to choose a way of life was a luxury toward which they could hardly aspire. Yet while Moore may have felt alienated from social action within his own country, he continued to engage himself in other spheres of action. If he was blind to the merits of human communities, he was acutely aware of how class, religion, and social conformity could stultify and destroy an individual.

Repeatedly, he depicts with sympathy those repressed by environmental circumstances and behavioral mores, be they stifled young debutantes, homosexuals, priests without vocations, or members of the underclass. His attitude toward the act of writing postulates creative labor as the antidote to that repression. Both the subject of his writing and his beliefs about work indicate just how imperative to him was the distinction between himself and "Mr Lazy Unproductive Landlord" and lead us to examine *Esther Waters* as, above all, a novel about work.

The results of Esther's labors seem to depend entirely upon the collusion of chance and inherited character. An event happens as "a mere accident"; whole estates and private lives hinge upon the horse race; characters debate the utility of prayer; fairy-godmother figures appear or not, unrelated to Esther's efforts; the word "luck" clangs as a constant refrain. Near the novel's beginning, Esther's mother and a shopgirl advise her to purchase one set of infant clothes and another only "if the baby lives": human life being set at even odds. The life of the consumptive William Latch, with whom she has reunited several years after her child's birth, depends upon his ability to win enough bets to pay for a trip to Egypt away from the unusually—and unluckily—severe English winter. Operating in conjunction with blind chance are factors of biological and environmental determinism. Latch's fate is early told in his "shallow chest" while his "low forehead and the lustreless eyes told of a slight, unimaginative brain." Esther too seems victimized by her inheritance of temper and pride. In addition to the negative force of genetic traits, nearly everything in her world of class-bound England conspires against her. As with Goncourt's Elisa and Flaubert's Emma Bovary, Esther's defenses against seduction are weakened by hearing her friend Sarah read titillating romantic novels—a taste symptomatic of the drudgery and tedium of Sarah's life.

Such naturalist elements of *Esther Waters* have been thoroughly studied, and readings since the 1970s have begun to distinguish the substantial differences between Moore's novel and more conventional naturalist fiction.[3] In truth, Moore gives himself the difficult project of writing both a naturalist novel and a success story. He chronicles in frank detail the systematic, institutionalized oppression that undermines all prospects of individual effort, while also presenting a tale of sustained resistance. These two very different kinds of narrative remain in steady if delicate balance throughout the novel; in this sense *Esther* resembles the familiar structure of those

Künstlerromane in which the primary character alone miraculously avoids the fully determining powers of heredity and environment that trap his or her compatriots. While the undertone of economic and biological determinism provides one of the most forceful components of the story, an equally persistent countertone echoes *Confessions of a Young Man* with its affirmation of a self that somehow predates environment, disclaims heredity, and with blind instinct creates itself by manifesting what it has always been.

We hear that counterpoint in Esther's answer to her husband when he remarks that she might have been happier married to "the other chap," the religious Fred Parsons: "I should 'ave liked quite a different kind of life, but we don't choose our lives, we just makes the best of them. You was the father of my child, and it all dates from that" (*EW* 298). Her response provides a significant self-commentary. She recognizes that she can exercise no control over chance, but within her limited sphere she responds to chance with actions that are themselves choices. Thus, while her assertion that "it all dates" from William's insemination of her body would appear to privilege some ineffable natural bond, the novel's insistent citings of parental neglect suggest that such bonds are made rather than inherently given. Faced with few opportunities to choose her course of action, Esther must decide between the claims of religion and convention, and between her pragmatism and her passionate desires. Throughout the novel, these claims and the forces behind them often conflict. In her efforts to maintain the life she has created—the child she calls Jackie—Esther repeatedly relinquishes her obedience to an abstract code and follows the leading of both her practical intelligence and unreasoned sensuous knowledge.

In *Parnell and His Island,* the process of defining one's own allegiances necessitated the rejection of potential selves, and the same design is apparent in *Esther Waters.* Margaret Gale, the former Woodview servant turned prostitute, represents one of Esther's possible destinies. Having recently lost a position because of the overtures of an employer's son, Esther searches for work, in the process of which she encounters Margaret on the street. Margaret discloses that she has been impregnated by "one of her masters," turned out by his wife, and that, without a character reference, she has lost all chance of finding another position. Nothing is said of her child, although enough has already been said of infanticide, malnutrition, and neglect to make Moore's silence at least as meaningful as a direct statement. Rather than assigning Margaret the character of a nymphomaniac or attributing other moral failing, Moore ascribes her downfall to the actions and attitudes of the upper and middle classes.[4] Wandering through the crowds of prostitutes in Piccadilly Circus, Esther notes that "their stories were her story. Each and all had been deserted; and perhaps each had a child to support. But they hadn't been as lucky as she had been in finding situations, that was all" (*EW* 172). Herself destitute and seeking a new position, Esther is just a moment away from answering the invitation of a well-dressed man. Light-headed from hunger, she apprehends the scene as "like a blurred, noisy dream." Moving into Charing Cross, "the dizziness left her, and she realized the temptation she had escaped" (*EW* 173). Moore concedes to public expectations in refusing to let his heroine consciously consider prostitution, yet the dreamlike quality of the scene also underscores one of the novel's primary thematic elements. Something besides conscious choice guides her away from prostitution, and Moore would call it the choice of her instincts as they are drawn together and focused by the maternal drive. She fears the workhouse most because of the humiliation Jackie would feel in later years at having once been there; surely the humiliation of prostitution would outrank that of the workhouse. Her motivation for life is set narrowly upon the welfare of her son, and she could be said to veer away from prostitution not only because of its moral repugnance, but because it will not serve her ends.

Another former Woodview servant, Sarah Tucker, presents an alternative to that of Margaret Gale; again, chance, choice, and instinct are the terms in which Moore presents the contrast between the two women. After Esther's marriage to William, Sarah reenters the story through a chance meeting in London. Sarah soon becomes erotically obsessed with a mutual acquaintance, an abusive, worthless gambler for whom she steals and at whose bidding she enters occasional prostitution. Her eventual imprisonment is brought on by bad luck, the hypocrisy of the judge, and her own susceptibility to false glamour, induced by years of hard work and a steady diet of romantic novels. Sarah's oppositional role comes across most directly in the first edition of 1894, in which long sequences are told from her perspective, and her obsession is more frankly and dramatically deliniated. While she attempts to leave the man, her erotic attraction overcomes any movement toward self-protection: "at odd moments remembrance, like a sob, caught her in the throat, and then she closed her eyes in a little sickness of desire."[5] Subordinating her financial imperative to her passion, Sarah ends with eighteen months at hard labor. Because Esther's passions are expressed for the most part through maternity, which necessitates a practical intelligence, she never sacrifices financial gain to desire as does Sarah Tucker.

Margaret and Sarah fulfill the prejudiced expectations of the society that terms them outcast. They are concerned with either survival or sexuality, but not both and certainly not in affiliation with motherhood. Rejecting the path of Margaret, who must utilize male desire to obtain her meager payment, and the path of Sarah, who must use money to obtain the erotic object of her desire, Esther steers a middle course and defies everyone's expectations. In this sense, she resembles a type Moore examined in an 1882 short story, "Under the Fan." In this story, a sympathetically rendered young actress manages through a collusion of accidents and quick thinking to get twenty thousand pounds from the tedious nobleman who pursues her, marriage with the actor whom she loves, and, with the nobleman's money, the opportunity to play the kind of drama to which she aspires. While this story is a light, ironic comedy, it nevertheless indicates an early interest in the problem of filling one's various and sometimes conflicting needs as well as an admiration for the character who is able to do so.

In Esther, Moore allows both pragmatism and passion to come together through the fulfillment of the maternal ambitions of an unmarried woman from the urban underclass. No English novel had proposed such a thing before, and no one besides Esther herself imagines motherhood to be practical or even appropriate for the poor—married or unmarried. At first glance, Moore may appear to be invoking the idealization of motherhood so much a part of middle-class Victorian rhetoric, but through the contradictory voices of his characters, he demonstrates his understanding that it was a highly restricted and class-bound concept. Esther's exhausted, undernourished mother, pregnant again by an alcoholic and abusive husband, warns early in the novel that "it is the children that breaks us poor women down altogether" (*EW* 94). Repeatedly, Esther loses her situation when her employers discover that she has a child or when she refuses to explain what she does with her money. Mrs. Rice and Mrs. Barfield are sympathetic employers, but neither advises that Jackie come to live with his mother (an unconventional option the novel never broaches). Mrs. Spires, the baby-farmer, and Mrs. Rivers, who employs Esther as a wet nurse, both assume the unworkability of her motherhood and offer infanticide as a solution. Given extraordinarily hostile circumstances, Esther, having once accepted as her axiom that the child should live, must pull together her intense and unreasoned love for the child with the most calculating intelligence she can muster. While she initially allowed William to kiss her merely because she desired him, she will never make that mistake again. After their reunion she represses her genuine desire for the handsome William Latch until he discloses his intent to provide for his son from a £3,000 fortune. His "great square shoulders" fill her imagination only after his pockets have proved full.

Yet neither is her interest in his money the sole determinant in her decision to marry the father of her child. She feels much more physical attraction toward William than toward the prim, high-voiced Fred. In the early part of the novel, Moore makes the revolutionary decision to depict a heroine who feels and acts upon her sexual desire, and the even more revolutionary decision to depict this sympathetically. Although she is said to be "fainting" during intercourse, Moore nevertheless depicts the scene in a way that quite clearly develops a silent pact with the reader as to the meaning of his words. As George Watt aptly observes, "His writing in *Esther Waters* is never to be as explicit as in Gautier or Zola, because he knew just how far he could go. He is provocative, but not stupid. Anything more directly describing Esther's growing passion would have been repressed, and would have had to join the underground circulation of dirty books like *Fanny Hill*."[6] With some concessions thus to his audience, Moore emphasizes the role that desire plays in Esther's choices. When William reappears many years later, she tries to exorcise his image by thinking of her other suitor, but finds that "William's great square shoulders had come between her and this meagre little man. She sighed, and felt once again that her will was overborne by a force which she could not control or understand" (*EW* 230).

If Esther's passion for William deviates from literary norms in being sympathetically depicted and coupled with pragmatic choice as a motivating force, it also differs from the model of female desire as father-love. This distinction offers interesting ramifications for the idea of the autogenous self. Esther's desire finds neither its source nor its end in the father. Esther's own father is dead, and her stepfather is indifferent to her pregnancy and an impediment to the welfare of her unborn child. In marrying William, she becomes mistress of a public house, the very kind of establishment to which her alcoholic stepfather was subject. Ignoring the religious code of her biological father, Esther becomes the powerful vendor of that which her stepfather craves. As in *Parnell* and *Confessions of a Young Man*—or later, in such works as *Memoirs of My Dead Life* and *Hail and Farewell*—the deposition of fatherly power proves imperative to self-generation. That such a demotion of the father should surface in *Esther Waters* testifies once more to the multiple forms by which even such an ostensibly determinist force as sexual desire is, instead, put at the service of the self-made man or woman.

Similarly, although Esther's attraction to William is portrayed vividly in terms that suggest her domination by unconscious forces, it is important not to stress these aspects to the neglect of the part played by Esther's maternal pragmatism. For Moore, the essential concept of "instinct" incorporates not only unconscious desire, but a shrewd capacity for self-preservation and development of one's talents. Moore differentiates instinct from what he terms "mere inclination" in an 1893 letter to Lena Milman in which he asserts, "If one does not follow one's inclinations the result seems to me to be complete sterilization. It is only those who are wanting in strength who do not follow them—will you allow me to substitute the word instincts? We must discriminate between what is mere inclination and what is instinct. All my sympathies are with instincts and their development. Instinct alone may lead us aright" (*GMT* 71). To see how this differentiation works in the novel, we might reexamine the decisive contrast with Sarah Tucker. Explaining why she has returned once more to her abusive lover, Sarah confesses: "whenever I meets him he somehow gets his way with me. It's terrible to love a man as I love him. I know he don't really care for me—I know he is all you say, and yet I can't help myself" (*EW* 313). In the 1894 edition of the novel, Esther is also contrasted with Sarah's older sister, who has casually borne three children from short-term affairs. Moore argues that there is little inherently "instinctive" in mere sexual activity or inherently creative in childbirth itself. The multiple pregnancies Esther's mother undergoes bring her nothing but hardship and, eventually, death. Esther is still of childbearing age when she marries William, but Moore chooses to stretch credibility by keeping her free of pregnancy, thereby allowing Jackie to continue to function as a sign of her deliberative labors rather than the first of a series of the unpreventable by-products of sexual activity. In this novel, neither the force of sexual desire nor maternity itself leads necessarily to the creative, and ultimately self-creative, work that is Esther's.

Esther's submission to instinct also differs from Sarah's or that of the older sister in that all evidence indicates William to be a prudent object of passion—someone who is not only attractive but wealthy, kind, and instantaneously attached to his son. Only the memory of her church upbringing draws her to the religious life Fred offers. Through a dream, Esther envisions this struggle between dogma and instinct as a struggle between chapel and public house: "Wishing she might go to sleep and awake the wife of one or the other, she fell asleep to dream of a husband possessed of the qualities of both, and a life that was neither all chapel nor all public-house. But soon the one became two, and Esther awoke in terror, believing she had married them both" (*EW* 232). Esther's bigamous fantasy captures the terror of divided consciousness. As Esther imagines her alternatives as either chapel or public house, she sees in her own terms a struggle between acquiescence and choice as well as between sexual suppression and its fulfillment. Acting upon her attraction to Latch and the appeal of his money, she merges what was initially only improvident desire with her discriminatory intelligence, thereby choosing to follow her instinct rather than acquiescing to either "mere inclination" or the religious training of her childhood. Whereas she finds in Fred the hope of re-creating her lost childhood among the Plymouth Brethren, William promises an unknown, adult future. Attracted to the varied life he offers her as mistress of a tavern, she, like Father Gogarty of *The Lake*—and unlike the narrator of *Hail and Farewell*—avoids the temptation of trying to return to what consciousness has rendered irredeemable. Torn between security and fulfillment, her adult nature moves her to accept the latter option.

Nora Glynn of the 1921 revision of Moore's 1905 novel, *The Lake*, embodies even more clearly the fusion of passion, generative activity, and individuality through unconventional maternity. Such fusion links both novels with the conception of self enacted in the autobiographies. Nora, too, is unwed and the mother of a child. Her affair with a soldier and consequent pregnancy receive only brief notice in the book; primarily she is a spokesperson for instinctive wisdom, self-knowledge, and allegiance to the demands of the self when challenged by convention or duty. Her sexuality and incidental maternity are offered as signs of her individualism. Her dissent from conformity greatly differs from that of Sarah Tucker or Moore's earlier characters, Kate Ede and May Gould. While they want a more intense life than their class and convention allow them, they act upon their longings without intelligence or discrimination. As a result, each ends in self-disgust. Esther, like Nora, also desires a broader life, and she chooses the variety and novelty of the barroom in the same way that she responds to the landscape at Woodview: instinctively. Because her instinct incorporates a high degree of self-interest, she survives.

In *The Lake*, Nora's child functions predominantly as a symbol of her self-confidence and her rejection of the Irish Catholic church. In *Esther Waters*, the child acts not only as a sign but, to a large part, as the source, of his mother's self-possession. It is true that Esther is introduced as a strong-willed character long before her pregnancy. At the end of the first chapter, Esther walks out of the kitchen at Woodview because the cook orders her to prepare vegetables immediately, before she can change her traveling dress. The woman's mockery of her worn dress, echoed by the housemaid's laughter, affronts Esther's dignity. Even before coming to Woodview, it is learned later, she had put an end to her stepfather's beatings by hurling hot water in his face, the only member of her family to have resisted his brutality. In each case, she defends her emergent sense of self against the full force of her economic dependency.

Despite the drudgery and monotony necessitated by her determination to raise her child, her labors also lead to an even fuller discovery of a sense of self formed by vigilant resistance to pressures around her. As Esther struggles for Jackie, she struggles also for unity of being, for purpose, and for meaning. Most of the decisions made for her son's sake are made in defense of her own integrity as well. In each aspect of her fight, all facets of the socially organized world oppose her. The pivotal standoff with Mrs. Rivers involves not only Esther's insistence that her child's life will not be traded for that of the rich woman's child, but an insistence that she will act as a whole human being. Moore seems to have recognized the centrality of the scene: no other section of the novel underwent such thorough and repeated revisions, and it occupies a large portion of the 1922 dramatic adaptation. The opposition between the two forces—unity and division—is powerful. Even Mrs. Rivers' name suggests a "river," one who splits or cleaves, forcing diversion of the "waters." On her first day at the Rivers household, Esther finds that "her self-respect was wounded" by the "constant mealing" meant to feed not the complete person, Esther, but a partitioned part of her body, the breasts, which in turn feed Mrs. Rivers' child. Not only does she resist the division of her own body, but likewise protests the separation of mother and child into replaceable units. Esther answers with silence Mrs. Spires's supposition that she might grow to love Mrs. Rivers's child as her own and argues that Mrs. Rivers immorally pur-

chases "the milk that belongs to another." In the dramatic adaptation, Moore draws even greater attention to this issue by having one
of Mrs. Spires's experienced clients profess that "one child is the
same as another at the breast."[7] Esther rejects these attempts at dis-
memberment, this partitioning of her body and family into discrete
and even interchangeable parts. She requires instead the integration
of herself as a totality and as a being conjoined with her newborn
son. Her individualism is paradoxically founded in her struggle to
build a communal structure from the basic but fragile unity of
mother and child.

In the world Moore depicts, the repressive codes that govern the
economy result in the extreme isolation of the underclass individual
and the breakdown of supportive communal structures. With few
exceptions, relationships are purely financial. Mrs. Rivers has not
the slightest interest in Esther's own child and, when pressed, blurts
out that its existence is an inconvenience to her and that it would be
better dead. She attempts to reduce the partnership of two mothers
and two children to a simplified relation of purchaser and product.
She has no medical need for a wet nurse, and her decision to employ
one only mimics what "a hundred other fashionable women were
doing at the same moment." The product itself she transforms from
a vital nourishment to a sign of her financial superiority. In a study
of Victorian medicine, Sally Shuttleworth contends that by the mid-
nineteenth century, it was common to see popular attacks on "idle
middle-class" women who reproduced sickly children or did not reproduce at all, "thus opening the door to the social domination of
the prolific working classes."[8] Moore's explicit condemnation of Mrs.
Rivers's decision not to nurse her own sickly child may draw from
this rhetoric, yet Mrs. Rivers belongs to Mayfair society rather than
the middle class, and Moore sees her action as an economic exploitation of the poor rather than the relinquishment of power to them.
Similarly, his condemnation of wet-nursing draws from a tradition
of upper-class queasiness over such arrangements, but places blame
not on the avarice of the lower-class woman—as was most common
—but upon a larger web of economic relations of which wet-nursing
was an integral part.[9] In his dramatic adaptation, Moore alters the
terms of the confrontation between Esther and her employer, perhaps with hopes of placating a potential theater audience, and this
weakening indicates just how strong his original statement was. Mrs.
Rivers follows Esther into the slums to explain that "it wasn't my
fault; I had no milk when baby was born" and to plead with Esther

to return out of the goodness of her heart. In the play, a circumstantial problem between two individuals thus sentimentally replaces the original depiction of a dehumanizing economic exchange between representatives of rich and poor.

At the novel's end, the now-widowed Esther with great relief withdraws from participation in that rigid yet erratic world of financial relationships and the mores that support them. She returns to the nearly deserted Woodview and to a friendship with Mrs. Barfield in which class distinctions are muted and punitive judgments of sexual behavior left behind. Beside the mother-and-child unit, the Plymouth Brethren who gather at what remains of Woodview represent the only supportive community within the novel. They are a peculiar, marginal group whose eyes are on the world hereafter. Wayne Hall is probably correct in drawing a parallel between Moore's exile from Ireland and Esther's retirement to Woodview and in viewing both as retreats from the given world. Yet the novel, like *Confessions of a Young Man,* is more than a book about failure. It recounts as well the individual's attempt to build an alternative community and to achieve value outside of failed structures. A repudiation of the established world, *Esther Waters* reads as an affirmation of meaning achieved through that most "Protestant" of virtues, work.

Whereas *Parnell* is a record of work undone or left unfinished, both *Confessions* and *Esther* are diaries of labor. In comparison with other fallen women of Victorian fiction, Esther would at first seem to be yet another heroine to be punished and redeemed by her labors. But as Esther retorts to Fred Parsons when he asks if she has repented, "I should think I had, and been punished too, enough for a dozen children. . . . If I am not good enough for you, you can go elsewhere and get better; I've had enough of reproaches" (*EW* 184–85). Like *Confessions,* the novel echoes the doctrine of work expounded in Carlyle's *Sartor Resartus,* and yet there is a great difference between Moore's understanding of work and that of Carlyle. Whereas Carlyle's Teufelsdröckh turns to work as a means of escaping the self, Moore's characters find in work a means to develop and recognize a self. Seen in conjunction with earlier writings, the novel offers work—with no guarantee of its ultimate success—not as punishment but as the primary way of establishing meaning and purpose for anyone who must attempt self-creation outside the realm of communal expectations.

In the novel, as in both of the early autobiographies, Moore is nevertheless ambivalent about the nature of work and profit. Part of his irresolution concerns the individual's responsibility to account for the source of his or her money. He seems unsure as to whether one can discriminate between acceptable and unacceptable sources of income. Dying of consumption, William Latch tells his son, "I worked hard enough that's true; but it was not the right kind of work. . . . No good comes of money that hasn't been properly earned" (*EW* 361). This deathbed repudiation may be out of character, but Latch's assertion that money can be properly and improperly earned accords with Moore's indictment of the prosperous classes who live on the bodies of their servants, prostitutes, and wet nurses.

Moore also suggests that earnings can never be made but at another's cost. The pregnant Esther imagines her child "learning a trade, going to work in the morning and coming back to her in the evening, proud in the accomplishment of something done, of good money honestly earned" (*EW* 110). In this novel, however, no one earns his or her money "properly." Esther's stepfather feeds his alcoholism on his children's piecework, itself a harsh employment in which their sore fingers stuff toy dogs for more prosperous children to enjoy; Esther's stepsister wheedles out of her half the money she has saved for the weeks following childbirth; the Barfields derive their fortune from horse-racing at the expense of their farming and the welfare of the neighborhood; William is a bookmaker living on the hopes of the impoverished. Even the pious Esther must work as a general servant in a whorehouse, and later her position at her husband's tavern contradicts her own beliefs of what is proper and good. All sources of income are suspect. As the narrator of *Parnell and His Island* asserts, "The socialistic axiom that capital is only a surplus-value coming from unpaid labour, either in the past or in the present, is in other countries mitigated and lost sight of in the multiplicity of ways through which money passes before falling into the pockets of the rich; but in Ireland the passage direct and brutal of money from the horny hands of the peasant to the delicate hands of the proprietor is terribly suggestive of serfdom" (*PI* 6–7). The harsh relations of rich and poor in Ireland, he contends, are only an exaggeration of a pervasive system in which profit derives invariably from exploitation.

If the world provides little opportunity to undertake "honest labour," Moore implies that the world deserves very little in return for that which is finally accomplished. The remains of an essentially corrupt community (be it Moore Hall or the racing world of Woodview) best serve the new generation in humble silence. Esther's return to

Woodview may not be quite the wish-fulfilling fantasy of the un-grateful son suggested by Wayne Hall, but parallels do exist between *Esther* and the autobiographies' recurring scenes of confrontation be-tween the narrator and Moore Hall. If a wish-fulfilling fantasy does operate here, it resides in the dispersal of two distinct features of the autobiographical persona into mother and son: the laborer and the landlord. The two characters hold in balance the chronic conflict between return and expatriation. Moore ends the novel with a loving embrace between Esther, the worker who creates with blind instinct against the powers of convention, and Jack, who receives by mail the last trickle of income from the wreck of Woodview. The narrative allows no condemnation of Jack and, in fact, highlights the legit-imacy of his claim by contrasting the relationship between the boy and his mother with that of Mrs. Barfield and her neglectful son, Arthur. Jack's letters to his mother are described as short notes re-questing money; Arthur, as Mrs. Barfield regretfully sighs, does not write at all. A "common racing man," Arthur could not care less about Woodview. He derives little money or status from it, has no desire to restore it, and his abrupt manner antagonizes the reader. By manipulating the fictional device of antithetical pairing—Jack and Arthur—Moore avoids the question of obligation. Jack actually functions as "landlord"; it is he who receives without labor whatever Woodview can still offer. But this financial relationship is obscured by sentiment and presented as a continuance of that devotion of mother to son we have witnessed throughout the novel. Although dear to the two women as a relic of their respective histories, Wood-view, the place of memory, is sacrificed to the needs of the next generation of life. Self-generating in all but physical form, Jack as an emergent individual owes no more to the old place than he does to the air he breathes.

"The old place," forming whatever social organization is left at the novel's end, is relevant to the individual's quest only through its monetary contribution. It provides little opportunity for purposeful labor. The alternative of urban London has been, if not irrelevant, directly hostile to Esther Waters's attempts to find for herself and in her own terms, a spiritual significance for her life. The particulars of her life seem to form what Julia Bently of *Vain Fortune* calls "a woman's life, —suppression of self and monotonous duty, varied by heart-breaking misfortune."[10] However, letters written during the novel's initial composition emphasize Esther's "fight," her "sturdy steadfastness," and her "heroism,"[11] suggesting that the novel is a story not of failure but of success—a success that is in accordance with certain culturally acceptable ideas of a maternal archetype, and is for the most part interior and purely individualist. As a symbolic record of motherhood, Esther's story constitutes a sequence of victories precisely where its particulars lead away from a historical understanding and into a mythic one. While Moore fully develops Esther as a character in the realist tradition, his early choice of a title, *Mother and Child*, invokes the world of symbol and the iconography of the Virgin.[12] Within the realm of human history, the Virgin appears as the mother deprived of a son; within the realm of myth, she is the mother forever triumphant, the Queen of Heaven. Although her transformation occurs in chronological sequence, the dual nature of her iconography is simultaneously apprehended by her devotee. Moore's novel asks the reader to experience a life of humiliation, fear, and physical pain within particularized historical circumstances, while also considering that life as transcendent.

In asserting Esther's capacity for transcendent knowledge and sublime joy, Moore attributes to Esther the capacity that Schopenhauer attributes to fathers; in utilizing the term "instinctive" to describe what the philosopher calls "metaphysical," he dissolves the opposition between the two terms. Schopenhauer, whose ideas Moore claims to have informed the novel, writes in "On Women": "As in animals, so in man, the original maternal love is purely *instinctive* and therefore ceases with the physical helplessness of the children. . . . The father's love for his children is of a different kind and more enduring. It rests on his again recognizing in them in his innermost self and is thus of metaphysical origin."[13] As articulated most clearly in *Confessions of a Young Man*, instinct culminates in the assertion of a self conceived and birthed in one's own work: painting, literature, music, and even maternity. With each revision of the novel, the instinct that leads Esther comes closer to a kind of metaphysical power. From a mere bestial drudge in the novel's earliest versions, she evolves as a figure whose instincts align her with the artist.[14] Instinct, far from being an inferior trait of animals and lower natures, instead acts as guide for the creative drive. That drive, when fulfilled, leads to profound pleasure in one's own being as manifest in its works.

As a mother, Esther is alive with wonder at the mystery of her productive capacity, both in the moment after birth when her life's energies find their focus and later when recounting the story of her hardship. In a letter of 1892, Moore noted that all of his character's suffering was depicted "in order to intensify the moment of sublime happiness when they put the baby into her arms."[15] After suffering the impersonal terrors of a charity maternity ward in which all her individuality is systematically denied, and after she is finally chloroformed for the difficult birth, Esther comes alive when the "pulp of red flesh rolled up in flannel" is laid beside her. "Its eyes were open; it looked at her, and her flesh filled with a sense of happiness so deep and so intense that she was like one enchanted. . . . Her personal self seemed entirely withdrawn; she existed like an atmosphere about the babe and lay absorbed in this life of her life, this flesh of her flesh, unconscious of herself as a sponge in warm sea-water. She touched this pulp of life, and was thrilled, and once more her senses swooned with love; it was still there" (*EW* 122).

Moore's emphasis upon Esther's obliviousness to anything outside herself and the child ties the passage to a similar one in *A Mummer's Wife,* but with a major difference. The lazy, irresolute Kate Ede is enraptured by the trancelike passivity of her postnatal state because "her very weakness and lassitude were a source of happiness; for, after long months of turmoil and racket, it was pleasant to lie in the covertures, and suffer her thoughts to rise out of unconsciousness or sink back into it without an effort."[16] Esther, in contrast, is alive with pleasure. In his description of Esther, Moore reverses the Darwinistic metaphor of the sponge, ridding it of its customary retrogressive implications; Esther's moment is one of metaphysical ecstasy, her being so thoroughly intertwined with its creation as to empower henceforward her struggle against the severing pressures of her world.

As Elliot Gilbert writes in his study of *Esther Waters* and scientism, she responds to the crush of an unchangeable world by "saying yes" to "the sovereignty of her own flesh."[17] While the maternal drive that defines her may seem at first a conventional one, as the expression of both her individuality and her embodiment of a transcendent archetype it opposes everything in the given world except the processes visible in the natural landscape.[18] Because her environment recognizes neither the rights of the individual nor the basic configuration of mother and child, she necessarily must war with her surroundings. She has to fight to assert her individuality because the social world opposes her instinctual choice to be what she is; in a society hostile to myth and nature, her individuality paradoxically lies in fulfilling an archetypal role. Not only does this role lie in conflict with environment, but with hereditary characteristics as well.

Under pressure, however, her inherited impatience and susceptibility to anger, which often function counterproductively, submit to
the dominance of the larger instinctual drive that, importantly, is
never described as an inherited capacity. She learns to compromise
for the sake of the child. Both standard categories of deterministic
force—environment and heredity—lead her toward self-alienation.
Her self-creation, which comes about through the birthing and rear-
ing of her child, leads her to apprehend the integration of life.

Esther and her creative activity are nevertheless constricted by
fundamental limitations. The struggle of Esther's life finally results
in fulfillment: the display of its intrinsic maternal quality. Yet we
hope to produce beyond our own lives, to create the objectified presence of ourselves in something else. In Esther's case, that production
would be Jack; in the case of the writer, some work of value. The last
scenes of *Esther Waters* cast serious doubt upon the fulfillment of
such expectations. One year before beginning *Esther*, Moore wrote to
the publisher W. T. Stead (correcting in a later letter his substitution
of the word "lust" for Schopenhauer's term, "will to live"): "Women
are lustful and the preservation of the race depends upon the lust
instinct . . . no good can be done in morals. Your bullets flatten
against the rock of the desire of the will to live. I am talking Schopenhauer, his book is a sad book, but it is a terribly true one."[19] Like
Schopenhauer, Moore sees the will to live in the urge to procreate
and recognizes that death eventually thwarts the will. The ordered
patterns of nature Schopenhauer and Moore acknowledge, but repetition comes to weariness and vivacity unfolds as a cruel joke. For all
of the novel's wonder at the self's own story, *Esther Waters*, like *Confessions of a Young Man*, combines a regard for the individual with a
sense of his, or her, ultimate futility. The last lines of *Esther Waters*
directly articulate that inherent sadness when the visible sign of
Esther's victory—the healthy, loving son who embraces her—falls
under the shadow of the red cloak and cap that identify him as a
soldier, subject to "the possibility that any moment might declare
him to be mere food for powder and shot" (*EW* 382).

In contrast to *Parnell*, where the overall sense of futility derives
from a failure of initiative in both character and culture, the pessimism of *Esther* recalls that of *Confessions of a Young Man*. Esther's
struggle to validate her own being by raising her son outside the
acceptable conventions of English life establishes a more than superficial parallel with the efforts of the young man to create something
of permanence outside the sterile world of Ireland. At the end of

Confessions it is not clear—in fact, it is dubious—whether the narrator will be able to accomplish his purpose. In a letter to John Mackinnon Robertson, Moore explains the inconclusive ending in which the young man withdraws to work on his novel. He writes, "the mainspring of the book is the persistency of the artistic instinct working blindly toward a goal it knows not of. Therefore I ended the book on the original theme."[20] In *Confessions,* the threat of final futility is subtly evoked in the reader's consciousness of the narrator's follies and the uneven quality of the work to be produced by its author, whose identification with the narrator is stressed. In *Esther,* that threat finds an objective form in Jack's army uniform. Death may or may not be imminent, but its eventual arrival is indubitable despite the persistence of labor, despite the power of the maternal instinct.

Moore's doubts about the final outcome of Esther's work and his own efforts compel a reexamination of the novel as a statement about the generative capacities and incapacities of self-descriptive narrative. Both *Confessions of a Young Man* and *Esther Waters* set a self-acquired language in opposition to the language one inherits. As *Esther Waters* was revised, Esther's control over her language became more pronounced; excepting the regressive dramatic adaptation, the revisions cut out snobbish acknowledgments of her ungrammatical phrasings.[21] As the young man of *Confessions* struggles to acquire a literary language out of the abyss of his failed education, Esther struggles to make sense of her experience, hampered by illiteracy and the obfuscating niceties of someone like Mrs. Rivers. In words parallelling those with which he describes Esther's fight for language, Moore writes of his own isolated development: "I had something to say and sought for the means of saying it, blindly, instinctively."[22] At several points in the novel, Moore wrote to his publishers, Esther "at last finds words, simple words, and tells what she thinks."[23] These "simple words" allow her to generalize from the harsh details of her experience and identify her victimization as part of a pervasive system. Without exception, they are scenes of angry confrontation: with Mrs. Rivers, when she identifies the wet-nursing system as genocidal; with the moralistic Mrs. Bingley, when she retorts that "there ain't much chance of temptation for them who work seventeen hours a day"; with the self-righteous Fred Parsons, when she argues that a woman "has to do the good that comes to her to do." Her language discovers itself precisely through its opposition to prevalent ideologies.

Her language being dependent upon the confrontational situation, Esther rarely reflects or speculates without an immediate purpose before her. The first three times she stops to tell her life story—to Mrs. Barfield, to Mrs. Rice, and to William—her retrospections, motivated by despair and the hint of kindness in the listener, serve in her ongoing combat with economic strictures. Hurled "as if they were half-bricks" at the despairing William, much of the detail of her story spells its own meaning. While "Mrs. Spires" may be a meaningless name to him, what she represents is not, and "the workhouse" needs no particularized explanation beyond its own connotation of horror. As told to all three listeners, her story arrives at no conceptual framework; the names and places pour out in a rush of emotion. Only when Esther has retired to Woodview can she provide any generalization about her own life, and that is to call it a "hard fight," a phrase borrowed from her former employer, the novelist Mrs. Rice. Esther's lack of meditative capacity narrows the possibilities of her self-generation. Her borrowed descriptive phrase, "It was a hard fight," does act as a corrective for Mrs. Barfield's reductive description of her life as a "long romance" and, as adopted by Esther, the phrase is left the defining one. Esther's limitations, however, become particularly clear through a comparison of this exchange with a vignette from *Memoirs of My Dead Life*, entitled "A Waitress."

Moore begins his vignette by attacking a passage of Robert Louis Stevenson in which Stevenson recalls his past misfortunes and the events that led him finally in flight to the South Seas, to be "cast . . . out in the end, as by a sudden freshet, on these ultimate islands." Contemplating his past, Stevenson writes that "I admire and bow my head before the romance of destiny." With evident anger at the way Stevenson's phrase sentimentally glosses over the real suffering many endure, Moore inquires

> For who does not feel his destiny to be a romance, and who does not admire the ultimate island whither his destiny will cast him? Giacomo Cenci, whom the Pope ordered to be flayed alive, no doubt admired the romance of destiny that laid him on his ultimate island, a raised plank, so that the executioner might conveniently roll up the skin of his belly like an apron. And a hare that I once saw beating a tambourine in Regent Street looked at me so wistfully that I am sure puss admired in some remote way the romance of destiny that had taken her from the woodland and cast her upon her ultimate island—in this case a barrow. (*MMDL* 17)

Despite the difference in tone, Moore's sarcasm parallels Esther's gentle repudiation of a similar phrase. He uses the phrase more ambiguously in an 1897 letter to Lena Milman in which he discusses the feelings of his character, Evelyn Innes, near the end of her stage career: "What a romance is destiny and how vain is the word. Why do we breathe, eat and aspire? Destiny is the only answer and how much happier we are when we pursue in quietness the inevitable path." Here, he would seem to be invoking the same sentiment for which he attacks Stevenson. However, turning his attention to his own compositional process, he continues, "The more I think of the subject the more I like it, the more it astonishes me. But I have not the power to write it, I mean to unravel its mysteries. I hold the skein and can follow the thread from end to end and yet cannot unwind it as I would like" (*GMT* 136). Moore reveals himself to be the true object of destiny's romance, not the passive Evelyn Innes who retreats from life to the "inevitable" path of a cloistered convent. If there is in operation "a romance of destiny," it lies in Moore's wonder at his own fate as the novelist who penetrates in vain the mysteries that elude him.

Similarly, at the end of his story about the sad life of the consumptive Irish waitress is the exclamation, "Poor little heap of bones! And I bow my head and admire the romance of destiny which ordained that I, who only saw her once, should be the last to remember her" (*MMDL* 25). Again, it is the writer, not the inarticulate or suffering character whose destiny is a romance. Moore openly acknowledges that the waitress is valuable to him only as she becomes the object of narrative. In the case of *Esther Waters,* birth remains—despite Moore's documentable and, to all appearances, very sincere concern for the problems of unwed mothers and neglected children—finally most significant as a subject for his own wonder and his own work. Without an observer, the object of observation attains no significance, just as the author becomes interesting only when the object of his own glance in the mirror or the topic of his own recollective reveries.

This positioning of the author as the object of his own gaze is important, for it is not only the female character who is placed in the role of object, but the male author as well. Whether in the role of perceptual object or of perceiving subject, Moore frequently takes on a feminine identity to describe his own persona. He can be the young author of *A Drama in Muslin* with "his sloping shoulders and his female hands" whom the older author of *Muslin* remembers seeing reflected in the Castle mirrors. Or, Moore may take the guise of a female author, as in his use of a feminine pseudonym for the serialized version of *Vain Fortune*. In discussing the composition of *Esther Waters*, he claims to have bettered George Eliot by becoming a better woman than she was, writing the novel a real woman would write. Reflecting on Hetty Sorrel, one of Esther Waters's best-known fictional predecessors, Moore remarks that "George Eliot sought a subject in Hetty Sorrel's murder of her child. A woman's moulding of the subject, a true moulding, would be Hetty living to save her child."[24] His dismissal of Eliot echoes those of a multitude of male writers at the end of the nineteenth century, who, as Elaine Showalter speculates, felt themselves threatened by a new generation of women writers who claimed Eliot's work as their matriarchal legacy. "One defense against the mother's reign," Showalter comments, "is to appropriate her power by repressing the maternal role in procreation and creation, and replacing it with a fantasy of self-fathering. . . . While fantasies of male self-creation and envy of the feminine aspects of generation were not new, they reemerged with a peculiar virulence in the 1880s. . . . In the male writing of the *fin de siècle*, celibate male creative generation was valorized, and female powers of creation and reproduction were denigrated."[25] With the psychoanalytic hypothesis that the male transvestite enjoys the sensation that he "assimilates femaleness into his maleness . . . so that he mysteriously owns the power of both sexes in a single, covertly but thrillingly male body," Sandra Gilbert and Susan Gubar correlate their own argument that male modernists who write about androgynous cross-dressing almost uniformly do so in order to project the disastrous ends of gender blurring for females and the continued privileges of the same phenomenon in males.[26] Male appropriation of the female voice or body, according to these arguments, has more to do with a usurpation of power than a utopian expression of androgynous understanding.

Elements of these discussions aptly correspond to Moore's own emphasis on autogenous development and his frequent analogies between maternity and his own generative acts as a writer. It is also true that he dismissed women's talents as writers or painters and utilized belittling metaphors of childbearing to describe what he alleged to be their inferior productions. However, as to his appropriation of Eliot's "subject," it could be argued that Moore felt bound to dismiss and insult almost any precursor, male or female. His deprecations of Eliot do not begin to equal in harshness his invectives against Stevenson and Hardy or his repudiations of the indubitable influence of such writers as Dickens and Zola. And as will be thoroughly examined in light of *Hail and Farewell,* he frequently usurps the voices of others, male and female, in a process that displays the polyglot, collective nature of authorship and at the same time dominates borrowed language by retaining the privilege of final arrangement.

As represented by Moore, the androgynous human subject need not always imply the superiority of the doubly gendered male and the contingent inferiority of the doubly gendered female. Rather, his stories condemn the social restrictions that cause the androgynous individual to suffer, while simultaneously finding gender identity to be inseparable from the "interpretive codes," the "glosses" by which the "text" of our lives is read (*CES* 192). Moore's claim to have bettered Eliot, seen in the context of his other representations of sexual identity, may reveal his insight into the very difficulty of establishing what "a real woman" or "a real man" is to be, especially in connection with the inherited body and the language with which identity is to be conceived.

"Quelque Hésitation de Sexe": A Sequence of Celibate Lives

To the 1889 French edition of *Confessions,* Moore added a passage that never appeared in any subsequent editions. Attempting to explain his fascination with women to "Conscience," the narrator remarks,

Je souhaitais d'être avec ce sexe, comme une ombre avec son objet. Jamais auparavant l'âme d'un homme n'avait été si embrouillée avec celle de la femme; et pour expliquer l'anormal de cette sympathie, je ne puis qu'imaginer qu'avant ma naissance il y avait eu quelque hésitation de sexe. Pourtant j'étais un joyeux garçon, amoureux de l'aventure, et excellent sportsman; une fois un cheval entre les jambes ou un fusil dans les mains, je quittais toutes morbides imaginations, tous étranges désirs de jouer les femmes en travesti, de porter leurs bottines et leurs peignoirs.[27]

I wanted to be with this sex, like a shadow with its object. Never previously had the soul of a man been so intermingled with that of woman; and to explain the abnormality of this sexual sympathy, I can only imagine that before my birth there had been some hesitation as to my sex. Nevertheless, I was a joyful boy, enamored with

adventure and an excellent sportsman; once I had a horse between
my legs or a gun in my hands, I gave up all such morbid fantasies,
all strange desires to dress up like women, to wear their little boots
and dressing gowns.

This confession is reminiscent of the narrator's proclamation in
English editions that he is "feminine, morbid, perverse"; it coyly
takes the signs of masculinity—the handling of guns and horses—
and renders these actions thinly veiled analogies to handling the
penis. In this passage, the gender of the speaker and the nature of
his desire are in question. Is the speaker male or female? Does the
interest in the male organ reflect that of a homosexual male or a
heterosexual female? And does the handling of horses and guns
provide a pleasurable—and more socially acceptable—substitute for
playing the woman's role, or does it turn the speaker against the
woman's role? Moore's flagrant articulation of gender ambiguity is
more than it appears to be at first perusal: that is, a mere affectation
of a bohemian gesture in keeping with his autobiographical portrayal of a youthful aesthete at large in Paris during the 1870s. Although figures of ambiguous gender were frequent subjects of the
art of this period, rarely did the artist produce doubly gendered self-
representations. As Michael Wilson has demonstrated in his study of
bohemian Montmartre, the society of artists during the period recalled in *Confessions* exhibited little tolerance for aberrants from
heterosexual norms except as objects of analysis, and then most frequently as objects of scorn or pity.[28] Given Moore's later cultivation
of the contradictory self-representations of ladies' man and impotent
celibate, this self-suppressed French passage evinces his own pervad-
ing preoccupation with the subject of mixed gender and a long-
standing desire to so characterize himself in the autobiographical
personae he presented to the public.

Crucial to understanding Moore's work in this area is sensitivity to his tone, particularly in regard to the ironic subtleties of his
autobiographies and short stories. In the suppressed passage from
Confessions d'un Jeune Anglais, he fashions an excruciatingly intimate
revelation with humor and objectivity. Frequently, as in this passage,
Moore displays a contemptuous amusement at sexual behavior and
the codes that would control it, while also holding up to scrutiny the
narrator or interlocutor who tells or hears the story of other people's private lives. Alternative sexualities and controlling norms are
treated with equal irony, as may be observed in the following two

examples: a biographical detail from the memoirs of publisher George H. Doran, and Moore's 1894 short story, "An Episode in Married Life." Doran relates how Moore approached William Heinemann with an idea for a new novel. Moore, he writes,

> outlined the plot of what he termed to be a great novel. In brief, a young man of family and distinction and title falls in love with a daughter of an equally distinguished house. The marriage is arranged. The wedding takes place at St. Margaret's, Westminster. On the bridal night the bridegroom discovers his totally unthought-of and unsuspected impotency. The following day in humiliation and despondency he arranges for the dissolution of the marriage. . . . He makes handsome settlement and departs immediately for a protracted voyage around the world on a sailing-ship. On board he meets a plump little sailor-boy and lives happily ever afterwards. "There," exclaimed Moore, "is a plot for you!" Heinemann protested that no such book could be printed and published in England. But Moore contended: "Why not! it is simply a modernizing of the Greek practice which pleased and thrilled the male and in addition gave protection to the innocence of Grecian women."[29]

Doran's anecdote appears in a chapter bewailing the increasing acceptance of homosexuality, and he gives the story as another distressing example of the trend. Moore's projected plot, however, sounds less like a plea for tolerance than a provocational satire aimed at many targets: then-current "Greek" apologias for male homosexuality, the standard of feminine sexual innocence, expectations of marriage as shaped by class values, the mores of English publishing, and sexuality itself, reduced to a matter of bodily function and viewed with a fascinated if ultimately contemptuous eye.

Similarly, in the story, "An Episode in Married Life," both sanctioned and unsanctioned sexuality are again subject to irony. As in many of his other prose narratives, Moore presents with greatest irony those figures of normative behavior who counterpose the abnormal. A young mother and wife who arranges an assignation at a costume ball feverishly kisses her child before going to the ball. "To free herself" from the "clutch" of passion, "she must appeal to her child; perhaps her baby's kisses would win her back to reason." For a moment she thinks "her little girl had saved her," but she is unable to resist her "intolerable desire." When she returns, having broken her appointment, she kisses the child so vehemently that it awakens and cries. For this story, Moore has borrowed a stock gesture in which the child functions as a moral control over a potentially way-ward woman. Yet in Moore's treatment, not only does the child pro-test being squeezed, but its mother's return has little to do with motherly feeling. She returns because her would-be lover, deciding he would test the depth of her passion, appears at the costume ball in the ridiculous dress and white-powdered face of a Pierrot. Any appeal of the childish goodness has been less decisive than her sud-den, and very physical, revulsion at the Pierrot. Underscoring his comically reductive treatment of the urgency of desire and the stan-dard gestures of conventional morality, Moore concludes, "And so did a powder-puff save a woman, when other remedies had failed, from the calamity of a great passion."[30] The "powder-puff," custom-arily the property of a woman, has here been applied to a male face, effecting a gender ambiguity that is so disorienting as to produce an effect more powerful than the attractions of either domestic virtue or commonplace adultery.

Despite his tendency to mock both desire and norms that con-trol, Moore's stories are by no means misanthropic. What distin-guishes George H. Doran's anecdote from Moore's fictions is that Moore's portraits of human beings confused and driven by sexual impulse and economic pressures register not only his amusement, but a sense of admiration and sympathy for the multifarious forms human behavior may take. Moore may well describe his own practice when he contends in an essay on Fielding that "a living and moving story related by a humorist very soon becomes a thing of jeers and laughter, signifying nothing. We must have humour, of course, but the use we must make of our sense of humour is to avoid intro-ducing anything into the narrative that shall distract the reader from the beauty, the mystery, and the pathos of the life we live in this world."[31] As he wrote to his friend Clara Lanza, "sex is full of myste-ries and subtleties" (*LGM* 153) and, however ironic and humorous, his fiction does demonstrate beauty, mystery, and pathos within the physical urgings, economic exigencies, and linguistic determinations that govern human sexuality.

At best, Moore successfully expresses both his irrepressible irony and that sense of wonder by adapting the objectivist techniques of French short fiction. His series of short stories on the subject of celi-bacy, published between 1895 and 1927, attempt intimate studies of characters whose sexual and even gender identities are uncertain as well as others whom economic circumstances have pressed into "sin-gle strictness." Although many initial reviews of *Celibates* predictably maligned Moore as a pornographer whose subjects "filter through the soiled substratum of his mind and come forth blemished," by the 1920s, reviewers of the new, revised editions were more willing to accept the controversial subject matter and to appreciate the restraint and maturity of his technique.[32] The technique demonstrates how very far Moore had come from the naturalism of Emile Zola or the Goncourt brothers. As minimally plotted psychological studies, his stories indulge in neither pseudoscientific theorizing nor rigid environmental causality. Long concerned with questions of origin, Moore here asks whether sexual behavior and gender identity derive from irreversible instincts, social conditioning, economics, or language. Although attracted to theories of innate psychological characteristics, Moore also proposes that gender roles are the product of culture and without absolute origin in the biological factor of sexuality. Several of his characters attempt to form gender identities that combine features of male and female, but repeatedly they find their language incapable of providing a self-description intelligible to themselves and others. Perhaps most important, the later stories in the series critique at length the problem of representing variegations of gender within a phallocentric language, as at the same time they call attention to the questionable ethical stance of the male observer-narrator. In several of the earliest stories in the celibate series, Moore tries to account for differences between social expectations and actual sexual behavior by explanations that trace sexual choices to congenital conditions. In the stories concerning the homosexual John Norton (later called Hugh Momfret) and the frigid hysteric Mildred Lawson (later renamed Henrietta Marr), he exhibits considerable confusion as to the origins of what he can only call an "instinctual" rejection of heterosexual norms. Mildred's seemingly innate psychological disturbance is symptomized by the conventional signs of anorexia, headaches, and such a hypersensitive nervousness that she is kept awake by "the aching smell of lilies" while "recollections of the day turned and turned in her brain, ticking loudly, and she could see each event as distinctly as the figures on the dial of a great clock" (C 1). Her sexual repression is so great that while chastity has become her waking obsession, she endures erotic bisexual nightmares. Although she can hardly bear to be touched, she thinks constantly about other people's "impurity." She finds herself in a dress "cut lower than she intended" reading a piece of what appears to be pornography; she perceives herself as a delectable "dainty morsel"; she dreams in horror of the "black slit" into which she might fall. Like Hugh Momfret, who explains his homosexuality as "an old original instinct" granted to him by God, Mildred too so accounts for her aversion to intercourse. Faced with the possibility of marrying a gifted and sexually vital painter, Mildred finds that "mysterious occult influences which she could neither explain nor control were drawing her away from him. She asked herself, what was this power which abided in the bottom of her heart, from which she could not rid herself?" (C 223–24).

Although Moore briefly suggests that Mildred is the product of her repressive education and Momfret the product of excessive exposure to Greek statuary and *Marius the Epicurean,* he resorts to a simplistic declaration of "instinct" as the final explanation. Throughout his other writings "instinct" has indicated a unique inner productive capacity; it is the term Moore uses to explain his own literary gifts and to explain the force that empowers Esther Waters to give birth and raise her son to adulthood against all odds. Echoing his own language, he wrote to a friend that "I wished to represent in Mildred Lawson a woman living in the shallows of vanity just as in Esther Waters I represented a woman living in the deepest human instincts" (GMT 110). In "Mildred Lawson" and "Hugh Momfret" he attributes to "instinct" a meaning inconsistent with his other writing and that, as an assertion of sexual essentialism, suppresses further analysis of the origins and nature of their sexuality. As a result, while the bourgeois conventions against which they rebel are openly satirized, the standards of the artistic bohemianism to which the protagonists aspire (and with which Moore sought to be associated) remain unquestioned. Similarly, the narrative authority invoked by the stories' rigidly realistic method precludes any self-reflexive examination of the terms by which either character is drawn.

In later stories like "Sarah Gwynn" and "Albert Nobbs," however, Moore either ignores or parodies simple congenital explanations, while reflecting on the difficulties of discussing a sexuality that neither follows heterosexual norms nor exists in simple binary opposition to them. In a passage from his *Conversations in Ebury Street* (1924), Moore articulates a view of gendered behavior that tends toward the behaviorist hypothesis: commitment to a particular kind of sexuality arises from social forces and desire consequently follows an established "sexual value system" that "drowns out competing alternatives":[33]

> I submit that it is rare to approach life except through interpretive codes: glosses learnt by heart before any attempt is made to read

the text. . . . The Dean of St. Paul's knows, too, that sodomy is essentially a Christian sin. He knows that the Greeks, to whom we owe our civilisation and to whom we are inferior in all the arts, married to continue the race but did not love their wives except in rare instances, yet modern conventions might compel him to advocate or at least to acquiesce in the persecution of those afflicted with abnormal love. (*CES* 192)

The idea of culturally perpetuated "interpretive glosses" by which the body is read differently in various historical periods here opposes the notion that certain individuals are "afflicted" with various forms of desire; typically, we find Moore straddling a middle ground between explanations. He both echoes and contradicts the influential theories of writers like Krafft-Ebing, Ulrichs, Carpenter, Ellis, and Symonds, all of whom argued for the congenital rather than the environmental origins of sexual orientation. In his very confusion, however, he can pursue lines of inquiry that deterministic essentialism had effectively closed off.

In "Agnes Lahens" and "Sarah Gwynn," Moore traces the relation between the sexual body and the symbolic systems by which it is known and interpreted; in the two stories, and to a much fuller degree in "Albert Nobbs," the sexual body functions as metonym for social or spiritual status. "Agnes Lahens" analyzes the environmental circumstances that drive a young girl toward the celibacy of the convent, but its powerful portrait of her mother offers the more explicit example of this process of metonymic conversion. The aging Olive Lahens maintains the illusion of beauty in order to maintain the illusion that she is involved in a passionate love affair, thereby gaining for herself a certain social standing as an object of desire. It is the illusion of gendered activity that matters, even for those who recognize it as illusion; for all concerned, Olive Lahens exists as an effigy of a desired object.

The metonymic function of sexuality is further explored in the story of the parlormaid, Sarah Gwynn, which was added to the series in 1922. In response to her employer's questioning, Sarah tells him that years ago she had escaped to Dublin from the hard life of a farm laborer near Belfast and was rescued from pauperism by Phyllis, a girl who took her home and found her work in a biscuit factory. There she discovered that the work paid for little more than lodging and that most of the girls spent several hours each night as prostitutes in order to buy food and clothes. Phyllis, she continues, met a man who paid her generously with the understanding that the money would be given to Sarah so that she might join a convent where she could pray for their souls. Having left the convent because she was not given sufficient time to pray, she is attempting to save enough money to enter another convent, and her evenings are spent searching the streets for Phyllis, whom she has not seen for these many years. She refuses an offer of marriage from her employer's gardener, an alliance she "shouldn't mind if things were different," because her lifework is to pray for Phyllis and the gentleman, even if both be long dead. In Sarah's view, the actions of Phyllis's body are external to what Sarah feels to be her essential identity as "a very good girl." Yet because she believes in the morality preached by the church, she must spend her life attempting to redeem Phyllis from eternal punishment. The sexual body constitutes the terms by which the two women express what they would probably define as their spiritual selves—the generous Phyllis and the devoted Sarah—yet those very identities demand a displacement of the body upon which they depend.

With "Sarah Gwynn," Moore begins to approach the problem of representing sexuality through language. Not only do Phyllis and Sarah's lives take place within worlds most explicitly established and dominated by men—that of prostitution and that of the church— but their story is heard and retold by a male interlocutor. Dr. O'Reardon, Sarah's employer, is a composite portrait of the men of Moore's own social circle. His mixed career in painting and medicine and his camel-like appearance match the description of Moore's friend Henry Tonks given in *Conversations in Ebury Street;* his bachelor habits and fussy acquisition of beautiful furnishings resemble the author's own self-descriptions, as does his interest in human beings for the sake of their stories. His patients, predominantly women, he finds tiresome, garrulous, perplexing; he desires that his life run smoothly without controversy or social embarrassment. Dr. O'Reardon enjoys finding metaphors to describe the people he meets and takes Sarah on as his servant because his "curiosity" is stirred aesthetically: her face and body are intriguingly shaped; there is the question of whether she most resembles a squirrel or a weasel. The mystery of her life's "plot" draws out in him the same kind of interest it does in the reader, who knows only as much as he knows at any point. In his desire to recover the details of this "plot," he writes to the friend who has recommended Sarah. "In the letter he was writing he would tell, too, of the secret which he was sure that Sarah was hiding from him. . . . His thoughts were brought to an end by the arrival of a patient, and it was not till many days after that he discovered the half-written letter among some papers on his writing-table" (*CL* 186). His actions are like those of a reader who puts down a novel, mildly interested in the story but not so much as to interrupt other business at hand.

The conclusion of the story satirizes the voyeuristic interlocutor with a suggestion of what has been lost from the lives of both O'Reardon, the inquiring subject, and Sarah, the disclosing object of his inquiry. As "Sarah Gwynn" ends, "The door closed. The doctor was alone again, and he continued his letter to Helena Lynch, hearing Michael's shears among the ivy." From within his elected celibacy, he now writes a letter that presumably retells the story he has just heard; his connections to life lie in listening and retelling. Meanwhile, the gardener continues clipping out the sparrow's nests, sparrows being in the doctor's view incompatible with sweet peas. Of this destruction Sarah had observed to O'Reardon: "He's sorry to do it sir. He showed me a nest with four little ones, and the moment I touched their beaks they opened them, thinking their father and mother were bringing them food" (*CL* 199–200). The destroyed sparrow nests parallel the nest never to be made by Sarah and Michael and, at the same time, point to the aesthetizing impulse that is behind Dr. O'Reardon's every interaction with human experience.

Moore's unflinching depictions of the observing and narrating male recall the candid parallels between the artist and the voyeur introduced very early in his career in such novels as *A Modern Lover* (1883) and *A Drama in Muslin* (1886) and that recur throughout his numerous autobiographies. When Moore portrays the voyeur-artist without any apparent criticism of the role, the result can be as disturbing as it is in "In the Luxembourg Gardens" from *Memoirs of My Dead Life* (1906). In the story, the elderly Moore recalls his youthful encounter with a young woman who delights in relating her erotic adventures to him. The younger Moore does not himself seem to be the object of her attraction. He is merely a looker-on who is in turn the object of the elderly man's recollection. The old man watches the young man who listens to the woman describe looking at herself through her lover's eyes: one night, she says, her lover and she "stood side by side before the glass without a stitch on. I did look a little tot beside him" (*MMDL* 179). Her comment is less a self-expressive phrase than the iteration of a male fascination with the female child as erotic object. While this young woman earns the author's approbation for her own mirror-gazing, it is nevertheless all too apparent that her self-observational act is in truth the object of the narrator's own observation. He retains the role of subject, not she. The elderly speaker is immune from her gaze by his existence in a future tense, while his youthful counterpart watches her, but is at no point watched by her. As a result, her self-observation and her self-narration primarily serve to amuse the narrator who then incorporates them into his own story. Because he is portrayed as a benign elderly man with no sexual ambitions of his own, he—like Dr. O'Reardon of "Sarah Gwynn"—behaves as would a reader: interested, even titillated, but safe from any active responsibility and maintaining rigorously the power to look without being seen.

The intrinsically exploitative relation between subject and object, or teller and tale, forms one of the most fascinating features of "Albert Nobbs," a story that of all the stories in *Celibate Lives*, most dramatically suggests the problematic relations of sex and gender. This tale of a woman who lives disguised as a male hotel waiter was selected from *A Story-Teller's Holiday* for inclusion in the last version of the celibate series. The transposition creates some awkwardness: without the context of *A Story-Teller's Holiday*, the reader does not know why the storytelling is occurring, or the identity of "Alec," the listener, or the identity of the storyteller. But by keeping the narrative frame intact, Moore achieves a superb story and a critique of the role of the male as observer, narrator, and audience.

"Albert Nobbs" has received renewed attention since being adapted for the stage in 1977 by the French feminist playwright Simone Benmussa. Her adaptation of the story has been widely praised as a drama that asks "the audience to understand female identity as a historical and cultural construction whose causes and consequences constitute the drama being enacted." As Elin Diamond argues in her study of the adaptation, the play's utilization of Moore's narrative frame presents Albert as a set of various signifiers, a person whose body, dress, name, and thoughts are "dispersed over a textual field; Nobbs is not singular at all but plural, a gesture, a line of description, with no wholeness of identity to structure the field." Diamond continues, "Albert as representation of non-Albert, the anonymous female body, lives at the limit of representation, knowing herself only as a 'perhapser,' a point cleverly made by the audience's first image of her as part of a *trompe l'oeil* setting, which implicates the spectator in Albert's misrecognition of her own sexuality."[34] Jill Dolan agrees that Benmussa's "representation of Albert's assumed role foregrounds . . . the construction of gender and gendered spectatorial positions in conventional narrative."[35] While Benmussa's play is brilliantly effective and original in its capacity to enact these ideas theatrically, much of what it said of her play is equally true of Moore's own story. It is Moore himself who foregrounds the problem of Albert's life as a story constructed, narrated, and heard by men: a tale told to ensure Moore's victory in a storytelling competition between himself and Alec, two men most tellingly described as "the Ballinrobe cock" and "the Westport rooster."

In "Albert Nobbs," the aesthetizing observer-teller-listener of "Sarah Gwynn" is developed into the aesthetizing author-narrator whose presence is crucial to the claustrophobic atmosphere in which the female characters move. Moore introduces Albert as a memory of the old days when his family came up to Dublin from Mayo in the 1860s; certain details are recited "for the pleasure of looking back and nothing else." Within the first paragraphs, Albert appears as a character in a story made of memory and nostalgia. Moore also integrates frame with story: when late in the story the hotel proprietress refers to "the little red-headed boy on the second floor," the reader remembers that the narrator's family stayed on the second floor of the hotel in which Albert works. The allusion also takes for granted the reader's familiarity with Moore's autobiographies, in which he describes himself in childhood as a little red-headed boy.

This intermingling of frame, tale, and allusion to other autobiography plays a significant role within the totality of the story precisely by exposing the story as narrative. The illusionary techniques of modern realism appear to be firmly in place: the narration proceeds almost entirely through indirect discourse and interior monologue, with a great deal of shifting between voices; authorial commentary is limited to a few transitional generalizations. However, the exposed frame and the reference to *Hail and Farewell* disturb that illusion of realism by reminding the reader that this is a narrated story. Their grounding in autobiographical context might be seen to entrench the story in yet another kind of realism, except that these allusions are intertextual references to an openly conventionalized narrative frame and to an autobiography Moore frequently described as fictive, a "novel about real people." As in so many of Moore's works, the rhetoric of realism and the rhetoric of sincerity actually serve to emphasize the artifice of the storytelling situation and to highlight the subjectivity in which any observation is enclosed. Just as Albert's identity is inescapable from what others think about her, "Albert Nobbs" cannot exist outside of a story narrated by another, regardless of any allusions to an existence as an unnarrated phenomenon.

Within the frame and the tale itself, Moore introduces the question of who may tell the story and even if it can or should be told. The characters have a great deal of trouble narrating their own stories, and pronouns provide the biggest stumbling block. The narrator withholds the male pronoun from Albert until Hubert Page, the house painter with whom she is forced to share her bed, discovers that she is indeed a "she." And not until Hubert divulges her own femininity, does Moore utilize the "she" in reference. Albert and Hubert themselves experience linguistic uncertainty and shift continually between male and female pronouns, sometimes within a single sentence. After death has exposed Albert's anatomical gender, the other characters have difficulty settling upon the appropriate pronoun with which to discuss her. They find themselves continuing to berate the kitchen-maid, Helen Dawes, for breaking Albert's heart until a scullion interjects that "after all, you wouldn't want her to marry a woman?" These voices are only occasionally identified and act as a chaotic chorus, groping together unsuccessfully toward some consensus. The secret of Albert's anatomy seems strangely irrelevant, inessential to their discussion of who she was or should have been.

Language, like dress, is tremendously confused and dislocated from the body, yet it also wields tremendous power. Being addressed as a male and wearing male clothes has altered Albert's interior life: "the clothes she wore smothered the woman in her; she no longer thought and felt as she used to when she wore petticoats, and she didn't think and feel like a man though she wore trousers." Despite the resources of this language of clothes and pronouns, Albert has no terms by which to describe herself; without those terms "what was she? Nothing, neither man nor woman" (*CL* 64). Only after Albert has told her own story and Hubert Page has commented upon it does she feel despair at the loneliness and futility of her life: "Seven years, Page repeated, neither man nor woman, just a perhapser. He spoke these words more to himself than to Nobbs, but feeling he had expressed himself incautiously he raised his eyes and read on Albert's face that the words had gone home, and that this outcast from both sexes felt her loneliness perhaps more keenly than before" (*CL* 59). Such words are echoed later when Page confides that she, too, is female and cries, "you can feel for yourself if you won't believe me. Put your hand under my shirt; you'll find nothing there" (*CL* 61).

With corresponding bewilderment, after Albert's death the servants wonder what might have happened on the wedding night had she succeeded in marrying Helen Dawes: "Nothing, of course." There seem to be no words, or only confused words, to represent what Hubert and Albert are. At the end of the tale, Hubert realizes that if she is to return to her life as a woman, her story cannot be told.

It might be possible to argue, as do Sandra Gilbert and Susan Gubar, that the limitations of the characters are, in fact, Moore's own limitations. Albert, argue Gilbert and Gubar, is "forced during her unsuccessful courtship to confront the lack that Moore identifies with her femininity. Almost as if he were glossing Freud's notion of female 'castration' the author delineates Albert's anxiety about erotic encounters." They continue, "At the end of the tale—with the story of Hubert's male life repressed because its truth wouldn't 'be believed'—the misrule of transvestism has been exorcised, proper patriarchal rule has been reestablished, and 'the Angelus [is] ringing.'"[36] But in addition to attributing untenably to the author the opinions expressed by the characters, Gilbert and Gubar overlook Moore's ironic presentation of authoritarian behavioral codes and fail to see that Moore challenges the idea of essential gender identity by counterbalancing it with the contradictory theory of cultural, and, in particular, linguistic determination.

Albert and Hubert may view themselves as castrated men, but this is one of many attempts at self-description and by no means is it offered as the story's ultimate assessment. Moore highlights rather than obfuscates the linguistic nature of gender identity by dispersing the narrative through the frame tale, dialogue, interior monologue, and indirect discourse. The failure of language to represent experience then conjoins with the failure of heterosexual norms to provide a successful basis for individual development. If we are to understand "patriarchal rule" to mean compulsory heterosexuality, then patriarchal rule is repeatedly scorned throughout the story. As a young girl, Nobbs was brutally treated by a man whom, she feared, would "pull her about" and make her pregnant; the husband of Hubert Page deserts her and her children; Helen Dawes is crudely exploited by a scullion. Although Albert cannot find the language to designate Hubert Page's marriage with another woman as a "real" marriage—that being signified by a heterosexual union—Moore repeats several times that "this marriage was as successful as any and a great deal more than most" (CL 63). If patriarchal society triumphs at the end, its drawbacks have been made more than obvious

throughout the story. The Angelus ringing no more signifies a celebration of authoritarian norms than does the little child grasped by
its would-be errant mother in "An Episode in Married Life." Additionally, the silencing effect to which Gilbert and Gubar allude is
itself counteracted as Alec disrupts Moore's narrative authority by
questioning him about subsequent events and complaining that he
has "left out some of the best parts."

Finally, what is "the lack that Moore identifies with her femininity"? The relegation of Albert Nobbs to the status of "neither
man nor woman, just a perhapser" does recall the pathetic figure of
the masculinist lesbian, a stereotype later popularized by Radclyffe
Hall in *The Well of Loneliness* (1928). However, these are the words of
Hubert Page, herself a woman who dresses as a man and who was
happily married to another woman until the latter's death. Alec
Trusselby's final judgment must also be taken with qualifications. At
the end of the story, he advises that Hubert should simply tell her
husband that she "was taken away by the fairies whilst wandering in
a wood" since "a woman that marries another woman, and lives happily with her, isn't a natural woman; there must be something of the
fairy in her" (*CL* 96). The story as a whole, however, indicates that if
a "natural woman" is to be understood as a heterosexually active
female who wears a dress, that generally unhappy state is less the
result of "nature" than of economic circumstances different from
those that led Albert toward a life as another sort of female in pants.

In his emphasis upon economic motivations for gender identity,
Moore contradicts the majority of the sexologists of the period who
interpreted the wearing of men's attire as a sign of lesbianism, and
lesbianism as firmly rooted in congenital factors.[37] Albert dresses as a
man, but is neither an active lesbian nor erotically stimulated by
transvestism; her reasons for choosing men's attire are exclusively
financial. Albert desires to marry primarily for company and because she wants a prosperous little shop. As she imagines which
woman she will court, she thinks almost entirely in terms of which
would make the best mistress of the shop. At the same time, once
Albert chooses Helen as the object of her attentions, she begins to
feel attraction, although she cannot bring herself to kiss Helen. Albert "liked Helen. Her way of standing on a doorstep, her legs a
little apart, jawing a tradesman, and she'd stand up to Mrs. Baker
and to the chef himself. She liked the way Helen's eyes lighted up
when a thought came into her mind; her cheery laugh warmed Albert's heart as nothing else did" (*CL* 76–77). Albert wants the

warmth of another being and secure nest: "a dream of a shop with two counters, one at which cigars, tobacco, pipes and matches were sold, and at the other all kinds of sweetmeats, a shop with a door leading to her wife's parlour" (*CL* 67). Now pursuant of her dream, she feels that "behind the show a new life was springing up—a life strangely personal and associated with the life without only in this much, that the life without was now a vassal state paying tribute to the life within" (*CL* 66).

But is this life male or female? The very problem is implicit in her vision of a single shop with "two counters," one selling men's items and another selling more feminine items. The problem is more explicit in her hope that while "she would continue to be a man to the world, she would be a woman to the dear one at home." What does it mean, however, to be a "woman"? Her projection of the role of wife is absolutely unrelated to heterosexual intercourse or to a feminine sexuality defined by its opposition to a male anatomy. Her thoughts break down into dreams of chintz sofas and a marble chimney piece, and of a little girl to parent: "What matter whether she calls me father or mother? They are but mere words that the lips speak, but love is in the heart and only love matters" (67–68).

This scene can be understood both as an indication of Moore's continuing reconsideration of the theory that gender characteristics are inherent in sex and as an indication of his perception, first articulated in *Confessions d'un Jeune Anglais,* that gender is frequently ambiguous in its response to a variety of influences. Moore would seem to offer this domestic maternal dream as a straightforward manifestation of Albert's "feminine instincts," yet Albert imagines the possibility that the dream can be fulfilled with herself playing the role of father: in this case a parodic father who in turn parodies maternal affections. A comparison might be drawn with a scene from Caryl Churchill's 1978 comic drama of gender confusion, *Cloud Nine,* in which a gay male, finding that he is erotically attracted to his sister, wonders aloud if he might be lesbian. Like Albert's feminized dream of chintz sofas and a little daughter, this character's dilemma could indicate the surfacing of some essential masculinity; much more likely, it reveals that matters of desire and gender identity fail to operate in clear oppositional categories.

Moore's own intimation of androgynous possibilities suggests his sympathy with the androgynous utopias so much a part of the vitalist theories that he echoes elsewhere in such works as *The Lake.* Imagining the homosexual as androgyne, homosexual apologists like Edward Carpenter proposed that an androgynous marriage might be free of the materialism and conflict of heterosexual marriages, thus leading to a more ideal society based on "the bond of personal affection" only.[38] As an individual starved for personal affection, Albert Nobbs wants security and tenderness. Attempts to stabilize her gendered identity either within or outside of her fantasized domestic refuge lead only to confusion and frustration. However, while living on the frontiers of gender might have led to the contentment Hubert Page enjoyed with her own wife, that utopian (and perhaps postlibidinous) alternative seems beyond the reach of the timid Albert.

Although Albert dies defeated and Hubert returns to heterosexual life, the story so effectively normalizes Hubert's same-gender marriage as to render that the most desirable of the various combinations possible. Through the two decades in which he wrote and revised his series of celibate lives, Moore viewed behavioral norms with an increasing skepticism matched only by his increasing disdain for the methods of realist narrative, especially the pretense of objective narration. From the authoritative omniscient narrator who clinically delineates Mildred Lawson's hysterical symptoms, to the ironically portrayed interlocutor who "reads" the life of Sarah Gwynn, to the narrator whose presence becomes an integral part of the self-reflexive examination of gender and representation that "Albert Nobbs" initiates, George Moore's *Celibate Lives* prefigures contemporary discussion of the problems of representation and the performative nature of gender. At the same time, Moore furthers his lifelong inquiry into the relation of the individual's procreative powers and the given forms of body, language, and social relations in which the individual must function and find a voice.

4

The Comic Body and the Tragic Soul
Satire, Caricature, and the Autobiographical Voice

—A man carved out of a turnip, looking out of astonished eyes
—A codfish crossed by a satyr
—The Grey Mullet
—A boiled ghost
—An over-ripe gooseberry
—The White Slug
—A large, distinguished carp

I N ADDITION TO SUCH COMPLIMENTS, George Moore's appearance inspired numerous other panegyrics. Max Beerbohm's descriptions of his friend's fluctuating chin, blank stare, and limpid hands are among the most vivid literary caricatures he ever wrote. In his memoirs, Havelock Ellis draws a resemblance between Moore and "some of the cat-mummies, one especially, in the Egyptian department of the British Museum." A visitor to Upper Ely Place remarked upon "his pasty face and vague eyes, and particularly his straw-coloured hair that looked as if it had been pitchforked on for the occasion." The sister of Oliver St John Gogarty called him "an aborted egg," and Yeats described his body as "insinuating, upflowing, circulative, curvicular, pop-eyed." Gertrude Stein compared him to "a very prosperous Mellon's Food baby," and to Lytton Strachey he was like "one of those very overgrown tabbies that haunt some London kitchens." Moore himself complained that a portrait by Jacques-Emile Blanche made him look like a "drunken cabby."[1] Clearly, Moore participated in a culture in which caricature flourished as a form of invention and commentary. In *Hail and Farewell,* he describes his own appearance as "comic," but reserves his most penetrating caricatures for others, not only drawing extraordinarily rich portraits of his friends, relatives, and associates, but developing more fully than ever before his meditations on what it is to know and describe the self.

In Moore's fiction, we have seen that the human body and the forms of nature are inseparable from the forms of language, the "glosses" through which they are understood. Language and the body are inextricably intermeshed. The body of Albert Nobbs perplexes herself and others because no words exist to describe it; in contrast, the sexual and maternal drives of the inarticulate Esther Waters lead toward the phrases she eventually finds. As Moore astringently represents the human form in *Hail and Farewell,* it becomes the ground of all knowing, although only as it is verbally caricatured by the articulate satirist. When Moore asserts that "only what my eye has seen and my heart has felt, interests me," he accurately expresses the faith and the practices of his career. Long intrigued by mysticism and the religious temperament, he was most of all interested in the claims that the physical body makes upon the would-be ascetic. And while he sought to depict the inner life of his characters rather than their incidental histories, he learned in his later fiction to accomplish this through the precise delineation of external detail as perceived by his protagonists. In *Hail and Farewell,* Moore demonstrates his allegiance to exteriority both as a literary technique and as a fundamental way of understanding his world. He places his trust in life's circumferences, the contextual detail of material being, which he sets against ideals, aspirations, and the language through which ideals and aspirations are made known.

Moore is keenly attuned to the discrepancy between the high principles by which people believe themselves to be living and the frequently bathetic realities imposed by their physical bodies. This disjunction provides him with a source of endless comedy. Yet he also openly entertains the theory that the material life in which he seeks to ground his satire is itself no more than the object of a highly subjective perceiver. To place the question in terms of Moore's literary influences, it is as if his naturalist's devotion to what can be observed conjoins with a more Paterian affirmation that nothing can be

seen save through the "wall of personality" alluded to in the conclusion of *The Renaissance*. For Moore, "personality" is a salutary concept, invoking not the limitations of the writer but his capacity for
originality and invention. The supposition that material life is dependent upon the experience of the perceiver can mean that one
with sufficient wisdom and ability might develop a subjective experience that can dominate that of others and, by its insight, transform
the physical world into a product of its own autogenic making.

Hail and Farewell both affirms and denies its narrator's success at
such a venture; its tale is simultaneously one of comic triumph and
tragically failed desire. Of the relationship between the creations of
his imagination and his own physical being, Moore announces that
"in my novels I can write only tragedy, and in life play nothing but
light comedy, and the one explanation that occurs to me of this dual
personality is that I write according to my soul, and act according to
my appearance" (*HF* 114). As a mixture of novel and life, his autobiography involves both the tragedy of the soul and the comedy of
the body. The tragic aspect of his three-volume comedy lies in the
incapacity of all its characters to realize their ideals in action, its finally impotent narrator having become "the equal of the priest, the
nun, and the ox," losing his lover and losing his friends to the fan-
cies their absurd and yet undeniable bodies have dictated to them.

In approaching this unusual genre of the comic autobiography,
I shall consider several issues. As the satirist of his own life story,
Moore sets up a critical distinction among past self, narrator, and
implied author, which differs radically from familiar autobiographical approaches to the speaking subject. Through the persona of the
wise fool who, like a child, insists upon the most literal evidence
while entertaining the most absurd theories, Moore's narrator asks
the essential question of how it is that we know anything about ourselves or other people. Although he shows material evidence to be
unreliable and susceptible to imaginative interpretation, his attraction
to it leads to his use of the verbal caricature as a revelation of the
human personality. Finally, I shall compare Moore's ideas on character
with those of W. B. Yeats and, in light of both Moore and Yeats, consider what it means to view one's life as a comic or tragic tale.

"A Second Self Which Spies upon the First": The Satiric Perspective

Writing to a friend in 1909, Moore described his book-in-progress as "written very lightly; the subject is serious enough; but I am

laughing all the while and turn myself and my contempor[ar]ies into ridicule" (*GMP* 171). The autobiographer who would satirize not only those around him but his own past follies faces a multiple task. Readers bring expectations of seriousness to both autobiography and satire; autobiography is rarely comic, and satire rarely pure farce. The author must convince his readers that his subject is serious: that the follies of others have brought forth calamities of a very real nature and that he is a serious man possessing peculiar wisdom and goodness, even if his narrator is engaged in the very acts the satire exposes.

In satire, the distinction between author and narrator is generally indicated by the use of different names or the use of speakers representing types easily recognized by readers familiar with classical satire. Many autobiographies, while presenting a distinct "past self" depicted in retrospect, assume the synonymity of author and narrator. In an essay on the autobiographical writings of W. B. Yeats, James Olney suggests that the distinction between the author-narrator and the past self accounts for what little comedy occurs in the majority of autobiographical writing. He offers the hypothesis that autobiography may be, despite its generally solemn tone, inherently comic in its ironic distancing of the past self from the narrating "I": "If, as has been claimed, classic autobiography depends for its existence on some sort of conversion in the autobiographer's life, then this great emotional and intellectual divide will almost inevitably be present in and will indeed rule the autobiography, giving an ironic, if not always nostalgic, distancing to the past."[2]

Moore's self-irony differs considerably from this paradigm. As a tour de force of autobiographical and satiric prose, *Hail and Farewell* combines seemingly contradictory elements of both. It achieves its laughter through ironic contrasts between past and present, a pattern, as Olney suggests, inherent in much autobiography. *Hail and Farewell*, however, also employs the distinction between author and narrator common to satire. Although the author, the naïve narrator, and the even more naive past self all share the same name, there is a clear differentiation between the author, on the one hand, and the narrator and past self, on the other.

Moore accomplishes this distinction through his novelistic structuring of narrative time. The narrator does not speak from the privileged position of the author; the narrator himself ages and changes throughout the book. Unlike most first-person narratives in which the speaker addresses the reader from the standpoint of one who has passed through all the events he is about to relate, *Hail and Farewell*'s narrator speaks most frequently from a moment coterminous with the events he describes. Occasionally he speaks a few days after an event has happened or, as in some sections, recalls his childhood and youth, but all such recollections are conducted from specific moments in his ongoing life rather than from the static vantage point of an author who controls the shape of the whole text. In his study of *Hail and Farewell*, Wayne Shumaker describes the way in which Moore "bring[s] several temporal planes into nearly simultaneous visibility so that each can be made to comment on the others," while the display is directed by "the mature Moore . . . pointer in hand, chuckling as he draws attention, with a note of irony in his voice, to the interconnections of the various actions. . . . Thus states of being are illuminated by juxtaposition with processes of becoming, and the complex total image gains a four-dimensional reality."[3] I would add, however, a crucial refinement to Shumaker's astute observations. The "mature Moore . . . pointer in hand" is also shown to be a character in process, one whose ideas alter as the book advances and a personage quite distinct from the George Moore who oversees the finished book from his London home and does not appear within it. Thus our sense of being spoken to in the present tense is a carefully crafted illusion created by an author writing long after a scene might have actually occurred. The first chapter, for example, begins, "In 1894 Edward Martyn and I were living in the Temple," and, despite the use of the past tense and the fact that Moore wrote this first chapter sometime in late 1909 or early 1910, his narrator has only the knowledge and experience of a man living at that precise moment in 1894.

Moore subtly yet emphatically distinguishes between the characterizations of self within the text and the George Moore whose name appears on the title page. As the narrator ages throughout the story, his increasing cynicism reveals the naïveté of his earlier ideas as articulated by the narrator in preceding sections of the book. The last chapters were written in 1913, but *Hail and Farewell* ends in 1911, and at its conclusion the narrative voice is satirized, presumably, by the author who stands outside the text but whose identity with the narrator is indicated by their shared name. In other works, and particularly in *Confessions of a Young Man*, Moore criticizes his narrator through prefaces and revisions added in later years. In *Hail and Farewell*, however, the one text includes commentary upon its earlier sections and the perceptions of their narrator. Outside his books,

Moore is similarly inclined toward ironic revision of his authorial posture; thus he writes to a friend that *Hail and Farewell* is "a messianic work which like most messianic works will be popular, though probably the Gospels will always keep the lead" (*GMP* 161). The wonderfully wry "probably" tells much about Moore's capacity to see, articulate, and satirize his own vanity without fully repudiating it or even attributing such a failing to a past, inferior self.

The process of self-revising enacted within *Hail and Farewell* is highly unusual in first-person narration of any kind and enables Moore both to speak as satirist and to appear as the object of satire. Irish poet John Montague has called the resultant story

> as great comedy as has ever been written, the kind of malicious yet loving detachment in *Don Quixote*, with Moore as Cervantes to his own Don Quixote, a lean and foolish writer, coming to Ireland on a grammatical crusade, and lost among the many windmills of a priest-ridden, fanatic little island. There is much in Moore . . . of Toad of Toad Hall, the outrageous landlord of Kenneth Grahame's animal story, with his inquisitive finger in every new-fangled pie, always reckless, and always being rescued by his long-suffering friends, especially poor dreamy Edward, the friendly Badger, who preferred the quiet wood. "We have gone through life together," said Moore, "myself charging windmills, Edward holding up his hands in astonishment." They became types and eternal figures, ineffectual and foolish immortals.[1]

Yet why would Moore assume the unusual role of comic autobiographer? Perhaps because he speaks not only as Cervantes and Don Quixote, but as the pragmatic survivor Sancho Panza. His mockery of his own past testifies to a nature that adamantly refuses the role of victim and that neither requests nor extends an attitude of pity, or even tolerance, toward its early follies. The description of his schooldays at Oscott, for instance, exposes the insensitive stupidity of the place, but demonstrates as well the ignorance and ineptitude of his own childhood self, an ugly little red-haired boy so repugnant as to thwart the reader's inclination to pity him. As one who places all value in labor and achievement, Moore would have his readers care for the clear-sighted and victorious author, not the fool whose story is recounted. Nor would he have us fully sympathize with the narrator until the last pages, when he is directly identified as the author of the first volume of *Hail and Farewell*. At that point the narrative present coalesces with the publication of first volume, and the narrator leaves Ireland to finish the book.[5]

To a degree, the past self, the narrator, and the author have much in common, as they all succumb too readily to pipe dreams. Yet, even in this regard, they remain distinct. The narrator replaces his initial disdain for Ireland with the dream of a Gaelic language revival, quickly recants that aspiration, and replaces it with the equally insubstantial hope for a revival of art in Ireland. At last, he leaves Ireland convinced that he will compose *Hail and Farewell* as a messianic message to the Irish that art and Catholicism are incompatible. Aspects of the latter dream are in part those of the author, who speculated throughout the letters written during its composition that he was writing a work of genius that would gain notoriety in Ireland. However, the nationalistic messianism of the plan belongs solely to the satirized narrator of *Hail and Farewell*, whom Moore describes as "a literary redeemer" (*GMP* 171). George Moore himself may have been an obsessive anti-Catholic, but the outlandish arguments presented in "Salve" humorously exploit his tendency to be irrationally swept up by a notion he will nonetheless defend. The religious debates with Colonel Maurice Moore in *Hail and Farewell* echo the pedantry and myopic concern with peripheral minutiae evidenced by the brothers' correspondence; in the book, these traits are heightened with the skill of a perceptive caricaturist, again suggesting that the narrator is an artfully exaggerated version of his author.

It has been frequently suggested that autobiographies depict the past self as intellectually inferior to the author and narrator, but spiritually superior in its earnest innocence.[6] Moore's narrator—who, it must be recalled, is closer to the past self rather than to the author—appears throughout the story as the gullible man of genuine goodness. Many autobiographies depict the past self as a wise fool; the wise fool is also a frequent protagonist of prose satires. Moore's figure is a particularly complicated one, as he can be alternatingly foolish and wise in both intellect and spirit. While the author is nearly always ironic, the narrator is sometimes ironic (and, by implication, wise) and sometimes a naïve enthusiast. Frequently, he is both at the same time, as he views his actions ironically but is incapable of controlling the enthusiasm that directs those actions. He is cautiously skeptical and childishly vulnerable to the sway of an attractive idea, and he can be defenseless against the enchantment of a sylvan mood. Early in the book, he wonders, "Was this visit to Ireland any thing more than a desire to break the monotony of my life by stripping myself of my clothes and running ahead a naked Gael, screaming Brian Boru?" "There is no one in the world that amuses one as much as oneself," he continues. "Whoever is conscious of his acts cannot fail to see life as a comedy and himself as an actor in it; but the faculty of seeing oneself as from afar does not save a man from his destiny. In spite of his foreseeing he is dragged on to the dreaded bourne like an animal, supposing always that animals do not foresee" (*HF* 111–12). Although the narrator prefers to stay in the role of prophet and, even more, in the role of an ironic elegist, as an autobiographer watching himself watch himself, he is still susceptible to the call of a spring morning and consequent involvement in the life of the present.

In spite of the distinctions among the childish past self, the weak-willed narrator, and the weary-if-wiser author, all three are estimated above the other characters in the book. If the persona acts cruelly when under the influence of his notions, he alone seems capable of delight in the world of nature that the others try to deny with their own abstract notions and that overcomes them all in the end. In the final paragraph, the bitter loss of friends is regretted; yet the reader is made to believe that an honest man could not have acted otherwise. And while the narrator feels he has wasted his time in Ireland, the period results in a self-acknowledged masterpiece of autobiographical prose.

This balance of wisdom and folly plays into an overall impression of the narrator as a guileless man. Jean-Jacques Rousseau's insistence upon his personal virtue, Moore points out, could have been repeated in his own claims to modesty in *Hail and Farewell*, "but my way is not Rousseau's"—implying that no one tells the truth about his own virtues and that his own brand of persuasion is more sophisticated than Rousseau's. Moore's presentation of his innocent simple-heartedness may bear little resemblance to J. B. Yeats's characterization of him as a "cesspool," "the big elderly blackguard who lives in Ely Place,"[7] but in Moore's lifewriting—correspondence, essays, and autobiographies—he represents himself as a childlike figure with little resistance to the force of either his instincts or the notions of others. Moore's friend Edmund Gosse recognized that the guise of naïveté allowed Moore to utter the most acidulous remarks while keeping the sympathy of his reader. Of *Conversations in Ebury Street*, Gosse comments: "Reticence, privacy, reserve—what have these to do with the revelations of Ebury Street? If there were the slightest tincture of ill-nature, so much as the twinkling of a tail or the whisper of a hiss, we should denounce the serpent and be all on fire with indignation. But how are we to face an innocency which resembles nothing so much as Sterne's naked infant rolling on the carpet—the Aubusson Carpet under the Lyre-shaped Clock? Not only does Mr. Moore mean no harm by his indiscretions, but he has no idea what it is to be discreet."[8] Here Mr. Moore is a naked infant rather than a naked Gael, but from this disarming, if not disarmed, persona comes forth acute observations on others and the self.

As in *Hail and Farewell*, the naïveté of the man seduced by pipe-dreams is matched by his insistence upon observable evidence and his capacity to see the incongruities between ideas and the context of the world around them. The operation of this "innocent eye" is also framed within a totality that suggests that the observable world is nothing if not purely self-reflexive. Like Manet, whom he loved as man and artist, Moore is fascinated by the outside of things while acknowledging that exteriors are perceived as refracted light. Such focus upon the exterior is closely related to the development of a persona who can be gullible, yet can also be shrewd enough to know that windmills are not castles even while he entertains the possibility. In a 1909 letter to his brother, Moore begs Maurice to give up his hopes for the restoration of Gaelic, passionately urging, "it is important not to waste the few years left to one following *what one knows* to be chimera" (*GMP* 167). The assumption here is that most people, including the speaker, are prone to follow chimeras, but that it is crucial to listen to the voice of doubt, most frequently a voice whose sardonic laughter begins in the deflating evidence of material context. AE, who is depicted in *Hail and Farewell* as so sweet as to be without humor, is also so susceptible to idealism that he never for a moment doubts the chimeras. Himself a painter of vague Blake-inspired pastels on cosmological subjects, he is indifferent to the collection of impressionist paintings Moore has hung in his newly acquired house on Upper Ely Place. As Moore portrays him, AE is incapable of appreciating the scrupulous attention to nature upon which impressionism depends. Disappointed, the narrator taunts, "I know what is the matter with you, AE; you're longing for Watts. You try to disguise it, but you are sighing for *Time Treading on the Big Toe of Eternity*, or *Death Bridging Chaos*, or *The Triumph of Purgatory over Heaven*" (*HF* 273). In addition to this incapacity to understand the close observation underlying impressionism, AE seems incapable of seeing accurately the life around him. Although AE is shown to be serious and earnest, and an energetic and capable organizer for the Irish Co-operative Society, Moore implies that he wastes his life on people who cannot follow through with what he begins. His deep idealism prohibits his recognition of the weaknesses of others and dooms him, finally, to ineffectuality.

Being able to see with shrewdness, Moore implies, is the key to extricating oneself from the vaporous world of illusions, be they nationalist, religious, social, or personal. The prerequisite to seeing others, he suggests, is seeing oneself. While he depicts himself as one frequently under the sway of an idea whose absurdity he grasps even as he finds it irresistible, still his insights inhibit full belief. Early in *Hail and Farewell*, the narrator is caught in a farcical tussle over the possibility of religious heresy in Yeats's play, *The Countess Cathleen*. He muses about the comedy that the self-observant man must see even against his will: "One does not like to speak of a double self, having so often heard young women say they fear they never can be really in love, because of a second self which spies upon the first, forcing them to see the comic side even when a lover pleads" (*HF* 114). The one who looks carefully at the lover who pleads cannot but be self-aware in turn. For Moore, self-awareness is the wellspring of art, and it begins with the capacity to see that which is around him. This material perspective is thus an epistemological and ethical position as well as an aesthetic one.

Moore's hermeneutic reduces to the most material terms the ideas that tempt him and entrap others. The dilemma of the Irish arts movement, for instance, all boils down to the Irish raising excellent beef without being able to create a sauce to flavor it. Although he hypothesizes that *sauce Béarnaise* could not exist because the rough sounds of Irish cannot accommodate so "buttery" a word, this language is afterward said to have been shaped by the life of the people, and their life shaped by the particular climate and topography in which they live. Suggesting that "the Irish race was never destined to rise above the herdsman," Moore finds evidence for such proclamations of fate in the absence of a steak sauce, a detail of the greatest import according to his method of knowing the world (*HF* 349–50). Thus Moore etches life's "facts": actual words and deeds that contrast, sometimes harshly, with the pleadings of ideals and aspirations. As the ambitions of the Irish aesthete are undercut by his nation's inability to cook well, the romance of the lover's pleas are discredited by a young woman's recognition of an equally bathetic comic dimension.

It is toward such material explanation that Moore turns with the guise of the wide-eyed child who sees the fabled emperor's nakedness: Lady Aberdeen's campaign against spitting overlooks the roots of tuberculosis in overwork, inadequate pay, poor food, and lack of decent housing; sexual restraint in young women, the narrator notes, is only of value in industrialized nations requiring dependable factory labor. Moore's eye fixates upon the details of the material context in which speech and action occur. Despite an ostensible wish to admire Yeats, the narrator finds himself unable to enjoy Yeats's "eloquent phrases" of mystical lore while recalling the deflating fact that Yeats and his fellow seekers hypnotize each other and cast horoscopes on a weekly basis in a prosperous London suburb.

The contextual life of an idea or belief may be simply too incongruous, or, on the other hand, it may be too artificially befitting the role one seeks to play. Moore first doubts Yeats's capacities as a poet because he finds Yeats's dress entirely too poetical, and notes that "as far back as the days when I was a Frenchman, I had begun to notice that whosoever adorns himself will soon begin to adorn his verses" (*HF* 79). One cannot become a poet by dressing as one, and he quotes the old adage that "a man's character transpires in his dress" (*HF* 121)—even, he insinuates, if the garb of the poet is a sure sign of a mere versifier. Suspicious of Yeats's posing and sharing the then-common view that Yeats's career as a poet had ended, Moore sees exposed in the poetical garb evidence of an interior lacking. Aspects of our appearance can belie the ideas we profess. Listening to Yeats thunder at the acquisitiveness of the middle classes, Moore cannot keep his eyes from "the magnificent fur coat which distracted our attention from what he was saying, so opulently did it cover the back of the chair out of which he had risen" (*HF* 541). Yeats's coat, as well as his paunch (both newly acquired in America), undercuts the authority of his ideological attack upon materialism. Whether dressed in poetical garb or a fur coat, Yeats can no more freely choose his clothes than his physiognomy, as mere artifice cannot alter "nature."

In Yeats's old green cloak and, later, his fur coat, as in T. P. Gill's beard or Maurice Moore's breeches and boots, Moore discloses what he believes to be the essence of a personality. Typical of his paradoxical approach to such questions, he draws together the naturalist's belief in dress as a sign of environmental determinism, Carlylian metaphors of clothing as dogma that may be deliberately acquired and shed, and his ever-invoked concept of "instinct." If Yeats's clothes brand him a versifier in spite of himself, Colonel Maurice Moore's piety and archaism place him in "dim grey hues" "because his natural garment, the doublet, is forbidden him." Speaking from his pose as the wise innocent in whom there is no subterfuge, Moore admits that he is "not good at clothes," never notices what he wears, and chooses according to instinct. Clothing reflects the inability of others to resist external pressure and the inherited qualities of their own inherited natures. The narrator's lack of concern for clothes indicates his imagined freedom from influence, environmental or hereditary.

While Moore constructs both an aesthetics and an ideology of appearances, he simultaneously rejects the reliability of observation. He asserts early that "only what my eye has seen, and my heart has felt, interests me," but then irreverently satirizes his theories of evidence. Exposing his own deductive process, he attempts to bring forth examples to support a hypothesis concerning poets and their clothing. Finally, he brushes aside the question of evidence: "But let us be content with the theory," he chides himself and the reader, "and refrain from collecting facts to support it, for in doing so we shall come upon exceptions, and these will have to be explained away" (*HF* 79). His narrator discovers through the progress of *Hail and Farewell* that neither the eye nor the heart will faithfully tell you where you are, who you are, or whom you are with. An adamant espousal of naturalistic evidence is coupled with a recognition of the linguistic basis of knowing and an intimation of solipsism.

The discomfiture caused by this epistemological confusion leads invariably to laughter. Carefully constructed confusion reigns in the following scene during which the narrator attempts to find evidence of his interior life in his exterior appearance. He searches his face for signs of his new Anglophobia and his conversion to the Irish cultural movement:

> I wandered across the room to consult the looking-glass, curious to know if the great spiritual changes that were happening in me were recognisable upon my face; but the mirror does not give back characteristic expression, and to find out whether the expression of my face had changed I should have to consult my portrait-painters: Steer, Tonks, and Sickert would be able to tell me. And that night at Steer's . . . I got up and walked round the room, feeling myself to be unlike the portraits they had painted of me. . . . The external appearance no doubt remained, but the acquisition of a moral conscience must have modified it. (*HF* 216–17)

The sheer pedantic literalness of the quest marks it as self-satire. As a self-characterization of a man in search of his characterization, its irony undercuts the assurance with which Moore has claimed the validity of external evidence elsewhere in his book. In search of his new reflection, the narrator here in his role as innocent fails to recall that a portrait is the representation of the painter's vision, not a representation of any unmediated reality. Under the influence of his new obsessions, the narrator in the role of innocent forgets his own dictum that "the world exists only in our ideas of it" (*HF* 222), and that what we think we see is in truth the reflection of our own desires, dictated to us by our undeniable "natures."

As in the story of his quest for the representation of the state of his soul, Moore suggests that "evidence" must be understood as the production of a perceiver whose imagination is subject at worst to societal expectations and at best to instinct. He makes a mockery of any naïve use of evidence to make assertions about the self or others (perhaps most particularly in the field of biography and autobiography) when he relates a fanciful account of an entirely fictional woman with whom the nineteenth-century politician Henry Grattan "may" have been involved. Soon the qualifying verb "may" gives way to the simple past. By the end of the paragraph Moore produces a letter to Grattan from this fictional woman in her destitute old age, so parodying the very apparatus of biographical documentation. As their own real correspondence testifies, the final breach between Maurice and George Moore was precipitated by the latter's insistence upon publicly calling their father's death a suicide when no evidence of any kind pointed toward that verdict. In response to his brother's threat to depict their father as having died at confession, Moore replied with apparent sincerity that the colonel should feel "quite free to write this. It doesn't happen to be true . . . but you can say it. I don't mind not the least bit. That I swear to you" (*GMP* 275). As Moore states in letters to his proposed biographer, John Freeman, and the literary critic Ernest Boyd, the most important consideration in choosing one's "facts" must be which version of a "fact" makes the most intriguing tale and follows the peregrinations of the storyteller's wandering mind.

Fancy becomes evidence, and evidence might well be fancy in service of a good storyteller who will base his stories upon close observation of human behavior. Crossing the Irish sea, the narrator recalls a legend that Ireland could seem "small as a pig's back to her enemies, and a country of endless delight to her friends," and wonders which it will appear to him. He thinks, "It was the hills themselves that reminded me of the legend—on the left, rough and uncomely as a drove of pigs running down a lane, with one tall hill very like the peasant whom I used to see in childhood, an old man that wore a tall hat, knee-breeches, worsted stockings, and brogues. Like a pig's back Ireland has appeared to me, I said; but soon after on my right a lovely hill came into view, shapen like a piece of sculpture and I said: Perhaps I am going to see Ireland as an enchanted isle after all" (*HF* 107).

The passage points to two different ideas about the power of evidence, both of which operate simultaneously throughout *Hail and Farewell*. On the one hand, the coarse, unpleasant nature of Irish life is evoked by direct observation of a particular Irish hill, by a specific childhood memory, and by the literary imagination's power to make a metaphoric link between the shape of the hill and the appearance of the peasant. On the other hand, the mind is also capable of making vague similes in which Ireland is "a piece of sculpture" or "an enchanted isle." The hackneyed quality of these similes warns of the unreliability of a subjective vision that is not rooted in the material. In this as in so many areas of his thought, Moore holds one idea in a dialectical relation to its contrary, and, from the paralysis of his contradiction, he looks toward his concept of instinct for release. Through *Hail and Farewell*'s exploration of how one establishes evidence for belief in anything—history, biography, ideas, or even the best way to interpret a landscape—Moore once again raids the larder of nineteenth-century positivism to cook up his own conception of a world whose forms and meanings reside at last in each individual perceiver, although each perceiver's vision has its source in his or her determinate nature: something that in most human beings is formed by environment and heredity, but derives instead from a transcendental instinct in artists like Manet, Balzac, and—so he would have it—Moore himself.

The autobiographical persona thus exists as a complex variation on the fundamentally wise and good (although often naïve) satiric speaker. His susceptibility to an idea and his capacity for observation are traits exclusively his, and if the world he sees is no more than his own illusion, *Hail and Farewell* is adamant that some illusions are superior to others. The simple-hearted man is driven to madness by the baroque hypocrisies of others, engaging in mock-heroic battles with offenders in his drive to uphold standards of art and behavior, ostensibly for the good of the community. As a man devoted to good writing, Moore's self-representation is legitimized rather than satirized, and valuable work—in writing, painting, or politics—remains an unquestioned standard of value throughout the text. Such an emphasis on productive capability should be unsurprising, since, as has emerged from the discussion of Moore's fiction, his criticisms of institutions and individuals center upon their relative incapacities to produce. When tempted by ideas that contradict his instincts and lead him away from productive work, the narrative persona is treated with cutting irony. The irony becomes particularly harsh when those ideas are, again, not grounded in the kind of material observation and attention to contextuality that produces such works as *Hail and Farewell.*

The instinct leading toward productive work has been demonstrated in previous chapters to be for the most part an unconscious force and often in conflict with prescribed ideology. Despite its dissociation from hereditary and environmental factors, Moore's idea of instinct finds a creative manifestation in sexual desire and the workings of the natural world. As part of its paean to the material world, *Hail and Farewell* explicitly condemns any belief system that threatens the workings of instinct, including those intoxicating abstractions that come "out of the mist." Listening to others' declarations of their self-effacing devotion to Ireland, the narrator muses

> as in a vision I saw Ireland as a god demanding human sacrifices, and everybody, or nearly everybody, crying: Take me, Ireland, take me; I am unworthy, but accept me as a burnt-offering. Ever since I have been in the country I have heard people speaking of working for Ireland. But how can one work for Ireland without working for oneself? . . . They do not know themselves, but go on vainly sacrificing all personal achievement, humiliating themselves before Ireland as if the country were a god. A race inveterately religious I suppose it must be! And these sacrifices continue generation after generation. Something in the land itself inspires them. And I began to tremble lest the terrible Cathleen ni Houlihan might overtake me. She had come out of that arid plain, out of the mist, to tempt me, to soothe me into forgetfulness that it is the plain duty of every Irishman to disassociate himself from all memories of Ireland— Ireland being a fatal disease, fatal to Englishmen and doubly fatal to Irishmen. (*HF* 213)

Typically, explanations confound and cancel one another: the Irish—including the author—are prone to nationalism because they are "inveterately religious" or because their topography inspires such worship. Because of such inherited and environmental factors, they are prone to the enchantments of the ultimate abstraction, "Cathleen ni Houlihan," an image ensuing from language and, according to this passage, the mist itself. Against Cathleen is invoked the absolute standard of free thought, personal development, and good art.

For this standard, Moore will subordinate himself and the personal relationships he most values. This tripart ideal toward which Moore claims to be drawn by instinct never receives satiric treatment. Other beliefs and preoccupations are put at its service, even his tornadic anticlericalism. While extratextual information confirms Moore's wholehearted distaste for Catholicism and his incessant provocation of his brother on the issue of a Catholic Ireland, as depicted in *Hail and Farewell*, this battle is a mock-heroic absurdity that enhances the comic texture of the book. The narrator seems to be succumbing to another chimera, and while he defends his anti-Catholicism with concrete evidence, his evidence is a ridiculous amassment of comically precise minutiae. His latest seduction is itself a story, and while the narrator's wide-eyed simplicity makes him again a fool in pursuit of an idea, Moore's narrative serves the larger pursuit of good writing.

If Moore was willing to portray himself as a fool for the sake of his story, he was more than willing so to portray others. Susan Mitchell quipped that while Rousseau wrote his own confessions, Moore wrote his friends', but it is equally true that in writing his friends' Moore also wrote his own. As AE remarked in 1923, "these vivid and malicious portraits . . . throw much more light upon the writer than upon his subjects. Indeed, if all the characters in *Ave, Salve, Vale*, were rolled into one they would constitute an admirable picture of the writer."[9] Moore himself seems to concur with AE's assessment, at least in theory, as he wrote to Ernest Boyd: "A delicate task is putting oneself into a book; a writer may tell all kinds of things about himself and yet put nothing of himself into the book, or he may put a great deal of himself into it while describing external things" (*GMP* 328). Moore subscribed to the latter method, and his portrayal of others serves as an integral part of his portrayal of the self. And most frequently, his depictions of others build from that key element of bodily gesture or form.

Verbal Caricatures:
Bodily Metaphors and Exterior Psychology

In *Everybody's Autobiography*, Gertrude Stein cheerfully proclaims that "writers did not really mind anything any one said about them, they might have minded something or liked something but since writing is writing and writers know that writing is writing they do not really suffer very much about anything that has been written." In case sympathy with such a view is not universal, Oliver St John Gogarty offers the following disclaimer at the start of *As I Was Going Down Sackville Street:* "The names in this book are real, the characters fictitious." Going even further to deny referentiality, Flann O'Brien begins his autobiographical novel, *At Swim-Two-Birds,* with the warning that "all the characters represented in this book, including the first person singular, are entirely fictitious and bear no relation to any person living or dead."[10] As one who saw himself most vividly amid a world of others, Moore's autobiographical writings depict others in order to depict "the first person singular." While he might have believed his work to be more imaginative than referential, others did not and some very much minded what was written about them.

Gogarty remarks that "making your rival ridiculous is the chief aim of Irish opponents since the duel was abolished" and accuses Moore of "feigned surprise" at the outrage his book precipitated.[11] From all apparent evidence, Moore did find the angry reaction of some of his "characters" genuinely baffling. He understood himself to be writing a combination of fantasy and fact: "a novel with no women in it" or "a novel about real people." A letter to John Eglinton echoes this frustration: "If those gentlemen [Rolleston and Hyde] sat for their portraits do you contend that they would have cause for complaint if the painter did not in one case omit a slice and in the other add a slice? Max Beerbohm has caricatured everybody, and ferociously—his representation of me hardly resembles a human being, but I have never complained and I have never heard of anybody complaining. Is this timidity, this care for personal appearance, confined to Dublin . . . ? I shall add five or six lines about my own personal appearance, which shall be savage enough" (*EG* 17). Defending what he called his "literary caricature" to Maurice Moore, he again cites Beerbohm as he tries to make his brother understand that his intentions were exclusively literary, his portraits "mere whimsicality" that "cannot be described as personal animosity" (*GMP* 248).

While autobiographers of even the slightest gifts almost invariably subject their lives to the form that the telling imposes upon life, in fact creating the form of their lives through that telling, they do so frequently with protestations of sincerity, claims to lapsed memory, or guilty confessions of artfulness. In contrast, Moore's fore-most aspiration seems to have been the creation of a design that would then reshape experience, submitting both facts and personal feelings to its rule. This seems to have been understood by many of Moore's friends, a striking case in point being the mutual satirizing that went on between Moore and Edmund Gosse, who nevertheless enjoyed a long and affectionate friendship. In the front of Gosse's copy of "Salve," Moore inscribed his gift, "To the great portraitist Edmund Gosse from a model in waiting." As evidenced by their correspondence, both men often put aside the issue of personal rela-tionship in order to create interesting characterizations of one an-other.[12] Beerbohm too professes that caricature is motivated less by personal likes or dislikes, or by any "moral judgment," than it is mo-tivated by "the sheer desire and irresponsible lust for bedevilling this or that human body." The caricaturist will make equally ridiculous people he admires and people he despises: "He portrays each sur-face exactly as it appears to his distorted gaze."[13]

Beerbohm places caricature in a sphere between imagination and observation, just as Moore acknowledges that *Hail and Farewell* is a "novel" whose characters may be encountered nonetheless in the Broadstone railway station. The vitality of the portrait derives from its placement between realms. While it is arguable that representa-tion is inherently metaphoric, caricature calls attention to itself as such. It rejects normative modes of portraying the body and through its distortions displays the very process of interpretation. Discussing Beerbohm's caricatures, John Felstiner posits that "as with the cubists, the implicit subject of his art was that very transit, or metaphor, between the original and the figure drawn. . . . In its transformations, caricature often works by creating a visual meta-phor—Gladstone a shark, Chesterton a stomach—and it entails un-likeness as well as likeness, as a metaphor does."[14] Beerbohm himself stresses the interpretive function of caricature, arguing that it "is not a mere snapshot. It is the outcome of study; it is the epitome of its subject's surface, the presentment (once and for all) of his most char-acteristic pose."[15] In similar language, Moore disparages what he be-lieves to be the camera's inability to distinguish crucial elements of a physiognomy from less significant aspects. In an essay of 1921, he complains that the camera can relate "only the facts in front of it impartially, the significant and the trivial, the ugly and the pretty. Impartially, I have said, but without attaining to the great impar-tiality of Nature; photography is finite, and whatever truth it is capa-ble of reflecting is disparate and fragmentary" (*MMDL* xi).

Moore claims, like Beerbohm, that in selecting an aspect of a subject's form as synecdochical of the whole, the artist expresses not a fragmentary element but a paradigmatic representation of the judgment upon his subject. Describing his own methods, Beerbohm writes: "The whole man must be melted down, as in a crucible, and then, as from the solution, be fashioned anew. He must emerge with not one particle of himself lost, yet with not a particle of himself as it was before. . . . And he will stand there wholly transformed, the joy of his creator, the joy of those who are privy to the art of caricature."[16] To see life metaphorically, to be "privy to the art of caricature" is to take pleasure in the space between the referent and the symbol: "the original and the figure drawn." Interpreting that space demands an act of imagination and trust in one's unique, and very possibly eccentric, understanding. In opposition to Matthew Arnold's "absurd line about seeing life steadily and seeing it whole, a line that led one generation gaping into the wilderness," Moore prefers that "distorted gaze" that focuses upon the one feature—often the obscure feature—that holds the key to the transposition of the whole.

To recognize the tension between the normative interpretation of a referent and the new symbol one seeks to make of it is to cast doubt upon the comfortable assumption that we all see the same way. It is to view the world ironically, with an eye to the windmill, the castle, and the distance between them. In *Hail and Farewell*, Irish susceptibility to ecclesiastical doctrine, disembodied mysticism, and impractical scheming blinds Moore's compatriots to everything but their imaginary castles and, in so doing, renders most of them humorless and incapable of recognizing the dissonance at the heart of comedy. AE is so "sweet" as to be without humor, and the agricultural reformer Sir Horace Plunkett is so purely quixotic that he "fears to meet any one with a sense of humour; he dreads laughter as a cat dreads cold water" (*HF* 565). Only a few, like Moore's fellow satirist Oliver Gogarty, retain their wit, although Edward Martyn is also capable of much laughter at the narrator's own inconsistencies. Martyn chuckles repeatedly over an incident in which the narrator asked "a very dignified old lady in a solemn salon in the Faubourg St Germain" who had declined a little game of cards if it were not true that "vous aimez sans doute bien mieux, madame, le petit jeu d'amour" (*HF* 309–10). Martyn, whose whole life aims at suppressing the conflict between his homosexuality and his ascetic piety, here acknowledges with delight the incongruity between body and word and marvels at the audacity of one who calls attention to it. According to Moore, most men are lost in the world of the symbolic word, incognizant of the referent, and certainly without the irony to see a discrepancy between the two. That discrepancy is the wondrous terrain of the comic metaphor and the realm of literature.

Throughout *Hail and Farewell,* Moore delivers metaphor after metaphor, caricatures, similes, synecdoches, reductive analogies, and parodies. Yet, with very few exceptions, Moore's portraits are not misanthropic in the tradition of satirists like Juvenal, Boccaccio, or Swift. "All things human interest me," Moore declares in *Memoirs of My Dead Life,* and his caricatures therefore communicate, as Wayne Shumaker writes, "a recognition of the marvelous inhering in the commonplace . . . the deep human sympathy that tempers much of the malice."[17] While he finds the variegation of the human form fascinating and frequently discovers in it some key to a character's greatest weakness, his caricatures betray no repulsion toward the body in and of itself. In much the same way that Beerbohm differs from Hogarth, Moore differs from his predecessors. As John Felstiner notes of Beerbohm, "his drawing of men does tend to bear out whatever imperfect drift their faces have, yet so as to celebrate their distinctiveness rather than condemn their vices."[18] Moore is not repelled by Edward Martyn's obesity, but intrigued by it as a sign of his character. An ascetic fat man, Martyn abhors women, upholstered chairs, and soft beds; yet his medievalism and his aesthetic and idiosyncratic piety, Moore repeatedly hints, are traceable to a severely repressed homosexuality and an inconsistency basic to Catholicism's rejection of the world it nevertheless seeks to govern. The portrait is a celebration of what Moore calls the intense originality of a man who has two thousand a year but "sleeps in a bare bedroom, without dressing-room, or bathroom, or servant in the house to brush his clothes, and who has to go to the baker's for his breakfast" (*HF* 595). All such abnegation of the flesh leads in Moore's analysis to Martyn's "monumental" appearance, since every twinge of conscience propels him toward the sideboard. Max Beerbohm recognized the genius of Moore's portrait and urged their mutual friend Edmund Gosse, "do read, if you have not read yet, *Hail and Farewell,* Vol I. The picture therein of Edward Martyn, built up touch by absurd touch, until . . . but no, this isn't the right image for that masterpiece. I see Martyn rather as a vast feather-bed on which Moore, luxuriously rolling and pommeling and crowing and (it goes without saying) stark naked, is borne towards immortality."[19] Like Beerbohm, Moore may find his subject's ideas absurd, but he remains endlessly fascinated by the incongruity between Martyn's thought and that "vast feather-bed" of his body.

In general, Moore finds attempts at sublimation of the body irritating, amusing, and deeply pathetic. Sitting at a formal dinner in honor of the literary revivalists, he complains to his neighbor that "Ireland is spoken of, not as a geographical, but a sort of human entity. You are all working for Ireland, and I hear now that Ireland begets you." As he is interrupted by someone eulogizing the idea that "the grey matter of Ireland's brain was at last becoming active" he marvels, "Ireland's brain! Just now it was the loins of Ireland" (*HF* 134, 135). While the abstract idea of the nation is given bodily properties, Moore despairs that in Ireland the bodies of men and women are singularly disregarded. Looking about him, the narrator observes

> not an opera-hat among them; and lowering my eyes, I noticed that some of the men had not even taken the trouble to change their shoes. Perhaps they haven't even changed their socks, and to pass the time away I began to wonder how it was that women could take any faint interest in men. Every kind seemed present: men with bellies and without, men with hair on their heads, bald men, short-legged men and long-legged men; but looking up and down the long tables, I could not find one that might inspire passion in a woman; no one even looked as if he would like to do such a thing. And with this sad thought in my head I sought for my chair, and found it next to a bald, obese professor." (*HF* 128)

Sexual unattractiveness, incapacity or indifference Moore closely associates with life in Ireland. At several points in *Hail and Farewell*, the narrator reiterates his youthful fear that he was so ugly as to never "win a woman's love," while in reality Moore insisted upon his irresistibility to sophisticated women as sign of his repatriation into the cosmopolitan world of letters. At the end of the "Vale," the narrator becomes indifferent to love, so entranced is he by his new mission to save Ireland by showing it the mirror of itself in *Hail and Farewell*. In characteristic ironic convolution, Moore accuses the Irish of inattention to the body while incorporating a satiric portrait of himself as similarly obsessed with a nationalist mission and similarly neglectful of his own sexuality. Even more paradoxically, the mission consists of writing a book that will expose the triumph of the body over dogma. Yet if his book is the masterpiece he thought it to be during its composition, his literature has indeed become, in his terms of value, more important than his lover—even though he is writing a book to expose the falseness of such a position. Through his extraordinary multiple ironies, Moore's testimony again acknowledges the compelling needs of the body while affirming his own distance from such need.

To analyze others, Moore utilizes bodily form in several ways. As a development of the naturalist techniques with which he began his novelistic career, descriptions of the body directly illuminate the interior life of his characters. In his portraits of Yeats and Martyn, for example, the thin man and the fat man live out two different responses to a shared conflict. Yeats is represented lying on a cushion declaiming the asceticism of the poetic life while being fed strawberries and cream by adoring young women; in context, his emaciated form suggests a crafty camouflage of his sensuous indulgences. Martyn's thick thighs and hands bespeak a more earnest conflict between spirit and flesh, originating in a sensuous nature so intense that when sexual expression is denied it, an outlet is found in voracious consumption of loin chops, stewed chicken, and plate after plate of curried eggs.

When Moore's descriptions of the human form rely particularly on overt metaphor and allusion, they form verbal caricatures that then self-consciously display the process by which description expresses a critical viewpoint. A case of this sort is his portrait of Douglas Hyde, nationalist and translator of Irish poetry and legend. Listening to Hyde speaking in Irish, the narrator glimpses "the great yellow skull sloping backwards," but, in an attempt to see life steadily and whole, refrains from judgment: "As nothing libels a man as much as his own profile, I resolved to reserve my opinion of his appearance until I had seen his full face. His volubility was as extreme as a peasant's come to ask for a reduction of rent . . . a torrent of dark, muddied stuff flowed from him, much like the porter which used to come up from Carnacun to be drunk by the peasants on midsummer nights when a bonfire was lighted." The appearance of the whole only reaffirms the insight of the narrator's first view of Hyde's skull: "when he turned, and I saw the full face . . . I sat admiring the great sloping, sallow skull, the eyebrows like blackthorn bushes growing over the edge of a cliff, the black hair hanging in lank locks, a black moustache streaking the yellow-complexioned face, dropping away about the mouth and chin. Without doubt an aboriginal, I said" (*HF* 139–40).

Moore's description draws directly from conventional simian representations of the Gael while also aligning Hyde's very physiognomy with the rough topography of the west. Hyde's language is all porter and rent strikes, the unaltered product of life in rural Ireland. This life and landscape, Moore insists, have nothing to offer until interpreted by artists. As the narrator says to Yeats somewhat earlier, "Who would care for France . . . if it only consisted of peasants, industrious or idle? . . . [T]he fields are speechless, and the rocks are dumb. In the last analysis everything depends upon the poet . . . it is for Ireland to admire us, not for us to admire Ireland" (*HF* 138). Through metaphor, Moore locates both the source of Hyde's "aboriginal" power and, in Moore's opinion, his weakness as a literary man. He is too much a reflection of his country and too little a sign of its transformation.

Through the metaphors that depict Hyde as a feature of Irish topography, Moore abrogates his power as someone with anything to say worth hearing. The metaphors found for Yeats and Martyn make one skeptical of their potential to transform Irish life through their writings. Yeats, for one, is a jackdaw, a crane, and a sparring cock, but, most of all, a rook attempting to build a nest with an owl: "Edward as great in girth as an owl (he is nearly as neckless), blinking behind his glasses, and Yeats lank as a rook, a-dream in black silhouette on the flowered wallpaper" (*HF* 76). The simile quickly becomes metaphor: the two men no longer merely resemble birds, but are birds. The metaphor extends for pages, implicitly reproaching Yeats as "the cunning rook [who] had enticed the profound owl from his belfry—an owl that has stayed out too late" and one distressed "lest the Dean and Chapter, having heard of the strange company he is keeping, may have, during his absence, bricked up the entrance to his roost" (*HF* 76). The narrator goes on to speculate, "Would the young owls cast out the young rooks, or would the young rooks cast out the young owls, and what view would the beholders take of this wondrous hatching?" (*HF* 78) The possibility of a literary theater is discussed entirely in terms of this extended metaphor, and that vehicle dooms it from the start.

By offering the comparison as extended metaphor rather than mere simile, Moore effectively rewrites nature, openly modifying its features to fit his own vision. The fact that owls are actually much fiercer than rooks is relevant only insofar as it underscores the difference between a natural owl and the owl of this story who is attempting an unnatural or "wondrous" hatching. The slow and timid owl is dominated by the nearly fleshless form of the Yeatsian rook (again emphasizing Moore's abhorrence of idealists who deny the senses). Not merely day-blind, the owl is also lost in the night's mysteries. Nowhere do we see the sharp claws and penetrating eyes of the night predator known to the ornithologist. Moore aptly describes the obese, pious, and conservative Martyn of his book and highlights those characteristics by encouraging the reader to think of the ways in which Martyn is both like and unlike the owl of nature.

Moore would see this reformulation as a very different procedure than, say, Yeats's attempt to remake Synge as a scholar: "I am sorry," he writes, "that Yeats fell into the mistake of attributing much reading to Synge; he has little love of character and could not keep himself from putting rouge on Synge's face and touching up his eyebrows" (*HF* 560). According to Moore, Yeats, having "little love of character," remade Synge as a wishful and idealized version of himself rather than presenting a personal interpretation of a very closely observed other. Yeats's portraits of his contemporaries in the *Autobiography* do demonstrate a very different perspective on the relation of model and portrait. Particularly in "The Tragic Generation," Yeats renders his subjects representatives of types and alters their unique forms to coordinate with archetypal figures, whereas Moore works more inductively: "We all have models," he writes, "and if we copy the model intelligently, a type emerges" (*HF* 564). In positioning himself as the artist who remakes nature, he nevertheless utilizes the peculiar characteristics of his subjects to develop analogies that even further accentuate human distinctiveness while simultaneously presenting comic types.

Many of the issues under discussion, and especially the encompassing question of how it is we know the self and others, converge in the short essay "Art without the Artist," which Moore added in 1925 as a preface to *Hail and Farewell*. A virtuoso performance of multiple comic ironies, the essay introduces most of the major themes of the book. Moore begins by playfully questioning if the Pre-Raphaelites began with Ruskin or Rossetti: with the theoretician or the practitioner? Noting that Ruskin was himself a practitioner as adept at drawing as at criticism, he dismisses the Irish Revivalists' tendency to theorize out of proportion to actual practice. He goes on to assert that neither the theorist nor the practitioner is so influential as what he calls "Nature": "Sometimes she undertakes the entire composition, as in *Hail and Farewell;* every episode and every character was a gift from Nature." "For years," he continues, "I believed myself to be the author of *Hail and Farewell,* whereas I was nothing more than the secretary" Finally, he decides that the composer is not Nature but "Erin," although since "the name Erin has been turned to derision by much bad poetry in modern times," he will designate the text's author "Banva," "Ireland's name when the Druids flourished" (*HF* 50–52). Yet how could "Banva," being itself an idealized illusion, "dictate" an exposé of illusions? And how could the artist as a remaker of nature be so subject to its dictations?

We shall need to return again to the distinction between the autobiographer and his narrator. To the narrator of *Hail and Farewell,* Ireland inspires the mission announced at the book's end, that of showing Ireland a reflection of itself in, as James Joyce said of his *Dubliners,* "my nicely polished looking-glass." A book composed by Banva will reflect, like all mirrors, a backward image. Its reflection of "Ideals in Ireland," to invoke the title of Augusta Gregory's 1901 anthology, betrays not a purist idealism but its opposite: the bodily forms that signify, in Moore's terms, the determinative power of heredity and history.

Distinct from the narrator, the autobiographer-satirist holds up this mirror, and whether made of ink drawing or typeset words, it reproduces his "distorted gaze" as it takes in the revelatory surfaces of experience. The power of the satirist-autobiographer to shape the materials provided by "nature" is asserted with much ironic subtlety throughout "Art without the Artist." Noting Whistler's proclamation that nature is at best a piano on which the musician plays, and that "Nature is rarely an artist," Moore retorts, "may we not say the same of Man? . . . Are not then Man and Nature equal, both of them being seldom artists?" (*HF* 49). While the essay thus explicitly declares the narrator to be merely Banva's secretary, it implicitly distinguishes Moore as the one real artist in the text. Others in *Hail and Farewell* attempt to play the role of interpreter of nature, yet like the mock-heroic knight he portrays himself to be, Moore vanquishes them in the one-sided verbal combat of his three-volume monologue. AE "has helped all and sundry through the labours of parturition," but Moore allows no others to give birth to themselves in the way that he does as autobiographer. In this sense, Moore's practice confirms James Olney's assertion of the autobiographical comedy implicit not only in the ironic distance between past and present subject, but in the autobiographer's position as "the master dramatist and stage manager, in control both of his own life and of the lives of others," assigning to others, if he or she wishes to, "bit parts as comic characters" in the new creation so frequently and so significantly titled, *The Life*.[20]

Moore assigns such a bit part to the nationalist T. P. Gill, and in one of the finest set-pieces in *Hail and Farewell*, he gleefully tells the tale of Gill's futile attempt at self-creation. An inconsequential man, Gill is prodded into his own birth throes quite accidentally. Having fallen asleep in a barber's chair in Paris, he awakens with a new Henri Quatre beard:

> It was not until the barber gave him the glass that he felt the sudden transformation—felt rather than saw, for the transformation effected in his face was little compared with that which had happened in his soul. In the beginning was the beard, and the beard was with God, who in this case happened to be a barber; and glory be to the Lord and to his shears that a statesman of the Renaissance walked that day up the Champs Elysées. . . . As he walked it seemed to him all the learning of his time had sprung up in him. He found himself like the great men of the sixteenth century, well versed in the arts of war and peace, a patron of the arts and sciences. (*HF* 130–31)

This beard Gill caresses "constantly, reminding one of a cat licking its fur, with this difference, however, that a cat is silent while it licks itself, whereas Gill could talk while he dallied with his beard." Gill's speech is itself born of this beard, and yet the more he talks the more evident it becomes that his Machiavellian beard reveals most fully his eternally weak chin. The narrator alludes to the monumental importance of this facial hair, using it to date events as one might use a king's ascension or a military battle: "About the time of Gill's beard . . ." or "As Gill was having his beard trimmed in Paris . . .". This bathetic symbol of Gill's ambitions serves to verify with some cruelty Moore's premise that only the caricaturist who detects that metaphoric space between chin and beard can negotiate between the determinism and autogeny they imply.

Fixity, Fate, and the Tragicomic: Moore and W. B. Yeats

In the very absurdity of the human attempt to remake the face, Moore discovers an aspiration worthy of unlimited interest. As one whose letters admit a habitual terror of the possibility that his ambitions might exceed his talents, he presents the failings of others with poignant recognition and lively malice. Of the attempts of W. B. Yeats at self-invention, he expressed both admiration and ridicule, just as Yeats later judged Moore's attempts with correspondingly begrudging praise, though with a particularly acrid rancor absent from Moore's assessment of him. Although Moore spent a good deal of his own career repudiating his father and fabricating a family history, he—derisively parodying Yeats' own language—relates how "one day whilst Yeats was crooning over his fire Yeats had said that if he had his rights he would be Duke of Ormonde. AE's answer was: I am afraid, Willie, you are overlooking your father—a detestable remark to make to a poet in search of an ancestry" (*HF* 540). Perhaps the outrageous nature of Moore's own versions of ancestry (which disclaimed his family's ties to Catholicism and in one instance denied being Irish at all) indicates that, in his mind, the fictionalization of family history should be taken for granted by both the teller and his audience. His mockery of Yeats may thus originate either in Moore's claim to exclusive rights of self-invention or in a belief that Yeats took with too much sincerity that fabrication of genealogy which he considered more playfully. Despite the differences between Moore and Yeats, one focusing sharply upon the exterior and the other turning his eye from it, their efforts at textual self-construction do provoke illuminating comparison, particularly in relation to issues of sincerity and artifice, the fixity or determined nature of the self, and the view of life as tragicomic experience.

In conversation and in their writings, both men were singularly unconcerned with sincerity or factuality. In his studies of Yeats's autobiographical prose, James Olney discovers a rhetoric of qualifications and memory lapses that conveniently clears the field of "fact"—the territory of the quotidian Self—so that the Soul who deals in the essential and archetypal nature of things may have free range. But by maintaining the referential status of memories, however faulty he claims his recollective capacities to be, Yeats holds his autobiographical speaker back from full entry into the domain of the archetypal Soul.[21] From the active combat of Soul and Self, Yeats imagined a life of heroic struggle and, from that struggle, poetry. Moore's own manipulation of autobiographical "fact," with its keen recognition of "the transit . . . between the original and the figure drawn," presents his version of a studied separation between self and soul. If it does not parallel exactly the Yeatsian division, it does indicate a similarity of vision in two men so otherwise opposed.

Moore's version of the life as a battleground between self and anti-self can be seen most particularly in the ambiguity of his sexual self-representation. In addition to his confession of a nature so feminine that he imagined his soul to have hesitated as to gender a moment before his conception, Moore offered contradictory and provocative descriptions of his own sexuality throughout his life. His perpetual recitations of his various and very dubious amours offended his listeners; even so ribald a conversationalist as Oliver Gogarty complains of them, and yet Moore would not cease. Max Beerbohm recalls that he would often prompt Moore to describe natural scenery—at which he was very gifted—but that "inevitably, the shepherdesses would come in. Never was a man so importuned by imaginary women! I have never met a shepherdess. Have *you*? But Moore was always running into them—rather, they kept running into *him*. Evidently, they revived their craft just to conquer Moore."[22] Such stories were so preposterous that he must have assumed that his listeners understood the artifice—as everyone who recalls them seemed to have done. His friend John Eglinton speculates that female listeners were unoffended by these stories because they intuitively knew them to be completely false (*EG* 10).[23] Yet just as autobiography resists the label of fiction at least as much as it resists the label of fact, Moore refused to identify these stories as either factual or fictional. In a 1914 letter to the *Evening Sun*, Moore indignantly protests any imputations that the romances recounted in his autobiographies were imaginary, although within the very same letter he offers the theory that "after five and twenty—certainly after thirty love adventures are no longer indiscretions, but matter for literary history."[24] Nancy Cunard, who ardently defends both Moore's virility and his good manners against what she dubs the malicious jealousy of the "legend-spiders," asserts that she "believed every word he said about those exploits and conquests," yet adds that "all of it seemed like a sort of 'self-editing' and so objective that he appeared to be talking less about himself than of some character created by him—exteriorising, externalising, 'ex-personalising,' even dramatising the little picture, with his merry innuendos."[25] While posing as a great lover, Moore encouraged rumors of his impotence to circulate, and, according to almost every memoir written about him, such rumors were fed by his stories of ludicrously unlikely affairs. "I never believed that your life is anything else but pure; it is only your mind that is indecent," jokes Edward Martyn in *Hail and Farewell*, giving voice to suspicion suggested by many other contemporaries (*HF* 309). The narrator of *Hail and Farewell* himself "confesses" to his impotence, as he confessed to transvestite fantasies in *Confessions of a Young Man* and to sexual awkwardness in *Memoirs of My Dead Life*.

Given the literary hay he was willing to make out of such potentially embarrassing conditions, it seems more than likely that, in introducing into society the rumor of his impotence, he was creating with deliberation the role of the lover who might be a celibate but who speaks and writes fiction from the standpoint of the lover. When we consider the rhetoric of sincerity dominant in nineteenth-century autobiography, this emerges as an astonishing self-construction: the pretense of being a lover who pretends to be a celibate in order to pretend to be a lover! Which role was fantasy and which experience? Or a better question: which expresses Moore's "instinctive" nature? It is impossible to do more than hypothesize biographically, but the point of the question lies less in its answer than in the fact that Moore's words and actions provoke it. He succeeded in presenting two opposing images of the self as an autobiographical battleground on which to work out his ongoing preoccupation with the issue of individual freedom.

In "Ego Dominus Tuus," Yeats praises Dante who, "being mocked by Guido for his lecherous life," wrote as a seeker of purity. Dante, he says, "set his chisel to the hardest stone" to fashion "from his opposite / An image that might have been a stony face / Staring upon a Bedouin's horse-hair roof." Yeats makes his point perhaps most clear in "The Death of Synge," where he reflects that "all happiness depends on the energy to assume the mask of some other self; that all joyous or creative life is a re-birth as something not oneself, something which has no memory and is created in a moment and perpetually renewed."[26] While Yeats would have heatedly denied that Moore found his antithetical self from the Anima Mundi (being, in Yeats's judgment, enslaved by the material world), Moore too seeks a voice that would be antithetical to his quotidian experience. If we look at his sexual tall tales as individual instances, they appear pathetic attempts to convince his listeners of his physical desirability. If they are considered as part of one long intertextual performance on the stage of the drawing room and at the podium of his autobiographies, these stories form yet another manifestation of a consistent way of seeing the self. The work of imaginative self-construction takes place precisely within the dissonance between body and idea, between self and antithesis.

Yeats claims a legitimacy for the deliberative artifice of his own self-making in a rhetoric of supernaturalism. Moore burlesques Yeatsian supernatural promptings while making repeated appeals to the authority of his instincts. In *Hail and Farewell*, the call to Ireland is issued forth by the mythical Cathleen ni Houlihan, who had arisen "out of that arid plain, out of the mist, to tempt me"; and the discovery of the narrator's anti-Catholic mission appears as a vision like that of St. Paul on the road to Damascus. Much as Yeats asserts the unchanging and transcendental nature of the daemon, Moore testifies to the unchanging and transcendental nature of instinct.

Like the paradoxical explanations of instinct in *Confessions* and in his fiction, Moore's argumentation about the origins of the instinct sometimes takes flexuous turns in *Hail and Farewell*. Edward Martyn attempts to answer the narrator's proposition that "as soon as the Irish Church became united to Rome, art declined in Ireland" by suggesting that the harsh suppressions of the Penal Laws had been responsible for the absence of a written literary tradition. "But the Penal Laws," the narrator counters, "are not hereditary, like syphilis" (*HF* 352). If historical conditions can be overcome, syphilis and other degenerative inheritances cannot—like the inability to produce *sauce Béarnaise*. When Martyn asks why he doesn't simply become a Protestant, the narrator insists that, despite his antipathy to Catholicism, he cannot "convert" to Protestantism. Invoking the rhetoric of the inner light, he argues that one doesn't become a Protestant; rather, one discovers oneself a Protestant. Yet the narrator disparages Martyn for believing that "if a little water is poured on the head of an infant in a Catholic Church the child remains a Catholic" despite its choices in later life. Is religion a matter of inherited disease, which cannot be overcome, or historical conditioning, which can be superseded? And if the latter, then why is conversion an inappropriate term? Moore's answer recalls the discussion of instinct in *Confessions of a Young Man* as, thinking again of Edward, the narrator reflects along the following lines: "He is a born Catholic, fell from my lips, and the phrase seemed to me to represent a truth hitherto unexpected or insufficiently appreciated. We do not acquire our religion, we bring it into the world. We are born Catholics or Protestants" (*HF* 630). While we may be taken in one direction by our training—"a little water . . . poured on the head of an infant"— nevertheless our instincts will eventually emerge and lead us toward a recognition of what we always were, which may have little to do with who our parents were or what they would have us be.

While elsewhere Moore has suggested that ideas are the product of culture and language and thus assumably subject to those conditions, he also offers the view that changes of opinion are actually stages in the gradual revelation of the ideas that are ours from birth, despite our imperfect knowledge of them. In a letter to Edmund Gosse, Moore metaphorically describes this process by which "an idea matures in the mind like a pear in a storeroom" (BK 51), but a passage from *Hail and Farewell* makes the point even more dramatically:

> A man of letters goes into a garden with an idea; he and his idea spend happy days under apple-boughs in the sun; he plays with his idea as a mother with her child, chasing it about the lilac-bushes; sometimes the child cries with rage, and the mother cannot pacify her baby, but, however naughty her baby may be, she never wearies; her patience is endless, and the patience of a man of letters is endless too. His idea becomes unmanageable, but he does not weary of it; and then his idea grows up, just like the child, passing from blue smock and sash into knickerbockers, in other words into typewriting. (*HF* 355)

One's idea may be truly an idée fixe, waywardly developing into its inevitable maturity, and the instinct that will eventually discard or embrace it finally may be equally intractable. However, the relation between instinct and the varying forms of ideas is itself forever changing and is represented in the impressionable "man of wax": the fluctuating "self" who remains in contrast with the unvarying "soul." Max Beerbohm points out this very phenomenon when he writes that "in Moore's face, immutable though the expression was, by some physical miracle the features were perpetually remoulding themselves."[27] Scrutinizing a physiognomical clue much as Moore himself might have done, Beerbohm observes that dynamic relationship between fixity and change.

Moore depicts the protean self struggling to reconcile instincts and ideas; the common incapacity to do so leads most frequently to absurd behavior and eventual failure. In one of the rare studies of Yeats as a comic writer, Hazard Adams postulates that Yeats's comedic spirit originates in his recognition of a not dissimilar effort in his own work. "The source of Yeats' comedy," Adams suggests, "is similar to that of fatalistic tragedy." "Yeats often sees us . . . in ridiculous conflict not only with our time and place ('body of fate') but also with the fate we ourselves apparently and mysteriously generate." Adams concludes that Yeats's tragicomic view "suggests that man inhabits a world where he will always look a bit foolish and will always confront something beyond his powers to understand. As a result, the gesture that man makes towards his situation is his most important function." From the gestures made to reconcile self and soul are forged heroic action and tragic aspiration, while the discrepancy between the attempt and the capacity to achieve such a unity of being ensures ironic comedy.[28] Despite vast differences in language and ideas, both Moore and Yeats attempt to recompose the determinism of the late nineteenth century into an idiosyncratic system that can also account for uniqueness or heroism. Both garner examples from literature, history, and the stories of their own lives to assert that one is born with a given nature and strives toward enactment of that nature. While Yeats formulates archetypes of tragicomic heroism from the foredoomed attempt at reconciliation, Moore documents the particulars of its failure. Yet both men see the human personality caught between deterministic models of being and see in that tragicomic entanglement the struggle that animates their art.

Certainly there is nothing in Moore of Yeatsian "tragic joy," that which R. Jahan Ramazani defines as the transformation of "the painful spectacle of destruction and death into a joyful assertion of human freedom and transcendence," "an ecstatic enlargement of vision" when human beings most fully confront annihilation or eternity.[29] (And here, the sublime tragic joy of the later poems and plays needs to be distinguished from the ironic tragicomedy of Yeats's autobiographical prose.) For George Moore, comedy has much more to do with the finite world than the transcendent; his is a comedy more pessimistic than tragic, and undeniably more derisive. It is perhaps this underlying pessimism that explains John Eglinton's characterization of his friend as "a soul in contact with some perennial source of caustic insight and salutary disillusionment."[30] As Moore represents human aspiration, the visions of most people are delusions from the start. That others should fail to enact their visions signals pathos—and occasionally bathos—rather than tragedy. Reflecting upon the life of J. M. Synge, for instance, Yeats praises him in poetry as one who "dying chose the living world for text," and in the *Autobiography* as a "sick man picturing energy, a doomed man picturing gaiety."[31] In the cloying deathbed scene Moore invents, Synge becomes instead a pathetic figure who died tearfully, the comic mask proving insufficient to snuff out the disappointments of the sickly man. Sir Horace Plunkett's inability to act out of his bewildering capacity for abstractions is also a matter of derision rather than tragedy, as is the inability of AE or Martyn to write well, or Yeats's apparent poetic exhaustion.

Instead of tragedy, then, Moore's comic perspective on the self incorporates the absurdism of tragicomedy, the pessimism of derisive satire, and the mournful quality of elegy. In *Hail and Farewell*, that elegiac mood produces extended sections of genuine poignancy and emotional power: vividly realized scenes from the "old life" of his father's world at Moore Hall, his youth in France, and the deterioration of his bond with his beloved younger brother, Maurice. This is not to say that the elegiac sections are not funny; they too make ample use of the satiric persona and such narrative tools as parody, caricature, and reduction. That comic element pits Moore's deep nostalgia against the deflating reminder that the lost world was one of barbarism and betrayals, both personal and public: a world of landlord despotism and peasant poverty in Ireland, manipulation and deceit in France, and a childhood of envy and bad faith on the part of the narrator toward his younger brother. There is an intoxicating quality to the sheer oddity and vitality of the Mayo estate where young "Masther George" ran waving pig bladders, tortured the laundry cats, tormented his good-natured brother, and greatly made a show of himself; or of the Paris where an older "Mr. Perpetual" attempted his love affairs, mingled with artists and writers in salons and cafés, and again made a great show of himself. Yet as the narrator emphatically asserts to his brother, who would preserve the past by attempting its restoration, "we have outlived our day, that is all; and in thirty years we shall be, as I have said, extinct as the dodo" (*HF* 636).

Such a reductive analogy between a past way of life and an absurdly named bird typifies the way Moore's allegiance to life in the present toughens the elegiac tone, mocking both the past and the deterministic historical demise he predicts for the landlord class. In various autobiographical works, Moore confesses his aversion to contact with that which has died, be it a human being or way of life. The sight of his father's face, changed in death, he tells us, forever replaced the image of the living man; the prospect of a vigil at his dying mother's bedside is as oppressive as the prospect of interment in the family vault. In *A Story-Teller's Holiday*, the narrator questions his hesitancy to confront that which belongs to the past. Attempting to explain to himself why he has avoided visiting Moore Hall, now empty of the brother who tried to restore it, he reflects:

> I walked up and down the platform at Athlone, seeking the reason why I was always diffident, shy, ill at ease at Moore Hall; and feeling myself nearer to apprehending a reason that had till now eluded me, I repeated the words: diffident, shy, ill at ease, ashamed, frightened, overcome by the awe that steals over one in the presence of the dead.
>
> Moore Hall is a relic, a ruin, a corpse. Its life ceased when we left it in 1870, and I am one that has no liking for corpses. The wise man never looks on the face of a corpse, knowing well that if he does it will come between him and the living face (*STH* 2:257).

Moore never admits to sadness greater than a transient melancholy and rarely envisions an imminent annihilative power surpassing that of the living world that holds it at bay. The past may be regretted and cherished, just as idealisms may be admired, but Moore delights most of all in the prospect of his own figure engaged in the act of inventive recollection. The past and the aspirations of idealists become material for literature, conceived by one who lives within the finite present.

Moore's comic perspective is rooted in his self-preservationist instinct and his relish of the present moment—even if it is the moment in which he dissolves in reveries over the past. In his *Christ and Apollo: The Dimensions of the Literary Imagination,* William Lynch aligns comedy with survival in simple, yet provoking, definitions of tragic and comic perspectives: "In the end the decision of every one of the great tragedies is that, left to itself, the human will at the very height of its straining stands broken and defeated." Comedy, on the other hand, finds "a kind of rock-bottom reality in man, the terrain of Falstaff and Sancho Panza, which is profoundly . . . unbreakable, which has no needs above itself."[32] Such a tragicomic synthesis of loss and recovery appears as *Hail and Farewell*'s narrator bitterly leaves his brother at Moore Hall, knowing that his relationship with Maurice—as with Ireland—is nearly at an end. As the train pulls away, he thinks, "So this is the end. He thinks that I have changed. We have both changed, and the fault is neither with him nor with me. He was born a Papist, and this is the end; unendurable words if we have given all our love. And thinking how much I had lost, I sat looking out on the wet fields of Mayo. So this is the end! I cried, scaring a fellow-passenger, who looked at me askance over his newspaper. He returned to his paper, I to my thoughts, which were no longer with the Colonel but with myself. In which direction does my life lie? I asked" (*HF* 641). Interrupting one of the most fully felt emotional moments of his story, Moore takes a brief moment of visual comedy as a bridge to a pragmatic consideration of his next step as a writer. His depiction of the narrator as so selfish a man suggests self-censure, but the humor of the scene drives home the recognition that such self-preoccupation is not only typical of human beings but also necessary and, in that sense, justifiable.

While betrayal and loss are conditions of life as depicted in *Hail and Farewell,* Moore implies that we shall all manage to survive in such a fallen world, although never so nobly as we wish we could. The narrator leaves Ireland "a very humble fellow, forgetful of Ireland, forgetful of Catholicism, forgetful of literature" and goes below the deck "to think of the friends he had left behind him—AE and the rest" (*HF* 644). Betrayed and betraying, the narrator puts aside the hobbyhorses that have plagued him and his compatriots and, without those ideas to tell him where or who he is, meditates on the loss of his friends: he is entirely alone at the book's end. The narrator will return to his friends in memory and imagination only as he finishes the book's last volume—an activity projected within it. And he behaves toward them much as he behaves toward all faces of the dead, having relegated them to a world that is as much a part of his past as the Mayo of childhood and the Montmartre of youth.

Autobiographies generally tell the story of one's life in the world; they are populated by a cast of figures drawn from experience. The speaking voice is created within the context of other voices at the same time that, through narrative, the autobiographer reconstitutes those others around him- or herself. The narrator of *Hail and Farewell* has been pushed to the periphery of his friends' experiences in the Irish Revival, but he now positions himself as its centerpiece, and their story becomes part of his own recollective consciousness. However, as the next chapter will explore, Moore undercuts by his own practice the supremacy of the world-dominating autobiographer; through its probing use of parodic discourse *Hail and Farewell* questions the ownership of the very language with which its author claims to generate his world.

5

Hail and Farewell's *Parodic Autobiography*

The Double-Voiced Utterance and the Singular Subject

MAX BEERBOHM'S CARICATURE of a conversation between the youthful George Moore and his aged self introduces a number of the issues pertinent to Moore's unique conflation of parody and autobiographical art. The elderly man and his younger counterpart engage in the following dialogue:

> YOUNG SELF: "And have there been any painters since Manet?"
> OLD SELF: "None."
> YOUNG SELF: "Have there been any composers since Wagner?"
> OLD SELF: "None."
> YOUNG SELF: "Any novelists since Balzac?"
> OLD SELF: "One."[1]

The two figures stand together before the viewer; they are united in a continuous present built upon their ongoing dialogue. As in Moore's autobiographies, past experience is pulled forward into the present tense. Memory revives experience, investing it with perhaps a greater liveliness than it had initially, then sweeps it away again into the past of the told tale or the written text. The younger Moore, wearing the dress of *Confessions'* narrator and dependent thus for his very existence upon a George Moore older than himself, persistently queries his elder. Just as the aging writer outranks the inquiring younger one in Beerbohm's cartoon, so Moore had ever jealously dismantled the authority of his younger self through decades of added revisions and prefaces to his earlier works, engaged in a drive to control, in addition to heredity and circumstance, all prior literary creators and their creations, including the younger George Moore as both author and subject of the works that bear his name.

Beerbohm also intimates, correctly, that Moore imagines himself most fully amid a world of other writers, artists, and talkers, including his antecedent selves. In Moore's autobiographical writings, the process of self-discovery and definition is less concerned with ontological identity than with his place in the world as he experiences it through talk, literature, and, to a lesser degree, landscape and landscape painting. (Characteristically, these latter areas are also understood to be forms of human discourse: Moore's descriptions of landscapes regularly incorporate an observer, and paintings are always discussed as the expression of specific painters he knew in France and elsewhere.) Although the narrator of *Hail and Farewell* is repeatedly described as having "lost the habit of reading," throughout his text Moore acts as the reader (and reviser) of the language of others. Janet Varner Gunn has proposed that autobiographical acts are intrinsically forms of reading and present a model of interpretive activity. She suggests that "as an act of orientation by means of which the self inhabits and not merely projects a possible world of significance, autobiography embodies the story of Antaeus and not, as so many are ready to assume, the story of Narcissus . . . the real question of the autobiographical self then becomes *where do I belong?* not, who am I? The question of the self's identity becomes a question of the self's location in a world."[2] In *Hail and Farewell*, this process is brought to the foreground, the life being self-consciously composed of readings and overhearings. Literature, speech, and gossip are so intertwined with observation and memory as to make both past and present experience interactions with antecedent forms of language.

Hail and Farewell memorializes Moore's dealings with a universe of talk. As early as *Confessions of a Young Man*, he had begun to incorporate without quotation marks or commentary the conversations he heard in Mayo, Montmartre, and Fleet Street. But more fully than these earlier books, and perhaps more than any autobiography before it, *Hail and Farewell* is a truly polyphonic work assembling the self through quotation, allusion, formal travesty, dialogue, and gossip. The digressive reveries of the narrator move associationally from one form of parodic discourse to another, while the transitional narrative is at times itself parodic. The voices heard throughout the book are, for the most part, those of scholars, journalists, and other writers. The voices of other numerous and memorable characters—bureaucrats, country people, painters, servants, relatives—also act as articulations of literary forms of language because all, Moore affirms, would surely have been the products of the great novelists and playwrights were they not already the handiwork of "the greater Aristophanes above."

In examining *Hail and Farewell*'s approach to the speaking self, I shall explore Moore's objectification of language as material phenomena, vulnerable to interpretation and domination by other, generally competitive, varieties of language. As a material phenomenon, language becomes subject to parody, much as the body was subject to caricature. With a tension similar to that operative in caricature between "the original and the figure drawn," parody depends upon a dissonance between the context of an original source and that of a parodic appropriation. In pointing out the discrepancies between modern Ireland and the imagined majesty of the ancient Ireland whose language and myths the modern writers wish to adopt, Moore determines their work to be predominantly parodic, although their parodies lack the crucial element of self-consciousness. Moore goes on to identify not only the work of the Irish revival but all art and all personality as parodic creations. The parodies of *Hail and Farewell* constitute social criticism and an occasionally spiteful exercise in literary competition; even more important, however, they expose the collective nature of authorship, particularly the authorship of the speaking subject. At the same time that Moore acknowledges collective authorship of both literature and the subject, he rejects its implications and again asserts the primacy of the final voicing, that of the self-born individual.

"To Gather Up a Great Mass of Speech": Parody and Materialism

For readers of *Hail and Farewell*, Mikhail Bakhtin and one of his foremost interpreters, Gary Saul Morson, provide ways of thinking about parody that help illuminate Moore's wide-ranging usage of the mode. As Morson explains, "Rather than viewing parody as a particular literary genre, or as a form of satire, or a special type of comedy . . . Bakhtin describes it in terms of the relation of any utterance, whether literary or nonliterary, to the context of its origin and reception."[3] As part of his analysis of the varieties of what he calls "double-voiced language," Bakhtin maintains that in parody

> the author again speaks in someone else's discourse, but . . . introduces into that discourse a semantic intention that is directly opposed to the original one. The second voice, once having made its home in the other's discourse, clashes hostilely with its primordial host and forces him to serve directly opposing aims. Discourse becomes an arena of battle between two voices. . . . One can parody another person's style as a style; one can parody another's socially typical or individually characterological manner of seeing, thinking, and speaking. The depth of the parody may also vary: one can parody merely superficial verbal forms, but one can also parody the very deepest principles governing another's discourse.[1]

In *Hail and Farewell,* parody is much more than a narrowly defined literary device. It is above all a form of satire, critiquing a previous utterance and the way of seeing (and way of life) that produced it. Moore parodies numerous kinds of previously existent languages in the form of quotation, allusion, represented dialogue, or the application of another's style and vocabulary to a content incongruous with the original. His parodies involve the recontextualization of syntax, vocabulary, content, or context of any previous utterance, oral or written. Disruption of any of these features results in a fundamental relocation of meaning. This new meaning will be controlled by the last speaker, often as a tool to counteract the original utterance. Any one of the disrupted features may itself be the target of the parodist's judgment. Such judgment may be of a favorable kind, indicating respect or nostalgia, but more frequently the verdict points to a denunciation.[5] In every case, parody presupposes the superiority of the last voicing, even when self-parody is involved or when it is parody that is being parodied.

Just as Moore self-consciously foregrounds the process of writing autobiography within his text, he places a high value upon self-awareness of oneself as a parodist. In one of several blatant borrowings from Dostoyevsky (an author the narrator finds unreadable), Moore comments that "to be ridiculous has always been *ma petite luxe,* but can any one be said to be ridiculous if he knows that he is ridicu-

lous? Not very well" (*HF* 487). In *Hail and Farewell*, Moore's compatriots appear completely obtuse regarding the nature of their own
activities: Lady Gregory "collates" and "quotes" translated Irish
texts; Douglas Hyde advocates Gaelic while being himself an "imitation native Irish speaker; in other words, like a stage Irishman";
Yeats seems "an Irish parody of the poetry that I had seen all my life
strutting its rhythmic way in the alleys of the Luxembourg Gardens,
preening its rhymes by the fountains." As one who is "naturally pro-
pense to thrust my finger into every literary pie-dish," the narrator
tastes each one of these imitative flavorings. By having the narrator
speak in this imitative language and then reject it in later parts of the
book, Moore repudiates the unconscious parodists whom his narrator naïvely parodied. In so doing, he repudiates his previous
enthusiasm for the language movement and for a way of seeing and
speaking he had sympathetically portrayed through the Irish mystic
Ulick Dean of *Evelyn Innes* and *Sister Teresa*. All Moore's compatriots
appear as participants in a misguided quest for some essential Irishness, some primary word to authorize their own discourse. As will be
further discussed, the voice of his autobiography is, in contrast, self-
consciously compiled of all these voices, and his identity a matter of
assimilation—with the crucial variation of being guided, of course,
by "instinct."

As might be expected of one who works through an aesthetic
and an ideology of circumference, Moore argues against the essentialism of the revivalists while using the decontextualizing technique
of parody to critique all language that seems excessively distanced
from its material location. As Morson states, "parody is most readily
invited by an utterance that claims transhistorical authority or implies that its source does not lie in any interests or circumstances of
its speaker. The parodist typically reveals the historical or personal
circumstances that led someone to make or entertain a claim of
transhistoricity. Parody historicizes: and in so doing, it exposes the
conditions that engendered claims of unconditionality. . . . In short,
denial of history is invitation to parody."[6]

Juxtaposed with other forms of discourse, a slight remark can
take on significance precisely through its contextual placement. *Hail
and Farewell* consists of hundreds of such remarks, dropped so casually as nearly to slip by unnoticed, asides whose resonance and import are glimpsed only after repeated readings of the whole text.
Moore's point concerning the necessary historical contextualization
of language is achieved by forcing the reader to consider the context

of his comment in order to ascertain a meaning. Early in "Ave," the narrator recalls idly searching many years ago for an old manor house in the hills above Dublin. He is diverted by stories of the nearby relics of druid altars and wanders off to look for them. A caretaker tells him that one had lately fallen and "in the words of a shepherd I'd consulted, the altar was out of repair" (*HF* 63). Upon examination, this seemingly insignificant aside betrays a multifaceted irony. The dissonance between the ancient past and such common- place modern language points to the absurdity of attempting to resurrect the glory of ancient Ireland in the fallen present. The lan- guage itself lacks cognizance of its subject, and Moore's quotation of it (as well as his own stridently businesslike word, "consulted") high- lights the neglect of the subject at hand, a neglect he diagnoses as endemic to Irish life. As a final irony, the search for a crumbling manor house—"some poetical spot"—in which to write an outdated novel of a departed way of life has been conducted by one pre- posterously "magnificent young Montmartrian," returned against his will from Paris to Ireland by "the ravages of the Land League." The land revolution to which Moore gives his fatalistic consent ren- ders the search anachronistic to begin with and the young man who ignores the irrelevancy of his project a figure of ridicule. Conse- quently, the herdsman's language is singularly in context with mod- ern life, while literary talk of druid altars is not.

Moore's double-voicing criticizes both a form of language and the cultural confusion symptomatized by what Patrick Scott has called "the disjunctions between literary and extraliterary codes," the observation of which he designates as a primary function of nine- teenth-century parody.[7] The literary sentiment here may express nostalgia for a golden age of druids, but Moore abjures either a liter- ature or a life based on that nostalgia. When old manor houses be- come "poetical," they become—as is said later of Moore Hall—of value only to millionaire Americans who want them precisely be- cause of their unreality. Similarly, when druid altars fall "out of repair," it is wiser to turn one's eye away from the ruin and onto something else: perhaps a satire of those still longingly eying the ruins.

Moore forces a recognition that language is grounded in speaker, place, and audience by his ironic historical contextualization of the herdsman's remark and, most importantly, of the young man who overhears and remembers it, as well as the narrator who recalls the whole episode while engaged in his own attempt to rediscover in

Ireland a "poetical spot" for still more anachronistic art. Throughout the book, Moore submits Martyn's drama, Yeats's poetry, the
utopian scheming of Plunkett, Gill, and AE, and even his own writing to a similar review of their location in time and place. The narrator's trip with AE to "the ancient divinities of the Gael," the passage
graves and altars north of Dublin, is related in self-consciously vague
and wistful language, parodying a nonsensical delving into Celtic
prehistory to find a sign of continuity in "a robin singing in a blackthorn, the descendant, no doubt, of a robin that had seen the
Druids" (*HF* 286). Ridiculing what Joyce's Leopold Bloom calls "the
like waves of the brain the poetical," Moore's use of parody historically locates those exceedingly abstract and anachronistic poetic discourses that avow their autonomy from a modern context. Of this
function of ironic quotation, Gary Saul Morson explains,

> while the parodist's ironic quotation marks frame the linguistic
> form of the original utterance, they also direct attention to the *occa-
> sion* (more accurately, the parodist's version of the occasion) *of its
> uttering*. The parodist thereby aims to reveal the otherwise covert
> aspects of that occasion. . . . By pointing to the unexamined presup-
> positions and unstated interests that conditioned the original ex-
> change, the parodist accomplishes what Fielding calls "the discovery
> of affectation" . . . the divergence between professed and un-
> acknowledged intentions—or the discovery of naivete, the differ-
> ence between belief and disconfirming evidence. He or she does
> not, therefore, quote "out of context," as the targets often respond,
> but rather in "too much" context—in a context the targets would
> rather have overlooked. Parody is the etiology of utterance.[8]

Moore mocks disembodied language, or language with a muddled
relation to its material context, because he sees all utterance as em-
bodied and not fully independent. In consequence, perhaps, Moore
had a predilection toward the ad hominem assault: for him, there
was no speech without a context in personality and experience. In
the essay "Art without the Artist," which introduces *Hail and Farewell*, he argues that theory cannot operate without practice, nor art
without nature, nor—as he adds later—theology without sex.

Moore's campaign against abstractions places his satire in what
Northrop Frye calls "the second or quixotic phase," which represents
"the collision between a selection of standards from experience and
the feeling that experience is bigger than any set of beliefs about it.
. . . The central theme . . . is the setting of ideas and generalizations

and theories and dogmas over against the life they are supposed to explain."⁹ Yet his assault upon the fixity of fact through the blatant invention of evidence (as in the story of Henry Grattan's mistress) destabilizes any agreed-upon universe of "experience." Without a referential reality against which to measure theories and dogmas, his story moves at times into the kind of ironic satire Frye associates with tragedy in its overwhelming sense of irrationality and imminent death. The closing section of *Hail and Farewell* has a sobriety un-matched by the rest of the book as the narrator recounts the death of his lover and projects the coming loss of Moore Hall. The narra-tor leaves Ireland accompanied only by his memories, wrapped up in the futile dream of saving his nation from Catholicism. If *Hail and Farewell* sings through its melody of deluded visionaries a hymn to the pragmatic and commonsensical, any easy confidence is repeat-edly subverted by that undertone which recognizes the absurdity of all effort and the subjective and probably self-deluding nature of any and all norms.

Nevertheless, the majority of the book takes on the task of set-ting abstraction—and, for that matter, language of any kind—against the life it is supposed to explain, a frame of reference that is presented as at least provisionally secure, if not ultimately. In order to demonstrate the material grounding of language, Moore utilizes the satiric technique of reducing words—especially abstract words—to a state of materiality. There are several reasons why he might have viewed language as an entity rather than as a transparent me-dium. Moore came of age in a society where many people thought of their own speech as an aberrant dialect and where one's accent was a clear sign of educational, religious, economic, and regional status. Young Catholic boys like the Moore brothers were sent off to En-glish boarding schools to rid them of "the terrible brogue" so viru-lently rendered in *A Drama in Muslin* and *Parnell and His Island*. Moreover, Moore served his literary apprenticeship in Paris sur-rounded by a language he imperfectly grasped. In compensation for his inadequate education, he had to teach himself English grammar and punctuation in midlife. "Until a few years ago," he wrote in 1888, "I could not punctuate a sentence. . . . For many years I had to pick out and strive to fit together the fragments of sentences with which I covered reams of paper."¹⁰ In his *Epitaph on George Moore*, Charles Morgan recounts that even in old age when Moore's reputa-tion was primarily that of an elegant prose stylist, his initial drafts were abominable messes of ungrammatical journalese requiring long and painstaking revision. Language, for Moore, could never be taken for granted, but it could be observed, analyzed, and molded as a nearly palpable entity.

In *Hail and Farewell,* words are described through concrete metaphors and regularly dissected for sound, weight, and etymology. Douglas Hyde's Irish is "porter," "a torrent of dark, muddied stuff"; English is "a wooly language without a verbal system or agreement between the adjectives and the nouns." In "Salve," the narrator undertakes a relentless debunking of Newman's *Apologia pro Vita sua* on the grounds of its awkward prose style, a process so convincing that it throws off the defenses of the hapless Colonel Moore, who is identified as a stand-in for the potential reader of the disputation to which he listens. The stylistic infelicities uncovered in the *Apologia* become the grounds upon which to condemn Newman's aesthetic sense, thereby "proving" the inadequacy of Roman Catholicism as a foundation for art. Because the narrator argues that style is character, poor style indicates poor character, and since in character is the origin of ideas, poor style indicates unworthy ideas. Newman's words are extraordinarily decontextualized by Moore in order that they may be weighed as discrete objects. He then recontextualizes the *Apologia* as the expression of Newman's weak personality and inadequate theology.

Moore objectifies words in order to ironically highlight their very materiality and historicity while, at the same time, he criticizes those—including his naïve narrator—who objectify language in order to dehistoricize it. In the initial stages of his repatriation, the narrator dreamily imagines "a vision . . . of argosies floating up the Liffey, laden with merchandise from all the ports of Phoenicia, and poets singing in all the bowers of Merrion Square; and all in a new language that the poets had learned, the English language having been discovered by them, as it had been discovered by me, to be a declining language, a language that was losing its verbs" (*HF* 106). The incongruity between the elevated ideal of classical Greece and the commonplace world of Merrion Square exposes the absurdity of an attempt to restore either the golden age of Greece or the lost world of ancient Ireland by substituting one verbal system for another.

Later, the still naïve narrator argues that Ireland desperately needs literature translated into Gaelic (*The Arabian Nights* being his suggestion), as if something would be accomplished by the mere translation without thought to content or context. The response of the Irish press "may be reduced to this sentence: Mr George Moore has selected *The Arabian Nights* because he wishes an indecent book to be put into the hands of every Irish peasant. We do not take our ideas of love from Mohammedan countries; we are a pure race" (*HF* 337). While the narrator sighs in frustration at this bigoted response, nevertheless, this view is not incongruous with Moore's own perception of language as a cultural signifier. Moore certainly knew that *The Arabian Nights* voices an appreciation of sexuality and aesthetic design at odds with a rigorously puritanical Irish Catholic outlook. *The Arabian Nights* in Gaelic is still *The Arabian Nights*, and, despite the narrator's ahistorical ambitions, its narrative cannot be divorced from the cultural assumptions that produced it.

The lesson is slow to be understood by the narrator and, according to Moore, never understood by Yeats. Earlier in the story, Yeats awakens him in the night to announce that, given their difficulties in collaborating on the proposed *Diarmuid and Grania*, Moore shall write the play in French, then "Lady Gregory will translate your text into English, Taidgh O'Donoghue will translate the English text into Irish, and Lady Gregory will translate the Irish text back into English." The narrator responds, "And then you'll put style upon it?" After considering the matter, he says, "as I was about to tell Lady Gregory that I declined to descend into the kitchen, to don the cap and apron, to turn the spit while the *chef des sauces* prepared his gravies and stirred his saucepans, the adventure of writing a play in French, to be translated three times back and forwards before a last and immortal relish was to be poured upon it, began to appeal to me" providing as it might, "literary adventures" and a release from English "which I had come to hate for political reasons" (*HF* 248–49). Through his reductive analogy to cookery and the several pages of *Diarmuid and Grania* he offers in the most execrably unidiomatic French, Moore drives home the point that a language cannot be adopted without taking on the consciousness of the culture which produces it. Yeats declares that he wants to take on the consciousness of Gaelic Ireland, and the currently Anglophobic narrator searches for any means of escape from English, which has become for him the obscene language of the Boer War. Yet neither Moore nor Yeats, despite the latter's desire to go out into the countryside to "gather up a great mass of speech," really desires the life of rural Catholic Ireland from which the most attractive idiom derives.

As Moore represents him, Yeats cannot come to confess that fact. Like Moore, he is "a literary magpie," but downplays the role of personality in speech for the sake of a nationalistic communalism. From this debate over communal language and the individual voice, a series of paradoxes emerge that will be central to a discussion of the double-voiced utterance in autobiographical writing. If *Hail and Farewell* is an example, speech is impossible without quotation, and all art, including autobiographical description, becomes a matter of quotation. The self, too, is a collage, or assimilation. Moore, however, also argues the contrary doctrine that all art is the expression of the instinctive personality. *Hail and Farewell* itself may effect a provisional resolution of the paradox; while the single speaker's tale is made up of double-voiced utterances, implying no originality or essentiality to its language, that latter voice is nevertheless the prevailing one. Moore demonstrates that while one cannot adopt speech without incorporating the context of the initial speaker, one can recount the comedy of such an attempt. Relentlessly, he draws our attention to the implicit quotation marks around all utterance (an emphasis even more pronounced after he deleted actual quotation marks in 1925). As with his caricatures, that which is unique comes from the space between the original and the assumed word.

As I shall suggest, the singular personal voice that speaks from that intermediate space still has its grounding within a cultural context, functioning in spite of itself within an Irish satiric speech community. Memory, too, emerges as a form of parody, and the very memories that would give the designated author an autonomous identity and unity of consciousness are shown to be themselves an assimilation of literary language. With characteristic contradiction, Moore will use such memories at the end of the trilogy to assert individual experience as the authoritative discourse of a single, autonomous speaker. We shall see also that the autobiographical subject exists in a world of gossip, the anonymity of which additionally displaces the voice of the author. Conversely, gossip as a structural component of *Hail and Farewell* also builds an illusion of intimacy between reader and narrator, reinforcing the sense of a singular speaker. Throughout, the text balances with comic precariousness between two hostile theories regarding the origins of autobiographical expression.

The Single Voice and the Communal World

One of Max Beerbohm's many caricatures of Moore, "Rentree of Mr. George Moore into Chelsea," depicts an encounter between the

author of *Esther Waters* and his "artist's model," a dowdy female servant. "Ought to be ashamed o'yerself," she accuses him, "coming an'
taking the bread out o' us poor girls' mouths."[11] In *Hail and Farewell*,
Moore confirms that the novel's commercial success, coupled with an
efficient land agent, plunged him into prosperity and "robbed me of
all my literary capital." His analogy between the utilization of sources
and mercantile exploitation develops as he goes on to admit his pal-
try farewell gift to the charwoman who inspired his best-selling
novel. "This confession," he says, "costs me as much as some of
Rousseau's cost him. . . . In bidding her goodbye I bade goodbye to
literature" (*HF* 102, 103). The comparison between himself and
Rousseau is both disingenuous and strangely accurate. Rousseau admits that as a youth he blamed a servant woman for his own theft of
a pink and silver ribbon, a crime that continues to haunt him. While
Rousseau reminds the reader of the difficulties that a servant faces
once so dismissed from a household, the fervency with which Rousseau belabors his guilt suggests either counterfeit emotion or mental
hysteria. Moore also delineates the disastrous consequences a dismissal might have upon a servant when he depicts a similar act by a
young gentleman in *Esther Waters*. But as the narrator confesses to
his act of cruelty in *Hail and Farewell*, the tone differs considerably
from either Rousseau's *Confessions* or *Esther Waters*. Moore implies
that the confession cost Rousseau nothing and in fact supplied him
with material for "literature," as did Moore's illiberality toward the
charwoman. In his capitalist metaphor and in his allusion to the voyeuristic Rousseau, Moore recalls the ethical problems of authorship
raised in *A Drama in Muslin* and *Parnell*, thereby suggesting that
using the language of others was for him not without ethical implications.

The Irish Renaissance aesthetic, characterized by Moore as a
search for primary sources to imitate or "translate," allows him to
consider the issue of authorship from a perspective other than that
of the guilty writer of documentary realism. In *A Story-Teller's Holiday*, Moore enthusiastically praises the folk tradition as emblematic
of the way all great stories develop from anonymous or many-au-
thored narratives that belong to all and no one. Moore's last decade
was preoccupied by the retelling of ancient and medieval tales, and
his efforts attest to more than passing interest in the mediumistic
role of traditional storyteller. At the same time, Moore refuses such
a diffident role, and his endorsement of communal authorship is
severely qualified by contextual irony in both *Hail and Farewell* and *A*

Story-Teller's Holiday. He dissents on two grounds, both of which will require some explanation: the first amounts to a rejection of the kind of communality of imagination projected by the Irish revivalists as Moore understood them. Second, he rejects the idea of communal art unless dominated by the final speaker: unless it acts, ultimately, as the expression of his personality or, as in autobiography, constitutes the creation of his personality.

As Moore represents literary nationalism, entering into a communal Irish authorship bespeaks agreement with an idea of essential Irishness and an adulation of an original, or first, voicing at the expense of adaptations or variations. As a confirmed iconoclast, Moore resists the ideological and behavioral authoritarianism implied in such a position. Although in his devotion to regional dialect, Yeats appears to be arguing for a wider definition of poetic speech and national identity, Moore suspects that he, like the pious Martyn, is actually searching for a single authoritative mode buttressed by the rhetoric of origin. In the first volume of *Hail and Farewell,* Moore recalls his own attraction to the idea of a pure and "unpolluted" original expression. Asked to give a speech at a literary luncheon, the narrator offers remarks that repeat almost verbatim "A Plea for the Soul of the Irish People," an essay Moore published in early 1901. Those ideas, which Yeats "begged of me not to go back upon," amount to a theory that "language after a time becomes like a coin too long current—the English language had become defaced, and to write in English it was necessary to return to the dialects. Language rises like a spring among the mountains; it increases into a rivulet; then it becomes a river (the water is still unpolluted), but when the river has passed through a town the water must be filtered. And Milton was mentioned as the first filter, the first stylist" (*HF* 235, 234).

As recounted in *Hail and Farewell,* the argument of his 1901 essay is undercut in several ways, most obviously the comic reduction of the Latinophile Milton to a filter that cleans polluted water of urban wastes. And by depicting the responses to his speech, Moore indicates that the idea of an "unpolluted" original language easily becomes the vehicle of other, related, authoritarian agendas.

Several of his phrases "intended to capture the popular ear" are cheered as he shouts them above the rattle of coffee cups, implying that the notion of a communal language is most zealously embraced by a mob mentality. Among his listeners at the luncheon are priests whose faces cloud at the "phrase that Ireland's need was not a Catholic, but a Gaelic University" (*HF* 235). Edward Martyn remonstrates that "Gaelic and Catholicism went hand in hand," and this hint of the authoritarianism the language movement by its very nature shares with the Catholic Church was "a remark which I did not understand at the time, but I learnt to appreciate it afterwards" (*HF* 235). Both Yeats and Martyn agree that a communal Irish consciousness could be revealed in uncorrupted language, and for this reason Yeats's belief in the supremacy of dialect parallels rather than contrasts with Edward Martyn's dogged reiteration that "I like the English language and I like the Irish, but I hate the mixture." As a parodist, Moore, in contrast, recognizes all language to be a mixture; as a realist he finds literary possibility everywhere, even in the most impure waters. He rejects the idea of communal authorship preached by his colleagues precisely because it limits rather than opens the possibility of what makes up the authorial voice and, by extension, the subject self.

In an irony that seems less than fully self-conscious, Moore's decision to stand outside of and to satirize the community of speakers he found in Dublin marks his participation in a well-established tradition of Irish satirists. Modern Irish autobiography may well be rooted more truly in satire than in any other form of discourse. Frequently, the speaker acts as an "editor" of the speech of others, a medium for gossip, plagiarism, and libelous invention. It is worth recalling that, as one scholar concludes, in early Irish literature "destructive spells and poems of slander or abuse were all thought of together as the work, and it sometimes seems almost the chief work, of the tribal man of letters."[12] Satire was so fully a part of early Irish culture as to be regulated by law. Centuries later, Moore's method brings in precisely those types of satire specifically indicated in ancient laws: a nickname that clings, recitation of a satire in the absence of its subject, satirizing of the face, laughing at all aspects of a subject, sneering at bodily form, and magnifying a blemish![13] Parody, in particular, was also an immensely popular form in the Paris of the 1880s and in such enclaves of British upper-class male society as Oxford and Cambridge. Yet a wide variety of evidence might be brought to support the premise that Moore's autobiography operates within a very localized world of Dublin art and politics where it was common and accepted practice to gossip furiously with little regard for fact, to openly attribute the wittiest sayings of others to oneself, and to admire the one whose oral and, in some cases, written satires were the most astute. In adopting the satiric voice Moore participates in a communal tradition, and in the autobiographies he provides original adaptations (an oxymoron perfectly in accordance with his theory) of a culturally inscribed practice of seeing oneself most fully through other people's voices, voices over which the ultimate speaker may exert imaginative sovereignty.

Within the Irish satiric community, art acts, then, as a display of dominance as well as a compendium of double-voicings, and the presentation of the public voice of "the author" remains paramount. When Colonel Moore objects that the narrator has spoiled his case against Cardinal Newman through ridiculous exaggerations, the narrator responds, "My concern is neither to overstate nor to understate, but to follow my own mind, faithfully, tracing its every turn" (*HF* 396). In the effort to trace that turning mind, the writer is at liberty to double-voice even his own prior utterances. Frequently repeating choice phrases within one work, or more commonly utilizing phrases from earlier texts in later ones, Moore disavows any guilt over this "auto-plagiarism"—to use the term Vladimir Nabokov invents to describe his own autobiographical practices. Early in *Hail and Farewell,* the narrator complains that while a sketch of his mother would be appropriate "in the present text," he has already written one in *Memoirs of My Dead Life* that is unfortunately too long to repeat, and "paraphrase is out of the question to a man who has written something that he felt deeply, and written, he thinks, truly" (*HF* 229). Were the portrait not overly long, he would simply incorporate it without scruple.

Moore's concern appears to lie always with the present articulative context rather than the original source of his language. He regularly had friends and paid assistants draft passages on topics with which they had a special familiarity, and he was not above "lifting" passages from published works without crediting the original authors.[14] He was unperturbed by the very accurate observations of his plagiarisms as a novelist and frequently tossed aside the issue by quipping that as quotations spoil the appearance of a text, his task in using others' materials was to search for synonyms. To a degree, he is describing the method by which he taught himself to write: "I always had a good memory," he recalls in a letter, "and I remembered all odd words and phrases, I strove to use them afterwards and I imitated the style of the author I was reading."[15] While it is true that the method of his self-education and the cultural milieu in which he lived might both encourage and even legitimize frequent borrowing, Moore also held to the concept of a single authorship, especially from a financial perspective. Although he often invited collaborations, he was incapable of relinquishing sufficient authorial control, and invariably the efforts ended in his angry suspicion of theft. Clearly, conflicting cultural expectations influence his concept of authorship.

The cultural expectations in question are, again, derived from that modern and localized milieu of literate satirists who repeated each other's best anecdotes, topped each other's invectives, and delivered with few qualms what Oliver St John Gogarty called in the subtitle of one of his autobiographies, "Phantasy in Fact." Of another sort of tradition, that of the communally authored folk tale or legend, Moore frequently counters his praise with misgivings over the lack of a prevailing authorial personality in either teller or tale. *A Story-Teller's Holiday* pits Moore, "the shanachie of Ballinrobe" in a contest with the peasant Alec Trusselby, "the shanachie of Westport." As Moore characterizes his rival, "when he is not telling a story he is as common, as witless, as any man picked out of the streets of Westport. . . . Not himself but his beautiful story is worth considering—the beautiful story whose origin we must seek further back than the Middle Ages" (*STH* 1:202). Pondering Alec's uninteresting character, he wonders that "very little of his gift of story-telling is personal to him—to himself. But can anyone say: This much belongs to me and to no one else? Is not all reflection and derivation?" (*STH* 1:173). Unwilling to repudiate the idea of personal authorship, he quickly dismisses "this blind alley" of inquiry, coming again to a temporary stalemate.

In contrast, the operas of Wagner provide an exemplary instance of individual genius and collectively authored tradition coming together to make a music that is autobiographical while also achieving the status of a cultural epic. Moore pivotally locates his extended sequence on Wagner near the beginning of *Hail and Farewell*. While Wagner worked from ancient stories, Moore would never categorize him, as he does his fellow Irish writers, as a mere "translator." In recognition of the intense individuality of Wagner's communally based art, the narrator responds to Wagner's music by meditating on the life and personality of "the Master." Moore's own text is also personal and autobiographical, but its place as a cultural epic comes about through its satiric exposure of the impossibility of re-creating Wagnerian art in Catholic Ireland. As a mock-heroic epic, it does not discredit the epic form or ambition, but a cultural situation that makes possible only the production of a comic inversion.

It is precisely within this comic mode that Moore is confident of his capacity to shape his borrowed materials in a way that will display a personality, so placing him in league with Wagner and surpassing his literary colleagues. In a letter to an American acquaintance, he writes, "I shall begin to write the book of my life, a[n] autobiography in three volumes, a book everybody will think very disgraceful, but which will sell longer than any of my novels. I do not feel that I can write novels as well as other people, I mean as well as Balzac or Turguenieff, but I do think I can write auto-biography as well as anyone that has yet written it. And this last sentence will tell you how the whole book will be written—with perfect candour and complete shamelessness" (*GMP* 123– 24). In addition to commercial success, he imagines artistic hegemony, as Wagner and Manet—neither writers nor Irishmen—remain his only rivals. Moore's use of double-voiced language in his autobiographies, like his temporary infatuations with various fictional models, thus gives evidence to Linda Hutcheon's idea that "the structural parodic act of incorporation and synthesis (whose strategy or function for the reader . . . is paradoxically one of ironic contrast or separation) might be seen as the means for some writers to shake off stylistic influences, to master and so supersede an influential predecessor. . . . Parody would then be one more mode to add to Harold Bloom's catalog of ways in which modern writers cope with the 'anxiety of influence.'"[16]

Moore might never "write novels as well as" Balzac did, but he has given himself an imposing rival in terms of originality. In an earlier essay on Balzac, Moore concludes that "As God is said to have created Adam from a handful of clay, so did Balzac create the French novel."[17] In *Hail and Farewell,* such originality is attributed only to "Banva," but as discussed in the previous chapter, "Banva" turns out to be a satiric mirror held by the autobiographer, George Moore: one who can also outdo his French progenitor. Upon hearing that the editor of the *Daily Express* wishes to meet him, the narrator remembers having read the previous winter "a newspaper so confused and disparate that I had never been able to imagine what manner of man its editor might be" (*HF* 121). At first it seems to the narrator that "only Balzac could solve the problem; only he could imagine the inevitable personality of the editor of the *Daily Express*," but upon further consideration it rests undecided as to "whether his father was Balzac or Turgenev." With no clear authorship in few, it becomes Moore's work to have T. P. Gill reborn into a new life as Flaubert's Pecuchet. Here Moore invokes parody not to deride Flaubert but to declare himself again a Frenchman, to mix his voice with that of the great French realist in order to develop through analogy a story he finds more original than any of Balzac or Turgenev. Because his characters have nonfictional referents and the hope of a nation behind them, he implicitly offers his story as more pathetically tragic and more ludicrously comic than even Flaubert's.

In *Hail and Farewell*, Moore's transposition of literature and gossip repeatedly assumes a confident authority over the previously read or spoken word. In a paradigmatic act of assimilation, the narrator creates a comic parody of Swinburne's quotation of the last words of the Emperor Julian. He plans to have Gogarty, the master of parody in verse, polish the lines somewhat. If the process continues as other such borrowings do, the reader might assume that he would retrieve and offer under his own name Gogarty's correction of his parody of Swinburne's quotation of the Emperor's words. The process begins to sound much like Yeats's plan for *Diarmuid and Grania,* with the crucial difference that no consensus is needed between the collaborators. This digression takes place as the narrator considers how, since the Council of Trent, Catholicism's monological doctrine has suppressed personality and art. His wildly playful manipulation of multiple sources evinces his own rejection of authoritarian control over language while it also implies the primacy of the final speaker.

Other parodies are similarly motivated by the urge to dominate, but simultaneously reveal the impossibility of being a truly original speaker. The narrator bemoans having lost the habit of reading; Shakespeare, Dostoyevsky, Sterne, and Cervantes all fall from his lap, and yet he attests to having acquired an ability superior to that of reading: thinking, which for Moore means remembering. From these memories, he creates for the reader *Hail and Farewell,* a book that draws from and resembles all of those the narrator cannot read.[18] If the narrator rejects his language's dependency upon pre-existent forms, the author develops parallels with those books his narrator supposedly never reads and exposes his own recognition of and dependency upon prior texts. In a 1914 letter to Edmund Gosse, Moore acknowledges the pressure of tradition and bewails the incapacity of his "individual talent" to blossom without its influence, regretting that "no likeness of Sterne could appear in my poverty-stricken prose. Ah Gosse, it is a pity that I would not read when I was young. It is impossible to write a language that has been in wear for three hundred years without study" (BK 86).

As Moore bewails what he feels to be his insufficient grasp of literary language, he comically postulates the autobiographical subject as an assemblage of the language of the world about him. At the same time, he postulates a single, authorial presence in command of its own nature. He stands equally ambivalent regarding the historical (and anatomical) materialism requisite to parody and caricature and the subjective interpretations from which both modes originate. Arguably, it is the comedy—the parody and caricature—of *Hail and Farewell* that most destabilizes the individual voice and demands the historicization of language. In this sense, Moore's comedy is the least conservative aspect of his lifework if conservatism is to be defined as individualist or, more broadly, as that which defends whatever is empowered at present. It has been frequently argued that individualist ideas of the self both derive from and in turn promote capitalist relations; the development of autobiography, consequently, has commonly been paralleled with the development of bourgeois capitalism. Satire is also frequently aligned with conservative political and cultural ideologies.[19] Yet this man who makes blatant essentialist proclamations concerning his "instinct," who depicts himself as a godlike author immune from communal ties, and who affixed himself to the upper reaches of conservative European society (as well as the urban bohemianism it patronized), effectively disrupts such claims through the methodology of his satiric autobiography.

Satire and parody have been defined as reactionary forms that act in one of two ways: either as attacks upon emerging alternatives that threaten to replace current powers or as attacks upon current powers that have displaced older authoritative forms. As Maynard Mack defines satire in his 1951 essay, "The Muse of Satire," it "asserts the validity and necessity of norms, systematic values, and meanings that *are* contained by recognizable codes . . . madness and blindness are usually the emblems of vice and folly, evil and good are clearly distinguishable, criminals and fools are invariably responsible (therefore censurable), and standards of judgment are indubitable."[20] As a form of satire, parody has been characterized by critics as diverse as Bakhtin, Barthes, Kristeva, and Jameson as a "legalized transgression," a mode that depends upon the recognized authority of that which it mocks, and which is therefore never truly subversive.[21] Linda Hutcheon provides a valuable corrective in her detailed argument as to why parody is never necessarily or inherently tied to one political agenda or another. She concludes,

> The presupposition of both a law and its transgression bifurcates
> the impulse of parody: it can be normative and conservative, or it

can be provocative and revolutionary. . . . [P]arody can suggest a 'complicity with high culture . . . which is merely a deceptively off-hand way of showing a profound respect for classical-national values' . . . or it can appear as a parasitical form, mocking novelty in the hope of precipitating its destruction (and, by implication, its own). Yet parody can, like the carnival, also challenge norms in order to renovate, to renew. In Bakhtin's terminology, parody can be centripetal—that is, a homogenizing, hierarchicizing influence. But it can also be a centrifugal, de-normatizing one. . . . Parody is normative in its identification with the Other, but it is contesting in its Oedipal need to distinguish itself from the prior Other.[22]

In *Hail and Farewell*, what Hutcheon calls the "paradox of parody"—its simultaneous incorporation and contestation of established forms—requires careful attention in part because Moore uses many forms of double-voiced language for various purposes, and in part because of the unusual historical situation in which he wrote. As Moore parodies his Irish contemporaries, attacking the very consciousness that produces their language, his rhetorical context becomes a crucial element: from what position does he speak, about what, and to whom? What Bakhtin calls an "externally authoritative discourse" figures in neither his own voice nor that which he parodies.[23] He cannot be said to speak from the most privileged position of power. As a colonized people, the Irish remained on the outside of normative English values; within the Ireland of the early twentieth century, economic and cultural relations had undergone such rapid and recent change as to make very difficult the identification of any one authoritative discourse within that nation. While the revivalists sought a language to articulate an essential Irish identity, their effort stayed at least one remove from the center of much Irish life. The language of the revivalists was by no means a principal, authorized discourse. As he represents himself in *Hail and Farewell*, Moore was a peripheral member of a peripheral movement in a peripheral nation.[24] If, as Linda Hutcheon notes, parody can rework forms that have become tyrannical, then the Celtic Twilight so parodied was, in Moore's mind, only a hapless tyranny of those with negligible influence over culture, revolutionaries whose cause he determines to be "a bubble." In the first paragraphs of *Hail and Farewell*, Edward Martyn blurts out that he'd like to write plays in Irish, and the narrator replies with amazement, "I thought nobody did anything in Irish except bring turf from the bog and say prayers" (*HF* 55). Three volumes later, he returns to the same conclusion; the life of poverty and piety articulated by that once-forbidden language of the outsider prevails still in the country of outsiders from whom he must live in exile.

In his study of parodic narrative satires, Frank Palmeri argues that satires which, like Moore's, involve no one authoritative discourse, create an "ongoing dialogicality that inverts the original inversion . . . divides the authority that informs the text, undercutting every singular perspective." He describes a "resulting multivoicedness, the unresolved clash of multiple alternatives," which certainly figures in *Hail and Farewell*. Palmeri argues that such dialogical satires, as I have claimed *Hail and Farewell* to be, most frequently appear at "certain historical moments—periods of collision between one cultural paradigm and an alternative."[25] *Hail and Farewell* indeed does take place during a period of experimentation and open competition for ideological authority in Ireland, making the identification of any externally authoritative discourse even more difficult. Given the univocal nature of much autobiographical expression, dialogical satire may be a surprising direction for an autobiographer to take. However, this "unresolved clash of multiple alternatives" is consistent with Moore's earlier representations of both the setting and the subject self. As in early works like *A Drama in Muslin* or *Parnell and His Island*, he depicts Ireland as a nation trapped by its inflexible religious and cultural attitudes, yet without stability and order. And since his first autobiography, Moore had set the subject self in opposition to nearly every form of preexistent life, stressing as essential to survival his protean capacity to embrace paradox and change.

If there is a cultural norm operative in Moore's work, it is, as ever, the Paris he experienced in the 1870s, a world alive only in his memory. His satire might be thus classified as conservative and nostalgic, except that this Parisian model was never Ireland's to begin with, and Dublin's transformation into Paris would involve a cultural revolution rather than a recovery. In the early editions of *Hail and Farewell*, Moore included an optimistic prediction that through the presence of French impressionist art, Irish people could develop the love of life that would then inspire great literature, art, and music. Without any apparent irony, he incorporated into his text a previously published essay in which he argues that impressionist painting could revitalize Ireland. In this instance, Moore seems to have fallen prey to the worship of the relic of which he accuses his compatriots. He imagines that a relic of Paris in the 1870s—the paintings Hugh Lane seeks to bring to Dublin—could potently transform the life about him and bring to Ireland the life of "la belle époque" of France. This section had been first delivered as a lecture in 1905, printed the next year as a monograph, and then used in *Hail and Farewell* until it was revised for the first Uniform Edition shortly before Moore's death. While his reasons for finally deleting the section will never be known, he may well have recognized that his narrator had, by the sixth chapter of "Vale," lost the innocence that could have allowed such optimism.[26]

If the Paris of the 1870s persists as the inviolable ideal, the only inviolable figures within the text, whose works are alluded to with reverence and with whom the narrator insinuates his own confederacy, are continental Europeans associated with music and painting rather than the verbal arts. Wagner and Manet occupy privileged positions: thus the long section that takes Moore to Bayreuth at the book's beginning and the extended memoir of the impressionists with which *Hail and Farewell* draws to an end. Moore uses the work of these two figures as what Bakhtin calls "internally persuasive discourse": a way of thinking to which one ascribes, and which, in turn, is assimilated. "Its creativity and productiveness," Bakhtin argues, "consist precisely in the fact that such a word awakens new and independent words. . . . It is not so much interpreted by us as it is further, that is, freely, developed, applied to new material, new conditions; it enters into interanimating relationships with new contexts."[27] The persuasive word in *Hail and Farewell* is best described as a faith in the subjective, even eccentric, reading of a carefully observed exterior life. In terms that might also flatteringly describe *Hail and Farewell* and the autobiographical persona he develops therein, Moore discusses Manet's work and character:

> It is often said that the personality of the artist concerns us not, and in the case of bad Art it is certainly true, for bad Art reveals no personality, bad Art is bad because it is anonymous. The work of the great artist is himself, and, being one of the greatest painters that ever lived, Manet's Art was all Manet . . .
>
> The artist must arrive at a new estimate of things; all must go into the melting-pot in the hope that out of the pot may emerge a new consummation of himself. . . . Art is a personal rethinking of life from end to end, and for this reason the artist is always eccentric. He is almost unaware of your moral codes, he laughs at them when he thinks of them, which is rarely, and he is unashamed as a little child. The word unashamed perhaps explains Manet's art better than any other. (*HF* 531–32, 533)

Personality is here a talismanic word, signifying both the origin and the product of one's work. Manet works as the artist, the melting pot, and the made object in a triadic sequence not unlike that of *Confessions of a Young Man*'s image of the autobiographer as architect of his own pyramid and the maker of his own mummy from the base material of his own corpse. As Moore describes Manet, personality (Moore might allow "instinct" here in substitution) is the crucible into which is poured experience. From these given ingredients, he concocts an art that will then display the artfully created persona, the "new consummation of himself." While the analogy between a writer and a "chef des sauces" invoked the Carlylian reductionism of "cookery," the model of the artist as chef or metalworker approaches the symbolist model of the artist-alchemist. The discussion of Manet displays common ingredients of the fin de siècle idea that art is exclusively a reflection of its creator and that the artist displayed in his work is entirely a product of deliberate construction.

However, in his focus upon Manet as a human being (and a similar focus upon the personalities and physiognomies of lesser artists), Moore qualifies any clear assertion of the artist as exclusively a product of his own mind. Moore's discussion of personality in art echoes the mid-Victorian concern with art as a revelation rather than a creation of the authorial personality. In an essay on Victorian parody, Terry Caesar remarks that Victorian aesthetics "stressed the content over the form . . . and, more, the inseparability of each from the man who authored it." He cites Cardinal Newman's 1858 essay, "Literature," which asserts that a writer's work transmits "the faithful expression of his intense personality . . . so that we might as well say that one man's shadow is another's as that the style of a really gifted mind can belong to any but himself. It follows him about *as* a shadow. His thought and feeling are personal, and so his language is personal." Caesar goes on to argue that parody, in contrast, exposes "that this is not so. Language does not originate with the individual. The very assumption of one man's verbal manner by another reveals it to be, alas, just that: a manner, or at least a structure of mannerisms. His personal speech is seized by its public face, whereupon it can be manipulated as so much rhetoric. . . . It was left to the parodists to reveal that literature is made not out of men but out of words."[28]

While many Victorians might have believed art to be a reflection of the author's morality, they nevertheless exercised a seemingly insatiable appetite for literary parody which, as Caesar argues, indicates a contradictory position. Moore's own view seems to reconcile these contradictions while eluding certain aspects of the question. In his dissection of Cardinal Newman's own language, Moore's purpose is less to expose Newman's personal lackings than to expose the failings he believes typical of the Catholic mind. While Newman the man is made to look foolish, Moore's concern centers upon the words themselves as an inadequate means of perception, words incapable of producing men who could, in turn, make better words that might then lead to more intensely experienced lives. Arguing implicitly the inseparability of culture, language, and the individual who creates and is created by such forces, Moore tempers his assertions of the independent life of individual genius. As artist and human being, Moore's persona is set within a world of literature and talk as a reviser rather than as a pure inventor.

Yet if Manet emerges from the melodious syllables, the sunshine, and the excellent food of France, whence comes Moore? From what he would call a priest-ridden, poverty-stricken, damp and boggy country of ruin and weed? Moore might answer, as he does throughout his career, that his unchanging and infallible instinct—an impulse toward genius of transcendental origin, beyond history or heredity—drives the whole process of his writing and living. Moore's enactment of this most essential contradiction of his lifework is especially striking in *Hail and Farewell*'s treatment of memory and gossip, two forms in which the most ostensibly personal discourse is found to be inexorably intertwined with the shared speech of a culture.

Reading One's Memory in Literature; Dispersing Oneself in Gossip

While the significance of memory in George Moore's construction of the self will be most fully explored in the final chapter of this book, several issues are critical to a study of Moore's postulation of the subject self within a world of double-voiced language. *Hail and Farewell* as a whole might be read as an extended consideration of the nature of memory, but two sections manifest perhaps the fullest emotional texture and the most provocative ideas. Both involve "the old life" of Mayo. The first, Moore's extravagant portrait of a man he calls his cousin Dan, comes immediately at the beginning of the book. The second, his memories of childhood and youth, makes up the major part of the final volume as he seals his estrangement from the colonel, the Irish revivalists, and Ireland itself.

If he is not indeed a fictional composite, Dan could well protest, as the colonel really did, that Moore transformed him into a character of fiction. In the short story "Enoch Soames," Max Beerbohm tells of a hopelessly ephemeral writer who sells his soul to Mephistopheles in exchange for the opportunity to visit the Reading Room of the British Museum one hundred years hence to see if he appears in the card catalog. Finding himself listed only as a character in a short story by Max Beerbohm, he reproaches his author with the accusation, "You aren't an artist. . . . And you're so hopelessly not an artist that, so far from being able to imagine a thing and make it seem true, you're going to make even a true thing seem as if you'd made it up. You're a miserable bungler. And it's like my luck."[29] While Dan and the colonel may seem "made up," that impression is due not to any "bungling" on Moore's part, but is the result of his capacity to create portraits that are so vivid and immediate that no extratextual information is required to make them fully realized characterizations.

Like most of Moore's familial memories, their stories are related solely to the reader rather than other characters, and the reader is brought into the illusion of intimacy with these memories. In the section that closes *Hail and Farewell*, the recollections of the brothers' boyhood are given with Maurice himself serving as interlocutor and audience, a role that the narrator has previously assigned him as stand-in for the eventual reader. This rhetorical frame even further enhances the aura of intimacy between writer and reader. We are thus brought into what seem to be the most deeply felt and personal memories. Yet fairly soon into the "Overture," the whole cozy alliance falls abruptly away when the narrator confesses that his memories are so intermeshed with the stock scenes and types of the nineteenth-century Irish novel as to blur the lines between a past "read" through memory and interpretation and a past literally "read" somewhere in a book. And most mournfully, Moore also suggests that memories, being dependent upon the absence of that which is remembered, imply always the transience of experience, the soon-to-be-lost life even of one who remembers. Memory—on which the self is constructed—becomes a pungent reminder of its fragility.

The first of these sections begins as the narrator strolls outside his London lodgings, pondering what kind of a book might be written about Ireland, a place of ruins both human and architectural. As the people of his Mayo past come to mind, he remarks, "to me they are clearer than they were in life, because the present changes so quickly that we are not aware of our life at the moment of living it. But the past never changes; it is like a long picture-gallery. . . . a cloth will fall as if by magic, revealing a forgotten one, and it is often as clear in outline and as fresh in paint as a Van der Meer" (*HF* 58). His thoughts seem to identify a past that is stable and recoverable, yet this is a past painted, aestheticized, and recoverable only as such. Augustine agonized over the subjective and selective nature of memory, but Moore does not expect personal memory to conform with any more authoritative version of events, be it God's or other people's. In compensation for the isolation of consciousness implicit within this doctrine of idiosyncratic memory, the past recalled from it can be at least grasped, possessed as events could not be while experienced. Near the end of the section, the narrator admires the lovely pattern of a leaf and "forgetful of my tale," thinks "how intense life seems here in this minute! Yet in a few years my life in the Temple will have passed, will have become as dim as those years of Dan's life in Dunamon. But are these years dim or merely distant" (*HF* 70)? The narrator of *Hail and Farewell* fears most the dimness of the past, suggesting that the real significance of the past lies in its capacity to play an active role in the narrating imagination. And the significance of the present lies in its eventual transformation into the stock of memory. Attention to the "intense life" of the moment, in contrast, requires the narrator to forget rather than develop his story.

Memory is interwoven with the act of telling stories and inseparable from them. While it may be subjective and peculiar, narrative memory is as dependent upon words as a painting is upon paint, and similarly indebted to generic expectations. Anticipating the postmodern contention that what we call a life story originates in given forms of storytelling, Moore's reflections imply what he later explicitly affirms, that as memories emerge in the process of composition, remembering and writing inevitably follow the forms required by previously existing utterances; in this case, that of the nineteenth-century "Big House" novel. Perhaps the best book about Ireland, the narrator decides in the "Overture," would be "a man's book, and it should be made of the life that lingered in Mayo till the end of the 'sixties: landlords, their retainers and serfs." At that decision, another type of memory "rose up before me," more fitted to the narrative expectations of the chosen literary form.

Moore then interfuses the language of fiction with that of personal memory. The story of a landlord at hounds and the peasants who follow him soon deteriorates into the trite phrases of its genre. Just as the story seems pure literature (and hackneyed literature at that), we discover that it is indeed memory, "the very words of the tinkers chiming in my head after many years." George Henry Moore is mentioned, and although his name would seem to be a signal that we are in the realm of memory, he makes his appearance as a character in "the novel I was dreaming." In a moment of compromise between memory and invention, the narrator announces that a scene between Dan and his pretty peasant mistress, Bridget, was never witnessed by anyone, "but it must have happened just as I tell it."

Confronting directly what he had handled obliquely in previous books, Moore considers both the epistemological questions of how fiction and memory intertwine and the ethical questions deriving from the rendering of real people into literature. If he is truly proud of "the tradition in the West that my family never yielded to such indulgences as peasant mistresses or the esuriences of hot punch," why, the narrator asks himself, "do you lift the veil on Dan's frailties?" His answer is fourfold: the preservation of Dan's memory, revenge upon Dan for having encouraged him to back the wrong horses, testimony to that which was best in Dan ("his love of beauty"), and, finally, the excellent story that it all makes. He writes, "It is no part of my morality to urge that nobody's feelings should be regarded if the object be literature. But I would ask why one set of feelings should be placed above another? Why the feelings of my relations should be placed above Dan's? For, if Dan were in a position to express himself now, who would dare to say that he would like his love of Bridget to be forgotten?" (*HF* 69). Dead for many years, Dan is not in a position to express himself, and the narrator imperiously recruits his memory into the literary camp. A Dan willing to be remembered for his love of the pretty Bridget is one who would stand with the narrator in defense of art against the pious Catholic relatives who would rather suppress the story.

According to Joseph Hone, Moore frequently remarked that "a man can only have one sort of conscience . . . and mine is a literary one" (*LGM* 309). As the literary conscience activates, it finds Dan and Bridget too predictable for its purposes, and as he considers the variety of stories which circulated as to Bridget's later years, the narrator concludes,

> Bridget is a type in the West of Ireland, and I have known so many that perhaps I am confusing one story with another. For the

purpose of my book any one of these endings would do. . . . But
the end of a life is not a thing that can be settled at once, walking
about in moonlight, for what seems true then may seem fictitious
next day. And already Dan and Bridget had begun to seem a little
too trite and respectable for my purpose. When he came to be written out Dan would differ little from the characters to be found in
Lever and Lover. They would have served him up with the usual
sauce, a sort of restaurant gravy which makes everything taste alike,
whereas painted by me, Dan would get into something like reality.
(*HF* 72)

If his personal memories take their shape from the novels of Lever
and Lover, the narrator's ownership over them will be judged by the
skill of his presentation, just as literary parody asserts the dominance
of the ultimate voicing, despite the evidence of its language's origin
in some prior source. The language of others is scrutinized always
with an eye to its potential usefulness as literature. Recalling the
wildly colorful language of an anecdote told to him long ago by a
peasant, the narrator records that "I closed my eyes a little and
licked my lips as I walked, thinking of the pleasure it would be to tell
this story." Like a cat who has come across the hiding place of a
delectable mouse, he imagines with relish the future consumption of
the story as material for his own writing.

The narrator also imagines that in writing his projected novel he
could, like "the predestined hero whom Cathleen ni Houlihan had
been waiting for through the centuries," restore literature to Ireland. However, he falls into sorrow over his own belatedness, having
been too far removed from the life of the west and too unwilling to
return in order to write the story properly. The humor here resides
in his having already told the story, and superbly. The story has
come, however, as part of the autobiographical examination of his
own composition process. Neither the personal world of memories
nor the public world of fictional discourse takes precedence in his
imagination. He has found his story in the process of sorting
through both and discarding neither, as they are so fully integrated
that there is no access to one without the other. Indeed, one might
not even exist without the presence of the other.

Moore opens the final volume with the chapters that, as he mentioned to a correspondent in 1914, he had "for years . . . been looking forward to writing" (*LGM* 309). That enthusiasm animates the
warm, colorful detail with which he evokes his early life. The section

begins with family history and chronologically takes the narrator through his childhood and his early days in Paris. Later, *Hail and Farewell* returns to the Moore Hall of memory, as he and his brother recall together their boyhood there. In this last volume, the tone and framework of recollection differ considerably from the "Overture." As much as Moore had openly investigated the origins of memory in reading and the inseparability of the life story's content from its narrative conventions, these last recollections give a greater authority to personal memory. Regardless of their dialogical and parodic nature, Moore's own memories dominate the final volume, imaginatively overpowering the idealized Ireland variously projected by the Irish revivalists.

The narrator finds himself spending the long evenings in recollection because he cannot find a book to interest him and because his friends are unavailable, being currently immersed in their own reading. Resigning himself to his thoughts, the narrator reflects that "though I may have lost the habit of reading, I have acquired, perhaps more than any other human being, another habit, the habit of thinking. I love my own thoughts; and the past is a wonderful mirror in which I spend hours watching people and places I have known; dim, shadowy and far away they seem, and pathetic are the faces, and still more pathetic is the way everybody follows his little prejudices; however unreasonable they may be we must follow them" (*HF* 461). Moore brings together here the traditional conception of art as a mirror, the folkloric motif of the mirror as a diviner of people and things far away, and the more literal definition of a mirror as a reflection of the observing self. The mirror reflects the viewer who sees the shadowy past, the foundation of his autobiographical art. His own little prejudices are, after all, a part of what appears in the mirror. Commenting on this same passage, Ronald Schleifer notes that "reverie is the narrative mode of Moore's work, and in it he tries to capture and present, as Monet did, the evanescent past and present, not by reading but in thinking, by *interrupting* reading with thinking. Reading passively follows the past, what has come before, while thinking, more active than reading, joins and engages the present and the past. Thus Moore's 'thinking' attempts to achieve a state of conversation rather than the logic of plot."[30] Schleifer highlights the dialogical nature of recollection for Moore, as well as its function as a creative rather than preservationist activity.

This definition of the recollective act bears a great similarity to

Moore's theories of painting. He consistently sets forth the idea of a painting as a personal, impressionistic reading of a very carefully observed exteriority, be it a landscape or human form. Painting, like caricature, is dialogic: nature perceived and transformed by one who is himself a natural being. Immediately following this evocation of the inextricability of the past and the recollector of the past, the narrator engages in a seemingly digressive consideration of his brother's own "unreasonable prejudice," his allegiance to the church. This apparent digression on the subject of Colonel Moore actually develops the narrator's prior line of thinking. The colonel admits that he cannot accept the immortality of the soul because "if Death deprives me of my senses of feeling and seeing, of my intellect, of everything that is me, how can it be said that I exist? he asked. . . . How can it be said that I, the personality connoted by the pronoun, exist?" (*HF* 461). If we recall that both the narrator's characterization of memory and his meditation on his brother are preceded by his lament at his inability to read Dostoyevsky (as "impersonal and vague as Nature"), then this whole section works as an integrated statement concerning the primacy of individual perception as it transforms experience from the vagueness of nature to the precision of recollective art.

Between the rich and deeply expressive memories that follow this digression and the elegiac return to Moore Hall, which precedes the final flight from Ireland, Moore delivers his memoir of the impressionists to an unregenerate Ireland of Bouvards and Pecuchets, discovers himself impotent, and—moving time three years forward—regrets the passing of his former lover who died in childbirth after leaving him to marry another man presumably more sexually able than himself. The narrator also accepts a new mission of liberating Ireland from Catholicism by writing the epic *Hail and Farewell*, a mock-heroic scenario accompanied by strains of Wagnerian music and the announcement that "since the day I walked into my garden saying: Highly favoured am I among authors, my belief had never faltered that I was an instrument in the hands of the Gods" (*HF* 609). As he entertains his brother in Dublin and then visits him at Moore Hall, the narrator fuels his argument against the church, but because Moore sees the church as the force most responsible for the repression of personality, the sequence also functions as an assertion of personality and subjective memory against his brother's brand of revivalism.

Colonel Maurice Moore was a true revivalist. He supported efforts to reestablish Gaelic and develop Irish art, and later he served as a senator in the Free State. He spent much of his money and several years of his life attempting the restoration of Moore Hall as an inheritance for his children. The colonel left Moore Hall in the summer of 1911; according to Joseph Hone and as is evidenced by the tone of the brothers' correspondence, he no longer felt comfortable living in his elder brother's house or being under financial obligations to him. After an angry quarrel in 1913, the two were permanently estranged despite the colonel's attempts at reconciliation. He and his family were entirely excluded from his brother's will and received nothing for their efforts to restore Moore Hall. Considering that this final estrangement occurred before the publication of the final volume in 1914, it is remarkable that the characterization of the colonel is so genial. An undisturbed picture remains of a kind, intelligent, and generous idealist deluded by faith in the church and the nation and by the greatest delusion of all in Moore's eyes: that the past of their Irish childhood might, or should, be brought to life again.

Amid the colonel's money-saving plans for water closets and sawmills, the narrator interjects his memories of the "old life" of racehorses and politics, obsequious peasants, eccentric cousins, preposterous schoolmasters, and, most of all, a house that functioned as the center of the community of servants, tradesmen, and tenants that surrounded it. The narrator's rejection of his brother's dreams becomes increasingly impassioned until he bursts out, "My dear Maurice, Moore Hall was built in feudal times. Read the tablet over the balcony, 1790, and feudalism continued down to 1870; a big square house on a hill, to which the peasants came every morning to work." Following a tirade on the former centrality and present irrelevancy of the house, he continues, "Moore Hall is out of date, and it astonishes me that you don't feel it. I wish in a way that I could summon sufficient courage to pull it down and sell it; it would make excellent rubble to build labourer's cottages, and if I could I would cut down every tree and lay the hillside bare. Why not, since I know it will be laid bare a few yeas after my death?" (*HF* 634–35). Like his repudiation of his father, the anguished refusal to listen further to the colonel's plans for restoration marks Moore's absolute distinction between the world of recollective art—with its discipline, craft, and beauty—and the pitiful, underbudgeted, hopelessly jerry-built products of the man of action.

As the argument progresses, the colonel is more frequently interrupted and his words twisted away from him. Dialogue is subjugated to the monocratic voice of the individual whose memories are preeminent, regardless of the imaginative origins of memory disclosed in the "Overture." The scenario is set up as a dialogue, yet, like the dialogues within his volumes of imaginary conversations or the dialogue of his epistolary relationships, Moore's attempt is to control his speaking partner. In *Hail and Farewell* he depicts the varied roles of his narrator as a listener, a reviser, and, as in the last sections of *Hail and Farewell*, a speaker who silences the voices of others.

As oral discourse is represented in Moore's autobiographical prose, the narrator can modify, restate, amplify, or even retract a previous utterance. He can engage in dialogue with himself (while overheard by an explicitly acknowledged reader-listener), or he can provide the last word in a conversation with another. The voice emerges through ongoing dialogue and in the presence of at least one listener. It follows that, for Moore, the self cannot be imagined in any realm that is not, to some degree, a public one. While it has been argued by some theorists of narrative that the "conversation" between narrator and reader is grounded in the illusion of privacy, the controlled intimacy with the reader that Moore builds is best seen as an aspect of the larger public language of gossip in which *Hail and Farewell* operates.[31] On the one hand, he substitutes for confessional monologue or precatory explanations the illusion of an intimate conspiracy with the reader: the narrator gossips with the reader about himself and others; his slow, insinuating voice seduces the reader into sharing his secrets, observing his follies, and noting his development. On the other hand, like the gossip who cannot keep a secret, even about himself, the narrator frequently ventures into the street in search of a companion to whom he might tell what he has just revealed to the reader. As the author of "a novel about real people," George Moore tells stories told to him by others and that others will in turn tell. In contrast to Rousseau who, while divulging his personal tale, makes reference to an alien and hostile world of gossip against which his autobiography might act as shield, Moore imagines his own confession as a site from which gossip will flow and out of which will flow more gossip. By encouraging friends to read drafts of his book and by tantalizing them with tales of what he had written about them and their mutual acquaintances, he seems to have welcomed that very world of language beyond his text that Rousseau finds so endangering.[32] He positions the autobiographical persona in the only place he can imagine it to be—in the midst of others' conversations.

That most disreputable form of doubled-voiced language, gossip, is important to such varied texts as *Confessions of a Young Man* or *Conversations in Ebury Street*, but the role of gossip is markedly pronounced in *Hail and Farewell*. Gossiping is a frequently depicted activity within the text, and the autobiography itself was received as gossip within the community in which it was produced and intended to be read. Of greater significance to this study is the correlation between the multiple authorship of gossip and Moore's ideas concerning the authorship of the autobiographical subject. In her examination of gossip, Patricia Meyer Spacks divides the activity into three sorts: maliciously purposeful speech, idle talk whose main function is the assertion of the speaker's presence, and a method of serious self-reflection involving no more than two persons.[33] By offering his idle talk to a potentially unlimited number of listener-readers, Moore operates within the public modes of gossip that Spacks castigates as universally destructive. The strongly dialogic—and dialectical—nature of the gossip *Hail and Farewell* perpetuated cannot be overlooked. Although most of his contemporaries understood his book to be a comic fiction, it was simultaneously seen as a public conversation about private topics. One acquaintance, for example, advised Yeats to write in retaliation "a little book all about him by you," and nearly all those talked about in the text did reply to it in their own writings.[34] Some, like Yeats, waited until Moore was safely dead and beyond the power of landing the last barb. Yet biographical evidence suggests that, as with his practice of caricature, whatever malicious purposes Moore himself entertained, he was more than equally motivated by a desire to develop themes and characterizations as one would in a novel.[35] Idle talk forms the very structural principle of this otherwise invertebrate book. The idle talk of *Hail and Farewell* has the serious aim of cultural and aesthetic criticism, as well as generating the self-construction of the autobiographical subject.

Moore lures readers into accepting gossip as a means of reflective thinking and then forces them to acknowledge the nature of the gossiping activity. After the narrator listens to the story of Gill's beard as told by a young man seated next to him at an honorary dinner, he expresses his appreciation for this and the other information his young acquaintance has provided, but finds that his blatant identification of such discourse as gossip almost closes off this form of language he has found so valuable:

> An excellent story that probably started from some remark of Gill's, and was developed as it passed from mouth to mouth. A piece of folk. If a story be told three or four times by different people it becomes folk. You have, no doubt, stories of the same kind about everybody?
>
> This last remark was injudicious, for I seemed to frighten my neighbour, and I had some difficulty in tempting him into gossip again. (*HF* 132)

Moore dangles in front of his critics a syllogism that would "prove" that as (1) folk speech is what Irish art needs and (2) gossip is folk speech, then (3) Irish art must therefore need gossip. By thus usurping the revivalist preoccupation with the merits of communal folk speech, he mocks that preoccupation and legitimizes his own speech. He is also simultaneously exploiting and dismissing the anonymity implicit in the collective authorship of both folk art and gossip. In his criticism of Alec Trusselby, the shanachie of *A Story-Teller's Holiday*, he argued the inferiority of an art that does not reveal an authorial personality. Here, he adopts the subterfuge of a legitimatized form of communal authorship, folk speech, in order to cloak his use of the illegitimate anonymous form of discourse, gossip. But by repeating gossip to the reader, Moore exposes his part in the authorship of that which has by this time, according to his syllogism, been rendered a form of art needed by Ireland. His dinner companion, however, retreats terrified at seeing his own signature on that particular title page.

While Moore's companion feels threatened by the prospect of being quoted as a repeater of gossip, Moore suggests that there is much greater danger in being talked about. When the narrator dismisses his compatriots as merely the subject material of literature rather than its producers, he suggests that little could be worse than to lose the position of speaker, even if one's discourse actually originates elsewhere or even if one is the subject of one's own gossip. Yeats bitterly remarks in "Dramatis Personae" that Moore "would destroy his reputation, or that of some friend, to make his audience believe that the story running in his head at the moment had happened, had only just happened."[36] Whether or not Yeats's assessment is accurate or fair, his observation corroborates the impression given in *Hail and Farewell* of a man for whom the position of speaker is the preeminent condition requisite to the construction and affirmation of the self.

Moore implies that positioning oneself as a speaker of gossip releases one from responsibility for its origin: if, that is, we accept the syllogism that transforms gossip into folk speech and folk speech into a communally authored form of art. Placement as the subject of gossip, however, can be dangerous if one is not also in the position of speaker or, even more crucially, in the position of writer. Oral discourse at least allows for immediate revisions and correction, and oral gossip may also remain within the relatively safe sphere of private conversation. In an 1898 letter to Maud Cunard, Moore remarks, "As for the news and gossip, that too is amusing but one cannot often write it . . . ink is an adjuvant which develops a dangerous quality in harmless ingredients" (*LLC* 29). This menacing possibility is realized in *Hail and Farewell* when the narrator recalls the journey taken through the Low Countries to look at art with "Stella" (Clara Christian), the woman who was to become his lover and accompany him to Dublin, and her friend "Florence": "An account of our aesthetic and sentimental tour would make a charming book; our appreciations of Ruysdael, Hals, Rembrandt and Van der Meer, and Florence's incautious confession that no more perfect mould of body than Stella's existed in the flesh—perhaps in some antique statues of the prime, though even that was not certain" (*HF* 183).

Why is such a confession "incautious"? Why does he repeat it and what does it cost him to do so? The reader can only hypothesize. The confession may have been incautious in that the narrator was thereby tantalized to pursue "Stella" and to disrupt the partnership between the two women who had been living and painting together and whose friendship apparently ended after Clara Christian became involved with Moore.[37] The confession may also have been incautious in that it intimates homoerotic feeling either on the part of "Florence" or between the two women. "Stella" is violated as the object of gossip, "Florence" is endangered through her authorship of it as well as her role as its object, and Moore might be censured for ungentlemanly behavior in repeating the story. But he who writes with "perfect candour and complete shamelessness" would dismiss any such charge as irrelevant, for by repeating "Florence's" confession he adds intriguing depth to these two otherwise minor characters in his book. By identifying himself as the transmitter of gossip, the primary function of which is aesthetic, Moore adds to his honor as the author of the text's design while refusing the responsibility of originating such a piece of intimate information.

From allusion, quotation, and parody to the equally mixed voices discovered in recollective utterance or gossip, Moore exhibits the multiplicity of sources from which autobiographical speech is generated. In his literary caricature, Moore's interpretive act openly depends upon cultural interpretations of the physical body; in his far-reaching use of parodic language, he indicates again the historical consciousness that tempers his assertions of his capacity to originate the self. Even the predominance of the autobiographer's final voice is undercut by Moore's exposure of its origins and contextual life. Wayne Shumaker has argued that the characterizations, images, and formal elements of *Hail and Farewell* all serve to advance what he identifies as Moore's ultimate purpose: to demonstrate the incompatibility of literature and Catholicism.[38] While I would dissent from this definition of Moore's intent as too narrowly that of his narrator, I would agree that, with unfailing precision and subtle juxtaposition of detail, Moore argues over three volumes the incompatibility of art and any exclusive claims to an authoritative discourse. As I shall next examine, George Moore's voluminous correspondence as well as his efforts in the epistolary novel and the "imaginary conversation" mark again his attempts to dominate the terms of exchange while, at the same time, engaging with great relish the other voices that challenge his own.

6

Writing the Life in Dialogue
Letters, Epistolary Novels, and Imaginary Conversations

> I become myself only by revealing myself to another,
> through another and with another's help. The most
> important acts, constitutive of self-consciousness, are
> determined by their relation to another conscious-
> ness. . . . To be means to be for the other, and
> through him, for oneself.
> —Mikhail Bakhtin,
> "Toward a Reworking of the Dostoevsky Book"

I F *Hail and Farewell* DEMONSTRATES MOORE to be an autobiographer whose voice openly displays its interfusion with the
voices of others, it should not be surprising that he was also attracted
to self-representation through letters and through essays in the form
of dialogues. Although as a writer he kept disciplined solitary routines, he also required near-instantaneous responses to the ideas developed in that solitude. Friends, acquaintances, and, for a period
of time, his brother Maurice were routinely sent drafts of work-in-
progress and called upon to answer his latest preoccupations
through conversation or letters. Ever-resistant to the telephone, he
was an inveterate correspondent who maintained numerous friendships for many decades with little contact beyond that of letters; in

some cases relationships were exclusively epistolary ones. For nearly forty years he wrote at frequent intervals to Maud Cunard and Edmund Gosse, although after 1911 he lived only a short drive away from either friend. His letters to Lady Cunard alone are thought to number in the thousands. Any sustained inquiry into Moore's theory and practice of self-construction must necessarily include an examination of the role of dialogue in the formation of his autobiographical voice.

Moore's achievements in what I have called "writing the life in dialogue" may be examined in terms of four distinct issues: the interplay between efforts at dominance and exchange in his letters and essay-dialogues; the creation of an epistolary persona and its relation to the autobiographical voice; the relationship between narrative and epistolary lifewriting; and the preoccupation with time and corporeal absence that emerges in Moore's erotic correspondence.

"There are claws in your velvet paws, my dear Gosse": Dominance and Exchange in the Epistolary Relation

As a boy of thirteen, George Moore was sentenced by his father to write home from boarding school a daily letter of three pages in an effort to improve his poor spelling, grammar, and handwriting. In the boy's desperate (and badly punctuated) complaints over such a loathsome task, certain characteristic gestures begin to appear. Through comic self-deprecation, assertions of goodwill, and what can only be described as a startling degree of presumption, he attempts to control the terms of the dialogue and involve his father in a self-serving collaboration: "It is of no good being cross with me any more," he writes, "if you will only correct the mistakes I make and send them to me I am sure that we by acting in concert will do a good deal more good than by scolding me. . . . I got a letter from my Aunt Browne who was kind enough to send me a post office order for a pound it was the hardest task I ever had to read her letter I will send you her letter by post. . . . Now my dear Papa we will be friends and you will not be cross with me any more I am sure that we will do much good if you will only follow the advice of this letter." With an audacity prefiguring that of his adulthood, the boy adds a postscript: "Please send me a translation of my aunt's letter I could only make out a little of it" (*LGM* 27).

The letters of Moore's maturity are not so different from this childhood effort. They remained casually punctuated and erratically spelled; more significant, however, he continues to invite his correspondents into an exchange as a stratagem to engineer his own dominance over the interchange. Just as he invites his father to cooperate in what is actually an effort to control the terms of letter-writing that had been set for him, so often the adult Moore asks for help, advice, and even affection while attempting to dominate the discourse of the relationship. These efforts can be seen both in his correspondence and in the essays he wrote in the form of imaginary conversations. In these essays, Moore's control over the whole is of course more certain; the dialogues are purely imaginary, and the simulated interchanges are planned and revised by their one author. Their failure to affectively reproduce the intersubjectivity of a dialogue can illuminate, by means of contrast, the nature of Moore's more successful ventures as a correspondent and as an autobiographer.

Unlike an actual correspondence, the imaginary conversation and the epistolary novel are produced by one omniscient author, and offer, at best, the illusion of intersubjectivity. It is in these subgenres that Moore demonstrates considerable difficulty representing the voices of others in a convincing manner. His epistolary novel *The Lake*, is a case in point. The young priest who is its protagonist learns through two important epistolary relationships to articulate the "instinct" that has lain dormant until the words of his correspondents stimulate his self-awareness. This process is rendered with great subtlety, and the story of Father Oliver's emergent consciousness is one of Moore's finest accomplishments. Yet, as Moore himself acknowledged, the letters of Rose Leicester were the least successful aspect of the 1905 version of the novel. When *The Lake* was extensively revised, few of her letters were retained. The choice was a wise one for many reasons, but perhaps most of all because Rose's letters distracted from what became a story singularly and unfailingly focused on one mind and its painful struggle to consciousness. Moore's autobiographies are resplendent with the voices of others, but controlling those voices is a narrating mind that filters, parodies, integrates, and utterly subjectifies them. The imaginary conversations, in contrast, present voices that speak independent of a narrator. If they do not appear as lively players in a narrator's fanciful meditations, neither do they emerge as rounded fictional characterizations. The interlocutors of *Conversations in Ebury Street* and *Avowals* (to whom Moore himself refers as "dummies" in his letters to Gosse) are wooden figures of undifferentiated speech, never realized as distinct individuals and never participating in any genuine dialogue.

The autobiographical persona is almost as colorless; in the midst of drawing-room conversations he can hardly indulge in his characteristic memorial reveries or confide the intimacies that Moore elsewhere proffers the conspiratorial reader. Nor do these conversations involve the element of suspense inherent in a letter exchange: the speaker is immediately answered and need not fear a letter's miscarriage or a possible misunderstanding of his words. Given these problems, why did the form appeal to Moore? In *Conversations in Ebury Street*, the autobiographical persona confesses that he is drawn to the form because he is "weary of essays, and I don't write them well." He planned to analyze various English novels after Defoe and to compare them with English poetry, but "this I could not do in an essay; the constant change of subject would have been irksome: to me at least it would have been" (*CES* 62). The attraction of the form would lie in its potential for easy management; it allows him to avoid the difficulties of sustaining a formal argument. But Moore's confessions are invariably as dubious as they are truthful. While the appearance of dialogue in the imaginary conversations is too often merely appearance, as a writer Moore is repeatedly drawn to the pretense, and one is pressed to consider why this is so.

The dialectic of genuine exchange has an unforeseeable and never entirely controllable direction: a condition with which Moore was distinctly uncomfortable. When Gosse objected to Moore's intent to replace him as a character in *Conversations in Ebury Street* with "a supposititious Mr. Arthur Mellowes," he rightly objected that "the whole point of a *dialogue* is gone if you argue with a non-existent adversary." In an earlier letter, he warned that "the thing will be great fun if you will only do it properly: but you start with the idea of humiliating your interlocutor, and I won't allow it. Come out in the open and be a hero."[1] Like the epistolary novel, the imaginary conversation represents a simulated rather than authentic exchange and may be planned and revised by its single author; but in order to be an effective simulation, it must imitate the way actual letters are formed with the addressee in mind.[2] Moore's imaginary conversations fail, as Gosse predicted, to allow that other voice in the dialogue a formative role. Moore appears to be nervous with even the most minor concession of autonomy (or autogeny) on the part of the primary speaking voice. "A letter is a bewildering thing," he writes. "Even the most ordinary letters often fill one with doubt."[3] In his efforts to circumvent the dangers of exchange (even a simulated exchange), Moore offers instead a monologue in two voices.

What I have called a monologue in the form of a conversation allows Moore to figure amid the world of process and change while remaining aloof from it. Despite the illusion of discussion, the opinions of the persona do not alter, time is relatively still, and while a setting is provided, there develops no narrative in which the voices can locate themselves. The autobiographies provide, in contrast, the story of both an individual and a culture in process. In *Confessions* and *Hail and Farewell,* the narrator is portrayed at the forefront of literary experimentation, but in both volumes of imaginary conversations the autobiographical persona poses as the last gentleman, a devotee of the eighteenth century and an elegist for the demise of English literature. In the narrator's aesthetic conservatism and in the calcified form Moore adopts, development has ceased and, with it, the dialectical process implicit in genuine exchange.

Like the imaginary conversations and his childhood letter to his father, the actual letters of his maturity articulate a resistance to the potential power of the other with whom he speaks. Moore solicits advice, but always of a practical nature and to aid him in reaching ambitions that have already been decided upon. A letter to his publisher T. Fisher Unwin provides an example. He requires suggestions as to how to modify his short story, "The Wild Goose," in order to avoid an outraged response on the part of reviewers. In the letter, however, he resolutely states, "I do not think you will deny that I have steered my course adroitly and avoided what would damage my reputation, advice. I think what really damages a reputation most is advice, and if I only take a little advice on this matter it will be because this is my firm belief" (*GMT* 267). Ironically but not atypically, a letter sent later on the same day indicates that Moore had, after all, taken Unwin's suggestions and thanks him for pointing out the "rigmarole" in his prose (*GMT* 270). His frequent requests for criticism from his friends almost invariably concern matters of style, and he could be effusive in his gratitude. With few exceptions, however, his ideological and artistic agenda remained unaltered.

The solicitation of practical help, a common feature of Moore's letters, is generally made in the defiant terms of his letter to Unwin, but in letters to friends like Dujardin and Eglinton the tone is muted by expressions of affection and self-depreciating references to his own ineptitude. And what I have been identifying as his strategies to dominate the epistolary dialogue are sometimes relinquished, particularly in the letters to Edmund Gosse. This is not to say that the letters to Gosse are utterly without attempts to dominate the relationship. Moore lectured Gosse at length about how to compose the work for which he is best known, *Father and Son,* and later took excessive credit for its success. Suggesting that they continue a discussion of the Romantic movement, he cannot resist adding, "I should like to for I think I have gotten you in a tight corner" (BK 130). His letters also frequently ask for public praise and quibble with Gosse's reviews of his own books. Yet both men utilized letters in such ways, and while Moore's letters are essayistic, they respond to and are altered by Gosse's own writing. The two men seem to have been temperamentally compatible: like Moore, Gosse's social interactions were characterized by what his biographer calls "a state of prickly agitation."[1] They were equally marked by hypersensitive egos and an absolute devotion to literature. Most of all, both men used their letters to pose, tease one another, and pontificate on a variety of subjects while entertaining carefully the views of the other in alternatingly caustic and affectionate terms.

A case in point is the dispute over Gosse's role in *Avowals.* The interlocutors of *Conversations in Ebury Street,* first published five years after *Avowals,* are a diffident lot: they timidly propose theories and cite various authorities, but rather quickly concede their points. They query, ask for further explanations and discriminations, but they are hardly allotted equal time to argue, and when they disagree, it is commonly with apologies and qualifications. Gosse was understandably uninterested in such a role, which is precisely what Moore offers him in a letter of 1918: "You apologize for interrupting me in my work—I am only too pleased to be interrupted. You ask me to give some account of the work I am engaged upon. I do so and express a wish that you should take the opposite side. But you say that you agree with me too cordially to make a good opposition. . . . Nine tenths of the dialogue will be by me, but a tenth must be by you. I will send you a draft of the whole and you will revise the bits I have written for you" (BK 132–33). In reaction, Gosse vehemently protests such a "degrading and subaltern position" and insists that they meet in a more "neutral" place. He concludes, "How DARE you propose that I should 'apologize for interrupting you at your work'? Damn your infernal cheek. . . . Don't think I am opposed to the scheme: it will be very amusing, but you *must* behave like a little gentleman, or else I won't play with you."[5] Pained, and baffled at Gosse's response, Moore wrote three impassioned letters of apology over the next two days. The last and briefest reads as both a recognition of Gosse's stature and an assertion of his own: "Your position in literature is so high and so secure that it can make no difference whether the imaginary conversation takes place here or on the balcony of your house. What I have to consider are the dramatic values" (BK 136). The two men could have "claws in their velvet paws," and neither one would take the role of subaltern that both expected of most of those around them, yet Moore and Gosse were above all concerned with the quality of their own productions and attentive to the work of the other.

The correspondence with Gosse also illustrates how much an artful self-presentation is, for Moore, integrated with the process of dialogue. Confined to a nursing home in his late years, seriously ill and in severe pain, he contemplated yet another series of imaginary conversations between himself and his friend, this time set amid the countryside of France. To Gosse, who was himself weakened, having lost much of his sight and fewer than three months from his own death, Moore writes: "As soon as you are well come to see me, and we'll improvise the five articles together. I am as agile as an Italian greyhound going through hoops at improvisation! Do come; we shall have such fun" (BK 248–49). Moore speaks to their friendship, their mutual obsession with work, and his own ongoing interest in the dialogue. But the last phrase is strikingly uncharacteristic. It is the kind of phrase Moore attributes in his fiction to giddy young ladies who are sending out invitations for tennis. Undoubtedly, Moore is wryly playing with authorial voice. As Gosse would have understood, given the nature of their correspondence, this ironic piece of ventriloquy functions paradoxically as a sign of its author's presence. It is a gesture employed to make less painful the recognition of absence that letters inherently bring about, a recognition intensified in this case by the precarious health of both parties. Perhaps of greatest interest to a consideration of autobiographical voice is that in this penultimate letter to one of his most abiding friends, Moore offers a parody of the conventions of heartfelt sincerity. And by such parodic language, Moore offers a representation of his own habits of mind and thus a curiously sincere self-representation.

The Epistolary Persona and the Autobiographical Voice

Moore might have been flattered by the suggestion of a constructed parodic voice in his letters; he bewailed his inability to write letters with what he considered literary interest, although he recognized their financial value. In a letter of 1924 he advises John Eglinton to keep his letters since those he wrote to Dujardin had brought his French colleague "a large sum" (EG 64). Three years later, he suggests that Eglinton translate the letters, announcing with satisfaction that "I think I have discovered a hoard for you" (EG 73). Bitterly ascribing nothing but monetary value to his correspondence, he remarks later the same year that "the letter takes time to write and will serve no purpose. I am wrong; it will increase your stock, which some day may be of use to you" (EG 75). He also frequently refers to his letters as a "hoard" from which genuine literature could be drawn, much the way one would look at a journal or notebook. Thus he admonishes Eglinton to use their letters to develop an article and asks Dujardin to "revise and re-touch" for publication an interesting letter exchange between Moore and his cousin—"for the correspondence of a man of letters is never wholly private."[6] Or in regard to one especially pleasing sentence in a recent letter from Gosse, he remarks, "it is one of those sentences that one doesn't forget; to waste so fine a phrase in a letter seems a pity. If you had mentioned it while I was writing the preface I'd have worked it in" (BK 107).

Although Moore viewed his own letters as little more than monetary and literary saving accounts, he believed in the aesthetic value of the letter as a literary genre. He enjoyed reading collections of letters and at various times refers to his delight in the letters of Marianna Alcoforado (the Portuguese nun), Lawrence Sterne, Balzac and Madame Hanza, Wagner and Mathilde Wesendonck, and Héloïse and Abelard. Of Gosse's letters, he spoke with open envy of the "epistolary genius" that enabled his friend to write with seeming effortlessness letters "so full of graceful wit" against which his own must "seem very dim and trite" (BK 161–62). To Mary Hutchinson he apologizes for a letter as "untidy as a man in a nightcap before he has had his bath" (*LGM* 316) and to Hildegarde Hawthorne he complains, "Songs do not chaunt in my head as they do in yours. My letters must read very tamely and lamely, sentences that halt like jaded mules or lie down like camels refusing to go any further" (*GMP* 140). Despite such appealing metaphors, Moore simply did not consider his own letters as art, primarily because in his experience art necessitated laborious revision. While he occasionally alludes to the possibility that his letters might be published and advised that his letters to Lady Cunard should form the basis of any biography of him, he was unwilling to spend time revising them. A 1910 letter to Maud Cunard provides an amusing instance of this point of view: Moore writes to apologize for his inability to articulate in conversation his admiration for her. Ostensibly providing a literary substitute in the letter, he proceeds to compare her to a goddess before interrupting himself abruptly to announce, "I hope this letter has not worded itself too stupidly. If it has it cannot be helped. I have to go out with Mrs. Williamson and it would be unpardonable to keep her waiting any longer" (*LLC* 77–78).

Few claims could be made for Moore as a master of the epistolary form. His letters do not really meet any of the three criteria of "autonomy, fertility, and versatility" proposed by Bruce Redford in his study of the eighteenth-century English letter. Unlike the letters Redford studies, a single letter of Moore's almost never creates a world of its own. While his epistolary output was prodigious, what I shall identify as an extraordinary compulsion toward self-presentation arguably outweighs as a motive the "campaign for intimacy with the other" that Redford sees at the heart of a copious epistolarium. Lastly, while Redford suggests that in great letters "details are pruned and inflections calibrated according to the identity and interests of the recipient," Moore's letters are frequently insensitive to the reader.[7] However, Moore's letters do achieve an end that is overlooked in Redford's focus upon the single letter as an artifact. Read in toto, they create a character with a recognizable and unique voice. Of more importance than their observations on art (that which both he and Eglinton prized in the letters), they build a psychologically complex portrait of resilience and intelligence coupled with self-doubt and incorrigible vanity, and, above all, an unfaltering energy. As his acquaintance Harold Acton suggested, what Moore says about the letters of Richard Wagner may well be said of his own: "Was there ever so garrulous a man? Was there ever a man so interested in himself? Well, he had the right to be, for he was the most interesting thing alive and he clearly knew it; and egotism is the god that inspires the letter-writer and good letters are all about the letter-writer" (*LLC* 40–41).[8] Of this autobiographical voice, which I have identified as Moore's chief epistolary accomplishment, Moore himself offers a commentary in a letter to Eglinton. Concerning the letters to Dujardin that Eglinton agreed to edit and translate, he remarks:

> I . . . find it hard to believe that all I sent to him during the last forty years have any particular literary merit. Of course there may be an odd phrase here and there that is funny, but an odd funny phrase isn't the substance of literature. Good letters are letters writ-

ten to be published, not letters written to a private individual. . . . I hope you will select the most interesting ones, saving me, so far as you can, from cutting a ridiculous figure. . . . But you have many letters to choose from, and I hope your selection will save me from a journey to Timbuctoo. (EG 78)

As to what he means by "cutting a ridiculous figure," an earlier letter may help to clarify: "I don't hope to shine as a letter writer, far from it, but I should like to appear as I shall be expected to appear. . . . The letters should be real letters, but it should be explained that the earliest were the letters of a very young man who wrote without thought of publication" (EG 75). Moore expresses the anxiety most public figures would feel in regard to the publication of their juvenilia, but beyond that commonplace response is a more interesting comment on epistolary voice. He is adamant that Eglinton make clear the same distinction between speaking voice in the letters (the young man) and author (the public figure of the mature George Moore) that forms the structural principle of autobiographies like *Confessions of a Young Man* and *Hail and Farewell.* As in those works, the "young man" should appear as one "with no thought of publication"—a natural, spontaneous, innocent persona. The author, in contrast, must be recognized as the artificer and the ironist, and there must exist signs in the text to indicate such a bifurcation of the authorial proper name.

Yet most letters are meant to be read as close to the time of their composition as is possible, and by a person whose reactions will directly affect their author (as distinct from their speaking persona). Is the epistolary voice then most related to the author who writes or to the persona who speaks? As may be true of letter writers as a type, Moore's epistolary voice intermingles the needs of the author with the constraints of the persona. The persona in use probably owes some of its features to received models of epistolary narration. In an essay on the familiar letter, English Showalter, Jr., addresses widely polarized answers to the question of the letter's origin. Does the letter function as "the spontaneous and direct expression of lived reality" whose forms emerge from unique personalities, or is it generated exclusively within "an epistolary system" defined by a social and cultural network? Showalter argues that "like any author, the letter writer brings an individual mind . . . to bear on the problem of encoding an experience and a set of referents within the forms available. The letter writer normally enjoys unusual freedom, both because the genre is loosely defined and because the communication is private and need please (or produce the desired effect upon) only one person, usually well known to the writer."[9] While Moore explained to a friend that "self is the essence of letter writing" (*GMT* 59), just what constitutes that self is determined both by certain consistent features of voice and the rhetorical context that reflects the personality of the addressee and the epistolary model in use.

Moore evidently modeled his lyrical, melancholy, and at times overly mannered erotic correspondence after that which he read in published collections. His letters to Edmund Gosse follow the aphoristic style and aesthetic subject matter common in the letters of other literary figures of the period. In letters to publishers and business associates, the pugnacious and oddly personal argumentation recalls the indignant posturing that stands out in the letters of George Henry Moore and other Irish landlords of the mid-nineteenth century. In letters soliciting the often very extensive assistance of his friends at research or proofreading, he sounds very much like his autobiographical persona: a figure whose egotism is so all-consuming that his apparent lack of self-consciousness grants him an appealing naïveté. Moore's letters home from his early days in Paris and London echo the language he heard about him. Assuming the guise of a man-about-town, he breezily recites to his aged mother his sexual adventures with married women and writes in an analogous vein to his morally conservative younger brother. Either this was deliberate antagonism or, more likely, an egotistical disregard for his addressee coupled with an intense desire to show himself "a *blase roue* . . . rotten with literature and art to which Wagnerism has lately been added" (*LGM* 188). Whatever his motivation, he writes no more such letters after the early 1890s.

Throughout Moore's epistolarium, however, there are repeated motifs that do not seem to be so much a part of an assumed persona. We see generosity, affection, and tact: all features at odds with the caustic public role Moore played in English and Irish letters. From the start, he voices doubts that he might ever write well and terror that the latest book might show some "falling off." In the letters of his old age, we hear the pleadings of an increasingly lonely man who in 1927, after repeated requests for letters, inquires if he might send Eglinton one hundred stamped envelopes with which to respond. But, as he quipped in *Conversations in Ebury Street:* "We are never altogether natural; the educated cannot be. Even dogs are actors; only cats are themselves and nothing but themselves" (*CES* 129). Although the sympathetic epistolary voice I have just described seems akin to the unself-conscious cat, Moore gives in one of the dialogues in *Conversations in Ebury Street* a warning about his persona which the reader of his letters might also heed:

> Mrs. Harley-Caton. Your books revealed your turn of mind to me; I was curious to learn the man who is behind the books, and I have come to you unable to forego my purpose. . .
> Are you unaware of how intimately you appear to us in your writing?
> Moore. I never thought of it.
> Mrs. Harley-Caton. And if you had sought the quality which attracts us it would have become by this time a mere literary trick.
> Moore. Mayhap you are destroying at this very moment the quality that brought you hither. (*CES* 142)

Moore would have hardly called his self-making "a mere literary trick," but it was decidedly something he had "thought of." The letter, as I have been arguing, was like the autobiographies an occasion for self-creation. Even when concerned with some practical matter, Moore used letters for self-analysis, autobiographical narrative, and philosophical and aesthetic speculation. The tone and diction of the voice most often works in accord with the nature of the self-defining statement Moore seeks to make, even more so than with the expectations of the addressee. The feelings of the addressee are at times recklessly ignored, and the message—generally a criticism of literature or a theological argument—dominates other features, even the genre conventions of, for example, letters of social invitation. A 1902 letter to the Celticist Kuno Meyer cordially and formally invites him to visit and expresses gratitude for Meyer's gift of his recent translation of two Old Irish poems. All very well—until Moore denigrates the translation as inferior to François Villon's and takes the opportunity to decry "the Irish mind" as inferior to the French.[10] Such a letter—unlike an autobiography—is addressed to one reader and, being primarily transactional, it requires a specific reply. At the same time, if the fact that the intended reader is Kuno Meyer stimulates and effects the tone and message (a formal invitation to visit), it nevertheless has a negligible effect upon that part of the letter concerned with self-dramatization. Without regard to the personal feelings of his addressee, Moore mixes the polite conventions of invitation with the tweaking criticisms that were apparently acceptable between literary men of the period. But above all, he must act the Francophile artist who has "thoroughly renounced his Celtic hopes." All else is subordinate to that activity.

An intriguing example of such self-dramatization occurs in a recently discovered 1898 letter to Maud Cunard. Given in entirety, it reads:

> I send you the proofs—I fancy that they are about a third of the book. I am feeling so depressed that I cannot come to tea; you would only think me hateful. Do you know what a black melancholy is? If there was only a reason but it is the sorrow of life, the primal sorrow. This sounds melodramatic, exaggerated, pedantic. Indifferent as the fiction doubtless is it is better than the horrible reality known as
>
> George Moore[11]

Here Moore has affected a diction he openly acknowledges as parody. Phrases like "the sorrow of life, the primal sorrow," occur almost exclusively in letters to women, just as cumulative lists of adjectives or nouns separated by commas appear primarily in the style he felt to befit the love letter. As in the autobiographies, he portrays himself as a man overwhelmed by instinctive forces without empirically traceable origins but so great as to alienate him from the niceties of social life. He identifies the role of melancholy artist as a trite fiction, but insists that his "real" self is in actuality a "horrible" incarnation of that fiction.

The letter's closure is an unusual one in that Moore's letters rarely experiment with closure and even more infrequently incorporate his signature within a sentence from the letter's body. One of the few other examples of this practice occurs in another letter to Maud Cunard, written some thirty-two years later. He closes the letter,

> Dearest woman, how can I thank? You cannot tell me and I cannot imagine, for I have no more love to give; you had it all years and years ago, but with the same love I am
>
> Yours always George Moore (*LLC* 181)

Here too, although to a less pronounced degree than in the letter of 1898, the signature is enclosed within a self-descriptive sentence, rendering the signature part of a constructed narrative about the self rather than an emanation from the self. The 1898 letter involves the signature in a paradoxical statement about the self's fictionality, and the letter of 1930 places the signature within a story perpetually retold in his letters to her: he was the man who would not marry, but would love one woman from afar and with a constancy that, while it did not preclude affairs on his or her part, would continue throughout their lives.

In his letters to Lady Cunard, Moore attempted to construct a retrospective plot of their lives, one to which the letter of the present moment would add another, if predictable, chapter. Yet if letters can include within themselves efforts to emplot a life, to what degree do actual correspondences provide a narrative? Can an epistolary narrative be directed by the letter writer? For a man who was seemingly compelled to dominate the terms of the discourse in which he participated, the answer could be of considerable consequence.

Narrative and Epistolary Lifewriting

If the construction of a self is integral to both the autobiographical persona and the fictional character, then what do the self-constructions performed in letters have in common with autobiography and fiction? Or, what fundamental differences exist? I have just discussed the peculiar characteristics of epistolary voice, specifically its relation with the voice of the other, but a related area of inquiry involves the degree to which letters do or do not involve narrative. In light of critical disagreement as to whether narrative is intrinsic to autobiographical writing, it becomes necessary to establish a working definition of narrative and to examine the relationship between narrative and epistolary self-presentation.

In what is to date the fullest discussion of narrativity and autobiography, Paul John Eakin draws upon Sartre's operative sense of narrative as "a manifestation of self-definition in terms of plot" and Peter Brooks's definition of plot as "less a structure than . . . a structuring operation, used, or made necessary, by those meanings that develop only through sequence and succession: an interpretive operation specific to narrative signification."[12] While much autobiographical writing includes passages that contain alternatives to sequential ordering, they are for the most part embedded within a primarily chronological narrative, a form that remains the dominant modus operandi of literary self-description. Other discussions of plot emphasize aspects that nevertheless depend upon sequence and succession: Booth, for example, concentrates upon conflict, Forster upon causal relations, and Hayden White suggests "a structure of relationships by which the events contained in the account are endowed with a meaning by being identified as parts of an integrated whole." (White's omission of the concept of sequentiality seems in context less a deliberate choice than an assumption of sequentiality's inherent presence in such a structure.)[13] In addition to sequence, theories of plot frequently emphasize its etiological aspect. In his *Reading for the Plot: Design and Intention in Narrative*, Brooks suggests that "we read only those incidents and signs that can be construed as promise and annunciation, enchained toward a construction of significance— those markers that, as in the detective story, appear to be clues to the underlying intentionality of event." Hence, "we are able to read present moments . . . as endowed with narrative meaning only because we read them in anticipation of the structuring power of those endings that will retrospectively give them the order and significance of plot."[14] Sequence, causality, and the integrative force of teleology: if such is narrative, how can epistolary writing be considered a life-narrative when by its very nature it is located within a fixed present and cannot see to its ending? How does epistolary writing manifest or refuse the temporal characteristics of narrative and how does this effect its potential status as lifewriting?

I would propose four basic ways in which letters can emplot a life. One can use letters interactively with other experience to effect the shape of future correspondence and the life outside it. This is a common and pragmatic use of the form, particularly in Moore's case, yet one that depends upon the willingness of others to go along with the plot one has designed. Second, one can embed narratives within letters. Moore writes to his friend Mary Hutchinson a long, lively travelogue of his trip through Palestine on camel-back, but this kind of retelling is a less noticeable feature of Moore's letter writing. The stories within his letters almost invariably relate the progress or frustration of his ongoing writing projects; one of his most frequent motifs is his own suspense as to whether a book will succeed or not. "I have strained every nerve to make it a masterpiece," he concludes in a typical letter to Maurice Moore. "It will decide what my position is. I am very nervous. It is sink or swim. I cannot do better, alas, I cannot do better."[15] One may also write letters with a sense of contributing toward an unfolding narrative—rather like composing one half of an epistolary novel. This was Moore's chosen way of corresponding with women to whom he was romantically attracted, and it will be discussed at length when looking at his erotic correspondence.

Finally, one may also use letters to make retrospective and predictive generalizations about life experience, locating the time of composition as the endpoint toward which prior experiences lead and by which their immanent structure may be revealed. The possibility of establishing in a letter a provisional endpoint is of critical importance to Moore's compositional practices, his chosen forms of storytelling, and the ideology informing both. Considering the question of teleology and epistolary writing, English Showalter, Jr. notes that "a correspondence is . . . a strange genre, in which one of the central prerogatives of the author, that of conceiving and implementing a coherent organization, is denied. Coherence can occur only if the letter writer's vision possesses such unifying power that, despite accidents and the randomness of daily events, it imposes a feeling of destiny on the writer's life."[16] In Moore's fiction and autobiographies, the significance of the present moment repeatedly derives from its place in a sequential chain of development leading up to the conclusion of the narrative or the moment in which an autobiographical narrator concludes his story. Moore explains in a letter to Nancy Cunard that he wrote always "with the end in view, almost gluttonously, like the child at the cake during dinner" (*LGM* 361). For one concerned with theories of origin and destiny and given to modes of recollective storytelling, the ending must thus always be the point of departure.

In correspondences of many years, Moore on occasion uses the present moment to reflect upon prior letters, discovering in them an emergent design or "plot." In so doing, he seeks to acquire that "authorial prerogative" of which Showalter speaks. If one writes as a single author, a story-in-process can be emplotted as one goes about telling it; one can also create a plot that incorporates the ideas of others. But one cannot predict another contribution nor control its contents. Although a letter writer might stop at points during a correspondence to seek and predict a plot, the whole of a correspondence can be emplotted only retrospectively. It has even been suggested that it is an editor's work to make a plot out of letters. This is precisely what is accomplished by the "life and letters" biography, and it is what Helmut E. Gerber has done in his two heavily annotated collections of Moore's letters.[17] A correspondence may be easily *read* as a life story; but only rarely is it *written* as one, with the narrative emphasis (and in particular, the teleology) implied by such a concept.

To make such retrospective analysis is to speak to the past from the present, a point of time frequently akin to the moment of composition in formal autobiography, although in *Confessions* and *Hail and Farewell* the moment of narration is distinctly prior to the actual time of composition. In general, autobiographies and letters differ greatly in their emphasis upon past and present. Comparing the temporal aspect of memoir-novels and epistolary novels, Janet Altman notes that "the present of the memoir narrator intervenes only to shed light on the past that interests us, to add the illuminating perspective of *now*'s reflections to the obscurity of *then*'s actions. In epistolary narrative, on the other hand, the past is the interloper, intervening to shed light on the present . . . in the memoir the present is subordinate to the past, in the letter the past is always relative to the present."[18] Altman's terms are too exclusive to be fully applicable to Moore's work, given that his autobiographical narrators speak from a point coterminous with the main line of action and that in much of *Memoirs of My Dead Life* and, to a lesser degree, in *Hail and Farewell*, the activity of remembering (conducted in the work's present tense) is of equal, if not greater, importance than the story that is remembered. Yet if we consider the temporal structure of the vast majority of autobiographies, her point is useful in that it suggests why those letters that highlight the present moment primarily as the conclusion to a story of the past might thus demonstrate a pronounced kinship to the formal autobiography.

But while many correspondences regularly incorporate retrospective analysis, Moore's do not. Most of his letters either briefly recount an immediate past or express the emotions and ideas of the present: they comprise requests for assistance with research or copy-reading, haggles over money, brief chronicles of various love affairs and struggles with composition or publishers, arguments over religion, sexuality, and nationalism, romantic paeans and fantasies, and —most of all—literary criticisms. Such elements are more akin to the essay than the story, and while on occasion Moore himself will note patterns or development in his actions and ideas, or in the letters that describe them, these brief reflections are for the most part meaningful only as part of a larger narrative imposed by a reader.

It could be argued that such letters, grounded as they are in the present moment, best fulfill the prescription of those who have found the narrative autobiography to be a limiting, and even evasive, form. They may offer a refutation of narrative architectonics and, in substitution, reflect the discontinuity that John Sturrock finds modeled in the immediacy and "sincerity" of the diary and Burton Pike finds reflective of the fragmented nature of contemporary cosmology.[19] While the letter is very different from the diary and is likely to be subject to more extensive rhetorical manipulation, a correspondence does come about through a succession of moments from which utterance has been made. Rather than pressing toward a "single, terminal point in time," which Sturrock claims is more rightly the province of biography, epistolary discourse would reveal "a whole, unfinished series of points in time."[20]

Yet if we choose to value those letters that more resemble Sturrock's model than do more overt narritavizations, we are perversely choosing to disclaim those very letters in which their authors have set out to order and seek meaning from their past. When at the beginning of *Metaphors of Self* James Olney proposes that autobiography is neither "a formal nor . . . an historical matter" but an expression of "the vital impulse to order," explicit in such a claim is that while autobiography may cross numerous generic boundaries, it will nevertheless embody the compulsion that presses its author to draw "out of the flux of events a coherent pattern," "a sufficient metaphor for experience."[21] The search for pattern and order, I would agree, marks the difference between archival material and the autobiographical self-presentation that may be developed out of it.

Letters that enclose narratives about the past or that make comments whose purpose is to analyze that past undoubtedly resemble most closely the struggle to order that characterizes most self-proclaimed autobiographies. But I would also suggest that those letters (and particularly, those prolonged correspondences) in which Moore is most concerned with voice may be read as efforts to construct an autobiographical presence, or metaphor. While the letters to Edmund Gosse, for example, often form generalizations about the events of Moore's past, they also represent a sustained self-presentation of the speaker as what Moore would have called "a man of letters": in both content and style, the frankness, the sparring debate, and the wry humor offer a consistent self-portrait. Correspondingly, in the fragments that remain of Moore's letters to Lady Cunard we see repeated forms of address, motifs and themes, even grammatical structures, that appear as part of Moore's presentation of himself as the faithful knight-errant of her life.

Voice may well be more significant to epistolary autobiography than issues of narrative emplotment. Yet convincing claims have been made by Janet Varner Gunn to the effect that autobiography is characterized precisely by "its anchorage in the phenomenon of temporality." Paul John Eakin has argued that "one of the most profound of human fictions," the belief that empty time could become significant when located within a teleological movement, renders narrative in autobiography "the archetypal form for human experience in and of time." Chronology, Eakin continues, is "a manifestation of the ineluctable temporality of human experience."[22] Even those letters that most eschew claims to narrative are yet highly conscious of their existence within time. A correspondence, while emanating from a series of presents, is nevertheless a record of change and contains individual letters that are themselves preoccupied with the past and the future. As Janet Altman has pointed out, the letter necessarily relates events in the past, communicates the most fleeting present, and is riddled with anxieties about its future.[23] A writer may or may not emplot a correspondence, but the presentation of voice I have identified as crucial to autobiographical expression must, in the letter, take place within and over time.

Like most love letters, Moore's letters to Lady Cunard are beset by anxiety about possible changes of heart, missing letters, misunderstandings, silences. As Rupert Hart-Davis explains, a letter bearing the fanciful signature of "Maud Emerald" (her favorite jewels were emeralds) sent Moore into an agony as to her marital status. "I beg you to send me a telegram," he pleads. "A yes or a no will be enough. You cannot fail to understand that it is unfair to leave a man who has loved you dearly for more than thirty years in doubt" (*LLC* 149). Thirty years collapses into two anxious days as letters, telegrams and searches through telephone directories for a Mr. Emerald were put to an end only by the arrival of an acquaintance who explained the nickname. Age and change were clearly factors in this long relationship, but by far the most prominent theme of Moore's letters to her is his insistence that their lives had been wound together inextricably in a masterplot whose story was to be endlessly retold: a story of desire without end, unaffected by time. As the expression of a consistent epistolary persona and all the various forms of emplotment I have outlined, their correspondence also constitutes a paradigm of the prevailing contradiction of Moore's career: on the one hand, a fervent belief in the autogenous instinct that made into one grand design the varied events of his life, and on the other, a sometimes devastating recognition of the force of historical change.

Writing to Freya: Love Letters

Repeatedly, Moore avowed to Maud Cunard that his love was unaltered by time, and in a brief note begging for her company, Moore addresses her as Freya, the mistress of the garden of eternal youth in Wagner's *Das Rheingold* (*LLC* 164). It is to her that the elderly Moore continues even from a nursing home to write passionate letters of anticipation and regret. He represents himself as the "Ebury Street Hermit" whose hours away from her are counted like the rosary beads of a penitent. He is also "the faithfullest of lovers" who, in characteristic melding of two motifs—the passage of time and the unchanging nature of his love—writes, "I love you more than I ever did, and I always loved you": a declaration followed by the assurance that he remains "the same as ever only more so" (*LLC* 168, 167, 181). Having had such a varied life, he counted this relationship as one of two vital continuities, the other being his profession as a writer. Of the latter, he had written in *Confessions of a Young Man* that out of "the labyrinth of my desires" "one cry was more persistent" and that he remained faithful to its summons throughout his life. Similarly, in old age he tells Maud Cunard that "you are the only woman that mattered . . . you are the one that I saw and heard most clearly; the others were but phantoms" (*LLC* 172–73). The vivacious girl of twenty-two years who sat opposite him at a society dinner was, he writes in *Memoirs of My Dead Life*, "the most beautiful thing that had ever appeared in my life, an idea which I knew from the first I was destined to follow" (*MMDL* 253). Their first meeting in 1894 is described repeatedly as an epiphanic experience as compelling as the revelation of his lifework.

While his last extant letters to Lady Cunard bespeak his sadness at his physical decline and incipient death, nevertheless, meditating upon the long years of his devotion and the prospect of death enriches rather than diminishes his personal myth of love's permanence. In a late edition of *Memoirs of My Dead Life*, he reflects that she had been "a constant but unfaithful mistress; in her own words she 'liked not continuity,' but was willing to pick up a thread again; and I forgave her certain caprices and take pleasure in remembering that I outlived them all, and that when my poor little reel of thread was empty, when there was no more thread to unwind, a great love passed into a perfect friendship as beautifully and serenely as summer passes into still autumn."[24] In *Confessions of a Young Man* he attributed his literary vocation to the soundings of "echo-augury," and in *Memoirs of My Dead Life* he answers his own query as to the origins of this second calling: "Who shall tell the mystery of love that time cannot change, What word conveys it, fate?" (*MMDL* 253).

He continued to tell this tale in various forms, and in the discourse that enables it—the love letter—he usually abstains from any retrospection besides the telling of that one story. Instead, he concentrates upon the present manifestation of his unaltering affection. In 1905 he remarks in a note to Lady Cunard that "if I were a letter-writer," she would receive a letter full of anecdotes about his brother Maurice, the progress of the latest book, or the delicious rusks "which when dipped into hot milk inspire the dull lagging brains of authors." However, he continues, he wants to write a different kind of letter, one that articulates the depth of his love (*LLC* 41). Narration of events in time is displaced by the assertion of a present moment whose feeling is unaffected by time. As he closes another letter, "With the longing and affection of a lifetime," he invokes the image of passing time only to counteract it with the simultaneous assertion of that feeling which has never passed.

The actual extent of this "grand passion," as he called it—that period before "my poor little reel was empty"—is unclear to biographers, but by Moore's own admission appears to have encompassed only a short period of time. Few of Moore's affairs lasted very long; as acknowledged in *Conversations in Ebury Street,* he had "always tried to avoid burdens" (*CES* 181). Responding to Mrs. Harley-Caton's confession of her irresistible attraction to priests, the narrator of *Conversations* assures her of his empathy: "We cannot desire what we possess, and love without desire is materialism" (*CES* 155). The time and space that letters must cross, a gulf which has agonized letter-writing lovers for thousands of years, was precisely what Moore needed to keep his ideal of unrealized desire. Earlier in his conversation with Mrs. Harley-Caton, the narrator argues that "the doctrine that our quest should be always the princess far away . . . is firmly established in the heart of man, which never changes. But the world is always at change; barriers disappear. The railway and the aeroplane have annihilated distance; the telegraph by day and the telephone by night have made the life of lovers promiscuous as marriage" (*CES* 146). Letter writers through the ages bewail the insecurity brought on by the hazards of epistolary communication, and the uncertainty over "Maud Emerald" attests that Moore could feel similarly distraught. Here, however, Moore finds most horrifying the changes in history that have mitigated our sensitivity to tensions produced by time and absence. The fear of a letter's possible miscarriage or misapprehension form part of the dynamic of "unchanging" human heart, whose loyalties, in fact, prosper under the threat of such change and become "promiscuous" when certainty is assured.

If Moore seems to be at greater ease with his feminine correspondent at some distance, so he also expresses no desire to hold close to him the letters he receives from her. The correspondent known only as "Gabrielle" sleeps with his letters in her bed, but such an inclination never seems to have entered his mind. To Gosse, Moore remarks that in writing the history of his love affairs for *Memoirs of My Dead Life*, "I do not have to look up the letters my old mistresses have written to me; my memory suffices" (BK 61). There are no kisses on the letters, no smelling of the paper, no analysis of handwriting, nothing of the fetishization of the object, which in one of its most extreme examples brings Moore's contemporary, the Anglo-Welsh painter Augustus John, to beg his lover to embroider the "sheets" of her stationery with her handwriting, then wrap herself in the paper so that he can feel the imprint of her "adorable self" on the sheets![25]

As has been suggested by several commentators on the love letter, fetishization of the letter may well be an effort to compensate for the bodily absence of the beloved. It has also been argued that epistolary romances depend upon that bodily absence.[26] Yet unlike the passionate correspondents he admired—the Portuguese nun, for example, or Wagner and Mathilde Wesendonck—Moore takes up the epistolary romance at will, as one might browse at odd moments through a familiar book. He begins a letter to Hildegarde Hawthorne, with whom he shared a sexually explicit correspondence, "It seems this evening a long time since I wrote to you and feeling the necessity of writing unless you are to drift out of my desire I began. Our first letters were full of sparkle—at least yours were—this letter will be dull; I should have answered your letter at once, that is the better way, and if you write again I'll write at once" (*GMP* 137). While he was intrigued by the sensation of desire, he appears to have been equally, if not more, anxious to participate in a literary form that recalled what was for him a more interesting world, a world before telephones, motorcars, and electric advertising signs.

In this world of epistolary romance, Moore could be both author and participant, a role amiably suited to a chronic autobiographer. The love letter allowed him to speak his cognizance of the uncertainty and force of time as well as his doctrine that time reveals a gradual unfolding of things that have always been: a literary vocation, an unalterable devotion, and—as articulated in letters to other women as well as to Lady Cunard—an eternal "springtime" present in the "compelling atmosphere" of women who "love life and desire to live" (*GMP* 129). In order to maintain the latter two of these personal myths, Moore recognized that physical distance from the women in question was of paramount necessity. He participated in at least three extended epistolary romances with women whom, with one exception, he never met; the woman who did contrive to meet him in Paris (Hildegarde Hawthorne) found their subsequent correspondence abbreviated and devoid of its former fervor.

As an author noted for his daring and frankness regarding sexual behavior, Moore was surely the recipient of many seductive letters from female readers. Why would he choose to respond to these three? The answer very likely may be that other such correspondences existed, but have not been recovered; there may also be biographical explanations.[27] Hawthorne, Emily Lorenz Meyer, and the unknown correspondent he called "Gabrielle" all exchanged letters with him during the first decade of the twentieth century. The correspondence with Gabrielle precedes the others (1903–6), and while letters to Hawthorne and Meyer continue past the war, his interest peaked between 1907–9. During that period, Moore was living in Dublin. By 1904 he had separated from Clara Christian and resumed his adoring letters to Maud Cunard, all the while circulating rumors of his impotence. If there were other women with whom he was seriously involved during this period, he made no remarks concerning them, and they are unnoted by his contemporaries and unknown to his biographers. With multiple projects in hand, he seems to have been, as he writes to Meyer, solely "indulging in a literary debauch" (*GMP* 137). As Adrian Frazier has remarked, Moore "is happiest when sex is polymorphous: that is, when it is transferred from genital intercourse to touch and talk, to sight and speculation, to future prospects or long retrospection, where it can be indefinitely prolonged through thought. Sex that is only speculative, or better yet, speculations that are sexualized, he preferred to the brief deed of procreation."[28]

Such a hypothesis provides an explanation of Moore's behavior, but the question remains as to how this need for corporeal absence affects epistolary self-construction. There are three possible answers to the question. First, perhaps because the correspondents shared no past beyond that of a brief epistolary acquaintance, these letters are almost devoid of retrospective narratives, although they do indulge in speculative scene-setting, a facet that will be addressed later in a discussion of them as fictionalizations. Unlike the letters to Maud Cunard, which tell over and over the story of their meeting, these letters contain no touchstones of a shared past. Describing the love letter's reflective obsession with the sexual interchange that commonly generates it, Roland Barthes suggests, "Amorous seduction . . . takes place *before* discourse and *behind* the proscenium of consciousness: the amorous 'event' . . . is my own local legend, my little sacred history that I declaim to myself, and this declamation of a *fait accompli* (frozen, embalmed, removed from any *praxis*) is the lover's discourse."[29] If the letters to Lady Cunard retell a "little sacred history," filling the present moment with its recollection rather than with any ongoing sexual activity, these letters to young women do not have even a "fait accompli" to recount.

"If we had been of the same generation," Moore writes to Hildegarde Hawthorne in 1910, "I am not sure that you might not have liked me as you liked the Hungarian. Bed is a wonderful thing; a thing none of us would have missed—not for anything: but one can be great friends without bed" (*GMP* 185). If one is neither lamenting nor longing for "bed," then letters of love will not necessarily be letters of passionate desire. While Moore invites female correspondents to recount their love affairs to him, he is not equally forthcoming. In fact, with all three correspondents, Moore rather quickly shifts from gallantries to ferret out any possible literary assistance that could be derived from his correspondents as translators or researchers. While he occasionally remarks upon Hildegarde's "beautiful body" and at one point wistfully indicates that he would happily trade places with her Hungarian, he simultaneously makes absolutely clear that this is more of a rhetorical flourish than a genuine desire. Nowhere is he the abject supplicant, and if most love letters are, to use Linda S. Kauffman's term, "discourses of desire," Moore's are for the most part discourses of domination. Thus my second point is that the motif of exchange is here replaced by the motif of sexual desire, but as with exchange, the language of desire becomes a strategy for gaining control over the epistolary relationship.

My third point with regard to corporeal absence involves the use to which such authorial control will be put, and that is the full fictionalization of the correspondence, a process involving characterizations, scenes, styles, and plots. As the editors of the letters to Gabrielle, Hawthorne, and Meyer point out, these exchanges were recognized by Moore (and to varying degrees by his correspondents) as, in Helmut E. Gerber's words, "a game," in which they saw themselves "as though they were characters in a work of fiction" (*GMP* 30–31). In his first letter to Gabrielle, for example, Moore writes, "I need not tell you that I have never met you in the flesh but your spirit I have known always—you are, to put it somewhat bluntly, one of my women and you recognized yourself as one, if you had not you would not have written to me."[30] Not only does she allow him to see her in these terms, according to his sense of what one of "my women" might be, but she is pleased by his statement and encourages the fictionalizing of herself and him. She writes a short time later, "I think I know what I want: to sit with you in a dark room and kiss you fervently. I have never seen your face, I don't know what your figure is like, I have never heard your voice. I won't see and hear you. It would be a catastrophe if I were to fall in love with the *man* in you. I will only be in love with the author."[31]

Imaginary scenes are also a recurrent aspect of the fictionalization process within these letters. Roland Barthes identifies the visual or aural "scene" of love's discovery as an episode with which "amorous time" begins; framed in memory, it involves a sudden awareness of the other, much like Moore's story of his first sight of the dazzling girl in a pink and grey shot-silk dress who was to become the perpetual object of his affections.[32] No such scenes could exist with women he had never met, so he was entirely at liberty to imagine them. As he indulges in fantasies of suddenly sailing to America or appearing in his correspondent's room, he invokes the element of suddenness that Barthes astutely identifies as the point from which the lover's discourse begins. "I should like to walk into the German inn and meet you in the passage," he writes to Emily Lorenz Meyer. "I see you in a large hat and you have a book in your hand" (*GMP* 172). Throughout his scene-making, Moore attempts full authorship, yet that privilege is limited by the evidence his correspondents send to him. He writes for photographs to help him imagine but is annoyed with their limitations, and he irritably contradicts or revises the scenarios developed by his correspondents.

As attempted fictions, his erotic letters demonstrate features of style and voice rarely seen elsewhere in his correspondences. For the most part, they are, as he promised Meyer, "long and pleasing" letters: gentle, coy, curious, with more questions than opinions, full of compliments undiminished by irony, and decorated with verbal felicities that sometimes border on purple prose. To varying degrees, he put into effect the aesthetic features he so admired in the letters of Marianna Alcoforado: "They contain not a single epigram or antithetical phrase. . . . We do not know if she was dark or fair, not whether she saw the officer on a cloudy day or a sunny day, nor are we amused with views of the surrounding country. I love you, come to me, I suffer, that is the simple substance of her letters; they are to me infinitely beautiful" (*GMT* 72).

Characters, scenes, and style—all the elements of fiction, and Moore did compose a play based upon his correspondence with Gabrielle. He tantalizingly suggests to her in 1906 that had he gone to Munich to meet her, she might well figure in one of the erotic vignettes in *Memoirs of My Dead Life*, as indeed she did in later editions. Passages from his letters were also reworked in other letters and used in his autobiographies. To Maud Cunard and Emily Lorenz Meyer he suggested literary collaborations involving their correspondence, but wisely, neither woman agreed to these proposals. As Helmut E. Gerber observes of Moore's many attempts to collaborate with friends, productive collaboration demands a relinquishment of authorial dominance of which he was never capable.

The writing of letters is thus an integral aspect of Moore's lifelong autobiographical project. He approaches the letter as yet another site for the representation of subjectivity. The voice of the other becomes another part of the experiential world to be observed and reconstituted by the autobiographical voice. It is a telling fact that one of Moore's last works, unfinished at his death and published posthumously, was an autobiographical memoir entitled *A Communication to My Friends*. The expectations of the familiar letter —the vehicle of communication in literate society and the very incarnation of textual intersubjectivity—is subsumed, finally, by what was for George Moore a much more powerful drive toward autobiographical self-construction.

7

"To Live Outside Ourselves in the General Life"

The Later Fiction and the Religion of Life

> It's life that matters, nothing but life—the pro-
> cess of discovering—the everlasting and perpetual
> process, not the discovery itself at all.
> —Virginia Woolf, *Night and Day*

IN THE SUMMER OF 1903, Moore wrote to his friend Edouard Dujardin, "Life has no other goal but life, and art has no other end but to make life possible, to help us to live" (*LGM* 245). This is a surprising statement for one who had espoused for years the doctrine that life only becomes significant as it is transformed into art and that art was worth any personal sacrifice. Moore had also shown himself a devotee of productivity, not process, and his works had repeatedly affirmed that a life had no point at all without the achievement of some end: some "honest work," in Esther Waters's words, or "useful work," in Alice Barton's. In accordance with Moore's assertion that "we do not change; we develop" (*LLC* 22), this seeming shift in his ideas may be best described as a development rather than a rejection of earlier principles. Without question, some modification was called for. Excepting the great success of *Esther Waters*, during the last years of the nineteenth century Moore had difficulty producing work that satisfied either himself or his public. It was a period of momentous transition in which he endured the maddening frustration of not one but a whole series of failed novels. Fortunately, his search for new subjects, a new style, and a new direction resulted in what are arguably his finest works, *The Lake* and *Hail and Farewell*. *Memoirs of My Dead Life* (1906), the subtle stories of *The Untilled Field* (1903) and *Celibate Lives* (1927), and the historical romances that preoccupied his last decade also reflect the surer hand of someone who had finally come into his full power. In the new century, Moore discovered the potential of a highly subjective mode of narration particularly suited to his belief in the power of memory to recast the terms of the given world.

This phase of Moore's development begins to be discernible in the fiction of the late 1890s. As is evident in works as different as *Confessions of a Young Man* and *Esther Waters*, Moore had long entertained the idea that our lives are driven by inward compulsions unique to each individual. Likewise, he had been long ambivalent as to whether this "instinct" is to be understood, according to the explanations of the German pessimists, as a terrible force that compels us to reproduce our own misery, or whether "instinct" is instead a power that weaves circumstantial experiences into a totality whose coherence is fulfilling. For many of the characters of Moore's later fiction, life turns out to have a design that is revealed as it is realized by the self-narrating act. For these characters, as for the autobiographical persona, the apprehension of that design leads to the strength, and in part the resignation, necessary to endure the constrictions of historical life.

As might be expected, characters who seek this inner design, spurred on by their burgeoning faith in the legitimacy of the private conscience, find themselves at odds with repressive forces. The restrictions of class battled by Esther Waters are conjoined with the restrictions upon intellectual and sexual freedom imposed by the church. Yet Moore's concern lies less with the destructive influence of oppressive powers than with the subjectivity that refutes them. In terms that describe much of Moore's later work, Joseph Stephen O'Leary remarks of *The Lake* that

> it belongs to a line of novels in which interest in the workings of society is almost eclipsed by the concern to communicate in all its primitive vigour a message of self-realisation, a gospel of Life. Gospels rather than novels are the typical produce of this generation, steeped in Nietzsche's *Zarathustra*, the daunting model of the genre.

> Whatever ironic distance the evangelist maintains towards his
> Christ-figure, the novels of Gide, Forster, Lawrence and Joyce's
> *Portrait* remain stirring affirmations of the self and of life which
> wrench the novel form away from its traditional social bearings. . . .
> The choices of Moore's priest, Gide's immoralist, Joyce's artist,
> Lawrence's lovers bear a purely negative, anarchic, relation to a
> social context, despite dreams of social regeneration. . . . Madame
> Bovary is no longer crushed by the world. Her reinforced rebel-
> lious subjectivity, now backed by the collusion of the artist, subverts
> the established order.[1]

The cultivation of subjectivity increasingly provides the means
by which social authority is refuted. While experience continues to
be what Esther Waters called "a hard fight" with a hostile world,
more and more it is also, to use the words of Mrs. Barfield, "a long
romance." As the latter phrase suggests, the novels begin to take a
retrospective turn through which the pattern of romance can be ascribed to what is otherwise a relentless series of battles with circumstance. Moore's later fiction and autobiographies depict protagonists
who are acutely aware of their own acts of memory and whose revi-
sionary recollections effect a compromise with the forces of the social world. Technically, this process is rendered through an indirect
discourse by which the thoughts and sensory experiences of the
characters replace the realist narrator. Guided by "instinct" and the
soundings of the natural world, his characters attempt to recover
their lives from the authoritarian structures that have molded them.
Their answers indicate a new direction in Moore's persistent attempt
to balance the need to live according to an ethic of free thought and
private instinct with the need to be part of a world greater than one's
own narcissistic self-cultivation.

"To Live Your Life or to Put Your Life Aside"

In *The Edwardian Temperament*, Jonathan Rose mentions T. E.
Hulme's complaint that whereas in previous eras God and, later,
Reason had dominated intellectual discourse, now "all the best peo-
ple take off their hats and lower their voices when they speak of
Life." Rose goes on to explain that for the Edwardians, "Life"

> could mean the surrogate religion of vitalism, the worship of the
> life process as a spiritual force. It could specifically mean the cre-
> ation of new life, an erotic impulse breaking out of Victorian con-

straints and sometimes worshipped as a religion in itself. Life could also be a mysterious spiritual quality that endowed human beings with identity, consciousness, a moral sense, and free will. . . . The cult of Life represented as well a reaction against the late Victorian cults of Art and Decadence. . . . In its most general sense, Life represented a demand for individual freedom and self-realization.[2]

Throughout the writings of George Moore, "life" is similarly tied to self-realization. Near the conclusion of *The Lake*, Nora Glynn admonishes Father Oliver that the most pressing need for each person is to "try to realize himself—I mean that we must try to bring the gifts that Nature gave us to fruition" (*L* 133). What, however, is constituted by such an aspiration? In his discussion of *The Lake*, John Wilson Foster succinctly states that for Moore "self-realization meant five related liberties: the expression of sexuality and acceptance of the body; unbridled curiosity of thought; freedom of conscience; the satisfying of the aesthetic instinct; and relish of nature."[3] The parallels between Rose's list and Foster's reveal how closely the debates of the Edwardian era echo Moore's persistent preoccupations.

I would add another crucial element, however, to a definition of Moore's sense of "life." Self-realization is closely tied to the capacity to articulate subjectivity, as seen in Esther Waters's struggle to find words or Albert Nobbs's inability to find them. For the protagonist of *The Lake*, the process begins with letter writing, continues through his symbolic interpretation of nature, and culminates in a new career as a journalist. As Moore imagines it, self-realization involves, in addition to the unfolding of one's gifts, the capacity to tell the story of that maturation. Self-articulation becomes a necessary aspect of the process and one that mitigates the primitivism of much vitalist discourse. Freedom of conscience and articulative capacity function in reciprocal relationship for his characters, and he also defines this reciprocity as the distinguishing feature of his authorial ambitions. In the introduction to the Carra edition of his works, "Apologia pro scriptis meis," he asserts: "Conventions there must be; we find them in savage as well as in civilised life; but man's instincts are always invading the moral law, and may loosen the conventions of prose narrative still further, and this Apologia serves as a rallying cry for seekers of a thoughtful and personal prose."[4] Moore here correlates the maintenance of individual liberty with the establishment of an innovative and subjective, or "personal," mode of narrative.

After the turn of the century, Moore's fiction steadily advances

toward a depiction of the process by which we progress from in-
tuition to consciousness. Having built his reputation on the realist novel, he wished to preserve its frankness and verisimilitude;
throughout his career, he would attack abstractions which, he believed, falsify experience and stunt human development. But he also
wished to trace the workings of that "undefinable, yet intensely real
life that lies beneath our consciousness, that life which knows, wills,
and perceives without help from us."[5] To combine realism and exploration of the unconscious, Moore had to create a new way of
telling a story. Conventional words, he wrote in *Sister Teresa*, were
"ineffectual to explain. . . . With words you can tell the exterior facts
of life; but you cannot tell the intense yet involuntary life of the
soul—that intricate and unceasing life."[6] As has been documented in
the numerous studies of Moore's evolving fictional technique, he began to borrow from Wagner's operas (and even more specifically
from French literary Wagnerism) the technique of recurring motifs
and seamless transitions between varying planes of narrative.[7] His
appreciation for the short stories of Turgenev and Dostoyevsky led
him to prize understated psychological observation and the construction of narrative as a series of waves: "each chapter rising out of the
preceding chapter in suspended cadence always, never a full close
. . . a smooth current, not very rapid, but flowing always, turning
sometimes east, sometimes west, winding, disappearing at last
mysteriously like a river."[8] Technique, he argued, could mirror the
very process of consciousness.

   Evelyn Innes (1898) and *Sister Teresa* (1901) represent his first
substantial moves toward a new kind of fiction, although his technical and thematic ambitions were greater than he could then handle
with complete success. Only a month after the first publication of
Evelyn Innes, Moore expressed his fears to Edouard Dujardin that he
"had given three years to the concoction of an imbecility."[9] The two
novels were repeatedly revised and substantially rewritten, yet neither satisfied him, and at the last he subjected the novels to blister-
ing mockery in *Hail and Farewell* and forbade their inclusion in the
Uniform Edition of his works. Although marred by melodramatic
scenes, overwritten passages, and digressions on such topics as Wagner and Celtic mythology, neither novel deserves quite the antipathy
its author came to feel. Both novels, at least in the far superior initial
versions, offer insight into the psychology of religious and sexual
experience. In addition to their innovations in narrative construction, the questions they raise remain compelling, even if their an-

swers are obscured by a lack of control over the totality of each novel.

Moore's story concerns an intelligent and musically gifted young woman of Catholic upbringing who is taken from the cloistered world of her father's home by Sir Owen Asher, a wealthy aesthete whose ambitions include making her his lover and training her to become a great Wagnerian soprano. Success follows, but so does terrifying moral confusion as Evelyn seeks to reproduce in life the sensual excitement she feels on the stage. She turns from Asher's agnostic positivism and his frantic pursuit of pleasure to the intellectual and spiritualist concerns of the Irish musician Ulick Dean. However, her own intense sexual response to both men, along with their aggressively unorthodox views, frightens her to such an extent that she succumbs to the influence of a priest. At his insistence, she takes refuge in a convent where she attempts to suppress her sexual and artistic longings by religious fervor. At the end, she purges herself of the need for either dogma or sensuality as a broken yet finally peaceful woman.

Through this tale, Moore probes several essential questions. Even the most trivial personalities in the story wonder what the purpose of their lives might be, although with few exceptions they lack the will and imagination to follow through on their intimations. If life's purpose is self-realization, Moore explores what precisely that quest involves. And, perhaps most urgently, he asks how one can heed the necessity to live in harmony with what he would call one's instincts, unhampered by social or religious codes, yet maintain an ethically responsible relation with one's fellows. Sir Owen Asher instructs Evelyn soon after they meet, "Is not our first duty toward ourselves? The rest is vague and uncertain, the development of our own faculties is, after all, that which is most sure."[10] That line of argument can be traced as far back as *Parnell and His Island,* and the very fact that Moore continues to pursue the question suggests that he was never entirely comfortable with the resolutions he projected. While later works demonstrate a more consciously controlled ambivalence, his attitude in *Evelyn Innes* and *Sister Teresa* projects a confusion that is clarified only at the conclusion of *Sister Teresa's* first edition. That clarity never effected a reconstruction of the whole in accordance with its insights. When Moore rewrote the story, he altered his ending in a way that was inconsistent with the psychology of his characters, and his failure to comprehend his subject is also betrayed by the clichéd, sentimental prose of the revisions. The first ending, however, is written with such skill and force as to serve as a center of interpretation for the admittedly muddled behemoth that is this double-novel.

From the start, *Evelyn Innes* confronts the problem of self-consciousness, one of the most perplexing difficulties within the ethic of self-realization Moore was trying to establish. Frequently in his work, as in much Edwardian literature, self-consciousness involves self-observation and, as such, impedes spontaneity, joy, and even sincerity —that troubled term so associated with the Victorian legacy, yet rekindled with fervor in the first decade of the new century.[11] Previously, Moore had voiced his discomfort with the figure of the observational artist through his character John Harding, the realistic novelist. Since he monitors himself as well as others, the autobiographical persona is suspect to an even greater degree than Harding, and *Hail and Farewell*'s self-watcher extraordinaire is redeemed only, perhaps, by his wide-eyed naïveté. Moore's irredeemable self-watchers, Mike Fletcher (of the truly disastrous novel of the same name) and Mildred Lawson of *Celibates*, observe themselves so closely as to be unable to love anyone. Mike is promiscuous, and Mildred's sexual impulse is as self-directed as her ambitions.

Owen Asher and Evelyn Innes embody similar tendencies. Sir Owen's obsession with elegant clothing bespeaks his hunger to acquire beautiful things: fabric, furniture, painting, houses, women. He collects such things in order to stimulate his senses, yet because he has so few inner resources with which to respond to them, he is forced to search out new sensations, which in turn stimulate him with equal brevity.[12] Despite his libertinism, he fails to live according to what Moore would call his instincts. Evelyn is capable of deeper responses, but they soon become susceptible to mechanical recall, and she nearly loses the capacity to act spontaneously. Because she learns to summon her emotions to the stage, she is an effective actress. But rather than simulating, she actually reproduces at will her deepest feelings.[13] Evelyn's incapacity either to perform without living or to live without performing is a source of grim amusement to her: when she returns with Owen to her father's house to seek a reconciliation, she imagines herself playing Brünnhilde and momentarily expects to hear Wotan's music issue from her father's mouth. Similarly, in the midst of her confession to the Reverend Mother, she becomes exquisitely aware of how fine a narrative her story makes and cannot resist adding the details that enhance its performative effect.

Despite her limitations, Evelyn's character is stronger than Owen's in that she is driven to find some way of reconciling her ideas with her behavior. She is also more fully endowed with a self-creative capacity that allows her a partial escape from the malaise of self-consciousness and inauthenticity. Near the beginning of *Sister Teresa*, Evelyn, having renounced her lovers, lies awake most of the night in the country house where she has gone to visit not knowing that Owen would also be there. Alone, she undergoes an agonizing test of her chastity and is saved from finally going to Owen's room by a remembrance of the *Veni Creator* as sung in the sweet, faint voices of nuns. Because the narrative perspective merges with Evelyn's own, the scene is given with minimal irony. Her struggle amounts to much more than an attempt to stay out of Owen's bed— a motivation Moore would have found amusingly absurd if that were all it amounted to. Instead, it is a test of her power to imagine herself, a power Moore finds crucial, even if the only language by which she can succeed is that of the church. Owen, on the other hand, has insufficient will to so succeed. Attracted to the pantheistic spirituality of Ulick Dean as an antidote to his own relentless materialism, he invites the young musician to dinner. The first dinner goes well despite their temperamental incompatibility, but although he knows such topics will repel the ethereal Ulick, Owen finally cannot restrain himself from talking about his acquisitions, his horses, hunting parties, and mistresses. Subject to loneliness and the pleasures of his senses, he is also painfully aware of his limitations. His aspirations to a life of the intellect and spirit are undercut by attachments common to his class. Unlike Evelyn (and perhaps unlike his creator) he cannot imagine himself sufficiently to bring that creation into being.

But how, finally, are we to understand the resolution, if indeed it is a resolution, to which Evelyn comes? At the conclusion of the double-novel, Evelyn has ceased to accept church dogma. Nor does her vow of celibacy alone give cause to believe that Moore condemns her choice to remain a nun: through most of the story, sexuality is an aspect of narcissism, stimulated by music and luxurious dinner parties. No one within the romantic triangle imagines marriage as anything besides a protective measure against Evelyn's becoming a nun or indulging in two lovers simultaneously. Early in *Sister Teresa*, she recognizes that hers is less a conflict between spirituality and sexuality than a conflict between her innate passivity and the call of some yet unnamed voice within her that requires strengths hitherto delitescent.

To look at the question of how to interpret Evelyn's decision, we must go to the final two chapters of *Sister Teresa*. It was the novel's ending that was most condemned by reviewers and eventually rejected by Moore himself; to a modern reader, however, accustomed to the ironic anticlimaxes Moore admired in French and Russian fiction, this ending is unquestionably the strongest part of either novel. The old prioress, who joined the convent after the sudden deaths of her husband and child and thus like Evelyn "renounced" rather than "refused" the world, dies leaving her friendless. Although the sudden loss of her beautiful voice dims any prospect of making a comfortable living outside the convent, Evelyn plans to escape as soon as she can complete her promise to the prioress to write a history of the order. She finishes the history, but the moment of opportunity only comes after many months of waiting, and finally, with the stolen keys in her hand, she opens the door to "the spring-tide." All nature is full of vitality and movement: birds call to one another and the fields are shimmering with light. But a change has taken place in Evelyn—"something had broken in her"—and she closes the door.

This decisive action is not unprepared for. The previous year, Evelyn had watched the flowers of the garden reach toward the sunlight and recognized that all things reach toward light. She imagines the darkest parts of the forest, the underswell of the ocean, "even the stones in the centre of the earth" turning toward this source of being. In the process, "The great secret was revealed; she understood the mysterious yearning which impels us in turn to reject and to accept life."[14] She comes to believe that the elevation of the Host is no more and no less than an instance of the interpenetration of the natural and the divine, which repeats infinitely through everything that lives. Although Moore wrote to an acquaintance that the subject of his book was the question of whether "to live your life or to put your life aside,"[15] everything about his conclusion suggests that the drive to embrace or to renounce is impelled by the same need to discover life's sacramental quality.

Evelyn's understanding is further elucidated in the final chapter, which starts immediately after the scene in which Evelyn closes the door upon the springtide. Beginning with the simple phrase, "In the middle of the following year Mademoiselle Heilbron called to see her, and Teresa came into the parlour," Moore effects the final transformation of Evelyn Innes to Sister Teresa and intimates that since closing the door, she had experienced time as a featureless continuum without struggle or change. In response to her friend's queries as to how she could bear to remain in a convent, Teresa answers, "The important thing to do is to live, and we do not begin to know life, taste life, until we put it aside. This sounds like a paradox, but it is a simple little truth. Life is the will of God, and to enter into the will of God we must forget ourselves, we must try to live outside ourselves in the general life." When she is asked how any can know the will of God, she responds, "What is your own breath Louise? You cannot explain it, and yet it is yourself. And there are times when the will of God seems as near to us as our own breath."[16] Evelyn has discovered a unanimity between herself and animated nature: to live in the general life is to feel her own life's breath most intently.

Sister Teresa's affirmation does not end the novel. Instead, Moore concludes on a skeptical note as the narrative perspective shifts to that of a minor character, Louise Heilbron, an opera singer from Teresa's past. Readers who find themselves doubtful of the epiphanies of the prior chapter will discover in the final scene their skepticism voiced by Louise, a shallow, sensual, and ambitious woman who is nevertheless kind and not without sympathy. Louise is puzzled by Teresa's laughter and wonders if she hears bitterness in it. She leaves the convent unsure how to interpret Teresa's words and can deduce only that perhaps it was the loss of her voice that caused her friend to remain a nun. In the final sentences of the novel, a carriage takes her back to the social world Evelyn has renounced: "'So this is the last stage,' she said as she drove back to London. And then Louise thought of her own life. She was now forty-five, she might go on singing for a few years—then she, too, would have to begin her packing up, and she wondered what her end would be."[17] Louise has a brief premonition of both the uncertainty of her own "last stage" and the certainty of her death, but is unable to understand her friend's response to the same dilemma. While Evelyn's growth is limited by her self-acknowledged need for authority, she nevertheless adapts the ecclesiastical dogma of the church to the answers revealed by her own pantheistic theology.

Moore's drastic revisions of this ending in later editions of the novel indicate the degree to which he was uncomfortable with the reconciliation of the contrary drives toward self-expression and submission, as well as by the reconciliation of vitalism and Catholicism so implied. An anecdote from *A Story-Teller's Holiday* (1918) offers another corrective revision, as the autobiographical narrator recalls a nun once seen at a railway station. Inventing a story for her, he imagines a tale of thwarted escape. She will eventually, he concludes, feel "nothing of the old desire, no faintest echo of it, and she'll be glad and believe the peace she is enjoying comes from God, unsuspicious that it is the absorption of the individual will in the will of the community" (*STH* 1:45). Here, nearly two decades after the first edition of the novel, Moore uses language echoing that of *Sister Teresa* to condemn this anonymous nun's decision. Within the context of her vision in the garden, however, Teresa's belief that she lives now within "the general life" reads as an acceptable compromise and a predecessor of those acceptable compromises between the individual will and the experiential world achieved by later characters. The same phrase, in fact, is used again a few years later in *The Lake* to describe the natural world toward which Father Gogarty is drawn. Yet the undeniable ambiguity of the ending, as well as Moore's apparent discomfort with it, places *Sister Teresa* with other early twentieth-century works as diverse as *Howard's End, Candida,* and *The Rainbow* in offering only the most inconclusive of conclusions to the conflict between self-development and the summons to become part of a wider life.

In the novel that followed *Sister Teresa,* Moore tells the story of a man who takes Evelyn's quest a crucial step further as he attempts to re-create himself outside the descriptive terms of the church. In one sense, *The Lake* is the record of an autobiography in the process of becoming. As Father Oliver finds a reader in his correspondent, Nora Glynn, he begins through this dialogical relationship to re-evaluate his past, leading him to reinterpret earlier letters and to produce revisions in subsequent ones. In the midst of this epistolary self-creation, he begins as well to reinterpret the voice of "the talking lake." Through this process, he acquires a new language from Nora, from some unidentified voice within himself, and from the soundings of a sexualized and resurrective landscape.

In order to chart the acquisition of a new language of self-description, Moore had to find ways of depicting a consciousness that had not yet found the words with which to represent itself. In many of the stories he wrote during this period, the characters envision their lives through a linear image incorporating time and space. In the final paragraph of *Sister Teresa,* Louise travels along the road and sees for a brief moment the path of her future. Young Agnes Lahens of *Celibates,* on the return to her convent, finds herself conscious only of "the remembrance of the road leading to the convent" and the path leading forward through it and through time to "the little cemetery at the end of the garden where the nuns go to rest" (*C* 559). For Louise and Agnes Lahens, the line leads out toward futility and, finally, death. In the final paragraph of "Homesickness" from *The Untilled Field*, it leads backward to the time and place where the protagonist feels his lost significance to be located. And at the conclusion of *The Lake*, Father Gogarty's mind moves back to the places and time preceding his present moment and forward beyond that moment, a motion that indicates his comprehension at some inarticulate level of the organic continuum of his experience.

In the years following the early editions of *Evelyn Innes* and *Sister Teresa*, Moore rapidly refined this device of the spatial representation of consciousness into a narrative technique that could govern an entire novel, and increasingly his fictions appear to emanate, like his autobiographies, from the consciousness of the characters themselves. During his stay in Ireland, he brought to this evolving technique his vivid memories of the Mayo landscape and a long-established dedication to placing his fiction in particularized settings. Within a landscape marked by the signs of Irish history, *The Untilled Field* and *The Lake* depict the interaction of consciousness and space. Characteristically, he polarizes the claims of nationality, family, and religion and that of what he would call "the instinct for life." However, to a much greater degree than Evelyn Innes, Moore's priest finds a way to follow the principle of living "outside ourselves in the general life" and, at the same time, "to taste life."

The Landscapes of Consciousness

The Lake opens as a young priest, Father Oliver Gogarty, paces the road bordering Lake Carra, near the town of Westport in County Mayo. We slowly learn that he is overwrought because his harsh sermon against sexual immorality has caused his friend the schoolmistress, whom he suspects of having an affair with a soldier, to flee the parish. Gogarty fears she has drowned herself in the lake by which he walks. He later receives a letter from a Father O'Grady in London informing him of her safety and chastising his harshness. With this letter Gogarty begins a correspondence with O'Grady and Nora Glynn, the schoolmistress. Through his letters and his long walks around the lake, he reviews the events that led him to the priesthood and gradually realizes that he entered the priesthood as an escape from the stultifying routine of his father's shop. Even more gradually, he recognizes that his condemnation of Nora was prompted more by sexual jealousy than by spiritual righteousness. His desire for Nora eventually reveals itself to be in truth the even more dangerous desire for the vibrancy she embodies. So as to avoid causing scandal to his small parish, he contrives to leave his clothes on a hill and to swim across the lake to a rail station on the other side, leaving his family and parishioners to assume he has accidentally drowned. He swims through the night, finally boarding the train that will take him to a boat for New York and an unknown, if not unpremeditated, future.

The edition of 1921 maintains the original ideas while providing many technical improvements. In this revision, Moore removed long digressions on Wagner, biblical history, and the Catholic church; deleted numerous facetious and merely topical passages; reduced and tightened elements of the plot; and effected subtle transitions between narrative and speech and between different temporal planes. By presenting Father Gogarty's perceptions of landscape, repeated like musical motifs in variations, Moore establishes a vocabulary through which Gogarty first describes and then understands his own conflicts. He is a man who by profession has sublimated a disruptive awareness of sensory stimulation and the self-examination of his disquieting desires. Only through the involuntary accumulation of harmonious or dissonant images—nearly always images from the natural world—can Gogarty permit himself to examine his creed or his motivations. With great restraint, the narrative voice of the final edition of 1921 allows Gogarty to render the features of the land around him into his own psychic geography, whose meaning he understands in varying degrees. The interpretation of this geography never appears as the willful imposition of an author; the land and its meanings appear entirely the protagonist's.

Despite the nearly faultless control over the final version and its tone of passionate sincerity, for any reader familiar with modern Irish literature one exceedingly jarring element persists: the name of the protagonist. Moore's friend Oliver Gogarty was an urbane Dublin physician known in his youth for his sexual adventures, ribald verses, and satiric assaults upon the church. Whereas Moore had long utilized the names of real people in his autobiographies and fiction, the characterizations therein are generally consistent with what else we know about the people described. Obvious use of models for characters who bear other names (for instance, the modeling of Owen Asher on Sir William Eden) provide insightful portraits of real people while enriching the density of the fictional characterizations for readers familiar with the extratextual allusions. But, in the case of *The Lake,* no apparent continuity can be established between the character and the real man from whom his name was taken.

It is difficult to discern Moore's intentions in appropriating Gogarty's name, although the effect of his choice can be analyzed with more success. Moore's explanation to Gogarty's mother concerning the irresistibility of a name with two dactyls is little more than a satire of conjectures of authorial intent. Gogarty himself professed to no annoyance, and the notion of Gogarty as a Baudelairean mock-priest may have been a familiar jest in Dublin literary circles, as James Joyce's depiction of him in *Ulysses* suggests.[18] Perhaps it was only a private joke intended either to underscore the dissimilarity between Gogarty and his namesake or, conversely, to intimate the suspicion finally given voice in *Hail and Farewell* that, despite his rebelliousness, young "Conan," as he is called there, would in middle age become a pious and upright citizen. Such little jokes might have seemed in keeping with the breezy, even fatuous tone of *The Lake's* early editions. Yet by 1921, one would think the joke would be over and that Moore, having transformed the giddy Rose Leicester into the wise Nora Glynn and the dandyish Ralph Ellis into the scholarly Walter Poole, would have taken the opportunity to revise Father Oliver Gogarty's name as well.

Because he did not, the book produces two distinct effects related to the configuration of Moore's autobiographical persona, his concept of authorship, and his portrayal of the priest as the emergent "author" of his own story. Near the end of the novel, Father Gogarty, struck by the possibility that some goatherd might take the clothes he has hidden in the rocks on the other side of the lake, contemplates the sight he would make huddled naked in a poor parishioner's cabin while the man went to fetch him a suit of clothes to wear home. He reflects, "If anyone comes to the cabin I shall have to hold the door to. There is a comic side to every adventure . . . and a more absurd one it would be difficult to imagine" (*L* 176). The comic side of *The Lake* can be found in the absurd appropriation of Oliver Gogarty's name, a reference that jolts us out of the earnest and self-contained world of the novel. By retaining this sign of his mocking presence, Moore makes his signature gesture. An analogy might well be made with the painter who always includes his own face or name as part of his design. We become aware of an author who refuses to relinquish his ironic, if frequently sympathetic, view of human aspiration.

While this explanation makes sense in light of Moore's obses-
sively subjective discussions of almost any subject, it also produces a
second effect which undermines the dominance of the author by
disturbing the self-containment of his text. In his study of the origins of the novel, Jon Stratton argues that "in works read by the
bourgeois reader the assumption is always that the text is enclosed.
It is the premise of confinement which enables the reader to experience the text as an object containing meaning . . . the confined text is
read . . . as free of all constraint. It becomes, in the realist novel, the
world in its final bourgeois production as an object which bourgeois
readers—and critics—can enter and observe, extrapolating situations and characterisations from the words on the page."[19] Stratton
goes on to argue that the book, as a self-enclosed world, acts as a
"virgin text" to be deflowered by the reader, fetishized into an object
of privately owned, if socially constructed, meaning. The closely
woven world of *The Lake* would be aptly described by Stratton's
terms but for this inexplicable intrusion. Like an irritant, the incongruous intrusion of Oliver St John Gogarty's name disrupts the
reader's capacity to possess an interpretive meaning with full confidence. As I have suggested of *Hail and Farewell*, Moore pivots between monologic and dialogic modes of art; once the novel enters
into a dialogue with a world outside itself, one whose meaning is left
unsettled and uncontrolled by the novel, the perfect, self-enclosed
universe produced by the novelist is disturbed, and an opening is
left for the uncontrollable impact of the world outside the text.

Even for the reader unfamiliar with Oliver St John Gogarty,
symptoms of an ironically reductive point of view remain, and frequently that perspective is Father Oliver's own. He habitually judges
a previous letter to have been silly and decides he must write another (at times equally silly) to correct the earlier one. At one point,
he crumples a sad letter-in-progress when he imagines Nora and her
employer laughing, "Poor Priesty," and tossing it into the fire. Later
in the novel, when Gogarty expresses a philosophical position akin to
Moore's own, he casts an ironic eye over even that set of beliefs.
After writing Nora an eloquent, ardently persuasive letter about the
vitalist ideals that now compel him to leave the priesthood, Gogarty
regrets his testament. The letter, it seems to him, "was written in a
foolish, vainglorious mood—a stupid letter that must have made
him appear a fool in her eyes. Had he not said something about—
The thought eluded him; he could only remember the general tone
of his letter, and in it he seemed to consider Nora as a sort of medi-

cine—a cure for religion. He should have written her a simple little letter . . . whereas he had written her the letter of a booby" (*L* 148). This scene, however, is followed by a visit from his curate that reinforces the convictions expressed in the letter, among them the idea incautiously declared to the curate that "the Church looks upon woman as the real danger, because she is the life of the world" (*L* 153). Thus while Gogarty is tempted to view sarcastically his notion of woman as "a sort of medicine—a cure for religion," he repudiates his self-sarcasm to confess the idea again in earnest terms that Moore himself echoes in a letter of 1913 characterizing Protestantism as a "vac[c]ine" against the "pox" of Catholicism (*GMP* 273).

In such scenes, Moore presents the ironic view while containing it within the consciousness of Father Oliver and eventually dismissing it. However, one scene continues to be as potentially disruptive in its dissonant irony as is the use of Oliver St John Gogarty's name. As the priest prepares to swim across the lake, Moore describes him standing on the rocks "as on a pedestal, tall and gray in the moonlight—buttocks hard as a faun's, and dimpled like a faun's when he draws himself up before plunging after a nymph" (*L* 178). Joseph Steven O'Leary finds the ludicrous image a reminder of Moore's tragicomic sense of life, and Jean Noel bravely attempts to explain the image in light of Mallarmé's "Afternoon of a Faun." Yet the image—as Joyce recognized in his parody of it in *Ulysses*—is much too incongruous to accept as an integral part of the narrative.[20] Whether Moore lost control over his stylistic mannerisms or whether he was intentionally parodying them cannot be determined. Like the cynical perspective of Louise Heilbron at the conclusion of the original *Sister Teresa*, this deflation of the ecstatic moment undermines the authority of Father Oliver's new knowledge. However, fully surrounded as it is by the crescendo of a wave that has been building faultlessly since the book's initial sentence, the note of ridicule itself seems out of place. Because this is the only moment when Gogarty is physically described, and thus the only moment when a viewer is implied, the scene jolts us into cognizance of an author behind the text. The "face" of the author appears in the picture, but its dominance is limited by the inadequacy of its mockery to refute so much assertion of belief. Despite these intrusions of the satiric perspective —a perspective integral to Moore's autobiographical representation —the novel abounds in affirmation, at the same time that it engages the most difficult problems of repression, displacement, and self-division.

At such points, Moore's ironic outlook seems to distort the work rather than function as an integral element within it. In general, his ironic outlook manifests itself most successfully in the portraits of characters of limited intellect or education who are either shrewd enough to get what they want, sufficiently good-natured to accept what they get, or too inhibited by the narrowness of their upbringing to know even what they want. While in his autobiographies articulate and self-conscious individuals become richly ironic comic characters, in his fiction such characters are frequently mere spokespersons who express various attitudes in overwrought prose. While such novels as *Mike Fletcher* or the 1909 revision of *Sister Teresa* indulge in forthright didacticism, it is perhaps Moore's inability to fully discard his comic perspective that most mars his attempts to be solemn. This is not to say that his humorous treatments are less serious; in truth they are more so. But in those works that eschew the comic, Moore best controls his intimations of the absurdity of all aspiration when depicting characters who are themselves inarticulate.

In *The Untilled Field,* the collection of stories to which *The Lake* was originally intended to belong, there are certainly stories of the kind I have just disparaged. "The Wild Goose," "In the Clay," "The Way Back," and a conflation of the latter two stories, "Fugitives," all concern painters and writers who embrace and reject Ireland. The stories gave Moore much trouble, and he rewrote and recombined their elements several times without real success. The mannered and callous behavior of their hero-protagonists presents formidable obstacles to establishing an interpretive position, and the characters do little but pronounce opinions on art and religion. Robert Welch has suggested that these stories be read as sustained ironic portraits of inadequate artists whose lives are also "untilled fields."[21] Yet if he is correct, the irony is so subtle (or undeveloped) as to remain ineffectual. Moore's final revision of "The Wild Goose" corroborates Welch's thesis in that it treats its artist-protagonist's aspirations with sardonic humor; however, it is uncertain as to whether the revisions represent an alteration in attitude or a clarification of original intentions. More certainly, the other stories in *The Untilled Field* present characters of the type Moore handles with delicacy, empathy, and unfailing psychological insight. All have visions that set them apart from and in conflict with their social environments, and all seek to imagine themselves.

Since the composition of *The Untilled Field* precedes that of *The*

Lake, it may be useful to look briefly at several of its stories in order to trace further the development of the techniques by which Moore was able to give the autogenous aspirations of his "swimming priest" without an incongruous and disabling cynicism. Most of the characters of these stories lack the capacity to explain just what makes them restless, and with meticulous probing Moore intimates the depth of their dissatisfactions. "In Ireland," Moore writes in *Hail and Farewell,* "men and women die without realising any of the qualities they bring into the world" (58), and the most compelling characters in *The Untilled Field* recognize this of themselves. In place of narratorial comments, he relates primarily through indirect discourse their actions and the comments of others, comments that are most illuminating in what they fail to perceive about those who seek "life."

Gérard Genette makes two distinctions regarding "point of view" that help describe what Moore does in these stories. He divides "point of view" into two categories: "mood" and "voice." The former addresses "the question *who is the character whose point of view orients the narrative perspective?*" and the latter addresses "the very different question *who is the narrator?*—or more simply, the question *who sees?* and the question *who speaks?*"[22] Narrative passages in the stories relate the perceptions of the characters in a prose similar to their own speech in diction and syntax. It is the characters who describe, recall, and comment on the actions of the stories. Because it is they who see and describe the action, they are perhaps best characterized by Genette's term, "focalizors." It is through their senses that we experience the world of the story, and it is through their eyes that we see. Their interior lives also emerge through psychologically revelatory actions and dialogue, the significance of which is hidden from the characters but clarified for the reader by means of ironic juxtapositioning. The seeing and speaking is divided among the whole cast of the story. However, the subtle juxtapositioning that elucidates without overt commentary the limitations of the characters' self-perceptions expresses the ironic point of view.

This technique is most evident in the triptych concerning Father MacTurnan, an intelligent and sympathetic priest. Moore sets up several frames through which it is told how Father MacTurnan attempted to build a theater for passion plays in the bogland of Mayo. After the project met with disaster (the work of ghosts, according to the local people; the will of God, according to Father MacTurnan; and an unfortunate accident, according to a traveling educator), the priest sits each night compulsively knitting more socks than he can possibly wear and haggling with the Board of Works for relief projects to feed his starving parishioners, projects that by cruel bureaucratic design are as useless as his basket of socks. The priest recognizes the futility of his efforts, but contains this recognition within a structure of meaning provided by his faith. He thus retains at least some productivity within the restricted circumstances in which he and his parishioners must live.

Although the three stories are related by an urbane narrator who hears them from the local people, his outlook is given no particular narrative authority. To use Genette's distinctions, he is neither the one who sees nor the one whose view orients the interpretive perspective. Instead, as Augustine Martin has shown in his analysis of the triptych, Moore puts to work "a flexible use of irony" operating "through his alternation of three voices, each speaking from a distinct view of the world." Of particular importance, it is Father MacTurnan's capacity to discipline his despair within an eccentric version of Catholicism that enables him to act at all and to be, as Martin writes, one of "the only manifestations of hope amid the damp and gloom . . . an indefatigable priest who writes letters to the great, plans impossible schemes, but finds a bedrock of consolation in humbly doing what he knows is God's will."[23]

As in the Father MacTurnan sequence, the sober irony of "Homesickness" resides in the degree to which we perceive the characters' lack of self-understanding to be limited—even comic—while at the same time we are encouraged to respect their aspirations. In this story, which of all those in *The Untilled Field* most prefigures the achievements of *The Lake* and *The Brook Kerith*, Moore employs a variation on the tightly controlled objective narrative of the MacTurnan stories and establishes a technique integral to his sense of how a life finds meaning through the recollective process of narration. As the story unfolds, James Bryden, ill and anxious from work in a subterranean Bowery bar, returns to his native village of Duncannon for a rest. Soon after arriving, he realizes that the barren countryside offers a disturbing contrast to the green land of his memory. Lying awake his first night in the loft of one of the town's more prosperous cabins, he feels the emptiness of the country he imagined as a refuge: "The cackling of some geese in the street kept him awake, and he seemed to realize suddenly how lonely the country was, and he foresaw mile after mile of scanty fields stretching all round the lake with one little town in the far corner. A dog howled in the distance, and the fields and the boreens between him and the

dog appeared as in a crystal."[24] This mental mapping of the countryside is one of many such representations by which subjectivity is expressed by its own wordless geographic imaging.

Like the narrator of *Hail and Farewell,* Bryden is intoxicated by
other, more attractive perceptions of the land around him, the relics
of castles and the reflection of glimmering water on a soft, sunny
day. He becomes engaged to a local girl and plans to settle in Duncannon until the censorious intrusion of the parish priest and a letter of greeting from New York quickly cause his fantasy of Ireland
to recede. All the incidents of his remaining years are compressed
into a few sentences: he returns to New York, buys the barroom,
marries, has children; his wife dies, he retires, and with his children
married, he begins to imagine the village he left behind:

> when he looked into the firelight, a vague, tender reverie floated
> up, and Margaret's soft eyes and name vivified the dusk. His wife
> and children passed out of mind, and it seemed to him that a
> memory was the only real thing he possessed, and the desire to see
> Margaret again grew intense. But she was an old woman, she had
> married, maybe she was dead. Well, he would like to be buried in
> the village where he was born.
>
> There is an unchanging, silent life within every man that none
> knows but himself, and his unchanging, silent life was his memory
> of Margaret Dirken. The bar-room was forgotten and all that con-
> cerned it, and the things he saw most clearly were the green hill-
> side, and the bog lake and the rushes about it, and the greater lake
> in the distance, and behind it the blue line of wandering hills.[25]

In addition to his thoughts, Bryden's deepest longings—all of
which exist below a verbal level—are represented in this passage,
as throughout the story, by his visualizations of the land. As in the
spatial representations I have already discussed, Bryden's visualization is also a representation of time: his childhood, his attempted
repatriation, his second exile, and his final return to be buried. By
so encompassing chronology, this visualization of space—a nearly
wordless process in Bryden's own consciousness—becomes his autobiographical act.

An indirect discourse incorporating thoughts and sensory impressions as well as spoken utterance thus intermingles throughout
The Untilled Field with dialogue and descriptions related by the participant or observed by another character. Yet something else happens as well in the conclusion to "Homesickness" that will be seen

again in *The Lake* and later works. As in many of Moore's writings of a decade later, the first sentence of the final paragraph signals an authorial voice reciting what is to be understood as a timeless parable. It brings in the figure of the narrator as storytelling author, and the visual impression of landscape is overtly acknowledged as part of that storyteller's tale: its position as fully narratized speech is made clear. Bryden's own self-narrating activity is absorbed into the frame of the story as related by the implied storyteller-author. This point is of more than technical importance. In the late novels and works like *Memoirs of My Dead Life*, we will see that action becomes much less important than the character's self-narrating act which describes it, and at times even that becomes less important than the self-conscious performance of the storyteller-author who relates the process.

In *The Lake*, Father Gogarty's capacities for explaining—or even telling—his life are as severely limited as those of any of the inarticulate characters of *The Untilled Field*. Much of the novel concerns his repeated revision of the life story he tells himself in the novel's opening chapter (a recollection that is itself identified as a revision of an earlier version of events). Gogarty negotiates among a wide variety of interpretive languages deriving from his ecclesiastical training, his reading, his conversations, the letters he exchanges with Father O'Grady and Nora Glynn, and the voice of "the talking lake." Through the novel's intricate interweaving of imagery, these sources of interpretation are frequently shown to contradict or alter one another. At points, a new voice may lead to the revision of the way another voice had been understood or may join together with it for an epiphanic moment of insight whose source baffles Gogarty as much as the reader. By juxtaposing these competitive interpretive languages, Moore demonstrates how poorly Father Oliver understands his motivations, how frequently he misreads those of others, and how often he must revise and revise yet again his interpretation and his interpretive method.

Once the novel moves into its epistolary mode in the third chapter, this process of revision becomes even more evident. Unlike the letters of Nora Glynn or Father O'Grady, Gogarty's letters are almost always stories; from the narrative of his actions, he then develops a question or expresses an idea. Most often, the stories lead him toward the voicing of repressed longings and dissatisfactions. His expressions surprise and shock him, and he frequently feels the need to write yet another letter repudiating the ideas of the last. These revisions are the primary method by which Gogarty's self-narrative evolves. They are interspersed with a few important conversations and numerous scenes of wandering near the woods and lake, places that speak to him in ways that affect his letters and are affected in turn by them. As in *Hail and Farewell*, dialogic exchange becomes the means to the discovery of an individual voice whose source may lie in "instinct" but that also derives from a world of discourse originating outside the self. Moore brings together letters—frequently a component of historical documentation or of the pretense of "found" discourse operative in the epistolary novel— with a highly subjective form and topic: the narratized representation of the priest's fluctuating mind, incorporating sensation, visual impression, and recollected utterances. That mind itself, however, is shown to be the product of prior and competing forms of language.

This process by which one interpretive code modifies another is best illustrated by two sequences of letter exchanges. After Gogarty learns that Nora's employer, Walter Poole, is a scholar of Christian history (and after he reads a newspaper description of Poole showing him to be a young and handsome man), he writes Nora a set of furious letters itemizing the spiritual dangers of Poole's influence upon her and asserting his own responsibility for her soul. Out of control, he finds himself breaking off his denunciations midsentence "to tell you that I think you are right when you say that we all want change. I feel I have lived too long by the side of this lake, and I am thinking of going to London" (*L* 91). A sudden storm interrupts him, and after he has wandered outside to watch the sky and the swirling birds, his letter is concluded in the gentle tone of a friend. The composition of the letter took Gogarty to a point of self-revelation whose ferocity was echoed by the passionate storm he describes to Nora; yet because the storm is also extraordinarily lovely, the tenderness of the man he is discovering himself to be is also made manifest. Two weeks later he writes again, vacillating among pious lecturing, apologies for the same kind of lecturing in earlier letters, depictions of the natural piety of the medieval ecclesiastics, and admissions of his despair. From early September to mid-December, he writes compulsively, each letter contradicting the one before and each contradiction fostered by the landscape reacting upon his consciousness or by the unpremeditated self-revelations his epistolary narrations prompt. "Why am I writing about myself?" he asks. "I want to escape from myself, and your letters enable me to do so" (*L* 93). His correspondence, however, accomplishes the opposite effect.

Nora's letters draw Gogarty closer and closer to the lake, which in Moore's symbolic geography mirrors the instinctual self. Classically, the mirror figures as a sign of moral danger, and Moore likewise frequently questions the ethics of self-reflection. To enter the lake in pursuit of one's image is to have accepted Narcissus's quest and, as well, the consequent danger of alienation from the rest of nature. Father Gogarty, thinking of the arduous swim that awaits him, "imagined the waves slapping in his face, and then he imagined them slapping about the face of a corpse drifting towards the Joycetown shore" (L 155). But to face the lake's solitude is also to enter the community of life in and around its waters, a world in which Gogarty sees woman as "a fountain, shedding living water," where the hedge exhales her perfume, the wind is her breath, and over the lake's water the blackbird calls to its mate.[26]

Through the letters and events of that autumn, the novel draws together the Narcissus parable, the doctrine of Catholic self-renunciation, echoes of Dante, the "talking lake," and the epistolary exchange itself to portray the multitude of voices that effect Father Oliver's final conversion to a creed of private conscience. Having sent throughout the autumn months a series of letters depicting the melancholy Irish season, a desperate letter inquiring if Nora is Walter Poole's mistress, and series of quotations from the self-renunciatory text, The Imitation of Christ, Gogarty engages in one of the most important conversations of the novel. His morose curate, Father Moran, has come to say good-bye before wandering out of the parish in search of whiskey, and Gogarty spends the night walking mile after mile with him along "the worn mountain road" until, as if by some miracle, Moran's burning need for drink disappears. Father Oliver returns exhausted to his chair before the fire to wonder if Nora would question the virtue of such a conquest over the self. Gogarty appears to know that Moran's drinking is a symptom of an illness they both share, and in suppressing the need for whiskey, Moran suppresses his self's cry for recognition.

Such questions are referred to Nora as if she had become Gogarty's new moral center, replacing the church. A new letter from Nora catches his eye as he rests at his desk after his long night's walk with Moran, and he imagines she has written to confess herself Poole's mistress. Delirious with grief, he wanders into the night without opening the letter. At the edge of the lake he finds himself, like Dante, lost in the midst of a great wood, "standing in an open space; about him were dripping trees, and a ghostly sky overhead, and no sound but that of falling leaves." He believes himself to be searching for a lost feminine soul, and an unnamed woman "white and cold" descends into his arms but will neither allow him to lift her veil nor escape with her into the wood. If Father O'Grady has acted as a kind of Virgil, a wise and virtuous guide who as a priest cannot himself enter the heaven Moore imagines, then Nora is a Beatrice, an untouchable vision who tells him that "he must abide by the shores of the lake." Yet she is also tantalizingly, painfully real. In this sequence, made dreamlike yet poignantly actual by his acute awareness of briarthorns, rushes, the great oak trees, and the peculiarity of Nora's walk, Gogarty develops yet another personal reading of the lake. The imagined voice of Nora, speaking for one aspect of his repressed self, tells another part—that which desires her—that the lake is neither a place for human relationship nor an expression of a pantheistic utopia. It reflects and contains instead within its water the dark, cold, terrifying solitude of the discrete self.

From this point, Gogarty's repertoire of explanatory discourses becomes hopelessly muddled as he moves from one to another seeking a way to describe his condition. He prays to God, but asks that Nora be kept for him in heaven and begs God's forgiveness for having impeded her ability to go quietly away to have her baby in Dublin and then return to him in Mayo. He composes a pitiful expression of his loneliness which he then throws away, imagining Nora's dismissive rejection of its sentiments, and seeks comfort not in *The Imitation of Christ* but in a passionate poem of unrequited longing. Again, he is searching for a vocabulary by which to interpret his life. Writing to Nora that he had been ill for many weeks, he notes with wonder that "after a severe illness one is alone with one's self, the whole of one's life sings in one's head like a song" (*L* 129). In this letter, he admits his love and the inadequacy of his "badly assimilated" ideas, yet resolves to bear his spiritual infirmity with stoic resignation and to fulfill his duties. Sensing that in his subjugation of the complex self he imposes an artificial arrangement upon the music of his life's song, she responds: "But we must not think entirely of our duties to others; we must think of our duties to ourselves. Each one must try to realize himself—I mean that we must try to bring the gifts that Nature gave us to fruition. Nature has given you many gifts: I wonder what will become of you?" (*L* 133).

What makes Nora's statement much different from the very similar statement of Sir Owen Asher in *Evelyn Innes* is her invocation of "nature," a concept foreign to the self-cultivated and unspontaneous world of the earlier novel. Nora affirms that there is a guide within each person greater than any other claim upon his or her allegiance and greater than any other teacher. It is Moore's subscription to this extraordinarily Protestant concept that for him places the individual at odds with almost any kind of community beyond a few mutually beneficial friendships. In part, we can ascribe his individualism to the privileged position he inhabited as a wealthy European male endowed with the ability to speak and be heard. In addition, Moore's liberationist model of "natural love" follows exactly the line of argument Michel Foucault traces to a fundamental misapprehension of the relationship between power and sexuality. In the vitalist theology of life, sex is aligned with "nature" as an ahistorical autonomous agency in rebellious opposition to power, which is defined primarily as an interdictory force located in political institutions. Even to speak about this forbidden sexuality "has the appearance of a deliberate transgression. A person who holds forth in such language places himself to a certain extent outside the reach of power; he upsets established law; he somehow anticipates the coming freedom."[27] In refutation, Foucault argues that the discourses of sexuality may themselves be created by the forces of power (power being here imagined as dispersed among many facets of a given society). In the light of such a critique, the role of transgressive hero, which Moore cultivated since his early years in Paris, would be very difficult to affirm. The definition of the self through repudiation of national origin depended upon his myth of autogeny, and in particular, the belief that his own discourse of nature was itself natural and unique.

Moore clearly makes claims for an instinctive language of liberationist nature throughout *The Lake*. Father Gogarty hears a voice akin to what in *Confessions of a Young Man* is called an "echo-augury": a latent urging of "natural" origin. Moore borrowed the term from De Quincey who defined it as that which occurs when "a man, perplexed in judgment, and sighing for some determining counsel, suddenly heard from a stranger in some unlooked-for quarter words not meant for himself, but clamorously applying to the difficulty besetting him . . . the mystical word always unsought for" (*CYM* 233). Father Gogarty hears the unsought-for word in the sounds of the lake and the life around it. He inquires how certain "thoughts could come into his mind" and decides that "the coming of a thought into the consciousness is often unexpected, but if the thought were not latent in the mind, it would not arise out of the mind" (*L* 27–28). The means by which Moore communicates this process develop di-

rectly from that narratized internal visualization of space and sensation seen earlier, in less developed forms, in *Celibates, Sister Teresa,*
and the conclusion to "Homesickness."

Early in the novel, the key "echo-augury" appears, and it is one
that will serve to focus the natural metaphors through which Gogarty reconsiders his past. Because he is confined and restless, his
eye most frequently falls upon the road as an image of constrained
movement: the road goes nowhere, but circles around the lake, or
leads out along a sandy, narrow spit. Because he suffers confinement in an abortive past as well as a circumscribed space, he sees the
roadway as a temporal metaphor of his brief passage through life
and a spatial metaphor of his isolation. To escape from full recognition of his condition, he allows his mind to be captivated by one
living creature at a time, one sound, one smell, one touch, one feature, exaggerated by his senses to a sensation that eclipses all others.
He encounters the "thick yellow smells" of the fox along the rough,
brushy shore, and he is drawn trancelike into a cloud of white but-
terflies. An unseen horse sighs near his cheek in the blackness of
night and, near dawn, he is watched by a great gull until the bird's
round head and black eye fill his consciousness. Many of these images are fearful, some are violent, and some suggest latent sexuality
and generation. All have a profound effect, and he discovers a new,
if still only partially understood, meaning to a lake that has been
seen until now only as the boundary of a prison. As he seeks an
explanatory metaphor, the mystical word appears:

> He could just distinguish Castle Island, and he wondered what this
> lake reminded him of: it wound in and out of gray shores and
> headlands, fading into dim pearl-coloured distance, and he com-
> pared it to a shroud, and then to a ghost, but neither comparison
> pleased him. It was like something, but the image he sought eluded
> him. At last he remembered how in a dream he had seen Nora
> carried from the lake; and now, standing among the scent of the
> flowers, he said: "She has always been associated with the lake in
> my thoughts, yet she escaped the lake. Every man," he continued,
> "has a lake in his heart." He had not sought the phrase, it had come
> suddenly into his mind. Yes, "Every man has a lake in his heart," he
> repeated, and returned to the house like one dazed, to sit stupefied
> until his thoughts took fire again, and going to his writing-table he
> drew a sheet of paper towards him, feeling that he must write to
> Nora. (*L* 35)

Father Gogarty's metaphors reflect his fear of what lies beneath the lake, as does his ambiguous remark that Nora has "escaped the lake." But the lake is also bound up in his mind with the lovely, living Nora Glynn, whose name suggests a stream-bisected glen. At this point, he recognizes that the lake contains a labyrinth of death, love, fear, and ecstasy. He still imagines, however, that all are best avoided, even if they are essential to each man's heart.

The aforementioned scene is atypical of the first part of the novel in that Gogarty verbalizes his experience. In most cases, the effect of his natural surroundings is seen in the letters, wherein such articulations of his latent consciousness are inadvertent and recognizable only to the reader of the letters. Much of the psychological accuracy and emotional power of the novel lies in its depiction of the way that events, physical sensations, and natural surroundings affect the protagonist, who is as of yet unable to interpret his reactions. Early in the novel, for example, long before Gogarty has recognized his love of Nora, his thoughts regarding a government bridge-building project suddenly break off: "And then Nora's name came into his mind, and he meditated for a moment, seeing the colour of her hair and the vanishing expression of her eyes. Sometimes he could see her hand, the very texture of its skin, and the line of the thumb and the forefinger. A cat had once scratched her hand, and she had told him about it" (*L* 29). With a precise concentrated effect, Moore here dramatizes what it is to long for the presence of another. Having been furious at Nora's refusal to identify the man who impregnated her, here he remembers acutely her telling him of how a cat's claw had broken through the threshold of her body. Gogarty may be incapable of acknowledging his desire, but his thoughts are nevertheless suffused involuntarily with the exquisite detail of Nora's hand.

Later in the novel, after Nora has requested an end to their correspondence, despair and desire manifest themselves as sensations of sound and presence: "Never had the country seemed so still: dead birds in the woods, and the sounds of leaves, and the fitful December sunlight on the strands . . . in these languid autumn days the desire to write to Nora crept nearer, until it always seemed about him like some familiar animal" (*L* 122). After she writes to him in May, challenging him to "bring the gifts that Nature gave us to fruition," he begins to make his own metaphors with greater frequency, and he establishes his own language, fusing Nora with the woods. A year after she left Mayo, he finds her in the sky "willful and blue"; in the cow-parsley, green like her eyes; in the camions, pink like the flowers of her hat. Her spirit lives in the birth of the young birds and farm animals, and in the aspens and willows. He decides that

> he must put his confidence in Nature; he must listen to her. She would tell him. And he lay all the afternoon listening to the reeds and the ducks talking together in the lake. Very often the wood was like a harp; a breeze touched the strings, and every now and then the murmur seemed about to break into a little tune, and as if in emulation, or because he remembered his part in the music, a blackbird, perched near to his mate, whose nest was in the haw-thorns growing out of the tumbled wall, began to sing a joyful lay in a rich round contralto, soft and deep as velvet. "All nature," he said, "is talking or singing. This is talking and singing time. But my heart can speak to no one and I seek places where no one will come." (L 136–37)

From out of his stupor, he wanders into the sunlight "trying to take an interest in everyone whom he met." His search for life among the tinkers and pig-drovers with whom he chats transforms his passive receptivity into an active effort to reproduce within himself the vital-ity of the world.

But does this process lead to self-discovery or self-creation? In her final letter to Gogarty, Nora avows the existence of a stable truth about the self that awaits discovery: "We live," she writes, "enveloped in self-deception as in a film; now and again the film breaks like a cloud and the light shines through" (L 131–32). Is this light the illu-mination of some essential nature, or does it illuminate the process of self-making toward some undeterminable end? In *Hail and Fare-well*'s metaphor of the sculptor who sculpts himself, the acts of cre-ation and revelation are inexorably intertwined; the design of the sculpture within the block can come into being only inasmuch as the artist can create it. When, in a letter to Edmund Gosse, Moore ad-mires his own novel's depiction of "the inner life of the priest, curl-ing and going out like vapour, always changing and always the same," he characterizes perfectly its double nature (BK 57). The novel is at once a story of movement outward, a *Künstlerroman* that leaves the protagonist-writer facing like Joyce's Dedalus the horizon he will enter to make his future; at the same time it is a spiritual biography like Augustine's, a circular tale of the recovery of what one has always been.

This paradoxical configuration of self-discovery can be compared not only with the conclusion to *A Portrait of the Artist as a Young Man* but with a lesser known work, Gerald O'Donovan's 1913 novel, *Father Ralph*. A former priest, O'Donovan was assisted by Moore when he abandoned his Galway parish in 1904 for a literary career in London, and his novels bore as advertisements letters of praise from Moore. O'Donovan's protagonist, Father Ralph O'Brien, is less influenced by "nature" in his decision to renounce the priesthood than by his outrage at the papal encyclical against modernism, an edict that Moore also found outrageous but so in keeping with Irish Catholicism that there was little point in protesting it in his own book.[28] Despite differences between the two novels, Father Ralph, like Father Oliver, embraces a creed of "life." "In the blind groping way which is the way of life," Father Ralph discovers that "life was larger than his vision of it." He stands on the deck of the Holyhead mailboat and, like Stephen Dedalus, beckons to "life":

> "I have found myself at last," he said under his breath. . . . The sun, falling slantwise on the foam in the wake of the boat, made a track of molten silver. On the horizon land had faded to a blue outline. He gazed at it longingly until the last faint grey disappeared, and the sea everywhere met the sky.
>
> He turned round and braced himself again to the east wind. Only one dream had faded into the sea, he thought . . .
>
> And then?[29]

Like the conclusion to *A Portrait of the Artist as a Young Man*, this passage differs markedly from the conclusion to *The Lake*. After Gogarty has swum the lake and found the clothes hidden amid the rocks on the other side, he climbs up and looks down across the waters he has struggled through:

> "A queer dusky night," he said, "with hardly a star, and that great moon pouring silver down the lake."
>
> "I shall never see that lake again, but I shall never forget it," and as he dozed in the train, in a corner of an empty carriage, the spectral light of the lake awoke him, and when he arrived at Cork it seemed to him that he was being engulfed in the deep pool by the Joycetown shore. On the deck of the steamer he heard the lake's warble above the violence of the waves. "There is a lake in every man's heart," he said, "and he listens to its monotonous whisper year after year, more and more attentive till at last he ungirds."
> (*L* 179)

Although Father Ralph looks backward with some longing on the passage over which he has traveled, the land drops from view and he turns to brace himself against the east wind. Stephen Dedalus calls to his father to "stand me now and ever in good stead," but faces outward across the sea. Gogarty, in contrast, gazes down from the rocks at the mysterious lake he has just crossed and retains it in his consciousness to such a degree that its light and sound overwhelm his present surroundings. Linear development and temporal change are suspended within the spatial image of the lake, containing within itself the passage of his life. To an even greater degree than in any of Moore's prior stories, self-narrative moves from a linear mode to that of a static metaphor: past, present, and future run concurrently within Gogarty's recollection.

As a whole, in his later work Moore places more value upon the *recollection* than he does upon the *repudiation* of one's struggles with the circumscriptions of historical life. Because of the similarity of their imagery, a brief comparison of *The Lake*'s conclusion and the first canto of *The Inferno* may help to elucidate this difference, although there is no apparent evidence to indicate that Moore had Dante in mind or even that he had read *The Inferno*. In the first canto, Dante's pilgrim tells of his passage through the "valley of evil" to a little hill whose light had assuaged the agony which "had wracked the lake of my heart / through all the terrors of that piteous night":

> Just as a swimmer, who with his last breath
> flounders ashore from perilous seas, might turn
> to memorize the wide water of his death—
>
> so did I turn, my soul still fugitive
> from death's surviving image, to stare down
> that pass that none had ever left alive.[30]

Gogarty's consciousness is illuminated not by a light shining from a distant hill—the night is dusky and without a star—but by the "spectral light" of the lake itself. His memory is flooded with what Dante calls "the wide water of his death," and he thus never fully departs from the lake. The place that has been his prison, his passageway, and his destination is one and the same. Located within his heart, the lake's light fills the darkness outside the train he rides; its sound rises above the noises of the ocean he crosses. Unlike the speaker in

Dante's Christian allegory, his worldly self is unveiled rather than repudiated. As he becomes that which he has always been, his essential nature is shown to be not the spiritual man known to God but the sensuous man known to a defied nature and the unique individual whose story lay dormant within his "instinct." As part of Gogarty's self-narrative, the lake of the heart is transformed into the symbol of a story inseparable, finally, from the remembering mind.

The interfusion of past and present through the spatial metaphor of the lake anticipates another issue critical to Moore's later work. Although the novel ends with the familiar motif of self-imposed exile, it is less pugnaciously repudiative of the past than Moore's other novels and autobiographies have been. The existence Gogarty imagines for himself in New York or London little resembles the Mediterranean adventures of Nora Glynn. Nor does it resemble the Parisian world of art with which Ireland is always held in unflattering contrast in Moore's writings and of which Gogarty himself dreams at the beginning of the novel. Gogarty's vision of his future instead bears notable similarities to a past spent along the narrow roads of Mayo. He writes to Nora, "I imagine myself in a threadbare suit of clothes edging my way along the pavement, nearing a great building, and making my way to my desk, and, when the day's work is done, returning home along the same pavement to a room high up among the rafters, close to the sky, in some cheap quarter" (L 146). Because he plans to describe the world he will observe as a journalist, in addition to continuing his self-observational correspondence with Nora, Gogarty looks with eager anticipation toward his future.

This future is distinctly urban and probably celibate. The narrator's prediction that Nora would become "the home of his affections" is sufficiently ambiguous to suggest that—as in the case of Moore himself, as well as many of his fictional characters—the memory or fantasy of love will play a greater role than does the experience. Much more crucial than domestic happiness is the discovery of a place in which Gogarty can continue his labors toward what Nora calls "self-realization." Just as Carlyle distinguished between happiness and the more imperative call of duty, so vitalist discourse held the search for "life" much higher than any corresponding quest for happiness. As Gilbert Murray complained to Bertrand Russell, "Utility," "Happiness," and "Pleasure" seemed vague terms that placed "too much stress on the future result to be obtained, whereas the truth is that The End of Life is in the Processes of Life."[31] While

Moore might have himself embraced such a sentiment, it must also be remembered that this new concentration upon the "processes of life" brought him a finer product than he had been able to achieve for some many years.

For both the writer and his characters, the contemplation of the passage of one's life leads to a poetic image through which the life story may be told. The observation of oneself engaged in the struggle of self-making culminates in the memory of this image—the meeting of sun and garden, the village of Duncannon, and, above all, the spectral lake of the always emanative self.

8

Narrating, Remembering, and the Autogenous Self

> Nothing is ever settled in this world. Everything is
> becoming. We can have no knowledge of anything,
> for nothing in this world is permanent, unless talk.
> —George Moore, *A Story-Teller's Holiday*

I N THE 1917 DEDICATORY LETTER to Robert Ross which pref-
aced the newly revised version of *A Mummer's Wife* (originally
published in 1885), Moore makes the most startling claims about this
second of his novels, a realistic study of an alcoholic actress modeled
after the works of Zola. Now eccentrically described as the chronicle
of "a band of jugglers and acrobats travelling from town to town,"
the novel is said to have reminded Ross of *The Golden Ass*, "a book,"
Moore suggests, "I might have written had I lived two thousand
years ago." "An antique story rises up in mind," he concludes, "a
recollection of one of my lost works or an instantaneous reading of
Apuleius into *A Mummer's Wife*—which?"[1] Two more incongruous
books could hardly be paralleled, and Moore's whimsical comparison
defies any simple attempt to explain it. Neither Apuleius's story nor
the prose version in *Marius the Epicurean* (with which Moore would
have been familiar for many years) bears any conceivable similarity
to Moore's naturalistic novel. The fascination of this passage lies in
what it tells us about Moore's theory and practice of narrative as it
evolved in the twentieth century. Not only does he foreground the

process of telling (rather than the ostensible subject of the narrative) but he suggests what had become as early as *Memoirs of My Dead Life* a much greater sense of the dramatic possibilities of the auto-biographical persona as a narrator of stories.

Moore described his preface to Eglinton as "an indictment of the English novel" (EG 32), but he seems compelled to reject even Balzac and Zola in his insistence therein that *A Mummer's Wife*, the one of his novels most concerned with contemporary lower middle-class life and then-contemporary modes of observational realism, could be thought to resemble a group of episodic tales arising from an oral tradition, a series of incidents related by a narrating persona who passes from master to master in the shape of a donkey. At the time Moore wrote his preface, he was also composing *A Story-Teller's Holiday*, a work that more obviously resembles *The Golden Ass*, and, even more so, *The Decameron*. In choosing to identify *A Mummer's Wife* as one of this type, Moore puts forth a serious aesthetic manifesto. With the aesthetic of "the told tale," he definitively replaces his earlier admiration for the realist method and its illusion of objective narration. It has been frequently argued that in offering themselves as replicas of the experiential world, realist novels produce highly self-enclosed, authoritarian texts.[2] In his preface, Moore implicitly rejects that type of narrative authority for another sort, based on a theory of fiction akin to his idea of autobiography as a record of the path taken by its author's remembering mind. Rather than providing a replica of the world, the more personalized texts offer a replica of consciousness. In *The Lake*, Father Oliver's letters tells us more about him than about his subjects of discussion, and despite the intrinsic interest of the engaging tales the narrators relate in *A Story-Teller's Holiday*, they also serve to demonstrate the character of their tellers. In *The Brook Kerith*, the crucifixion is retold by Joseph of Arimathea, Jesus, and Paul, not because any one of the three supplies information missing from the other's version, but because what and how they remember exposes that aspect of their character Moore wishes to explore.[3]

The subjective consciousness becomes, then, the overt concern of Moore's later fiction and concomitant with that development, the recollective storyteller takes on a more expansive role. Imagining himself the author of "an antique story," Moore queries with fanciful uncertainty whether that which rises up in his mind is a lost work from his "prior life" as an ancient writer or some phantasmagoric blending of classical and modern texts. While preoccupied with mortality and change, his narrative voice nevertheless claims to speak simultaneously from the present and from a distance of two thousand years. Before looking at the novels that so fully demonstrate the process of recollective narrative in characters who are themselves from worlds of long ago, some attention must be paid to the work that was the first of Moore's to place at its dramatic center the retrospective narrator, and, in so doing, to dissolve conventions of temporality in the autobiographical speaker's relation to his story.

Memoirs of My Dead Life: Time, Death, and Memory

Throughout 1904 and early 1905 Moore was finishing *The Lake* and revising the pieces that were to become *Memoirs of My Dead Life*. Until the 1921 revision, *The Lake* was still primarily an epistolary novel, and so it is *Memoirs* that first treats in detail the interdependence between the recollection of a shared historical world and the self-creation occurring within the act of narrating one's memories. In the fiction prior to *Memoirs,* Moore's characters demonstrate the difficulties of telling one's own story. Kate Ede of *A Mummer's Wife* hides her story from others, and Alice Barton of *A Drama in Muslin* composes popular fiction that belies the depth of her understanding. Evelyn Innes writes the history of her convent rather than of herself, while Sir Owen Asher trivializes his experiences in cocktail chatter. Esther Waters relates her story with a powerful effect upon her listeners, but the reader is not made privy to her retelling, and its details confuse her attempts to generalize from it. In contrast to such earlier fictional characters, the autobiographical narrator of *Memoirs of My Dead Life* allows his primary activity to be that of remembering and retelling, placing as much attention upon the recollective act as he does upon the story remembered.

Like *Confessions of a Young Man* and *Hail and Farewell* (on which Moore was to begin work very soon after the publication of the first edition of *Memoirs*), *Memoirs of My Dead Life* experiments with time and perspective in ways that demonstrate his assessment of the creative aspects of memory. From the beginnings of his career, Moore's autobiographies reject the familiar trope of a narrator who is assumed to be coterminous with the composing author and who offers the judgments of maturity concerning his chronologically rendered life. Although *Confessions* is organized by means of a skeletal chronology, in certain scenes its autobiographical narrator acts and speaks within the present tense, while elsewhere he looks back from a perspective that could be identified with his position at the end of the text (a position that can be dated approximately five years before *Confessions* was actually written). As I have described in detail, *Hail and Farewell* develops chronologically through the illusion of a continuous present in which the time of narration is concurrent with the time of the main line of action; within that line of action, the narrator often remembers prior events and conversations. Perhaps because it emerged first as a collection of previously published essays, *Memoirs* has no discernable chronological organization. A narrator speaks directly to his readers from various moments in what appears to be the same general period of his late middle age. From these points he frequently falls into reveries on lost love. It is memory itself, rather than the narrative plot, that hovers over time, pulling the narrator through a variety of tenses, and sometimes inducing the disturbing sensation of the simultaneity of different temporal spheres.

Despite its wry humor and its elegant, worldly tone, *Memoirs of My Dead Life* is a somber book. While the remembering mind is fluid and expansive, overcoming in its reveries conventional boundaries of time, it is nevertheless repeatedly faced with death, impotence, and powerlessness. The book, after all, was conceived as a record of loss. The title, as he explains to his anonymous correspondent, "Gabrielle," was an "affectation intended to indicate that my love life is over."[4] The narrator professes his enjoyment of the prospect of days spent in meditations on art, women, and "what I once heard dear old McCormac, Bishop of Galway, describe in his sermon as 'the degrading passion of 'loave'" (*MMDL* 65). "The old," he writes, "have a joy that the youths do not know—recollection . . . without memory we should not have known ourselves or others. We should have lived like the animals" (*MMDL* 138). Yet the narrator protests too much, and repeatedly he finds that memory and imagination, like Keats's "viewless wings of poesy," are insufficient to hold back the premonition of a future that must soon bring death.

Keats is in fact a strongly felt presence in "Bring in the Lamp," one of the concluding episodes of *Memoirs of My Dead Life*. This story echoes the language, theme, and plot of "Ode to a Nightingale" and demonstrates a handling of imaginative time commensurate with that of the poem.[5] The narration begins in the present tense, as the autobiographical persona finds himself alone in the early evening. His language is luxurious in its description of the London twilight, but he is dulled and weary. He might, he thinks, escape his state could he but tell himself a story, and he projects this possibility in the conditional future tense. His tale of two lovers then materializes in the present tense as it appears before his imagination, just as Keats represents his own journey to "the embalmed darkness" as if it were actually in progress. Speaking again in the conditional future, he wishes he could be an "accomplished story-teller" so that he could ingeniously conclude his tale, but because the events *did not happen that way,* he becomes despondent. The story suddenly is revealed to be rooted in his own past. Unlike the speculative dream of Keats's ode, the story is an all-too-poignant moment from an earlier life. The speaker's questioning as to what the story's outcome will be (here he uses the future tense) is answered by the past. The story is fixed now within the actuality of the past as it overwhelms the present moment. There is no future, or what future there is intimates a foreboding emptiness:

> All this happened twenty years ago: perhaps the earth is over her charming little personality, and it will be over me before long. Nothing endures; life is but change. . . . Death and life always overlapping, mixed inextricably, and no meaning in anything, merely a stream of change in which things happen. . . . Twenty long years ago, and there is no hope, not a particle.
>
> I have come to the end of my mood, an ache in my heart brings me to my feet, and looking round, I cry out, "How dark is the room! Why is there no light? Bring in the lamp." (*MMDL* 213)

In this story, the life of the present is "overlapped" by the absence of the past and the mortality of the future. As Carl Dawson observes in his study of *Memoirs of My Dead Life,* the story "posits something like 'it happened tomorrow.'" "The entire book," he suggests, "deals with metamorphoses of present-into-past-into-present, a landscape emerging which is at once of the moment and in the mind. Consciousness becomes a kind of scanning process, either active or passive, which memory articulates by tenses. And memory, however personal, self-indulgent, and private in origin, becomes— through narrative—historic, archetypal, and ultimately public."[6] Dawson argues that as much more than a narcissistic recital of one man's amours, *Memoirs* provides a rigorous inquiry into the relationship between memory and creativity and an assertion of the "remembering individual mind" as a paradigm of cultural memory, a replication of "history and civilization, all that need not die by the workings of time."[7]

Memoirs of My Dead Life is at heart a panegyric to memory, but in this book, more than in any other of his writings, Moore gives voice to the darker aspects of recollection. Like the letter, whose presence is predicated on the absence of its sender, memory too is accompanied by a recognition of the absence of that which is remembered. As in "Bring in the Lamp," recollection may provoke an acute awareness of the transience of the present, a moment soon to enter the realm of memory: life soon to enter the realm of death. "Sometimes I think I only do things in order that I may brood upon them," Moore wrote to Lady Cunard (*LLC* 49), and if life is predicated on its future as a memory, it is experienced always with the cognizance of its future absence.

Moore also suggests that only in the perception of absence—that is, when a moment is remembered—is that moment truly felt. "Reality clouds, our actions mitigate our perception," he writes, "we can only see clearly when we look back or forwards."[8] In "Resurgam," the final section of *Memoirs of My Dead Life*, the narrator regrets that he cannot mourn his mother, who has just died, because he is in mourning for another woman who had left him some weeks ago: "But from too deep thinking of her a madness crept up behind the eyes, and in it the thought . . . that it were an exquisite despair to know that I should never possess her sweet personality again, never again hold her dainty oval face in my hands, so that I might better steep myself in her eyes, and that all the intimacy of her person was now but a memory never to be renewed by actual sight and touch. In these moments of passionate memory one experiences real grief" (*MMDL* 254). The too-precious adjective, "exquisite," aestheticizes the speaker's despair all the while that his description of the woman testifies to the intensity of the loss. That the woman was most certainly Maud Cunard is especially interesting since Moore was to spend some thirty years making literature out of what he called his ever-present memory of her loss, as well as basing their long friendship on the memory of their brief affair. Her sexual absence from him, continually reinforced by her presence as a friend rather than a lover, became a vehicle for imaginative re-creation of himself as her faithful devotee.

The autobiographical narrator, however, seeks to keep other memories in the past as if to eradicate their ever having been. In the story of his journey back to Mayo at the time of his mother's death, the narrator endures great distress at the sight of the localities of his childhood: a "curious agony of mind caused by a sudden recognition

of objects long forgotten—a tree or a bit of bog land." "How terrible
was all this resurrection! The present hides the past; but there are
times when the present does not exist at all, when every mist is
cleared away, and the past confronts us in naked outline. . . . Two
more turnings and we should be within sight of the house! This is
how men feel when condemned to death. I am sure of it" (*MMDL*
242, 245).

Why should this resurrection be so terrible? First of all, the
speaker is no longer a child, his mother has died or is about to die,
and his own death is forthcoming, as is underscored in his encounter
with the stone mason who assures him of a place in the family vault.
But much more precisely and more important, what the narrator
fears most is a Catholic burial and his final entombment within a
familial line he had attempted, since the days of *Parnell and His Island,* to reject with utter finality. From the beginning of Moore's career, County Mayo and the world of the Irish landlord had been
identified as both the source of a requisite income and that which
had to be unequivocally left behind. This past is still too potent; except as it pays tribute to the present in the form of income, it has to
be kept, absolutely, in the past.

In his discussion of what he terms "modern pastmindedness,"
Rockwell Gray notes that many modern autobiographers express "a
simultaneous fascination and impatience with the past," feeling it to
be at once a potentially revelatory place of origin and "an intolerable
weight, a suffocating presence which threatens to reduce what is, or
will be, to what was." From this latter perspective, the "stream" of
time "binds us." "Continuity becomes deadening repetition, and tradition, a yoke of oppression. . . . We begin to experience time as a
series of discontinuities, a jagged and disruptive rhythm (or absence
of rhythm). Sharp breaks appear in the 'flow' of history."[9] Although
Moore's narrator exhibits that ambivalence of which Gray speaks
and condemns the old world of Mayo as a dangerous threat to his
present and future, Moore rarely represents time in terms of discontinuity and fragmentation. Rather, he establishes, like Yeats, an
imaginary continuity with a tradition that is even older than that of
his family's past, and from it postulates an unending cosmic recurrence from which the autobiographical speaker may take reas-
surance.

That continuity with tradition is explicit in Moore's projection of
himself as a reincarnation of Apuleius. He may thus see his own life
as a passage between worlds and as paradigm of cultural recovery.

In the last pages of "Resurgam," Moore envisions his final escape from Mayo and his return to the ancient world he proclaims to be his true place of origin. The future comes into being as a chosen form of death. Because "I am of the Romantic temperament," he foresees being burnt atop a magnificent funeral pyre fifty feet high while his mourners feast upon roast meat to the music of the "Ride of the Valkyries." Considering a visit to the family solicitor in Dublin to ensure that his wishes be followed, he sadly resigns himself to the thought that there are probably laws against public burnings. Nevertheless, he foresees a means of assuring that the Irish past and his own future never overlap, and it is with this picture that *Memoirs of My Dead Life* concludes: a cremation abhorrent to Catholic doctrine but linked with the classical past, his ashes placed in an antique urn decorated with a motif of Pan, to be deposited in an ocean of eternally recurring primal life and to be recovered some billion years hence when the vital past of the classical world will begin again.

Although I noted earlier that *Memoirs of My Dead Life* has no operative chronological overstructure, in "Resurgam" Moore chooses to end the book by projecting his funeral. Unlike many autobiographies that grasp the moment of speaking as a provisional ending from which one may then discover a plot within the incidents of a life, the autobiographical narrator here looks toward a time beyond the text. However, as I have been suggesting, the forward motion is equally a looking back, a sign of continuity and even rebirth as the classical past is imagined reemerging at some point far in the future. Like "Bring in the Lamp," which, as Carl Dawson remarks, "posits something like 'it happened tomorrow,'" the ending of "Resurgam" offers the claim, "yesterday will happen in the future." The drive toward an ending may often be in actuality a movement paradoxically characterized by recurrence. In his *Reading for the Plot: Design and Intention in Narrative*, Peter Brooks suggests that

> the stories of many young protagonists of the nineteenth-century novel, while ostensibly a striving forward and upwards, a progress, may also be, perhaps more profoundly, the narrative of an attempted homecoming: of the effort to reach an assertion of origin through ending, to find the same in the different, the time before in the time after. . . . Repetition, remembering, reenactment are the ways in which we replay time, so that it may not be lost. We are thus always trying to work back through time to that transcendent home, knowing, of course, that we cannot. All we can do is subvert or, perhaps better, pervert time: which is what narrative does.[10]

It is also precisely what the storytelling characters of Moore's late novels do in their ongoing efforts to forestall time by talking and, in talking, to find the point of conjunction between the deprivations of temporal life and the sacramental origins of that life which they seek to assert in the face of its tragedies.

The Religion of Life-Remembered:
The Historical Romances

Immediately following *Memoirs of My Dead Life,* Moore concentrated his energies upon *Hail and Farewell* and the revision of earlier books. His next major prose works were *The Brook Kerith* and *A Story-Teller's Holiday,* written only a few years before the final revision of *The Lake.* Both feature protagonists who, like Father Gogarty and the autobiographical narrator of *Memoirs of My Dead Life,* seek the terms in which to understand their own stories and for whom the act of remembering and retelling is of more value than further action in a constricting and broken world. Of the three principal characters of *The Brook Kerith,* Joseph of Arimathea searches from one sect to another for an explanatory narrative that will accommodate both his human affections and his passion for the divine. After he recovers from a failed crucifixion, Jesus revises his interpretation of his own life as he learns to remember anew. Paul, however, discovers one story that for him remains unrevisable, and from its rigid affirmations he builds a course of action that points to Rome and the establishment of the Catholic church. Similarly, in *A Story-Teller's Holiday* each character must find a way to understand his or her own story, even if the result is isolation, persecution, or death. In the short novel, *Ulick and Soracha* (later revised and incorporated into the final version of *A Story-Teller's Holiday*), an old man's retelling of a tale of lovers separated by the church becomes itself a means of overriding the power of the church, transforming the place of their elopement into a popular miracle shrine where pilgrims come to hear the story of their love and rendering the timid, pious harper who tells their story into a man who finds joy and delight in contemplating the body of the young wife the church forces upon him for the sake of propriety.

In each of these works, characters seek to bring into mutual accordance their lives and their philosophic and religious understandings. Despite severe oppression by those who can see little or no resemblance between the world and the divine, certain characters are able to develop their own reconciliatory theologies. The pantheistic Jesus of *The Brook Kerith* recognizes in his later years that God is "not without but within the universe, part and parcel, not only of the stars and the earth, but of me, yea, even of my sheep on the hillside" (BK 479).[11] In *A Story-Teller's Holiday*, the medieval Ireland Moore imagines also allows for a pantheistic Christianity, admitting even sexual passion, at least to some degree, within an elemental Christian vision.

In contrast to the distant past stands the censorious present, where the local shanachie Alec Trusselby cowers in fear at the clergy's probable disapproval of his tales and fails to see that what he mocks and bewails in the clergy of old exists to an even greater degree in the church of his own era.[12] Not only Ireland, but modern Europe in general is dismissed by Moore as wayward and perhaps even irrelevant to the values he holds forth in these works. Both *The Brook Kerith* and *A Story-Teller's Holiday* were written during World War I, which Moore viewed even in its early stages with consummate disgust. When to friends like Edmund Gosse or Emily Lorenz Meyer he writes that the war was not worth discussion or thought, his response is that of a man who sees an endless and pointless debacle too appalling to consider and too much the product of a civilization gone horrifically awry.[13]

Given Moore's revulsion toward the war and the concurrent violence in Ireland, it is not surprising that *The Brook Kerith* ends in the assertion of a most Quakerly doctrine of the inner light, as throughout it has enacted such a philosophy through its very mode of narration. By means of the elaborate indirect discourse I have described in the previous chapter, the novel proceeds through the speech, thought, physical activity, and sensory perception of alternating characters. The story of the birth of Christianity is given from three perspectives: that of Joseph of Arimathea, a very minor figure in the Gospels and a very ordinary man in the novel; Jesus himself, who does not die on the cross, but, nursed by Joseph, recovers from a coma and spends the remainder of his life as an Essene shepherd; and Paul, who encounters Jesus in his Essene retreat but cannot alter his belief in Christ's death and resurrection. The novel suggests that we know God only through conscience, and that conscience differs in each person as a result of upbringing and psychological constitution. Because no one can ever share the same mind, as Jesus attempts to explain to Paul, we must resist the temptation to put our sense of the divine into words, an attempt that leads to frustrated proselytizing and eventual persecutions.

Moore never associated his theology with the Quakers, although he did write to Eglinton that "I suspect that it inclines toward Buddhism" (EG 30). Perhaps Moore was thinking both of the universalism of Buddhism and its relative indifference to an evangelical mission. In a letter to Alfred A. Knopf, Moore describes his Jesus as an "ironical mystic who no longer believes in the conversion of the world" in contrast to Paul, "a man of action" (*GMP* 289). Throughout these late novels, action is frequently synonymous with persecution while the suspension of action signals a kind of spiritual grace. Suspended action is perhaps the key term for understanding these late novels so fully concerned with the remembering and telling of stories.

As in *The Brook Kerith*, the illusion of orality and the suspension of action are integrally associated in *A Story-Teller's Holiday*. On the outer edge of the many frames in which the tales are enclosed is George Moore, the autobiographer whose tellings echo the rhythmic digressions of intimate spoken discourse. Within the frame defined by the narrator's contiguity with the name upon the title page is a narrator who is both an oral storyteller and figure of exile: the cosmopolitan novelist visiting from London, a man who declines to travel the few miles from Westport Lodge to his ancestral estate near Ballintubber. Keeping aloof from this profound emblem of the familial and historical life into which he was born, he engages in a storytelling contest with Alec Trusselby. The stories enable him to hold his historical life at a distance. Like the stories of *The Decameron*, with which he compares his own book, they keep at bay the cognizance of loss and death. In his study of books modeled upon oral narrative, Robert Kellogg finds this characteristic of such works:

> the tellers and their listeners are usually removed, at rest, and frequently exhausted in one way or another. . . . The restless power of the imagination builds worlds of its own to confound and forestall the chaos and desire that is just outside the pleasance where stories are told . . . even deep sorrow, thus revived and shaped by fantasy and memory, is a greater pleasure than sleep. The interdependence of art and life, of contemplation and active intelligence, of pastoral and heroic, of contrary worlds of every kind, are themes which necessarily attend a book's pretense to be a story told within a story.[11]

Storytelling does provide a hiatus in the life of the aging and self-exiled narrator of *A Story-Teller's Holiday*. Many of the stories also involve characters who live in a state of suspension, in which the culminating moment of mortal life—the sexual union of lovers—lies either behind or in front of them, remembered or anticipated, but only momentarily in the present. Moore renders through the delayed action and the suspended cadences of his prose both the anguish and the pleasure of longing, as well as the comic or tragic results of fulfillment deferred. The stories do not depict the cessation of desire, but rather the endless postponement of its completion.

Moore borrows numerous folkloric motifs to conclude his adaptations of these stories from the Old Irish in which love is fulfilled for the most part in the spirit, and only once—if at all—in the body. The poets Curithir and Liadin are pulled apart by the church after their intense love causes Curithir to forget his poems and Liadin to compose songs of such a troubling nature that the passions of her listeners run wild. After death, however, intertwining rowan trees grow from their graves with "berries, that were red as Liadin's lips" (*STH* 1:93). Dinoll and Crede, separated by the same kind of ecclesiastic interference, come at last together in old age to live "lying side by side in warmth on the winter's night without the dread of sin to keep us apart" (*STH* 2:234). The ribald story of Father Moling and the nuns of Cuthmore ends with an appropriately comic victory of Moore's own invention. The two lovers—Moling, a cleric, and the nun Ligach—are also painfully separated, but their son, "Martin," is revealed to be none other than Martin Luther, founder of the Protestantism that Alec Trusselby reviles as "no better than a whore," but that Moore's autobiographical narrator lauds at the end of the book.

As in his indictments of contemporary Ireland, Moore castigates the early church for its denial of the very sacramental aspect of sexuality on which its faith is founded. When the ecclesiastical poet and hermit, Marbar, is made an outcast for having succumbed to sexual temptation he fervently replies to his accusers,

> Luachet is beautiful, but it wasn't her body altogether that drew me . . . there is something beyond the lust of the eye and the desire of the flesh, something that is beyond the mind itself, and maybe that thing is the soul; and maybe the soul is love, and whosoever comes upon his soul is at once robbed of all thought and reason, and becomes like a flower. . . . I somehow cannot believe it true that my love of her will rob me of my love of Jesus, nor that her love of me will rob him of her love, for in our hearts it is all one and the same

thing, and aren't we more sure that God made our hearts than of anything else? (*STH* 1:134)

The passage recalls a scene in *Hail and Farewell* in which the narrator lashes out at the Jesuitical renunciation of the natural world, bitterly remarking that "he that reads often of the beatific faces in Heaven, and the flames that lick up the entrails of the damned without ever consuming them, is not troubled with doubt that perhaps, after all, the flower in the grass, the cloud in the sky, and his own beating heart may be parcel of Divinity" (*HF* 340). In both passages, Moore accuses the clergy of sins against life, and the anger of *Hail and Farewell*'s narrator joins with the pleading of Marbar to identify this as an impassioned and recurrent concern underlying what sometimes seem to be frivolous or merely testy attacks upon the church.

In seeing medieval Ireland as a time in which, despite the growing puritanism of the church, faith might yet include sexuality (which for Moore stands with art as the fullest expression of "the religion of life"), Moore differs distinctly from his Irish contemporaries for whom, as John Wilson Foster argues, medievalism "was a force in the Revival meant to counter realism and romantic self-expression in literature; democracy and individualism in politics; science and rationalism in our understanding of the universe; Protestantism in religion; machinery and industrialism in our transactions with nature; and the Renaissance as an influence in the history of culture."[15] In *A Story-Teller's Holiday*, the Middle Ages are, despite evident repressions, still a time when one could love God and the natural world in such a way that individualism could flourish and free adapting of dogma (what Moore would call "Protestantism") might be tolerated. As Foster has noted elsewhere, "Moore's clerics deny the claims of the flesh, and are reprehensible for that, but in doing so with such perilous intimacy they exhibit the fearlessness and earthiness of Irish Catholicism, as Moore sees it, before it imported a Continental puritanism. *A Story-Teller's Holiday* is . . . a lament for Ireland between the seventh and twelfth centuries—sensual and aesthetic at once, alive to the beauties of woman and of art, those 'halcyon days,' as Moore calls them, echoing his earlier creation, Father Gogarty."[16]

Despite Moore's nostalgia for this imagined past, these stories cannot be called escapist fictions, however much they depend upon the suspension of action for their telling and describe, in many cases, the suspension of action as well. If the telling of the stories keeps

Moore Hall at a distance from the narrator, he is still aware of its presence a few miles off and confronts his own deliberate absence in the book's final chapters. By means of satiric contrast, the tales themselves point to the repression of contemporary Irish rural life, and if the medieval church depicted therein has not completely lost its tolerance of a pantheistic sexuality, it still harshly punishes transgressors. And although nature in this preindustrial world is lovely, still, as vividly depicted in *Ulick and Soracha* it is part of a world where poverty, war, and religious oppression devastate human affections as much as the wolves destroy human life itself.

The wonder of *Ulick and Soracha* is that bonds are made at all amidst the harshness of war and religious persecution. It seems as likely as it does absurd that in a landscape filled with displaced and lonely individuals blown about by endless fighting, Tadgh the harper is most loved by a goose, the loyal Maria who follows him as he escapes seven years of slavery in Scotland to sail across the Irish Sea, finally to cross a war-torn Ireland in search of his master, Ulick. While the church destroys the lovers Ulick (a troubadour) and Soracha (a nun), it is Tadgh the harper who finally and successfully brings together religious faith and human love. As he and a young peasant woman, Bridget, oversee the shrine that has developed on the island to which Ulick and Soracha eloped, Tadgh begins to recount Ulick's stories of love and romance to the pilgrims who travel to the site, drawn by its erotic associations as much as by any pious ones. The clergy insist that the aged harper marry his companion, which he does much against his wishes and with no intentions to consummate the marriage; he is, in fact, impotent. But needing to see a woman naked in order to better tell Ulick's stories (and so keep the church prosperous from the pilgrims' donations), he asks his wife to allow him to look at her. At the sight of her, he cries "Biddy, you're just Mother Eve herself, come out of the word of God. . . . I shall leave this world happy now, for though I have never sinned with a woman I have seen God's creation" (*STH* 2:219). The old man enters what Moore in *Memoirs of My Dead Life* calls the "Great Procession" of sexual life in which "one does feel more conscious than at any other time of rhythm, and, after all, rhythm is joy" (*MMDL* 204). He does so by an ecstatic synthesis of his love of life and the religious system through which he has been taught to comprehend his world.[17]

Tadgh's admiration of his wife carries with it no anticipation. Because he is outside the world of potential action due to his age, infirmity, and the knowledge of his oncoming death, he may well be the only happy character in *A Story-Teller's Holiday*. If life, to invoke again Virginia Woolf's words, is at best a process of discovering, then what one discovers is most frequently more longings unfulfilled. In his rendition of the early Semitic folk tale of Lilith, Moore tells of an Adam and Eve who (like Daphnis and Chloe, whose story he was to translate and publish several years later) deliberate as to how sexual intercourse is to be accomplished. They have been commanded not to imitate the methods of the animals and are quite bewildered until Eve is finally given the secret by Satan's emissary, Lilith, Adam's first wife. But of much more thematic importance than their eventual— and comic—consummation, is Adam's apprehension that while he may have Eve, he will always dream of Lilith. "Does the imagination dwell the most / Upon a woman won or a woman lost?" Yeats asks in "The Tower." Moore's Adam realizes as does Yeats's speaker that the woman for whom he longs is as "evanescent . . . as the mist, yet she was very real, more real than Eve sitting by him." She is "the reality behind the appearance," the object of desire who comes "between waking and sleeping and in dreams" (*STH* 1:230, 229).

Union with another human being becomes a form of union between the subject and the object of his imaginings: an act to be dreamed of in retrospect or longing. If Adam's desire will never be fulfilled because his dreams are always more wonderful than the reality of another, if Tadgh the harper's participation in the sexual world is more observational than experiential, we would seem to be in the realms of narcissism and voyeurism. Would this condition not prohibit an entry into the "Great Procession" of life? Moore's younger contemporary, D. H. Lawrence, reviled self-observation as pornographic and hypothesized a sexual unity in which consciousness of self would disappear; for Moore, however, self-observation becomes the key to a reconciliation of self and other. In fact, it is the very passageway into that "Great Procession."

What one seeks to embrace is frequently as evanescent as Lilith. The past often amounts to a legacy of failure, as emblematized by the shell of Moore Hall. The present bespeaks violence and catastrophe, vividly captured in the ruins of the General Post Office through which the narrator walks at the beginning of *A Story-Teller's Holiday*. But Moore shifts attention to the prospect of himself, in a perpetual admiration at that which comes to him: bits of speech, landscapes, books, the unique and fascinating shapes of the people around him, and most of all the seeming miracle of his own imagination transforming these openings into fictions. Amid the ruins of the General

Post Office, Moore finds the deepest pleasure in the fact that "nature" has given *him*—not Balzac nor anyone else—the key element of a displaced cat to complete his picture of the scene. From first to last, Moore marvels at the spectacle of the "mystery of destiny" that he should tell the story: Father Oliver looking back on the lake he has crossed, Adam lost in the wonder of his own dreams, Tadgh delighted not only at Biddy's backside but at his newfound satisfaction in its prospect.

This self-reflexive subjectivity does not, however, preempt Moore's acknowledgment of the historical world that conflicts, while sometimes colluding, with his aspirations to autogenous self-creation. To concentrate as Moore does upon the act of remembering is to place at center a consuming sense of the present; yet that present is constructed of its ongoing, even relentless, researching of the past. The subjective perceiver is always fully intermingled with the object of his perception, as in *The Lake*, where even the boundaries between the subject and the object of his contemplation seem to disappear, the process of consciousness replicating the forms of its natural surroundings. In *Hail and Farewell* the unique voice of the autobiographical persona is shown to be constructed, in part, of the voices of others, and in fictional works like *Esther Waters* and *Celibate Lives,* the protagonists are never fully independent of the constraints of their material surroundings, the language in which others describe them, or their own physical bodies. And in Moore's earliest works, the figure of the cosmopolitan artist exists in an uneasy contraposition with the world of western Ireland it so repudiates.

These contradictions bring to mind again Malcolm Brown's brilliant formulation of the essential "Moorism" as that which at once puts forward and ironically undercuts its own proposition. The representations of the self in Moore's fiction and autobiographies are Janus-faced ones, and the autogenous self remains intertwined with its opposite. The achievement of Moore's long career resides in this bold predication of the created face with the simultaneous recognition of that against which it is defined. "I seek an image," Yeats asserted, thinking of Dante whose worldly nature found its opposing image in the pilgrim of the *Divine Comedy.* As Yeats surely knew from his own experience, it is the sense of a vital interaction between historical life and aesthetic representation upon which art depends. And in the case of George Moore, it is that necessitous tension that was so fully realized in his life's exploration of the multifold mysteries of the speaking self.

Notes
Bibliography
Index

Notes

Preface

1. Christopher Hassall, *A Biography of Edward Marsh* (New York: Harcourt, Brace, 1959), 395.

2. In the first chapter of her dissertation, Cynthia A. Merrill offers an original and carefully argued history of what she terms a "dialectic" between assertions of transcendence and self-creation and theories of historicity and determinism. She describes "the wrenching tension between two competing positions" into which "philosophically . . . the self was born" in the eighteenth century: a self "at once acutely aware of its dependence upon temporality, circumstance, language and culture, and yet perpetually in quest of autonomy and transcendence." See "Self-Reflections: The Dialectics of Autobiography," (Ph.D. diss., Univ. of Washington, 1990), 8, 2.

3. Moore to Clara Lanza, 12 Aug. 1891, in Robert Stephen Becker, "The Letters of George Moore, 1863–1901" (Ph.D. diss., Univ. of Reading, 1980), no. 338.

1. The Discourse of Repudiation:
A Drama in Muslin and *Parnell and His Island*

1. As quoted by Charles Morgan, *Epitaph on George Moore* (London: Macmillan, 1935), 3.

2. For a study of formal elements in the narration in *Drama*, see Judith Mitchell, "*A Drama in Muslin:* George Moore's Victorian Novel," *English Literature in Transition* 25, no. 4 (1982): 211–24.

3. The Land League was declared an illegal organization on 20 Oct. 1881 and was reconstituted as the Irish National League on 17 Oct. 1882. The main action of *A Drama in Muslin* takes place between the spring of 1881 and the autumn of 1883, but Moore does not specifically differentiate between the organizations. Dr. Reed, who would be the character most aware of such changes, does refer to the National League in conversation with Alice near the end of the novel. See *Drama in Muslin*, 293.

4. Paul Sporn, "Marriage and Class Conflict: The Subversive Link in George Moore's *A Drama in Muslin*," *Clio* 3 (1973): 17.

5. Moore to Frans Netscher, sometime between late 1885 and early 1886, cited in J. G. Riewald, "From Naturalism to Lyrical Realism: Fourteen Unpublished Letters from George Moore to Frans Netscher," *English Studies* 58 (1977): 137.

6. Moore's urgent sense of the need for vocation is evident not only in his letters, but in nearly all his fiction and autobiographies, as has been noted by numerous commentators. See particularly chap. 3 of *George Moore in Transition*.

7. Moore to Netscher, in Riewald, 137.

8. George Moore, *Muslin* (London: Heinemann, 1915), xi.

9. Eduard von Hartmann, *Philosophy of the Unconscious*, vol. 3, trans. W. C. Coupland, 1884, as cited in Patrick Bridgwater, *George Moore and German Pessimism* (Durham, England: Univ. of Durham Press, 1988), 31. Bridgwater identifies the source of Alice's remark although he does not note the discrepancy between Moore's version and the original. Since Bridgwater cites the same translation and edition with which, he argues, Moore would have been familiar, alternate translation cannot be held responsible for the differences between the original and Alice's statement.

10. That Moore thought of Alice's development as integrally linked to its precise historical moment is further indicated by the nature of his revisions in the 1915 *Muslin*. As he deemphasizes the historical framework, he also shifts attention away from Alice. As suggested by his proposed new title, *The Baiting of Mrs. Barton*, he transfers the point of view to that of Alice's mother. Clearly, he felt Alice's story and the story of the Land War to be inexorably related, and when he downplayed the one, he diminished the other as well.

11. See Frank Harris, *Contemporary Portraits*, 4th ser. (New York: Brentano's, 1923), 292–94. Moore dismisses Schreiner's novel in *Confessions of a Young Man*, although this is an unreliable testament of his opinion during the middle of 1885. See also Christopher Heywood, "Olive Schreiner's Influence on George Moore and D. H. Lawrence," in *Aspects of South African Literature*, ed. Christopher Heywood (New York: Africana, 1976), 42–53. While discussing *Esther Waters*, Heywood argues that Schreiner distinguishes between rival claims of motherhood and independence, but a more accurate reading of both Moore's novel and hers indicates that in the tradition of Mary Wollstonecraft, Schreiner was contrasting the common experience of motherhood with what she felt to be its ideal form. See also Schreiner's *Women and Labour* (London: T. F. Unwin, 1911) for her comparison of motherhood as practiced by the bourgeois "sex-parasite" to its ideal state as a mode of intelligent creation.

12. Olive Schreiner, *The Story of an African Farm* (Chicago: Academy Press, Cassandra Editions, 1977), 181.

13. Ibid., 180–81.

14. Ibid., 183

15. It appears that Moore utilizes the conventional assumptions of his time, which correlate sensuousness with hunger, and sexual frigidity and religious spirituality with an antipathy to food. Many studies of the subject exist, but especially interesting in its evaluation of nineteenth-century advice books, sex manuals, and cookbooks is Helena Michie's *Flesh Made Word: Female Figures and Women's Bodies* (Oxford: Oxford Univ. Press, 1987), 12–29.

16. Although letters and biography indicate that Moore considered marriage twice (both times for financial reasons), his letters to his mother and brother Maurice also indicate his early prescience that he would never marry. In spite of his penchant

for explicit stories about himself and various women, most of his friends disbelieved the tales. Frank Harris speaks for all when he describes Moore as exhibiting "astonishing moderation in desire." Similarly, Oliver St John Gogarty claims Moore's particularity regarding his food to be based in an actual lack of real taste or pleasure in food. See Frank Harris, *Contemporary Portraits*, 2d ser. (New York: privately published, 1919), 117–18; Oliver St John Gogarty, "Next Door to George Moore," *Saturday Review of Literature* 14 (18 July 1936), 15, and *It Isn't This Time of Year at All: An Unpremeditated Autobiography* (Garden City, N.Y.: Doubleday, 1954), 137.

17. Revised passages and their originals are reproduced side-by-side in E. Jay Jernigan, "George Moore's 'Re-Tying of Bows': A Critical Study of the Eight Early Novels and Their Revisions" (Ph.D. diss., Kansas State Univ., 1966).

18. Charles Stewart Parnell, *Freeman's Journal* 29 Oct. 1881.

19. See Paul Bew, *Land and the National Question in Ireland* (Atlantic Highlands, N.J.: Humanities, 1979), and his "The Land League Ideal: Achievements and Contradictions," in *Ireland: Land, Politics and People*, ed. P. J. Drudy (Cambridge: Cambridge Univ. Press, 1982), 77–92.

20. Sporn, "Marriage and Class Conflict," 15–17. In his excellent book on Moore's novels, Richard Allen Cave, I believe, misreads the happy ending of *A Drama in Muslin* as unqualified by irony and only slightly overshadowed by the limitations of the Reeds' income. See Richard Allen Cave, *A Study of the Novels of George Moore* (Gerrards Cross: Colin Smythe, 1978), 62–63.

21. Sporn, "Marriage and Class Conflict," 16.

22. I am not here considering all facets of the concept of authorship, but am drawing from Foucault's discussion of the author's proper name as designating not a historical person but a set of utterances understood according to culturally accepted codes. See Michel Foucault, "What Is an Author?" in *Textual Strategies: Perspectives in Post-Structuralist Criticism*, ed. Josué V. Harari (Ithaca: Cornell Univ. Press, 1979), 141–60.

23. Moore usually sent proofs and copies of books to friends and relatives, quizzing them impatiently as to their reactions. Sometimes reactions were vehement if people felt themselves to have been portrayed unflatteringly. In the case of *A Drama in Muslin*, Moore writes to his mother, "I am very sorry indeed I cannot go to Moore Hall this year. Nothing would give me greater pleasure than to spend a few months with you in the old place but I hear my book has given so much offence that it would be better from me to keep away." Moore to Mary Blake Moore, 8 Feb. 1886, in Becker, "Letters of George Moore," no. 119.

24. Gogarty, "Next Door to George Moore," 4.

25. Moore, *Muslin*, viii.

26. Walter Pater, *The Renaissance* (Chicago: Academy Press, 1977), 235.

27. Malcolm Brown, *George Moore: A Reconsideration* (Seattle: Univ. of Washington Press, 1955), 15.

28. The Ardilauns and Moores appear as themselves, and the names of other people living in the area—such as the Blakes and Dalys—are applied to fictionalized composite characters. The hard-drinking, sadistic Miss Barrett may have been suggested by Harriet Gardiner, a female landlord highly unpopular with the tenants for her frequent forced eviction, although she was neither drunken nor a bisexual profligate as is the fictional Miss Barrett.

29. Francis Hart, "Notes for an Anatomy of Modern Autobiography," *New Literary History* 1, no. 3 (1970): 488.

30. An insightful correlation between Moore's rejection of his responsibilities as landlord and the pessimism of his novels is given by Wayne E. Hall in his *Shadowy Heroes: Irish Literature of the 1890s* (Syracuse: Syracuse Univ. Press, 1980), 83–112.

31. George Moore, *Terre d'Irlande*, trans. Felix Rabbe (Paris: Charpentier, 1887), 11.

32. Joseph Hone, *The Moores of Moore Hall* (London: Jonathan Cape, 1939), 182.

33. David Thornley, *Isaac Butt and Home Rule* (Westport, Conn.: Greenwood, 1976), 89–91. J. H. Whyte remarks of G. H. Moore that "his tongue and pen were quite unbridled," and offers as an example an address in which Moore castigated a landlord who punished a tenant for voting against the landlord's interests: "The only difference that exists between Mr. H. de Burgh and the greater part of the landlords in Mayo is, that he has the imbecile manliness to acknowledge what they have the wise cowardice to conceal and disavow." J. H. Whyte, *The Independent Irish Party, 1850–9* (Oxford: Oxford Univ. Press, 1958), 129, 126. While Moore's words are sharp, it is worth noting that Mayo politics were as a rule combative and even slanderous. Lord Sligo can thus write a letter to G. H. Moore accusing him of speaking "claptrap," adding "you . . . do more ruin and injure and persecute and exterminate your tenants than any man in Mayo," yet end the letter, "Yours affectionately." Hone, *Moores*, 159–60.

34. In addition to the biographies prepared by Maurice Moore and Joseph Hone, informative summaries of the political career of G. H. Moore are best provided in Whyte, and Donald Jordan, "Land and Politics in the West of Ireland: County Mayo, 1846–82" (Ph.D. diss., Univ. of California, Davis, 1982), 49–72.

35. Hone, *Moores*, 155–56, 158–60.

36. See Moore's comments (and particularly the comparison of his father and Sir William Gregory) in *Hail and Farewell*, ed. Richard Cave (Gerrards Cross: Colin Smythe, 1976), and his introduction to his brother's biography of their father, *An Irish Gentleman, George Henry Moore* (London: Laurie, 1913).

37. Jordan, "Land and Politics," 268.

38. Moore, *Terre d'Irelande*, 161–62.

39. G. Moore to the Editor, *Court and Society Review* 24 (Dec. 1885): 511.

40. Cited in Donald Jordan, "John O'Connor Power, Charles Stewart Parnell and the Centralisation of Popular Politics in Ireland," *Irish Historical Studies* 25, no. 97 (1986): 46.

41. T. W. Moody, *Davitt and Irish Revolution 1846–82* (Oxford: Clarendon, 1981), 394–95.

42. As much as Moore inserted references to the body and to sexuality into his revised *A Drama in Muslin*, he extracted them from the text of *Parnell*. Correspondence indicates that the text was expurgated by its publishers and that, at one point, printers refused to set the type. Deleted scenes include one in which Miss Barrett, the rough and drunken female landlord, reaches with relish to feel the male sexual organs of a bull; or in which certain members of Parliament are said to have engaged in "fastes de la honte" in "la saleté et les ordures de Ship Street." George Moore, *Terre d'Irlande*, 176–77, 23–24.

43. Hall, 91.

44. See, for example, James Olney, *Metaphors of Self: The Meaning of Autobiography* (Princeton: Princeton Univ. Press, 1972), 20–22; and Georges Gusdorf, "Conditions and Limits of Autobiography," in *Autobiography: Essays Theoretical and Critical*, ed. James Olney (Princeton: Princeton Univ. Press, 1980), 28–48.

2. The Autobiographical Pyramid:
Confessions of a Young Man

1. Moore wrote to Edouard Dujardin of his desire to use his own name on 12 Feb. 1888, before the issue of the French edition of 1889. See G. Moore, *Letters from George Moore to Ed. Dujardin, 1886–1922*, ed. and trans. John Eglinton (New York: Crosby Gaige, 1929), 25. In the preface to the 1889 English edition, Moore indicates that he had originally intended to do so.

2. Max Beerbohm, *Mainly on the Air* (New York: Knopf, 1958), 83, 82. A detailed study of the similarities between Wilde and Moore is given in David B. Eakin, "The Man in the Paper Mask: Epistolary Autobiography in Oscar Wilde and George Moore" (Ph.D. diss., Arizona State Univ., 1980).

3. AE to George Moore, 6 Apr. 1916, in *Letters from AE*, ed. Alan Denson (London: Abelard-Schuman, 1961), 109–10.

4. W. Eugene Davis and Mark J. Lidman, "'I Am Still a Young Man': George Moore's Last Revisions of *Confessions of a Young Man*," *Bulletin of the New York Public Library* 79, no. 1 (1975): 83–95. The revisions of *Confessions* have been thoroughly examined by Susan Marie Dick in her dissertation and the subsequent edition of the text that is used throughout this book. See "*Confessions of a Young Man* by George Moore: A Variorum Edition" (Ph.D. diss., Northwestern Univ., 1967).

5. The relationship among Moore-author, Moore-narrator, and Moore-character is much debated by *Confessions'* critics, although all agree that the problem bears relationship to the author's unusual use of the present tense. Michael M. Riley speaks of Moore's attempt to "embrace all that he has been and thought while at the same time making clear that he has outgrown much of it." Jean C. Noel argues that Moore "does not try to dissociate himself from his past self even when he casts ridicule upon it." Of the indulgent yet critical interpretations most make of their past lives, Jon Lanham notes in reference to Joyce, "We are rarely, and then fondly, embarrassed by the emotions of our youth; we are nearly always embarrassed by our jejune convictions." See Riley, "Persona and Theme in George Moore's *Confessions of a Young Man*," *English Literature in Transition* 19, no. 2 (1976): 87–95; Noel, "George Moore's Pluridimensional Autobiography: Remarks on His *Confessions of a Young Man*," *Cahiers du Centre d'Etudes Irlandaises* 4 (1979): 49–66; and Lanham, "The Genre of *A Portrait of the Artist as a Young Man* and 'the Rhythm of Its Structure,'" *Genre* 10 (1977): 77–102.

6. While there are other biblical models for nineteenth-century autobiography (e.g., the model of the Genesis as utilized in Wordsworth's *Prelude*), the predominance of the Exodus has been explained in John N. Morris, *Versions of the Self: Studies in English Autobiography from John Bunyan to John Stuart Mill* (New York: Basic, 1966); Linda H. Peterson, *Victorian Autobiography: The Tradition of Self-Interpretation* (New Haven: Yale Univ. Press, 1986); and Heather Henderson, *The Victorian Self: Autobiography and Biblical Narrative* (Ithaca: Cornell Univ. Press, 1989).

7. To Maurice Moore, 20 Mar. 1888, in Seamus MacDonncha, "Letters of George Moore (1852–1933) to His Brother, Colonel Maurice Moore, C.B. (1857–1939)" (Ph.D. diss., National Univ. of Ireland, Galway, 1972–73), 6.

8. Arthur Schopenhauer, "On Thinking for Oneself," in *Parerga and Paralipomena: Short Philosophical Essays*, trans. E. F. J. Payne (Oxford: Clarendon, 1974), 2:491–92. For a precise historical study of Moore's reading of Schopenhauer and Nietzsche, see Bridgwater.

9. In arguing that *Confessions* forcefully posits its persona as an essentially un-

changing character, I am differing in emphasis from commentators like Robert Langenfeld who, in support of his thesis that *Confessions* follows the genre of farce, stresses the psychological and ideological fragmentation of the narrator. See Robert Langenfeld, "A Reconsideration: *Confessions of a Young Man* as Farce," in *Twilight of Dawn: Studies in English Literature in Transition*, ed. O. M. Brack, Jr. (Tucson: Univ. of Arizona Press, 1987), 91–110.

10. Esther Waters's capacity to raise her son rests on exactly such a small increase in salary; in the difference between fourteen and sixteen pounds is the failure or success of Esther's life. The ambiguity of the novel's ending, however, questions just how much this two pounds has really come to. Despite the triumphant language of the conclusion, Jackie has been reduced to soldiery, and Esther wonders if he will not soon "be mere food for powder and shot" (*Esther Waters*, 382).

11. Arthur Schopenhauer, *The World as Will and Idea*, as cited in Bridgwater, 35.

12. See "Salve," chaps. 12–17. The issue is more complicated than whether or not Newman could write a passable sentence. Moore's theory of the incompatibility of art and Catholicism has everything to do with the justification of his own failure to be warmly received by Irish artists or the Irish public. Yet Moore insists on reducing the terms of argument to a trivial debate over Newman's syntax. Within the narrative of *Hail and Farewell*, the strategy is quite convincing. Moore's sentence parsing becomes the only aesthetic criterion; Newman cannot withstand Moore's stylistic criticism, and as the debate's sole representative of a Catholic artist, his failure becomes Catholicism's. At the same time, the argument seems such an insignificant basis for the dissolution of a fraternal relationship that Moore appears to be, once again, in the grip of irrational "instinct."

13. See MacDonncha; and *George Moore on Parnassus*, ed. Helmut E. Gerber (Newark: Univ. of Delaware Press, 1988).

14. Paul de Man, "Autobiography as De-facement," *Modern Language Notes*, 94 (1979): 920–21.

15. I have reproduced the 1917 text of the dedication as given by Susan Dick. The remainder of Dick's text is the 1888 English edition. Dick and Gilcher both state that the dedication was first added in the French edition of 1889, then slightly expanded in the 1889 English edition, then altered again in 1917 with the correction of two minor failures in idiomatic usage.

16. Louis A. Renza, "A Veto of the Imagination: A Theory of Autobiography," in Olney, *Autobiography*, 286–88. The question of Moore's compulsion to assert the authority of his text over that of other preexisting ones is treated in chap. 6.

17. Roland Barthes, "An Introduction to the Structural Analysis of Narrative," *New Literary History* 6, no. 2 (1975): 261. This essay first appeared in French in 1966.

18. Useful summaries are given in Paul John Eakin, *Fictions in Autobiography: Studies in the Art of Self-Invention* (Princeton: Princeton Univ. Press, 1985); Janet Varner Gunn, *Autobiography: Towards a Poetics of Experience* (Philadelphia: Univ. of Pennsylvania Press, 1982); and Michael Sprinker, "Fictions of the Self: The End of Autobiography," in Olney, *Autobiography*, 321–42.

19. de Man, 919–30. Interestingly, Moore's American contemporary, Henry Adams, also refers to autobiography as self-murder in an 1884 letter to John Hay. See *The Letters of Henry Adams*, vol. 2, *1868–1885*, ed. J. C. Levenson et al. (Cambridge, Mass.: Harvard Univ. Press, 1982), 532.

20. J.-K. Huysmans, *A Rebours* (Paris: Charpentier, 1925), 100.

21. In numerous instances, Moore expresses surprise at the offense others took

at their appearance in his works. His brother, for example, was furious at his portrait in *Hail and Farewell*, but Moore's letters to him (see *George Moore on Parnassus*) show no understanding of the colonel's position. Even earlier, his letters to his mother after *Le Figaro* published his defamatory "Letters sur l'Irlande" indicate his bewilderment over his neighbors' anger at what they took to be their portraits. Whether Moore's surprise in such cases was real or feigned is a matter of speculation, although fictionalized autobiography was not at all uncommon during the period. Yeats's disdain for factuality, for example, has been noted in every study of his autobiographical writings. In his 1936 reminiscence "Next Door to George Moore," Gogarty reports meeting Maurice Moore the night before George Moore's "at-home" and discussing the controversial preface to *An Irish Gentleman;* he identifies himself as having suggested to the colonel that he enter a disclaimer slip into the preface. Yet the letters collected in *Parnassus* indicate that Moore sent his brother the preface the day before he left for Paris, where he remained until the book was published. Therefore this conversation on Ebury Street could not have occurred. This kind of fictionalization may well have been typical and expected within Moore's circle.

22. Philippe Lejeune, "The Autobiographical Pact," in *On Autobiography*, ed. Paul John Eakin, and trans. Katherine Leary (Minneapolis: Univ. of Minnesota Press, 1989), 3–30.

23. Renza, 278–79.

24. Moore to Herbert Wigram, n.d., cited in Edwin Gilcher, *Supplement to A Bibliography of George Moore* (Westport, Conn.: Meckler), 5. Gilcher also provides documentation of Moore's desire to withdraw the unflattering photograph from distribution.

25. An unsigned review in *The Hawk*, Augustus Moore's periodical, compares *Confessions* to *Sartor Resartus*. If the review was not actually written by George Moore himself, it may well have been written by Augustus or someone else who had discussed the work with Moore. Moore has "borrowed" so many motifs from *Sartor Resartus* and *Past and Present* that he could not have been unaware of his debt to Carlyle.

26. Moore's inability to become "English" has been noted with some amusement by Joseph Hone who reports that Moore dropped his membership in the aristocratic Tory Club because one of its members persisted in talking of horses, a subject Moore equated with the cultural barbarism of Mayo. Hone also relates Moore's discomfort with the dress, manners, and hunting preferences of the English aristocrat (*Life of George Moore*, 191–93). A similar picture is presented by Beerbohm in *Mainly on the Air*, 95–96.

27. Moore to Edouard Dujardin, *Letters from Moore to Dujardin*, 30.

28. Moore to W. T. Stead, May, 1889. In another letter, Moore wrote to Stead, "I have laughed at philanthropy because all philanthropy except that of not bringing any children into the world seems to me superficial." Moore to W. T. Stead, 3 Apr. 1889, in Becker, "Letters of George Moore," nos. 271 and 267.

29. Huysmans, 124.

30. Richard N. Coe, *When the Grass Was Taller: Autobiography and the Experience of Childhood* (New Haven: Yale Univ. Press, 1984), 146–47.

31. Jean-Paul Sartre, *The Words*, trans. Bernard Frechtman (Greenwich, Conn.: Fawcett, 1964), 11.

32. Ronald Schleifer, "George Moore's Turning Mind: Digression and Autobiographical Art in *Hail and Farewell*," *Genre* 12 (1979): 486.

3. Moore's Own Everlasting Yea:
Sexuality and Production in the Fiction of the Middle Period

1. Hall, 83–112.

2. From a speech delivered in County Sligo, 1879. See Moody, 350.

3. Brief summaries of the critical response to Moore's realist fiction appear in more recent studies refuting exclusively naturalistic interpretations. Among the best of those are Cave, *Study of the Novels*, Elliot L. Gilbert, "In the Flesh: *Esther Waters* and the Passion for Yes," *Novel* 12, no. 1 (1978): 48–65; and Judith Mitchell, "Fictional Worlds in George Moore's *A Mummer's Wife*," *English Studies* 67, no. 4 (1986): 345–54. Brian Nicholas rejects the novel precisely because of its blending of naturalist doctrines with those of free will and because Esther is motivated both by unconscious desire and lucid choice. His judgments perhaps indicate a lack of familiarity with the way such polarities function throughout Moore's total corpus. See "The Case of Esther Waters," in *The Man of Wax: Critical Essays on George Moore*, ed. Douglas A. Hughes (New York: New York Univ. Press, 1971), 151–83.

4. In her historical study of Victorian prostitutes, Judith Walkowitz argues that "the stereotyped sequence of girls seduced, pregnant, and abandoned to the streets fitted only a small minority of women who ultimately moved into prostitution." She concludes that in the second half of the nineteenth century most prostitutes were motherless local girls in their teens who often were infertile or bore infants who did not survive due to neglect, disease, and infanticide; that many operated independently of male keepers and entered prostitution by choice as an alternative to other low-paying and arduous employment; and that approximately two-thirds had a clientele drawn exclusively from their own class. Moore's description of the circumstances of common prostitution emphasizes economic distress rather than moral failing, but otherwise contradicts the picture drawn by Walkowitz. See *Prostitution and Victorian Society: Women, Class, and the State* (Cambridge: Cambridge Univ. Press, 1980), 13–31.

5. See app. 1 to *Esther Waters: A Novel*, 347.

6. George Watt, *The Fallen Woman in the Nineteenth-Century English Novel* (Totowa, N.J.: Barnes and Noble, 1984), 187. It is worth noting that as he revised *Esther Waters*, Moore became much bolder in his articulation of Esther's sexuality. Watt (who uses only the 1920 revision) argues that Moore was the first novelist in English to sympathetically represent sexual desire in a "fallen woman." In defense of his thesis, I believe he overstates the sexual motivation in Esther's decision to choose William instead of Fred. While, as Watt persuasively demonstrates, desire plays a large role in the novel, it is counterpoised by Esther's practical considerations. The blending of unconscious desire and the pragmatic is, as I argue, crucial to Moore's working concept of "instinct."

7. George Moore, *Esther Waters: A Play in Four Acts* in *The Celebrated Case of Esther Waters: The Collaboration of George Moore and Barrett H. Clark on "Esther Waters: A Play*," ed. W. Eugene Davis (Lanham, Md.: Univ. Press of America, 1984), 57.

8. Sally Shuttleworth, "Female Circulation: Medical Discourse and Popular Advertising in the Mid-Victorian Era," in *Body/Politics: Women and the Discourses of Science*, ed. Mary Jacobus et al. (New York: Routledge, 1989), 67.

9. Paul Sporn identifies a periodical article on wet-nursing and baby farming which was very likely one of Moore's sources of information. Sporn points out that whereas the article takes pains not to condemn the well-to-do (and in fact portrays them as benevolent), Moore directly attacks them for their role. It is therefore all the

more likely that his changes in the dramatic adaptation arose from the desire to pacify a potential paying audience. See "*Esther Waters:* The Sources of the Baby-Farm Episode," *English Literature in Transition* 11, no. 1 (1968): 39–42. An example of upper-class disquiet regarding the wet-nursing system can be observed in such an archconservative as W. S. Gilbert, whose parody, "The Baby's Vengeance" details the life of a wet nurse's child whom "*she slighted.* Tempted by a lot / Of gold and silver sent to her." Neither Esther nor the other poor women in the novel are made rich by their occupations, despite Mrs. Spires's promise that wet-nursing offers a lucrative employment. See W. S. Gilbert, *The Bab Ballads,* ed. James Ellis (Cambridge, Mass.: Belknap Press of Harvard Univ. Press, 1970), 226.

10. George Moore, *Vain Fortune* (London: Walter Scott, 1895), 264.

11. Referring to his novel-in-progress he says, "The human drama will be the servant girl's fight for her child's life among the baby farmers." To Charles Scribner's Sons he writes, "The girl I am trying to depict represents the simple sturdy steadfastness of the saxon race." In a later letter to them he refers to "the heroism of the working woman." Moore to Michael Field, 25 Aug. 1890, in Becker, "Letters of George Moore," no. 314; Moore to Charles Scribner's Sons, cited in Moore, *Esther Waters: A Novel,* xiv, xv.

12. Moore explained very late in life that he had rejected the title as "sententious." *A Communication to My Friends* (London: Heinemann, 1937), xlvii. I have no verification that this was his reason for rejecting it at time of composition.

13. Arthur Schopenhauer, "On Women," in *Parega,* 625.

14. Jay Jernigan, "The Forgotten Serial Version of George Moore's *Esther Waters,*" *Nineteenth-Century Fiction* 23, no. 1 (1968): 99–103; Royal A. Gettmann, "George Moore's Revisions of *The Lake,* '*The Wild Goose,*' and *Esther Waters,*" *PMLA* 59 (1944): 540–55.

15. Moore to Charles Scribner's Sons, 28 Jan. 1892, in Becker, "Letters of George Moore," no. 350.

16. George Moore, *A Mummer's Wife* (London: Heinemann, 1937), 279.

17. Elliot L. Gilbert, 62.

18. Richard Allen Cave discusses the association of Esther with natural landscape, citing as a critical scene her moment of ecstatic apprehension of nature while on the hillside of Woodview. He also argues that the overgrown garden at Woodview acts as a sign of nature's regenerative power, echoing the theme of mother and child. See Cave, *Study of the Novels,* 88–91.

19. Moore to W. T. Stead, Sept. 1888, in Becker, "Letters of George Moore," no. 243.

20. Moore to John Mackinnon Robertson, 13 Mar. 1888, in Becker, "Letters of George Moore," no. 210.

21. In the earliest version of the story, Moore suggests that Esther is stupid and coarse, "a regular Joe Blunt." In the play, he repeatedly calls attention to her grammar and has Mrs. Barfield assert that "she is none the worse for her mistakes of speech and is much more intelligent than many who speak correctly." Perhaps he was trying to acknowledge the biases of his imagined theater audience, or his own position simply may have been unsettled. See Jernigan, "Forgotten Serial Version," 102, and Moore, *Esther Waters: A Play,* 68.

22. Moore to an unknown journalist, 15 Sept. 1888, privately published as "George Moore on Authorship" (Cherry Plain, N.Y.: Privately printed, 1950).

23. Moore to Charles Scribner's Sons, cited in Moore, *Esther Waters: A Novel,* xv.

24. Cited in Moore, *Ester Waters: A Novel,* xiii.

25. Elaine Showalter, *Sexual Anarchy: Gender and Culture at the Fin de Siècle* (New York: Viking, 1990), 77–78.

26. Sandra Gilbert and Susan Gubar, *Sexchanges*, vol. 2 of *No Man's Land: The Place of the Woman Writer in the Twentieth Century* (New Haven: Yale Univ. Press, 1989), 335. The theory that male transvestism involves a rigidification rather than a blurring of gender roles is also argued by Annie Woodhouse in *Fantastic Women: Sex, Gender and Transvestism* (Basingstoke, Hampshire: Macmillan, 1989).

27. George Moore, *Confessions d'un Jeune Anglais* (Paris: Savine, 1889), 247–48.

28. Michael Wilson, "'Sans les femmes, qu'est-ce qui nous resterait?': Gender and Transgression in Bohemian Montmartre," in *Body Guards: The Cultural Politics of Gender Ambiguity*, ed. Julia Epstein and Kristina Straub (New York: Routledge, 1991), 195–222.

29. George H. Doran, *Chronicles of Barabbas, 1884–1934* (New York: Harcourt, Brace, 1935), 269–70.

30. George Moore, "An Episode in Married Life," in *In Minor Keys: The Uncollected Short Stories of George Moore*, ed. David B. Eakin and Helmut E. Gerber (Syracuse: Syracuse Univ. Press, 1985), 169, 170.

31. George Moore, *Avowals* (London: Heinemann, 1936), 74.

32. Summaries of reviews are provided in *George Moore in Transition*, 110–17 and in Robert Langenfeld, ed., *George Moore: An Annotated Secondary Bibliography of Writings about Him* (New York: AMS Press, 1987).

33. For references and discussion, see Lillian Faderman, "The Morbidification of Love between Women by 19th-Century Sexologists," *Journal of Homosexuality* 4, no. 1 (1978): 88–89; and David F. Greenberg, *The Construction of Homosexuality* (Chicago: Univ. of Chicago Press, 1988), 1–21.

34. Elin Diamond, "Refusing the Romanticism of Identity: Narrative Interventions in Churchill, Benmussa, Duras," *Theatre Journal* 37, no. 3 (1985): 277, 279.

35. Jill Dolan, *The Feminist Spectator as Critic* (Ann Arbor, Mich.: UMI, 1988), 105.

36. Gilbert and Gubar, 336–37.

37. For treatment of the historical association between transvestism and lesbianism, see Marjorie Garber, *Vested Interests* (New York: Routledge, 1991); Greenberg, 380–83; and Esther Newton, "The Mythic Mannish Lesbian: Radclyffe Hall and the New Woman" in *The Lesbian Issue: Essays from Signs*, ed. Estelle B. Freedman et al. (Chicago: Univ. of Chicago Press, 1985): 7–25.

38. A useful discussion of this issue is found in Barbara Fassler, "Theories of Homosexuality as Sources of Bloomsbury's Androgyny," *Signs* 5, no. 2 (1979): 237–51; and in Jonathan Rose, *The Edwardian Temperament, 1895–1919* (Athens: Ohio Univ. Press, 1986), 64–66. Nancy Cunard reports Moore's judgments on homosexuality to be less tolerant of homosexual practice than either his fiction or the selection from *Conversations in Ebury Street* would indicate. However, the condemnatory views expressed to Nancy Cunard may result from confusion over her term, "pederasty," which may broadly refer to male homosexuality in general, but which carries a more specific reference to sexual activity with children. See Nancy Cunard, *GM: Memories of George Moore* (New York: Macmillan, 1957), 187–88.

4. The Comic Body and the Tragic Soul: Satire, Caricature, and the Autobiographical Voice

1. Verbal caricatures are from W. B. Yeats, *The Autobiography of William Butler Yeats* (New York: Collier, 1965), 271; Gertrude Atherton, *Adventures of a Novelist* (Lon-

don: Jonathan Cape, 1932), 161; Cartoon in *The Irish Times*, 5 Feb. 1910; Lady Gregory's diary of 1899, as quoted in Mary Lou Kohfeldt, *Lady Gregory: The Woman Behind the Irish Renaissance* (New York: Atheneum, 1985), 135; Susan Mitchell, *George Moore* (New York: Dodd, Mead, 1916), 14; Julia Frankau, as quoted in Gilbert Frankau, *Self-Portrait: A Novel of His Life* (New York: Dutton, 1940), 101; Cunard, 27; Havelock Ellis, *My Confessional: Questions of Our Day* (Boston: Houghton Mifflin, 1934), 209–10; James H. Cousins, as quoted in Robert Hogan and James Kilroy, *The Irish Literary Theatre, 1899–1901* (Dublin: Dolmen, 1975), 36; Mayflo Gogarty, as quoted in Ulick O'Connor, *Oliver St John Gogarty: A Poet and His Times* (London: Jonathan Cape, 1963), 108; Yeats, 283; Gertrude Stein and Lytton Strachey, as quoted in Michael Holroyd, *Lytton Strachey: A Critical Biography*, vol. 2 (London: Heinemann, 1968), 76; Moore, as quoted in Jacques-Emile Blanche, *Portraits of a Lifetime*, trans. Walter Clement (London: J. M. Dent, 1937), 152.

2. James Olney, "The Uses of Comedy and Irony in *Autobiographies* and Autobiography," in *Yeats: An Annual of Critical and Textual Studies*, ed. Richard J. Finneran (Ithaca: Cornell Univ. Press, 1984), 2:197. See also Eugene R. August, "Darwin's Comedy: The *Autobiography* as Comic Narrative," *Victorian Newsletter* 75 (1989): 15–19.

3. Wayne Shumaker, *English Autobiography: Its Emergence, Materials, and Form* (Berkeley: Univ. of California Press, 1954), 194–95. Shumaker's essay and that of Schleifer remain the most penetrating studies of *Hail and Farewell*. In general, the book has been inexplicably ignored in studies of autobiographical literature, and what examinations of it do exist tend, with a few exceptions, to explain Moore's attitudes toward particular historical figures rather than the structure and technique of the text.

4. John Montague, "George Moore: The Tyranny of Memory," in *The Figure in the Cave and Other Essays*, ed. Antoinette Quinn (Syracuse: Syracuse Univ. Press, 1989), 95–96.

5. Moore left Ireland early in 1911; the "Overture" was published in the *English Review* in March 1910, and vol. 1 of the trilogy was published by Heinemann in Oct. 1911.

6. See, for example, Jean Starobinski, "The Style of Autobiography," in Olney, *Autobiography*, 83; and R. Victoria Arana, "Sir Edmund Gosse's *Father and Son*: Autobiography as Comedy," *Genre* 10 (1977): 63–76.

7. J. B. Yeats to W. B. Yeats, 21 May 1909, in Richard J. Finneran, George Mills Harper, and William M. Murphy, eds., *Letters to W. B. Yeats* (New York: Columbia Univ. Press, 1977), 1:213.

8. Edmund Gosse, "The Carpet and the Clock," in *Silhouettes* (New York: Charles Scribner's Sons, 1925), 398.

9. AE as cited in Jack W. Weaver, "AE, George Moore, and *Avatars*," *English Literature in Transition* 19, no. 2 (1976): 98.

10. Gertrude Stein, *Everybody's Autobiography* (New York: Cooper Square, 1971), 31; Oliver St John Gogarty, *As I Was Going Down Sackville Street* (New York: Reynal and Hitchcock, 1937), vi; Flann O'Brien, *At Swim-Two-Birds* (New York: New American Library, 1966), 7.

11. Gogarty, *As I Was Going*, 110.

12. E. H. M. Cox, *The Library of Edmund Gosse* (London: Dulau, 1924), 185–87. A very amusing satire of the repartee between Moore and Gosse is given by Beerbohm in *Mainly on the Air*, 89–92.

13. Max Beerbohm, "The Spirit of Caricature," in *The Incomparable Max: A Collection of Writings of Sir Max Beerbohm* (New York: Dodd, Mead, 1962), 94, 98.

14. John Felstiner, *The Lies of Art: Max Beerbohm's Parody and Caricature* (New York: Knopf, 1972), 113.

15. Beerbohm, "Spirit of Caricature," 101.

16. Ibid., 101.

17. Shumaker, 212.

18. Felstiner, 105.

19. Max Beerbohm to Edmund Gosse, 11 Nov. 1911, in *Letters of Max Beerbohm, 1892–1956*, ed. Rupert Hart-Davis (New York: Norton, 1988), 81.

20. Olney, "Uses of Comedy and Irony," 204–5.

21. James Olney, "W. B. Yeats's Daimonic Memory," *Sewanee Review* 85 (1977): 583–603. See also his "Some Versions of Memory/Some Versions of Bios: The Ontology of Autobiography," in *Autobiography* 259–67.

22. Max Beerbohm as quoted in Samuel Nathaniel Behrman, *Portrait of Max: An Intimate Memoir of Sir Max Beerbohm* (New York: Random House, 1960), 272.

23. One notable exception to this feminine tolerance was Edith Wharton, who was deeply offended by his conversation and described Moore in 1909 as "so monstrous, incredible & repulsive a bounder that I had to annihilate him; which I did to my satisfaction, so competely that there were no recognizable fragments to gather up." See *The Letters of Edith Wharton*, ed. R. W. B. Lewis and Nancy Lewis (New York: Charles Scribner's Sons, 1988), 173.

24. *The Evening Sun*, 31 July 1914. Joseph Hone also provides examples of this contradiction in *Life of Moore*, 266–70.

25. Cunard, 170–71.

26. Yeats, 340.

27. Beerbohm, *Mainly on the Air*, 84.

28. Hazard Adams, "Some Yeatsian Versions of Comedy," in *In Excited Reverie: A Centenary Tribute to William Butler Yeats, 1865–1939*, ed. A. Norman Jeffares and K. G. W. Cross (New York: Macmillan, 1965), 155, 156, 167.

29. R. Jahan Ramazani, "Yeats: Tragic Joy and the Sublime," *PMLA* 104 (1989): 163. In certain poems, as in the final stanza of "Vacillation," the modes of tragicomedy and tragic joy are interfused, thereby producing a multitonal effect and a much compressed complexity of thought and emotion.

30. John Eglinton, *Irish Literary Portraits* (1935; reprint, Freeport, N.Y.: Books for Libraries, 1967), 86.

31. Yeats, 307.

32. William F. Lynch, S.J., *Christ and Apollo: The Dimensions of the Literary Imagination* (New York: Sheed and Ward, 1960), 67–68, 91.

5. *Hail and Farewell's* Parodic Autobiography: The Double-Voiced Utterance and the Singular Subject

1. Max Beerbohm, "The Old and the Young Self: Mr. George Moore" (1924) from *Observations* (1925), reprinted in *Beerbohm's Literary Caricatures: From Homer to Huxley*, ed. J. G. Riewald (Hamden, Conn.: Archon, 1977), 255.

2. Gunn, *Autobiography*, 23.

3. Gary Saul Morson, *The Boundaries of Genre: Dostoevsky's "Diary of a Writer" and the Traditions of Literary Utopia* (Austin: Univ. of Texas Press, 1981), 108.

4. Mikhail Bakhtin, *Problems of Dostoevsky's Poetics*, ed. and trans. Caryl Emerson (Minneapolis: Univ. of Minnesota Press, 1984), 193–94.

5. The idea that parody may in some cases express respect toward the discourse it parodies is explored by Linda Hutcheon in *A Theory of Parody: The Teachings of Twentieth-Century Art Forms* (New York: Methuen, 1985), 50–55. As discussed later in the chapter, Moore's use of Flaubert's "Bouvard and Pecuchet" valorizes the text from which it borrows in order to denounce the historical personages who find themselves allegorized within Moore's adaptation of it.

I am not interested here in minute distinctions between the formal features and rhetorical effects of various types of parody, although studies of the genre abound in such distinctions. Moore utilizes such an extraordinarly wide variety of parodic approaches in *Hail and Farewell* as to discourage exclusive definitions regarding the methods or targets of parody.

6. Morson, 118–19.

7. Patrick Scott,"From Bon Gaultier to *Fly Leaves:* Context and Canon in Victorian Parody," *Victorian Poetry* 26 (1988): 251. Terry Caesar argues in contrast that it is misguided to convert Victorian "parody into the spokesman for some sort of morality or value. First of all, parody is a vehicle for specifically literary criticism before any other kind." Terry Caesar, "'I Quite Forget What—Say a Daffodily': Victorian Parody," *ELH* 51 (1984): 798. From *Parnell and His Island* on, however, Moore portrayed literary expression and cultural well-being as mutually symptomatic and interdependent, and the distinction Scott and Caesar make is not applicable to his work.

8. Morson, 113.

9. Northrop Frye, *Anatomy of Criticism: Four Essays* (Princeton: Princeton Univ. Press, 1957), 229–30.

10. "Moore on Authorship," n.p.

11. Max Beerbohm, "Rentree of Mr. George Moore into Chelsea" (1909) from *Fifty Caricatures* (1913), reprinted in *Beerbohm's Caricatures*, 253.

12. Fred Norris Robinson, "Satirists and Enchanters in Early Irish Literature," in *Satire: Modern Essays in Criticism*, ed. Ronald Paulson (Englewood Cliffs, N.J.: Prentice-Hall, 1971), 3.

13. Ibid., 8. Surprisingly, with the exception of Michael Kenneally's attribution of Sean O'Casey's autobiographical method to a tradition of oral invective, the relation between satire and autobiography in Irish literature has been little studied or even acknowledged. See Michael Kenneally, *Portraying the Self: Sean O'Casey and the Art of Autobiography* (Totowa, N.J.: Barnes and Noble, 1988).

14. For the most thorough study of Moore's plagiarisms, see Graham Owens, "A Study of George Moore's Revisions of His Novels and Short Stories" (Ph.D. diss., Univ. of Leeds, 1966).

15. "Moore on Authorship," n.p.

16. Hutcheon, *Theory of Parody*, 96.

17. George Moore, "Balzac," in *Impressions and Opinions* (1891; reprint, New York: Benjamin Blom, 1972), 64. In the final version of this essay, included in the 1924 *Conversations in Ebury Street*, Moore deletes this phrase and emphasizes Balzac's debt to the era that produced him. In his last years, Moore repeated more emphatically that great literature could be produced only in certain periods, the modern era not being among them.

18. Moore's denunciations of Dostoyevsky ("Gaboriau with psychological sauce," "sculpture in snow") and the incapacity of *Hail and Farewell*'s narrator to read *The Brothers Karamazov* ("a marsh") are particularly interesting given certain similarities between the two writers. Most striking are the variety of nature and motive in their

use of previously existent speech and the desire to impose, finally, an authoritative voice to govern the multiple voices within the text. I continue to maintain, however, that this assertion of what Bakhtin calls the "internally persuasive word" exists in tandem with Moore's skepticism regarding narrative authority. See Nina Perlina, *Varieties of Poetic Utterance: Quotation in "The Brothers Karamazov"* (Lanham, Md.: Univ. Press of America, 1985).

19. Correlations between conservatism and satire are ubiquitous in studies of the genre, as is the historical parallel between the rise of capitalism and the emergence of European autobiography in histories of that genre. Recently, some critics have postulated a relation between capitalist ideology and autobiographical criticism, with varying degrees of persuasiveness. An influential predecessor of this kind of approach is Michael Ryan's polemical review of Philip Lejeune's *Le Pacte autobiographique* in *Diacritics* 10, no. 2 (1980): 2–16.

20. Maynard Mack, "The Muse of Satire," in Paulson, 190–201.

21. For citations and further discussion, see Hutcheon, *Theory of Parody*, 69–83; and her *Poetics of Postmodernism: History, Theory, Fiction* (New York: Routledge, 1988), 22–27.

22. Hutcheon, *Theory of Parody*, 76–77.

23. Mikhail Bakhtin, "Discourse in the Novel," in *The Dialogic Imagination: Four Essays by M. M. Bakhtin*, ed. Michael Holquist; trans. Caryl Emerson and Michael Holquist (Austin: Univ. of Texas Press, 1981), 342–45.

24. The relation of Moore's peripherality to the digressive structure and autobiographical design of *Hail and Farewell* is given detailed consideration in Schleifer, 473–503.

25. Frank Palmeri, *Satire in Narrative: Petronius, Swift, Gibbon, Melville, and Pynchon* (Austin: Univ. of Texas Press, 1990), 8, 17. Bakhtin makes similar claims that those periods in which dialogical elements in the novel flourish are frequently periods of ideological transformation. See Bakhtin, *The Dialogic Imagination*, 370–71.

26. In his notes to *Hail and Farewell*, Richard Cave speculates that Moore may have felt that the tone of the original sixth chapter of "Vale" detracted from the climax in the twelfth, or that Lane's death had ended any hope for the picture's return to Dublin, thus draining the chapter of its urgency. See *Hail and Farewell*, 734–36.

27. Bakhtin, *Dialogic Imagination*, 345–46.

28. Caesar, 810.

29. Max Beerbohm, *Seven Men and Two Others* (London: Heinemann, 1950), 44.

30. Schleifer, 478.

31. For a discussion of the intimate nature of the narrator-reader relationship, see Wolfgang Iser, "Interaction between Text and Reader," in *The Reader in the Text: Essays on Audience and Interpretation*, ed. Susan R. Suleiman and Inge Crosman (Princeton: Princeton Univ. Press, 1980), 106–19.

32. Moore showed portions of the manuscript to friends for their correction and to lawyers for their advice concerning any possible libel charges. As AE and Yeats indicate, he also appeared to enjoy provoking gossip about his book and disquiet among his "models." For example, AE writes to a friend that Moore had recently said, "'Russell, I have just written over 2000 words about you.' I nervously enquired whether I might see them, but he said: 'No, you will see them later on,' and I don't know what the fiend has written." AE to John Quinn, 27 Apr. 1909, in *Letters*, 67.

33. Patricia Meyer Spacks, *Gossip* (New York: Knopf, 1985), 4–6.

34. Lennox Robinson to W. B. Yeats, 27 Feb. 1928, in Finneran, Harper, and

Murphy, 2:483. He precedes this comment with the cruel suggestion that Moore, who had been hospitalized for prostate disease, "lay a-dying" from envy of Thomas Hardy's Order of Merit.

35. One revealing case concerns Moore's portrayal of Sir Horace Plunkett, whom he hardly knew when he characterized him as Flaubert's Bouvard. After having finally conversed with Plunkett in 1915, Moore expressed his admiration and, according to Susan Mitchell, remarked "How fortunate it was I wrote my book before I knew him." Plunkett's own remarks are equally interesting, given the theory of an Irish satiric community. Plunkett is reported to have said of Moore that "as nobody takes him seriously, much as they admire his craftsmanship in literature, I bear him no ill will whatsoever." Citations and an interpretive discussion are provided in Robert Langenfeld, "Comic Techniques in the Major Autobiographical Writings of George Moore" (Ph.D. diss., Arizona State Univ., 1983), 110–17.

36. Yeats, 291.

37. See Richard Allen Cave, "George Moore's 'Stella'," *Review of English Studies* 28 (1977): 181–88.

38. Shumaker, 185–213.

6. Writing the Life in Dialogue:
Letters, Epistolary Novels, and Imaginary Conversations

1. Edmund Gosse to George Moore, 11 Apr. 1918 and 21 Mar. 1918, in Evan Charteris, *The Life and Letters of Sir Edmund Gosse* (New York: Harper and Brothers, 1931), 422 and 420–21.

2. See Janet Gurkin Altman, *Epistolarity: Approaches to a Form* (Columbus: Ohio State Univ. Press, 1982). As part of his taxonomy of the letter, Charles A. Porter stresses as one of its vital characteristics that the letter "usually *is a reply* to another letter and / or *invites a reply.*" He does not, as does Altman, go on to discuss the effects of that expectation on the rhetoric of the letter itself. See Charles A. Porter, "Forward," *Yale French Studies* 71 (1986), 5.

3. From "The George Moore Calendar" (London: Frank Palmer, 1912), 56.

4. Charteris, 486.

5. Edmund Gosse to George Moore, 21 Mar. 1918, in Charteris, 420–21.

6. Moore to Edouard Dujardin, 31 Jan. 1911, in *Letters from Moore to Dujardin,* 87–88.

7. Bruce Redford, *The Converse of the Pen: Acts of Intimacy in the Eighteenth-Century Familiar Letter* (Chicago: Univ. of Chicago Press, 1986), 9–10.

8. Harold Acton, "George Moore and the Cunard Family," *London Magazine* 5 (1958): 55–56.

9. English Showalter, Jr., "Authorial Self-Consciousness in the Familiar Letter: The Case of Madame de Graffigny," *Yale French Studies* 71 (1986), 113–14.

10. Seán Ó Lúing, *Kuno Meyer 1858–1919: A Biography* (Dublin: Geography Publications, 1991), 19.

11. Moore to Maud Cunard, 14 Feb. 1898, in Robert Stephen Becker, "Private Moore, Public Moore: The Evidence of the Letters," in *George Moore in Perspective*, ed. Janet Egleson Dunleavy (Totowa, N.J.: Barnes and Noble, 1983), 83.

12. Cited in Paul John Eakin, 160.

13. Hayden White, "The Value of Narrativity," in *On Narrative*, ed. W. J. T. Mitchell (Chicago: Univ. of Chicago Press, 1981), 9.

14. Peter Brooks, *Reading for the Plot: Design and Intention in Narrative* (New York: Knopf, 1984), 94.

15. Moore to Maurice Moore, n.d., in MacDonncha, 50. Happily, the work in question was *Esther Waters*.

16. English Showalter, 129.

17. Porter, 14.

18. Altman, 123.

19. John Sturrock, "The New Model Autobiographer," *New Literary History* 9 (1977–78), 54–55; Burton Pike, "Time in Autobiography," *Comparative Literature* 28 (1976), 340–42. Both arguments are countered by Paul John Eakin, 164–75.

20. Sturrock, 56.

21. Olney, *Metaphors of Self*, 3, 45.

22. Janet Varner Gunn, "Autobiography and the Narrative Experience of Temporality as Depth," *Soundings* 60 (1977), 194–99; Paul John Eakin, 174, 172.

23. Altman, 123–29.

24. George Moore, *Memoirs of My Dead Life* (New York: Boni and Liveright, 1920), 35.

25. Michael Holroyd, *Augustus John: A Biography* (New York: Holt, Rinehart and Winston, 1975), 228.

26. This issue is discussed in Linda S. Kauffman, *Discourses of Desire: Gender, Genre, and Epistolary Fictions* (Ithaca: Cornell University Press, 1986); and Roland Barthes, *A Lover's Discourse: Fragments* (New York: Hill and Wang, 1978).

27. Helmut E. Gerber notes a correspondence with another young woman Moore called "Leah." Her nineteen extant letters to him are all dated in 1924. From 1907 until his death, Moore corresponded with and occasionally met the young American woman Honor Wolfe, whose name was given to the heroine of his "Euphorion in Texas." In his investigation of their relationship, Adrian Frazier gives evidence that suggests some sort of sexual contact, although the nature of that contact is difficult to determine. Joseph Hone also remarks that in his old age, Moore was "pleased to receive the homage of young admirers, especially when they were young women of an attractive appearance. He would reply to their enthusiastic letters without condescension, interest himself in their personal affairs, even accept the role of a sort of pagan Father Confessor." See *George Moore on Parnassus*, 694–97; Adrian Frazier, "On His Honor: George Moore and Some Women," *English Literature in Transition* 35, no. 4 (1992): 423–45; and Hone, *Life of Moore*, 389.

28. Frazier, 428.

29. Barthes, *Lover's Discourse*, 94.

30. Moore to Gabrielle, Nov. 1903, in George Moore, *George Moore's Correspondence with the Mysterious Countess*, ed. David B. Eakin and Robert Langenfeld (Victoria, B.C.: English Literary Studies Monograph Series, no. 33, 1984), 21.

31. Gabrielle to Moore, 11 Dec. 1903, in Moore, *Correspondence with the Countess*, 26.

32. Barthes, *Lover's Discourse*, 190–94.

7. "To Live Outside Ourselves in the General Life": The Later Fiction and the Religion of Life

1. Joseph Stephen O'Leary, "Father Bovary," in *The Way Back: George Moore's The Untilled Field and The Lake*, ed. Robert Welch (Totowa, N.J.: Barnes and Noble,

1982), 106–7. Recent studies of Victorian literature, particularly novels by women, have revealed the challenges to the social order within works that heretofore had been thought to confirm it. While Victorianists would thus take issue with O'Leary's argument, he is nevertheless accurate in arguing for a much more conspicuous subversion in the early modern novels he cites.

2. Rose, 74.

3. John Wilson Foster, *Fictions of the Irish Literary Revival: A Changeling Art* (Syracuse: Syracuse Univ. Press, 1987), 133.

4. George Moore, "Apologia pro scriptis meis," in his *Lewis Seymour and Some Women* (New York: Boni and Liveright, 1922), xxxiii.

5. George Moore, "Since the Elizabethans," *Cosmopolis* 4 (1896): 57.

6. George Moore, *Sister Teresa* (London: T. Fisher Unwin, 1901), 207.

7. Among the best studies of the evolution of Moore's later fictional technique are Graham Owens, "The Melodic Line in Narrative," in *George Moore's Mind and Art*, ed. Graham Owens (New York: Barnes and Noble, 1970), 99–121; William F. Blissett, "George Moore and Literary Wagnerism," in *The Man of Wax: Critical Essays on George Moore*, ed. Douglas A. Hughes, 185–215; and chaps. 5–8 in Cave, *Study of the Novels*.

8. George Moore, "The Nineness in the Oneness," *Century Magazine* 99 (1919): 65–66. In his preface to Lena Milman's translation of *Poor Folk*, Moore praises narrative in which "the life upon the written page is as mysterious as the life around us; we know not how or whence it came, its origin eludes our analysis . . . we watch the unfolding of the story as we watch the unfolding of rose leaves." While the analogy between narrative and the rose leaves points to Moore's desire to rid his fiction of much of its mechanical apparatus, the analogy is inferior to that of the wave or cadence, as it fails to describe the way leitmotifs surface and then submerge, only to resurface in a different context or form, thus by repetition and variation pulling the narrative forward. See Preface to *Poor Folk*, by Fyodor Dostoyevsky (London: Elkin Mathews and John Lane; Boston: Roberts Brothers, 1894), xii–xiii.

9. Moore, *Letters from Moore to Dujardin*, 43.

10. George Moore, *Evelyn Innes* (London: T. Fisher Unwin, 1898), 61.

11. Jonathan Rose argues that "sincerity" became an important term again in reaction against the ethical discomforts of self-observational aestheticism and decadence. For a discussion of self-consciousness as antithetical to vitalism, as well as the frequent Edwardian conflation of nature, divinity, and sexual relations, see Rose, chaps. 1–3.

12. Sir Owen Asher's debilitating narcissism is given thorough treatment in Cave, *Study of the Novels*, 148–50.

13. According to Mary Burgan's study of musical women in Victorian fiction, music was in the last decade of the century frequently depicted as a morally dangerous stimulation of female sexuality and hitherto repressed rebellion against societal constraints. Moore's treatment incorporates basic elements of this view: Owen seduces Evelyn by playing Wagnerian chords on the harpsichord (an interesting thematic symbol if musically unlikely); her sexual passions are repeatedly aroused on the stage; in the convent, the sensuousness with which she sings even sacred music forces another nun to recognize her own lesbianism. What Moore seems to criticize, however, is not the presence of sexuality in music but more specifically the confusion of spontaneity and artifice that is brought about in the performer herself. See Mary Burgan, "Heroines at the Piano: Women and Music in Nineteenth-Century Fiction," in *The Lost Chord: Essays on Victorian Music*, ed. Nicholas Temperley (Bloomington: Indiana Univ. Press, 1989), 42–67.

14. Moore, *Sister Teresa*, 233.

15. George Moore, *George Moore in Quest of Locale: Two Letters to W. D. Stead* (N.p.: Harvest Press, 1931), n.p.

16. Moore, *Sister Teresa*, 234–35.

17. Ibid., 236.

18. O'Connor, 107–8. I have been unable to examine all Irish reviews of the novel to ascertain whether Irish reviewers made note of the use of Gogarty's name. In a letter responding to my inquiry, Richard Allen Cave reports that he does not recall from his own reading of the Irish reviews any observation of the similarity between the character's name and that of the Dublin author and surgeon.

19. Jon Stratton, *The Virgin Text: Fiction, Sexuality, and Ideology* (Norman: Univ. of Oklahoma Press, 1987), 33–34.

20. O'Leary, 114; Jean C. Noel, "Rambling Round *The Lake* with George Moore," *Cahiers du Centre d'Etudes Irlandaises* 5 (1980): 84–85. Joyce's letter to his brother parodying the same passage from *The Lake* is discussed by Albert J. Solomon in "A Moore in *Ulysses*," *James Joyce Quarterly* 10 (1973): 219.

21. Robert Welch, "Moore's Way Back: *The Untilled Field* and *The Lake*," in Welch, *The Way Back: George Moore's The Untilled Field and The Lake*, 35–39.

22. Gérard Genette, *Narrative Discourse: An Essay in Method*, trans. Jane E. Levin (Ithaca: Cornell Univ. Press, 1980), 186.

23. Augustine Martin, "Julia Cahill, Father McTurnan, and the Geography of Nowhere," in *Literature and the Art of Creation*, ed. Robert Welch and Suheil Badi Bushrui (Totowa, N.J.: Barnes and Noble, 1988), 109, 111.

24. George Moore, *The Untilled Field* (Gerrards Cross: Colin Smythe, 1976), 38.

25. Ibid., 48–49.

26. Geert Lernout has located the origin of these repeated motifs in Wagnerian opera. See "George Moore: Wagnerian and Symbolist," *Cahiers du Centre d'Etudes Irlandaises* 5 (1980): 55–69. There is no question, however, that Moore had fully assimilated the Wagnerian metaphors into his own active vocabulary. He wrote to Maud Cunard in 1905, "You come into a room filling the air with unpremeditated music. The best comparison I can think of is the indefinite hum of a fountain. . . . The water surges compelled by a force unknown and we are cooled, refreshed, soothed and charmed; the water falls back full of fleeting iridescent colour." To Maurice Moore he wrote that "men are moved to reject dogma instinctively just as the swallows are drawn by the spring tide. Rose Leicester [later Nora Glynn] represents the spring tide and her breath awakens Gogarty." Even beyond the composition of *The Lake*, Moore closely associated through the metaphor of water an abstract principle of instinctual life and a very real woman's liveliness. *Letters to Lady Cunard, 1895–1933*, ed. Rupert Hart-Davis (London: Rupert Hart-Davis, 43; Hone, *Life of George Moore*, 262.

27. Michel Foucault, *The History of Sexuality: An Introduction*, trans. Robert Hurley (New York: Vintage, 1980), 6.

28. T. P. Foley and Maud Ellman, "A Yeats and George Moore Identification," *Notes and Queries* 25 (1978): 326–27. Discussions of *Father Ralph* in connection with *The Lake* are provided in Foster, *Fictions*, 138–41, and in Peter Costello, *The Heart Grown Brutal: The Irish Revolution in Literature, From Parnell to the Death of Yeats, 1891–1939* (Totowa, N.J.: Rowman and Littlefield, 1977), 58–64. In 1908, Moore wrote to Edouard Dujardin, "You ask what is thought here of the Pope's Encyclical. Well, people here think nothing at all about it—nothing whatever. They have all the sacra-

ments they want, rosaries, cheap indulgences, and these are enough to satisfy my countrymen. Ireland is the cemetery of Catholicism." *Letters from Moore to Dujardin*, 64.

29. Gerald O'Donovan, *Father Ralph* (London: Macmillan, 1913), 494.

30. Evidence points directly to Armand Renaud's poem "Les Cygnes" for the image of the soul or heart as a lake. See *Letters to Lady Cunard*, 46. Having no evidence that Moore read Dante, I am not arguing for direct influence and thus have not attempted to ascertain which translation he might have seen. I have chosen instead to cite John Ciardi's translation as that which makes my point most persuasively. *The Inferno*, trans. John Ciardi (New York: New American Library, 1954), 28.

31. Gilbert Murray, as quoted in Rose, 109.

8. Narrating, Remembering, and the Autogenous Self

1. Moore, "A Dedication to Robert Ross," in *A Mummer's Wife*, n.p.

2. See Stratton, xi–xxii.

3. This point is effectively argued by Richard Cave in *Study of the Novels*, 222. See also Thomas C. Ware, "The Source of the Christian River: The Function of Memory in George Moore's *The Brook Kerith*," *English Literature in Transition* 30, no. 1 (1987): 27–37.

4. Moore to Gabrielle, 17 Feb. 1906, in *Correspondence with the Countess*, 69. Joseph Hone suggests that Moore may have borrowed his title from one suggested in the *Journal des Frères Goncourt*. See *Life of Moore*, 255.

5. See Carl Dawson, *Prophets of Past Time: Seven British Autobiographers, 1880–1914* (Baltimore: Johns Hopkins Univ. Press, 1988). Dawson briefly notes the similarity between "Bring in the Lamp" and "Ode to a Nightingale," and I have elaborated on his suggestion.

6. Ibid., 139.

7. Ibid., 147.

8. George Moore, *Memoirs of My Dead Life* (London: Heinemann, 1906), 298.

9. Rockwell Gray, "Time Present and Time Past: The Ground of Autobiography," *Soundings* 64, no. 1 (1981): 52–53.

10. Brooks, 110, 111.

11. Moore is anticipated here by G. B. Shaw's 1912 preface to *Androcles and the Lion*, which similarly characterizes Jesus as a pantheist universalist. Other contemporary attempts to associate Jesus with nature, Buddhism, and the cult of Pan are explored in Rose, 78–91.

12. Moore's implied ironic contrasts between medieval Ireland and modern Ireland are discussed in detail in Foster, *Fictions*, 273–76; and in Robert Langenfeld, "George Moore's *A Story-Teller's Holiday* Reconsidered: Irish Themes Expressed Through Comic Irony," *Cahiers de Centre d'Etudes Irlandais* 9 (1984): 15–29.

13. Moore's attitude toward World War I is not entirely clear. He did join in the denunciation of Kuno Meyer, the German scholar of Celtic literature who, on a pro-German lecture tour of America, had advocated Irish collaboration with the Germans in a war against England. Moore's decision to publish his denunciation of his former friend in the *Daily Telegraph* was cruel (and an act he later regretted), but the terms of his dismissal—"not because of the German that is in you, but because of the man that is in you"—may have had more to do with his revulsion at militant nationalism rather than with any anti-German hysteria on his part. See Ó Lúing, 174. See also the letters concerning World War I in *George Moore on Parnassus*.

14. Robert Kellogg, "Oral Narrative, Written Books," *Genre* 10 (1977): 656–57.

15. John Wilson Foster, "The Artifice of Eternity: Medieval Aspects of Modern Irish Literature," in *Medieval and Modern Ireland*, ed. Richard Wall (Totowa, N.J.: Barnes and Noble, 1988), 124–25.

16. Foster, *Fictions*, 276.

17. Anyone familiar with Moore's life is immediately struck by parallels between Tadgh the harper and his author. A detailed comparison is offered in *George Moore on Parnassus*, 690.

Bibliography

Acton, Harold. "George Moore and the Cunard Family." *London Magazine* 5 (1958): 54–57.

Adams, Hazard. "Some Yeatsian Versions of Comedy." In *In Excited Reverie: A Centenary Tribute to William Butler Yeats, 1865–1939,* edited by A. Norman Jeffares and K. G. W. Cross, 152–70. New York: Macmillan, 1965.

Adams, Henry. *The Letters of Henry Adams.* Vol. 2. *1868–1885.* Edited by J. C. Levenson, et al. Cambridge, Mass.: Harvard Univ. Press, 1982.

AE [George Russell]. *Letters from AE.* Edited by Alan Denson. London: Abelard-Schuman, 1961.

Altman, Janet Gurkin. *Epistolarity: Approaches to a Form.* Columbus: Ohio State Univ. Press, 1982.

Arana, R. Victoria. "Sir Edmund Gosse's *Father and Son:* Autobiography as Comedy." *Genre* 10 (1977): 63–76.

Atherton, Gertrude. *Adventures of a Novelist.* London: Jonathan Cape, 1932.

August, Eugene R. "Darwin's Comedy: The *Autobiography* as Comic Narrative." *Victorian Newsletter* 75 (1989): 15–19.

Bakhtin, Mikhail. "Discourse in the Novel." In *The Dialogic Imagination: Four Essays by M. M. Bakhtin,* edited by Michael Holquist; translated by Caryl Emerson and Michael Holquist, 259–422. Austin: Univ. of Texas Press, 1981.

———. *Problems of Dostoevsky's Poetics.* Edited and translated by Caryl Emerson. Minneapolis: Univ. of Minnesota Press, 1984.

Barthes, Roland. "An Introduction to the Structural Analysis of Narrative." *New Literary History* 6, no. 2 (1975): 237–72.

———. *A Lover's Discourse: Fragments.* New York: Hill and Wang, 1978.

Becker, Robert Stephen. "The Letters of George Moore, 1863–1901." Ph.D. diss., Univ. of Reading, 1980.

———. "Private Moore, Public Moore: The Evidence of the Letters." In *George Moore in Perspective*, edited by Janet Egleson Dunleavy, 69–83. Totowa, N.J.: Barnes and Noble, 1983.

Beerbohm, Max. *Beerbohm's Literary Caricatures: From Homer to Huxley.* Edited by J. G. Riewald. Hamden, Conn.: Anchor, 1977.

———. *Letters of Max Beerbohm, 1892–1956.* Edited by Rupert Hart-Davis. New York: Norton, 1988.

———. *Mainly on the Air.* New York: Knopf, 1958.

———. *Seven Men and Two Others.* London: Heinemann, 1950.

———. "The Spirit of Caricature." In *The Incomparable Max: A Collection of Writings of Sir Max Beerbohm*, 94–103. New York: Dodd, Mead, 1962.

Behrman, Samuel Nathaniel. *Portrait of Max: An Intimate Memoir of Sir Max Beerbohm.* New York: Random House, 1960.

Bew, Paul. *Land and the National Question in Ireland.* Atlantic Highlands, N.J.: Humanities, 1979.

———. "The Land League Ideal: Achievements and Contradictions." In *Ireland: Land, Politics and People*, edited by P. J. Drudy, 77–92. Cambridge: Cambridge Univ. Press, 1982.

Blanche, Jacques-Emile. *Portraits of a Lifetime.* Translated by Walter Clement. London: J. M. Dent, 1937.

Blissett, William F. "George Moore and Literary Wagnerism." In *The Man of Wax: Critical Essays on George Moore*, edited by Douglas A. Hughes, 185–216. New York: New York Univ. Press, 1970.

Bridgwater, Patrick. *George Moore and German Pessimism.* Durham, England: Univ. of Durham Press, 1988.

Brooks, Peter. *Reading for the Plot: Design and Intention in Narrative.* New York: Knopf, 1984.

Brown, Malcolm. *George Moore: A Reconsideration.* Seattle: Univ. of Washington Press, 1955.

Burgan, Mary. "Heroines at the Piano: Women and Music in Nineteenth-Century Fiction." In *The Lost Chord: Essays on Victorian Music*, edited by Nicholas Temperly, 42–67. Bloomington: Indiana Univ. Press, 1989.

Burkhart, Charles. "The Letters of George Moore to Edmund Gosse, W. B. Yeats, R. I. Best, Miss Nancy Cunard, and Mrs. Mary Hutchinson." Ph.D. diss., Univ. of Maryland, 1958.

Caesar, Terry. "'I Quite Forget What—Say a Daffodily': Victorian Parody." *ELH* 51 (1984): 795–818.

Cave, Richard Allen. "George Moore's 'Stella.'" *Review of English Studies* 28 (1977): 181–88.

———. *A Study of the Novels of George Moore.* Gerrards Cross: Colin Smythe, 1978.

Charteris, Evan. *The Life and Letters of Sir Edmund Gosse.* New York: Harper and Brothers, 1931.

Coe, Richard N. *When the Grass Was Taller: Autobiography and the Experience of Childhood.* New Haven: Yale Univ. Press, 1984.

Costello, Peter. *The Heart Grown Brutal: The Irish Revolution in Literature, From Parnell to the Death of Yeats, 1891–1939*. Totowa, N.J.: Rowman and Littlefield, 1977.

Cox, E. H. M. *The Library of Edmund Gosse*. London: Dulau, 1924.

Cunard, Nancy. *GM: Memories of George Moore*. New York: Macmillan, 1957.

Dante, Alighieri. *The Inferno*. Translated by John Ciardi. New York: New American Library, 1954.

Davis, W. Eugene, and Mark J. Lidman. "'I Am Still a Young Man': George Moore's Last Revisions of *Confessions of a Young Man*." *Bulletin of the New York Public Library* 79, no. 1 (1975): 83–95.

Dawson, Carl. *Prophets of Past Time: Seven British Autobiographers, 1880–1914*. Baltimore: Johns Hopkins Univ. Press, 1988.

de Man, Paul. "Autobiography as De-facement." *Modern Language Notes* 94 (1979): 919–30.

Diamond, Elin. "Refusing the Romanticism of Identity: Narrative Interventions in Churchill, Benmussa, Duras." *Theatre Journal* 37, no. 3 (1985): 273–86.

Dick, Susan Marie. "*Confessions of a Young Man* by George Moore: A Variorum Edition." Ph.D. diss., Northwestern Univ., 1967.

Dolan, Jill. *The Feminist Spectator as Critic*. Ann Arbor, Mich.: UMI, 1988.

Doran, George H. *Chronicles of Barabbas, 1884–1934*. New York: Harcourt, Brace, 1935.

Eakin, David B. "The Man in the Paper Mask: Epistolary Autobiography in Oscar Wilde and George Moore." Ph.D. diss., Arizona State Univ., 1980.

Eakin, Paul John. *Fictions in Autobiography: Studies in the Art of Self-Invention*. Princeton: Princeton Univ. Press, 1985.

Eglinton, John [W. K. Magee]. *Irish Literary Portraits*. 1935. Reprint. Freeport, N.Y.: Books for Libraries, 1967.

Ellis, Havelock. *My Confessional: Questions of Our Day*. Boston: Houghton Mifflin, 1934.

Faderman, Lillian. "The Morbidification of Love between Women by 19th-Century Sexologists." *Journal of Homosexuality* 4, no. 1 (1978): 73–89.

Fassler, Barbara. "Theories of Homosexuality as Sources of Bloomsbury's Androgyny." *Signs* 5, no. 2 (1979): 237–51.

Felstiner, John. *The Lies of Art: Max Beerbohm's Parody and Caricature*. New York: Knopf, 1972.

Finneran, Richard J., George Mills Harper, and William M. Murphy, eds. *Letters to W. B. Yeats*. 2 vols. New York: Columbia Univ. Press, 1977.

Foley, T. P., and Maud Ellman. "A Yeats and George Moore Identification." *Notes and Queries* 25 (1978): 326–27.

Foster, John Wilson. "The Artifice of Eternity: Medieval Aspects of Modern Irish Literature." In *Medieval and Modern Ireland*, edited by Richard Wall, 123–34. Totowa, N.J.: Barnes and Noble, 1988.

———. *Fictions of the Irish Literary Revival: A Changeling Art*. Syracuse: Syracuse Univ. Press, 1987.

Foucault, Michel. *The History of Sexuality: An Introduction.* Translated by Robert Hurley. New York: Vintage, 1980.

———. "What Is an Author?" In *Textual Strategies: Perspectives in Post-Structuralist Criticism,* edited by Josué Harari, 141–60. Ithaca: Cornell Univ. Press, 1979.

Frankau, Gilbert. *Self-Portrait: A Novel of His Life.* New York: Dutton, 1940.

Frazier, Adrian. "On His Honor: George Moore and Some Women." *English Literature in Transition* 35, no. 4 (1992): 423–45.

Frye, Northrop. *Anatomy of Criticism: Four Essays.* Princeton: Princeton Univ. Press, 1957.

Garber, Marjorie. *Vested Interests.* New York: Routledge, 1991.

Genette, Gérard. *Narrative Discourse: An Essay in Method.* Translated by Jane E. Levin. Ithaca: Cornell Univ. Press, 1980.

Gettmann, Royal A. "George Moore's Revisions of *The Lake,* 'The Wild Goose,' and *Esther Waters.*" *PMLA* 59 (1944): 540–55.

Gilbert, Elliot L. "In the Flesh: *Esther Waters* and the Passion for Yes." *Novel* 12, no. 1, (1978): 48–65.

Gilbert, Sandra, and Susan Gubar. *Sexchanges.* Vol. 2 of *No Man's Land: The Place of the Woman Writer in the Twentieth Century.* New Haven: Yale Univ. Press, 1989.

Gilbert, W. S. *The Bab Ballads.* Edited by James Ellis. Cambridge, Mass.: Belknap Press of Harvard Univ. Press, 1970.

Gilcher, Edwin. *A Bibliography of George Moore.* DeKalb: Northern Illinois Univ. Press, 1970.

———. *Supplement to A Bibliography of George Moore.* Westport, Conn.: Meckler.

Gogarty, Oliver St John. *As I Was Going Down Sackville Street.* New York: Reynal and Hitchcock, 1937.

———. *It Isn't This Time of Year at All: An Unpremeditated Autobiography.* Garden City, N.Y.: Doubleday, 1954.

———. "Next Door to George Moore." *Saturday Review of Literature* 14 (18 July 1936): 3–4, 15.

Gosse, Edmund. *Silhouettes.* New York: Charles Scribner's Sons, 1925.

Gray, Rockwell. "Time Present and Time Past: The Ground of Autobiography." *Soundings* 64, no. 1 (1981): 52–74.

Greenberg, David F. *The Construction of Homosexuality.* Chicago: Univ. of Chicago Press, 1988.

Gunn, Janet Varner. "Autobiography and the Narrative Experience of Temporality as Depth." *Soundings* 60 (1977): 194–209.

———. *Autobiography: Towards a Poetics of Experience.* Philadelphia: Univ. of Pennsylvania Press, 1982.

Gusdorf, Georges. "Conditions and Limits of Autobiography." In *Autobiography: Essays Theoretical and Critical,* edited by James Olney, 28–48. Princeton: Princeton Univ. Press, 1980.

Hall, Wayne E. *Shadowy Heroes: Irish Literature of the 1890s.* Syracuse: Syracuse Univ. Press, 1980.

Harris, Frank. *Contemporary Portraits.* 2d ser. New York: privately published, 1919.

———. *Contemporary Portraits.* 4th ser. New York: Brentano's, 1923.

Hart, Francis. "Notes for an Anatomy of Modern Autobiography." *New Literary History* 1, no. 3 (1970): 485–511.

Hassall, Christopher. *A Biography of Edward Marsh.* New York: Harcourt, Brace, 1959.

Henderson, Heather. *The Victorian Self: Autobiography and Biblical Narrative.* Ithaca: Cornell Univ. Press, 1989.

Heywood, Christopher. "Olive Schreiner's Influence on George Moore and D. H. Lawrence." In *Aspects of South African Literature,* edited by Christopher Heywood, 42–53. New York: Africana, 1976.

Hogan, Robert, and James Kilroy. *The Irish Literary Theatre 1899–1901.* Dublin: Dolmen Press, 1975.

Holroyd, Michael. *Augustus John: A Biography.* New York: Holt, Rinehart and Winston, 1975.

———. *Lytton Strachey: A Critical Biography.* Vol. 2. London: Heinemann, 1968.

Hone, Joseph. *The Life of George Moore.* New York: Macmillan, 1936.

———. *The Moores of Moore Hall.* London: Jonathan Cape, 1939.

Hutcheon, Linda. *A Poetics of Postmodernism: History, Theory, Fiction.* New York: Routledge, 1988.

———. *A Theory of Parody: The Teachings of Twentieth-Century Art Forms.* New York: Methuen, 1985.

Huysmans, J.-K. *A Rebours.* Paris: Charpentier, 1925.

Iser, Wolfgang. "Interaction between Text and Reader." In *The Reader in the Text: Essays on Audience and Interpretation,* edited by Susan R. Suleiman and Inge Crosman, 106–19. Princeton: Princeton Univ. Press, 1980.

Jernigan, Jay. "The Forgotten Serial Version of George Moore's *Esther Waters.*" *Nineteenth-Century Fiction* 23, no. 1 (1968): 99–103.

———. "George Moore's 'Re-Tying of Bows': A Critical Study of the Eight Early Novels and Their Revisions." Ph.D. diss., Kansas State Univ., 1966.

Jordan, Donald. "John O'Connor Power, Charles Stewart Parnell and the Centralisation of Popular Politics in Ireland." *Irish Historical Studies* 25, no. 97 (1986): 47–66.

———. "Land and Politics in the West of Ireland: County Mayo, 1846–82." Ph.D. diss., Univ. of California, Davis, 1982.

Kauffman, Linda S. *Discourses of Desire: Gender, Genre, and Epistolary Fictions.* Ithaca: Cornell Univ. Press, 1986.

Kellogg, Robert. "Oral Narrative, Written Books." *Genre* 10 (1977): 655–65.

Kenneally, Michael. *Portraying the Self: Sean O'Casey and the Art of Autobiography.* Totowa, N.J.: Barnes and Noble, 1988.

Kohfeldt, Mary Lou. *Lady Gregory: The Woman Behind the Irish Renaissance.* New York: Atheneum, 1985.

Langenfeld, Robert. "Comic Techniques in the Major Autobiographical Writings of George Moore." Ph.D. diss., Arizona State Univ., 1983.

————. ed. *George Moore: An Annotated Secondary Bibliography of Writings about Him.* New York: AMS Press, 1987.

————, "George Moore's *A Story-Teller's Holiday* Reconsidered: Irish Themes Expressed Through Comic Irony." *Cahiers du Centre d'Etudes Irlandaises* 9 (1984): 15–29.

————. "A Reconsideration: *Confessions of a Young Man* as Farce." In *Twilight of Dawn: Studies in English Literature in Transition,* edited by O. M. Brack, Jr., 91–110. Tucson: Univ. of Arizona Press, 1987.

Lanham, Jon. "The Genre of *A Portrait of the Artist as a Young Man* and 'the Rhythm of Its Structure.'" *Genre* 10 (1977): 77–102.

Lejeune, Philippe. "The Autobiographical Pact." In *On Autobiography,* edited by Paul John Eakin; translated by Katherine Leary, 3–30. Minneapolis: Univ. of Minnesota Press, 1989.

Lernout, Geert. "George Moore: Wagnerian and Symbolist." *Cahiers du Centre d'Etudes Irlandaises* 5 (1980): 55–69.

Lynch, William F., S.J. *Christ and Apollo: The Dimensions of the Literary Imagination.* New York: Sheed and Ward, 1960.

MacDonncha, Seamus. "Letters of George Moore (1852–1933) to His Brother, Colonel Maurice Moore, C.B. (1857–1939)." Ph.D. diss., National Univ. of Ireland, Galway, 1972–73.

Mack, Maynard. "The Muse of Satire." In *Satire: Modern Essays in Criticism,* edited by Ronald Paulson, 190–201. Englewood Cliffs, N.J.: Prentice-Hall, 1971.

Martin, Augustine. "Julia Cahill, Father McTurnan, and the Geography of Nowhere." In *Literature and the Art of Creation,* edited by Robert Welch and Suheil Badi Bushrui, 98–111. Totowa, N.J.: Barnes and Noble, 1988.

Merrill, Cynthia A. "Self-Reflections: The Dialectics of Autobiography." Ph.D. diss., Univ. of Washington, 1990.

Michie, Helena. *The Flesh Made Word: Female Figures and Women's Bodies.* Oxford: Oxford Univ. Press, 1987.

Mitchell, Judith. "*A Drama in Muslin:* George Moore's Victorian Novel." *English Literature in Transition* 25, no. 4 (1982): 211–24.

————. "Fictional Worlds in George Moore's *A Mummer's Wife.*" *English Studies* 67, no. 4 (1986): 345–54.

Mitchell, Susan. *George Moore.* New York: Dodd, Mead, 1916.

Montague, John. "George Moore: The Tyranny of Memory." In *The Figure in the Cave and Other Essays,* edited by Antoinette Quinn, 86–97. Syracuse: Syracuse Univ. Press, 1989.

Moody, T. W. *Davitt and Irish Revolution 1846–82.* Oxford: Clarendon, 1981.

Moore, George. *Avowals.* London: Heinemann, 1936.

————. *Celibate Lives.* London: Heinemann, 1938.

————. *Celibates.* London: Walter Scott, 1895.

————. *A Communication to My Friends.* London: Heinemann, 1937.

————. *Confessions d'un Jeune Anglais.* Paris: Savine, 1889.

————. *Confessions of a Young Man.* Edited by Susan Dick. Montreal: McGill-Queens Univ. Press, 1972.

————. *Conversations in Ebury Street.* London: Heinemann, 1930.

————. *A Drama in Muslin.* Gerrards Cross: Colin Smythe, 1981.

————. *Esther Waters.* London: Heinemann, 1938.

————. *Esther Waters: A Novel.* Edited by Lionel Stevenson. Boston: Houghton Mifflin, 1963.

————. *Esther Waters: A Play in Four Acts.* In *The Celebrated Case of Esther Waters: The Collaboration of George Moore and Barrett H. Clark on "Esther Waters: A Play,"* edited by W. Eugene Davis, 37–89. Lanham, Md.: Univ. Press of America, 1984.

————. *Evelyn Innes.* London: T. Fisher Unwin, 1898.

————. "The George Moore Calendar." London: Frank Palmer, 1912.

————. *George Moore's Correspondence with the Mysterious Countess.* Edited by David B. Eakin and Robert Langenfeld. Victoria, B.C.: English Literary Studies Monograph Series, no. 33, 1984.

————. *George Moore in Quest of Locale: Two Letters to W. D. Stead.* N.p.: Harvest Press, 1931.

————. *George Moore in Transition: Letters to T. Fisher Unwin and Lena Milmann, 1894–1910.* Edited by Helmut Gerber. Detroit: Wayne State Univ. Press, 1968.

————. "George Moore on Authorship." Cherry Plain, N.Y.: Privately printed, 1950.

————. *George Moore on Parnassus.* Edited by Helmut E. Gerber. Newark: Univ. of Delaware Press, 1988.

————. *Hail and Farewell.* Edited by Richard Cave. Gerrards Cross: Colin Smythe, 1976.

————. *Impressions and Opinions.* 1891. Reprint. New York: Benjamin Blom, 1972.

————. *In Minor Keys: The Uncollected Short Stories of George Moore.* Edited by David B. Eakin and Helmut E. Gerber. Syracuse: Syracuse Univ. Press, 1985.

————. *The Lake.* Gerrards Cross: Colin Smythe, 1980.

————. Letter to the Editor. *Court and Society Review* 24 (December 1885): 511.

————. *Letters from George Moore to Ed. Dujardin, 1886–1922.* Edited and translated by John Eglinton [W. K. Magee]. New York: Crosby Gaige, 1929.

————. *Letters of George Moore.* Edited by John Eglinton [W. K. Magee]. Bournemouth: Sydenham, 1942.

————. *Letters to Lady Cunard 1895–1933.* Edited by Rupert Hart-Davis. London: Rupert Hart-Davis, 1957.

————. *Lewis Seymour and Some Women.* New York: Boni and Liveright, 1922.

————. *Memoirs of My Dead Life.* London: Heinemann, 1906.

————. *Memoirs of My Dead Life.* New York: Boni and Liveright, 1920.

————. *Memoirs of My Dead Life.* London: Heinemann, 1936.

————. *A Mummer's Wife.* London: Heinemann, 1937.

————. *Muslin.* London: Heinemann, 1915.

————. "The Nineness in the Oneness." *Century Magazine* 99 (1919): 63–66.

————. *Parnell and His Island.* London: Sonnenschein, Lowrey, 1887.

————. Preface to *Poor Folk,* by Fyodor Dostoyevsky. Translated by Lena Milman, vii–xx. London: Elkin Mathews and John Lane; Boston: Roberts Brothers, 1894.

————. "Since the Elizabethans." *Cosmopolis* 4 (1896): 42–58.

————. *Sister Teresa.* London: T. Fisher Unwin, 1901.

————. *A Story-Teller's Holiday.* London: Heinemann, 1937.

————. *Terre d'Irlande.* Translated by Felix Rabbe. Paris: Charpentier, 1887.

————. *The Untilled Field.* Gerrards Cross: Colin Smythe, 1976.

————. *Vain Fortune.* London: Walter Scott, 1895.

Moore, Maurice. *An Irish Gentleman, George Henry Moore.* London: Laurie, 1913.

Morgan, Charles. *Epitaph on George Moore.* London: Macmillan, 1935.

Morris, John N. *Versions of the Self: Studies in English Autobiography from John Bunyan to John Stuart Mill.* New York: Basic, 1966.

Morson, Gary Saul. *The Boundaries of Genre: Dostoevsky's "Diary of a Writer" and the Traditions of Literary Utopia.* Austin: Univ. of Texas Press, 1981.

Newton, Esther. "The Mythic Mannish Lesbian: Radclyffe Hall and the New Woman." In *The Lesbian Issue: Essays from Signs,* edited by Estelle B. Freedman, et al., 7–25. Chicago: Univ. of Chicago Press, 1985.

Nicholas, Brian. "The Case of Esther Waters." In *The Man of Wax: Critical Essays on George Moore,* edited by Douglas A. Hughes, 151–83. New York: New York Univ. Press, 1971.

Noel, Jean C. "George Moore's Pluridimensional Autobiography: Remarks on His *Confessions of a Young Man.*" *Cahiers du Centre d'Etudes Irlandaises* 4 (1979): 49–66.

————. "Rambling Round *The Lake* with George Moore." *Cahiers du Centre d'Etudes Irlandaises* 5 (1980): 71–88.

O'Brien, Flann. *At Swim-Two-Birds.* New York: New American Library, 1966.

O'Connor, Ulick. *Oliver St John Gogarty: A Poet and His Times.* London: Jonathan Cape, 1963.

O'Donovan, Gerald. *Father Ralph.* London: Macmillan, 1913.

O'Leary, Joseph Stephen. "Father Bovary." In *The Way Back: George Moore's The Untilled Field and The Lake,* edited by Robert Welch, 105–18. Totowa, N.J.: Barnes and Noble, 1982.

Ó Lúing, Séan. *Kuno Meyer 1858–1919: A Biography.* Dublin: Geography Publications, 1992.

Olney, James. *Metaphors of Self: The Meaning of Autobiography.* Princeton: Princeton Univ. Press, 1972.

———. "Some Versions of Memory/Some Versions of Bios: The Ontology of Autobiography." In *Autobiography: Essays Theoretical and Critical*, edited by James Olney, 259–67. Princeton: Princeton Univ. Press, 1980.

———. "The Uses of Comedy and Irony in *Autobiographies* and Autobiography." In *Yeats: An Annual of Critical and Textual Studies*, edited by Richard J. Finneran, 2:195–208. Ithaca: Cornell Univ. Press, 1984.

———. "W. B. Yeats's Daimonic Memory." *Sewanee Review* 85 (1977): 583–603.

Owens, Graham. "A Study of George Moore's Revisions of His Novels and Short Stories." Ph.D. diss., Univ. of Leeds, 1966.

———. "The Melodic Line in Narrative." In *George Moore's Mind and Art*, edited by Graham Owens, 99–121. New York: Barnes and Noble, 1970.

Palmeri, Frank. *Satire in Narrative: Petronius, Swift, Gibbon, Melville, and Pynchon*. Austin: Univ. of Texas Press, 1990.

Pater, Walter. *The Renaissance*. Chicago: Academy Press, 1977.

Perlina, Nina. *Varieties of Poetic Utterance: Quotation in "The Brothers Karamazov."* Lanham, Md.: Univ. Press of America, 1985.

Peterson, Linda H. *Victorian Autobiography: The Tradition of Self-Interpretation*. New Haven: Yale Univ. Press, 1986.

Pike, Burton. "Time in Autobiography." *Comparative Literature* 28 (1976): 326–42.

Porter, Charles A. "Forward." *Yale French Studies* 71 (1986): 1–14.

Ramazani, R. Jahan. "Yeats: Tragic Joy and the Sublime." *PMLA* 104 (1989): 163–77.

Redford, Bruce. *The Converse of the Pen: Acts of Intimacy in the Eighteenth-Century Familiar Letter*. Chicago: Univ. of Chicago Press, 1986.

Renza, Louis A. "A Veto of the Imagination: A Theory of Autobiography." In *Autobiography: Essays Theoretical and Critical*, edited by James Olney, 268–95. Princeton: Princeton Univ. Press, 1980.

Riewald, J. G. "From Naturalism to Lyrical Realism: Fourteen Unpublished Letters from George Moore to Frans Netscher." *English Studies* 58 (1977): 118–50.

Riley, Michael M. "Persona and Theme in George Moore's *Confessions of a Young Man*." *English Literature in Transition* 19, no. 2 (1976): 87–95.

Robinson, Fred Norris. "Satirists and Enchanters in Early Irish Literature." In *Satire: Modern Essays in Criticism*, edited by Ronald Paulson, 1–36. Englewood Cliffs, N.J.: Prentice-Hall, 1971.

Rose, Jonathan. *The Edwardian Temperament, 1895–1919*. Athens: Ohio Univ. Press, 1986.

Ryan, Michael. Review of *Le Pacte autobiographique*, by Philip Lejeune. *Diacritics* 10, no. 2 (1980): 2–16.

Sartre, Jean-Paul. *The Words*. Translated by Bernard Frechtman. Greenwich, Conn.: Fawcett, 1964.

Schleifer, Ronald. "George Moore's Turning Mind: Digression and Autobiographical Art in *Hail and Farewell*." *Genre* 12 (1979): 473–503.

Schopenhauer, Arthur. *Parerga and Paralipomena: Short Philosophical Essays.* Vol. 2. Translated by E. F. J. Payne. Oxford: Clarendon, 1974.

Schreiner, Olive. *The Story of an African Farm.* Chicago: Academy Press, Cassandra Editions, 1977.

———. *Women and Labour.* London: T. F. Unwin, 1911.

Scott, Patrick. "From Bon Gaultier to *Fly Leaves:* Context and Canon in Victorian Parody." *Victorian Poetry* 26 (1988): 249–65.

Showalter, Elaine. *Sexual Anarchy: Gender and Culture at the Fin de Siècle.* New York: Viking, 1990.

Showalter, Jr., English. "Authorial Self-Consciousness in the Familiar Letter: The Case of Madame de Graffigny." *Yale French Studies* 71 (1986): 113–30.

Shumaker, Wayne. *English Autobiography: Its Emergence, Materials, and Form.* Berkeley: Univ. of California Press, 1954.

Shuttleworth, Sally. "Female Circulation: Medical Discourse and Popular Advertising in the Mid-Victorian Era." In *Body/Politics: Women and the Discourses of Science,* edited by Mary Jacobus et al., 47–68. New York: Routledge, 1989.

Solomon, Albert J. "A Moore in *Ulysses.*" *James Joyce Quarterly* 10 (1973): 215–27.

Spacks, Patricia Meyer. *Gossip.* New York: Knopf, 1985.

Sporn, Paul. "*Esther Waters:* The Sources of the Baby-Farm Episode." *English Literature in Transition* 11, no. 1 (1968): 39–42.

———. "Marriage and Class Conflict: The Subversive Link in George Moore's *A Drama in Muslin.*" *Clio* 3 (1973): 7–20.

Sprinker, Michael. "Fictions of the Self: The End of Autobiography." In *Autobiography: Essays Theoretical and Critical,* edited by James Olney, 321–42. Princeton: Princeton Univ. Press, 1980.

Starobinski, Jean. "The Style of Autobiography." In *Autobiography: Essays Theoretical and Critical,* edited by James Olney, 73–83. Princeton: Princeton Univ. Press, 1980.

Stein, Gertrude. *Everybody's Autobiography.* New York: Cooper Square, 1971.

Stratton, Jon. *The Virgin Text: Fiction, Sexuality, and Ideology.* Norman: Univ. of Oklahoma Press, 1987.

Sturrock, John. "The New Model Autobiographer." *New Literary History* 9 (1977–78): 51–63.

Thornley, David. *Isaac Butt and Home Rule.* Westport, Conn.: Greenwood, 1976.

Walkowitz, Judith. *Prostitution and Victorian Society: Women, Class, and the State.* Cambridge: Cambridge Univ. Press, 1980.

Ware, Thomas C. "The Sources of the Christian River: The Function of Memory in George Moore's *The Brook Kerith.*" *English Literature in Transition* 30, no. 1 (1987): 27–37.

Watt, George. *The Fallen Woman in the Nineteenth-Century English Novel.* Totowa, N.J.: Barnes and Noble, 1984.

Weaver, Jack W. "AE, George Moore, and *Avatars.*" *English Literature in Transition* 19, no. 2 (1976): 97–100.

Welch, Robert. "Moore's Way Back: *The Untilled Field* and *The Lake.*" In *The Way Back: George Moore's The Untilled Field and The Lake*, edited by Robert Welch, 29–44. Totowa, N.J.: Barnes and Noble, 1982.

Wharton, Edith. *The Letters of Edith Wharton.* Edited by R. W. B. Lewis and Nancy Lewis. New York: Charles Scribner's Sons, 1988.

White, Hayden. "The Value of Narrativity." In *On Narrative*, edited by W. J. T. Mitchell, 1–23. Chicago: Univ. of Chicago Press, 1981.

Whyte, J. H. *The Independent Irish Party, 1850–9.* Oxford: Oxford Univ. Press, 1958.

Wilson, Michael. "'Sans les femmes, qu'est-ce qui nous resterait?': Gender and Transgression in Bohemian Montmartre." In *Body Guards: The Cultural Politics of Gender Ambiguity*, edited by Julia Epstein and Kristina Straub, 195–222. New York: Routledge, 1991.

Woodhouse, Annie. *Fantastic Women: Sex, Gender and Transvestism.* Basingstoke, Hampshire: Macmillan, 1989.

Yeats, W. B. *The Autobiography of William Butler Yeats.* New York: Collier, 1965.

Index

George Moore and the Autogenous Self

was composed in 10 on 12 Baskerville on a Mergenthaler Linotron 202
by Eastern Composition;
printed by sheet-fed offset on 50-pound, acid-free Natural Smooth,
and bound over binder's boards in Holliston Roxite B,
and with dust jackets printed in 2 colors,
by Braun-Brumfield, Inc.;
and published by
Syracuse University Press
Syracuse, New York 13244–5160

Richard Fallis, *Series Editor*

Irish Studies presents a wide range of books interpreting important aspects of Irish life and culture to scholarly and general audiences. The richness and complexity of the Irish experience, past and present, deserves broad understanding and careful analysis. For this reason, an important purpose of the series is to offer a forum to scholars interested in Ireland, its history, and culture. Irish literature is a special concern in the series, but works from the perspectives of the fine arts, history, and the social sciences are also welcome, as are studies that take multidisciplinary approaches. Selected titles in the series include: